EIGHT PLAYS BY
MOLIÈRE, *1622-1673*

The Precious Damsels

The School for Wives

The Critique of The School for Wives

The Versailles Impromptu

Tartuffe

The Misanthrope

The Physician in Spite of Himself

The Would-Be Gentleman

TRANSLATED, WITH AN INTRODUCTION, BY

ÆONIAN PRESS

MATTITUCK

© Copyright, 1957, by Morris Bishop

TO THE READER

It is our pleasure to keep available uncommon titles and to this end, at the time of publication, we have used the best available sources. To aid catalogers and collectors, this title is printed in an edition limited to 300 copies.

——— Enjoy!

ISBN 0-88411-448-1

AEONIAN PRESS, INC.
Box 1200
Mattituck. New York 11952

Manufactured in the United States of America

Contents

Introduction

Molière is the best beloved of French authors. "The French see themselves in his work as in a mirror," says the playwright Émile Fabre; "whoever knows Molière knows well the French."[1] But this is a parochial judgment. What is his meaning for us who are not French? What is his standing in the gigantic literary Olympics?

In his class, Dramatic Comedy, he is the unquestioned champion. He created the popular comedy as we know it today. The formula for the Hollywood comedy and farce can be traced back to Molière, not to Shakespeare or Aristophanes. His own work is still vital and universal. He is one of the most popular playwrights for the contemporary French stage, and in translation he delights the theatregoers of every land that has a theatre.

He was and is a mighty laugh-getter. He knew all the tricks: the cumulative effect of repetition, the echo-dialogue, the change of pace, the big word out of place, the double take, dignity's pratfall, and so on. But he must be more than a laugh-getter, or this edition would not exist. Where are the comics who convulsed our grandfathers? Who wrote *Our American Cousin?* Or *Abie's Irish Rose?*

The fact is that Molière made of comedy not only an art form, but a means of revelation. Eventually we ask of literature not distraction or instruction, but understanding of ourselves. Molière gives us an answer, by revealing to us the follies and absurdities of our behavior.

Typically he does so by picturing a positive character, dominated by a passion, a vice, a conviction, or even an ideal. This character is at odds with society, convention, normalcy. The revelation, and the humor, lie in the conflict, and in the revenge

[1] *Notre Molière* (1951) p. 7.

vii

which normalcy takes upon the exceptional person. In the farce, the exceptional character is grotesque; in the comedy, he is realistic. Arnolphe, in *The School for Wives*, errs by his passion to dominate and possess his bride, in contempt of her rights as a human being. Tartuffe is the hypocrite, the frank evildoer. Alceste, the Misanthrope, sins by excess of virtue. The moral is constant: that nature has given common men a racial wisdom, an instinctive virtue leading to happiness within the group, and the excessive person tampers at his peril with the profound imperatives of humanity.

Jean-Baptiste Poquelin was born in Paris, and was baptized on January 15, 1622. His father was a master upholsterer, or interior decorator, Furnisher by Appointment to His Majesty; he held the honorable and profitable post of *valet de chambre du roi*. He was a well-to-do bourgeois, of the type that Molière was later to picture and puncture. His wife, also of an upholstering family, died when our subject was ten. The father, who evidently had ideas above his station, sent the boy to the Collège de Clermont, the aristocratic Jesuit school. Here he had an excellent classical grounding, and also an introduction to the stage, for the students were constantly producing Latin plays of the classic repertory, and novelties written by a stage-struck master. He then, apparently, took a degree in law at Orléans. He did not practice, but returned to work in his father's shop.

On his twenty-first birthday, in 1643, he came into a bequest from his mother, and informed his horrified family that he was renouncing the succession to his father's privileges, abandoning the benefits of his education, and entering a profession proscribed by the Church and condemned by moral, right-thinking bourgeois —the stage.

In June of the same year he signed a contract establishing the Illustre Théâtre, in partnership with an actress, Madeleine Béjart, who rewarded him as leading ladies reward angels, and who

brought the rest of her acting family into the company. And
Jean-Baptiste Poquelin took the stage name of Molière. We do
not know quite where he found it, any more than we know why
François Marie Arouet became Voltaire.

The Illustre Théâtre promptly belied its name, and Molière,
after a sojourn in a debtor's prison, fled from Paris with the remains of his troupe, some time in 1645 or 1646.

Now begins a period of the utmost importance in the forma-
tion of Molière's art, but of which we know almost nothing. For
twelve years, as actor-manager of a bedraggled company of players, he wandered about France, barnstorming in actual barns, inn
yards, and indoor racquets courts. He learned a great deal about
life: how to handle grafting officials, unruly audiences with
apples in pocket for missiles, drunks and stage-door johnnies, and
also his own temperamental, grumbling troupers. He learned the
trade of the utility actor, ready to play any kind of part at need.
And he began to learn the playwright's business, adapting the
familiar repertory, writing skits and scenarios, trying them out on
live audiences, observing what goes over, revising what falls flat.

In October 1658 he dared to return to the capital. He opened
with a tragedy by Corneille, a failure; and one of his own farces,
a hit.

Thenceforth his theatrical career is a record of almost continual success. Installed in his own theatre, under the patronage
of young King Louis XIV, he led for fifteen years a life of har-
ried activity, managing, directing, acting the star roles, and writing twenty-nine plays, everything from tragicomedy to knock-
about farce.

Happy with success, he was less happy in what private life an
actor may possess. At the age of forty he married Armande Béjart, the twenty-year-old daughter of his former mistress, Madeleine Béjart, by an unknown father. It was an awkward, disturbing, even scandalous match, a defiance to all his own counsels of
conventional wisdom. But he loved her. He had watched her grow

from babyhood to womanhood; he had taught her the profession of the actress and had made her a star. She was a part of half his life, and she was what he wanted for the remainder of it.

But to Armande, her husband was as familiar as a father. He could not fill her life; there was nothing thrilling and adventurous about him. Gossip said that she was soon unfaithful to him, as the dukes and marquises practiced on her their art of seduction, which reached its apogee in the gallant court of Louis XIV.

The great creator of laughter was unhappy, and also ill. His wandering actor's life, with its strain and hardship, its irregular, hasty meals, had given him a chronic nervous indigestion. Later, he contracted tuberculosis. He forced himself to overwork, he sought the peace of love in vain, while his health gradually failed, while the solemn physicians proposed only treatment that would weaken him further. Characteristically, he turned sickness, death, and a wife's falsity into uproarious farce, in *Le Malade imaginaire*.

At the fourth performance of *Le Malade,* on February 17, 1673, Molière was seized by a hemorrhage of the lungs during the final scene. He succeeded in playing out the scene, took his bows, and was carried home. He died in a few hours. His wife was absent, trying fruitlessly to persuade a priest to give him the last rites. God was displaying his anger against Molière, said Bishop Bossuet.

It was one of the great exits of history.

Molière's art derives inevitably from the dramatic conceptions current in his time, from the example of Corneille and others. But his comedy is less a reworking of classic principles and devices than it is a development from two popular traditions—those of the old French farce and of the Italian *commedia dell' arte*. The French farce, vigorous in the later Middle Age, was still the delight of common people at country fairs. The action was gross and brutal, usually a deception practiced on a simple gull, ending in a rain of blows. The characters were familiar types, presented with crude realism.

The *commedia dell' arte* was introduced to France in Molière's youth. In the *commedia,* a troupe of skilled actors develop a set scenario with improvised dialogue. The actors, in white-face or wearing masks, represent invariable characters. They were masterly mimics; being masked, they developed to a high point the art of posture and gesture. They played in an "expressionistic" style which Molière took much to heart. Such types as Harlequin, Pantaloon, Punch, and Columbine are not forgotten today. One may still see a form of the *commedia* at the Tivoli Gardens in Copenhagen, and one may recognize the old dress and devices among our circus clowns.

The influence of the French farce and the *commedia dell' arte* is clear in Molière's work. In *The Precious Damsels,* Mascarille was masked, Jodelet played in white-face, and Gorgibus was a stock figure of the *commedia.* More essentially, the conception of a stage character as something fixed and unchanging derives from the masked types. The elaborate mystifications of which Molière seems overfond were inherited from the same conventions. One perceives the tradition also in Molière's balletlike stylization or formalization of comedy, as when, in *The Would-Be Gentleman,* the two girls pursue the obdurate young men about the stage; then, as at a dance signal, the young men reverse, to pursue the obdurate maidens.

Molière wrote, then, on the basis of a current convention. He accepted another limitation—or opportunity: the capacity of his actors. Each of his plays was written for a cast, and was designed to display his actors' abilities and minimize their shortcomings. In short—and this has been sometimes overlooked—each play is primarily a *performance,* and only secondarily a study of character or a social critique.

With this fact in mind, one may defend Molière against certain reproaches. His plays are certainly ill constructed, according to all the rules of the well-made play. In *The Would-Be Gentleman,* for instance, the first two acts consist entirely of gags; the action does not begin until Act III. But the gags are good enough to have amused three centuries of theatregoers, and the public, little inclined to analyze a musical comedy, has not complained. The gags are more important than the plot, the performance more important than the dramatic structure.

Or take the question of Molière's dénouements. In such plays as *The School for Wives* and *Tartuffe,* the problem is resolved by the introduction of a new and surprising element, for which no proper preparation has been made. This is not good, certainly, and there is no use dragging in the *deus ex machina* of the Greeks. But, aside from the fact that the theories of the well-made play had not yet imposed themselves, Molière was bound by a stage convention. Comedies regularly ended with a salute of all the players to the audience (our curtain call); it was customary to have all the characters on-stage, and the obvious way to arrange this was to show some massive imbroglio, settled by the appearance of an outside agent to resolve the situation with a minimum of explanation.

However, we cannot acclaim Molière as a master of dramatic composition. His plots and developments were sufficient, but hardly more. They can carry the weight of his characters and of his ideas.

His characters are forever memorable; they have their little life in every literate mind. Molière depicts universal types rather than particular individuals. He shows us the Miser, the Hypocrite, the Pedant, the Arrogant Noble, the Libertine, the Coquette. He generalizes, reinforces the dominant characteristic, suppresses the accessories. He simplifies psychology in order to gain dramatic effectiveness. This is the esthetic method of the French classical period. And since it is reinforced by observation of life, it is realism.

When we come to his ideas, or his philosophy, or his ethical purpose, we are on somewhat difficult ground. As a French citizen under Louis XIV, Molière accepted the governing ideas of his time. He did not question, for instance, that Church and King rule absolutely, and for our good. As an educated bourgeois and a prosperous businessman, he applauded the business and family virtues of the prudent social man. And as the producer of plays before the court aristocracy, which determined success or failure with the larger public, he had to consider the settled opinions of his audiences.

Thus, in general, his heroes and heroines are of the nobility, his villains and especially his ridiculous characters are of the bourgeoisie. The code to which he refers implicitly as admirable is the noble attitude toward life. His ideal is that of the *honnête homme,* the honorable man of the world, the gentleman. A gentleman is gentle by birth and *honnête* by training; the bourgeois, condemned to money-grubbing, can hardly be *honnête.*

And yet he was no sycophant to his public. He dared to satirize the futile, beribboned marquises of the court; and when the King laughed, the marquises laughed too. He went further; in *George Dandin,* his noble family is stupid and despicable. His strange and troubling *Don Juan* is a full-length portrait of *le grand seigneur méchant homme.* In *The Would-Be Gentleman,* the noble Dorante is a liar, a crook, and a parasite. No doubt the implied criticisms were covered by the broad farce of the presentations.

He had his convictions. He implied, timidly and even cryptically, that nature is a better guide than authority. Nature is the healer, and physicians' dogmas are in opposition to nature. Marriage should be based on love, not worldly advantage. Essential religion resides in the upright spirit, not in forms and ceremonies.

Critics were long wont to find in Molière's work a proclamation of his faith, and a revelation of his private life. *The Misanthrope,* for example, spoke the protest of a sincere and sensitive man against the falsities of convention. *The School for Wives* reflected Molière's own passion for the budding Armande, and so forth.

Most present-day writers treat such subjective, such "romantic" criticism with scorn. The plays, they insist, are merely plays and nothing more. The professors, they say, who have never written a play and know nothing of stage necessities, speculate windily on the text, unaware that the text is merely a pretext for action. These critics consider it absurd to seek and find personal confessions in performances which were designed only to be hits of the season. The professors should go to school to some popular practicing playwright.

I am not entirely convinced. If Molière were merely a popular practicing playwright, he would now be deservedly forgotten. The point is that he was something more, as Shakespeare was something more. It is because of the something more that we read and study him, that we examine his creative process with the same respect that we give to a poet's, that we find in his work evidences of his character and spirit. We expected to find an author and we find a man, as Pascal said.

Thus it cannot be mere coincidence that when he was wooing and wedding he wrote two plays about the marriage of a middle-aged man to a young girl, and another on jealousy; that when he was persecuted by the Church he wrote a play on religious hypocrisy, and fought for years to produce this alarming, dangerous work; that as his health worsened and he could find no help from the doctors he wrote five plays consisting wholly or in part of mockery of medical follies. Of course these productions do not baldly state Molière's convictions, but surely they betray his preoccupations. Literary men, if not popular playwrights, are like that. They want to speak of their secret concerns, though they may disguise their thought, or even state its contrary. They find a strange pleasure in imprudence; they like to make a public confession in words that few or none will understand. Thus the cartoonist may delight in a subtle indecency, invisible to the million conners; thus the sculptor carves his own face on a gargoyle.

And thus we have a right to seek and find Molière in his work. In *Le Malade imaginaire,* Molière played the imaginary invalid. He describes his symptoms to a doctor; they are the symptoms of a man dying of tuberculosis. The episode ends in an enormous laugh, but Molière surely found his own piercing pleasure in his moment of truth. In the last act of *The School for Wives* the middle-aged lover pleads with the girl for her love. Suddenly the comedy drops away, the agonized aging man speaks desperate, moving words. Such words are not invented, says Maurice Donnay, they are recovered. True, Molière played them for laughs, but did he write them for laughs? And finally, in *The Would-Be Gentleman,* Madame Jourdain forgets that she is playing in a farce, and imagines her daughter married to a noble and returning to her quarter, under the suspicious, supercilious glances of the neighbors. Madame Jourdain asks rather a son-in-law to whom she can say: "Sit down there, my boy, and have dinner with us."

These are moments of truth. There are many such in Molière. Without them he would be only a supremely competent writer of comedy. With them, he can offer us the kind of revelation of life and spirit which we have a right to ask of every author whom we call great.

EIGHT PLAYS BY
MOLIÈRE

The Precious Damsels

A FARCE IN ONE ACT

Les Précieuses ridicules was presented on November 18, 1659, after Molière had been established in Paris for a year. It was an immediate success, Molière's first real smash hit in the capital.

In form, it is a farce, showing the influence of the *commedia dell' arte*. Gorgibus and Mascarille were stock names and stock types. The names of the other characters are the actors' stage names. Molière, wearing a mask, played Mascarille. Jodelet, an old slapstick performer, appeared in white-face. He was allowed some of his popular gags, such as the peeling off of his many layers of clothing. The playlet ends with the ritual shower of blows with stuffed clubs.

The novelty of the play is its combination of farce and social satire. The mockery of preciosity would have been beyond the reach of the *commedia dell' arte*.

Preciosity is essentially an effort toward distinction, in thought, speech, literature, behavior. There is certainly no harm in this, and the preciosity which flourished in the second quarter of the seventeenth century was a praiseworthy reaction against coarseness and brutality of manners. But the effort toward distinction became an effort for novelty at all costs, and the *précieux* tumbled into absurdity. Many of the examples given in the play are exact, not exaggerations. The Map of Loveland is the *Carte de tendre* in Mlle de Scudéry's novel, *Clélie*.

The *précieux* had looked sourly on Molière and his broad, certainly unrefined, farces. *Les Précieuses ridicules* was a counterattack, which turned into a major victory. It made the current preciosity ridiculous. It did not, of course, kill the spirit which seeks precious expression, for this is a condition of mind, a constant. The condition of mind was forced, however, to change its manner of manifestation. This is not a hard task for preciosity, whose essence is the search for novelty in thought and word. James Joyce, Dylan Thomas, Gertrude Stein are *précieux*. Preciosity thrives today, in the cenacles of riddling poets, even on the sports pages of our newspapers. And *The Precious Damsels,* avowedly a burlesque of a passing fad, is still immensely successful on the stage. There must be something permanent about it.

The Characters

LA GRANGE, young gentleman

DU CROISY, young gentleman

GORGIBUS, well-to-do bourgeois

MAGDELON, daughter of Gorgibus

CATHOS, niece of Gorgibus

MAROTTE, maidservant in Gorgibus' household

ALMANZOR, lackey in Gorgibus' household

MASCARILLE, manservant of La Grange

JODELET, manservant of Du Croisy

LUCILLE, CÉLIMÈNE, neighbors

TWO SEDAN-CHAIR BEARERS

FIDDLERS

TWO HIRED BULLIES (may be omitted in stage presentation)

The scene is in the house of Gorgibus, in Paris.

LA GRANGE *and* DU CROISY *are discovered.*

DU CROISY: Seigneur la Grange—
LA GRANGE: What?
DU CROISY: Look at me for a moment . . . And don't laugh.
LA GRANGE: All right. Well?
DU CROISY: What do you think of our visit? Are you happy about it?

LA GRANGE: Well, in your opinion, do you think we have any reason to be?

DU CROISY: To tell the truth, not much.

LA GRANGE: To speak for myself, I admit I was thoroughly disgusted. Has anyone ever seen two scatterbrained country girls put on such airs? Or two men treated as offhandedly as we were? They could hardly bring themselves to the point of asking us to sit down. I've never seen so many mutual confidences in the ear, so much yawning, so much eye-rubbing, so much repetition of "What time is it?" And to everything we could think of to say to them, could they find any answer except "Yes" and "No"? So won't you admit that if we'd been the scurviest people on earth, they couldn't have treated us worse than they did?

DU CROISY: It seems to me you're taking the matter very much to heart.

LA GRANGE: Certainly I take it to heart. So much so that I want to get revenge for their impertinence. I know what made them so haughty toward us. [They are precious.

DU CROISY: Precious?

LA GRANGE: Yes. The precious are people who go in for preciosity.

DU CROISY: Preciosity?

LA GRANGE: Exactly. Preciosity is the new fashion among the intellectuals. They're so pure and sensitive and dainty that they can't stand anything common or real. They can't call anything by its right name; they play a kind of literary game, to see who can make the most far-fetched allusions, according to their special code of affectation.][1] This precious fashion has not only infected Paris, it has spread into the provinces, and our ridiculous damsels have taken a good dose of it. In short, they are combinations of the precious and the coquette. I can see the sort of thing they would appreciate; and if you'll agree,

---

[1] The passage between brackets is interpolated by the translator.

we'll play a trick on them which will show up their folly, and may teach them to judge people better.

DU CROISY: How do you mean?

LA GRANGE: I have a valet named Mascarille. In the opinion of a good many people, he passes for a wit in the modern manner, for there's nothing cheaper than wit nowadays. He's a fantastic fellow, who has taken it into his head to play the gentleman of quality. He makes a specialty of elegance and refinement; he writes poetry; and he looks down on the other servants; coarse brutes, he calls them.

DU CROISY: Well, what do you expect to do with him?

LA GRANGE: What do I expect to do? The thing to do—but first let's get out of here.

(*Enter* GORGIBUS.)

GORGIBUS: Well, gentlemen, you have seen my niece and my daughter. How are things going? What is the result of your visit?

LA GRANGE: That is something you can learn better from them than from us. All we can tell you is that we thank you for the favor you have done us, and we remain your very humble servants.

(*Exit* LA GRANGE *and* DU CROISY.)

GORGIBUS: Well now, what's this? They seem to be leaving in a very bad humor. I wonder what's the reason. I'd better find out. Hey there, you!

(*Enter* MAROTTE.)

MAROTTE: What do you wish, sir?

GORGIBUS: Where are the ladies?

MAROTTE: In their boudoir.

GORGIBUS: What are they doing?

MAROTTE: Making lip salve.

GORGIBUS: Too much salve. And too much lip. Tell them to come down. (*Exit* MAROTTE) Those hussies are trying to ruin me, with their lip salve. All I see around is whites of eggs, virgin-milk, and a hundred other groceries I don't recognize. Since we have been here they have used up the fat of a dozen pigs at least; and four menservants could live on the sheep's trotters they get rid of. (*Enter* MAGDELON *and* CATHOS) Girls, you've got to stop spending so much money to grease your mugs. Now tell me, what did you do to those gentlemen, so that I just saw them go out with a very chilly air indeed? Didn't I order you to receive them as gentlemen I proposed to give you as husbands?

MAGDELON: What regard, Father, do you expect us to bestow upon the irregular proceedings of those persons?

CATHOS: And how, Uncle, could a somewhat reasonable girl make shift with their characters?

GORGIBUS: What objection can you find to them?

MAGDELON: What kind of gallantry did they display! What! To begin right off with marriage!

GORGIBUS: What do you expect them to begin with? Concubinage? Isn't their procedure one you ought to approve, as I should too? Isn't that the gentlemanly thing to do? And that sacred bond that they propose, isn't it an evidence of their honorable intentions?

MAGDELON: Father, you're so utterly bourgeois! It makes me ashamed to hear you talk that way. You ought to take a course in conversation as a fine art.

GORGIBUS: I use conversation as a fine way of saying what I mean. And I say that marriage is a holy and sacred matter, and it's only decent to begin with it.

MAGDELON: Dear me, if everyone were like you, novels would be very short! A nice thing it would be, if the Great Cyrus married his Mandane right at the beginning, or if Aronce married Clélie in the first chapter!

GORGIBUS (*to* CATHOS):   What is she trying to say?

MAGDELON: Father, my cousin will tell you, just as well as I, that marriage should never occur until after the other adventures are over. A lover, in order to be acceptable, should be able to toy with noble fancies, and play the gamut of emotion, sweet and tender and impassioned. And he should woo according to the rules. First he should see the future object of his affections in church, or on the promenade, or in some public ceremony. Or else he should make a fatal visit to her house with a relative or friend; and he emerges in a trance, all melancholy. For a while he hides his passion from the loved one, but nevertheless he pays her a few calls, when some problem of gallantry is always brought up to exercise the wits of the assembly. The day of the declaration arrives; this should usually take place in a garden path, while the rest of the party has gone on. This declaration is followed by immediate anger on our part, which shows itself in our blushes; and for a time our fury banishes the lover from our presence. Then he finds some way to calm us down, and little by little he accustoms us to his description of his passion, and he draws from us that admission which causes us so much distress. Then come the adventures: the rivals who cross an affection which has been established, the persecutions of fathers, the jealousies which are conceived on some false basis, the reproaches, the despairs, the abductions and all the consequences. That's how matters are treated according to proper etiquette; those are rules of gallantry which can hardly be set aside. But to come right out at the beginning with proposing a matrimonial union, and to put all your love-making in the marriage contract, and to start the romance at the wrong end, really, Father, nothing could be more hucksterish than such a procedure, and the mere thought of it makes me sick at my stomach.

GORGIBUS: What kind of rubbish is all this? I suppose that's the highfalutin style in fashion.

CATHOS: In fact, Uncle, one could barely be righter than my cousin. How can one properly receive persons who are quite grotesque in matters of gallantry? I'll wager they have never even seen the Map of Loveland, and that the towns of Sweet-notes, Deference Minor, Truelove-Tokentown, and Prettyverse Village are strange country to them. Don't you see that their persons breathe the dreary dullard, and that they don't make a good impression on people? To come courting without frills at the knee, with a hat naked of feathers, a head uncurled, and a coat confessing a dearth of ribbons! Good heavens, what kind of lovers are those! What paucity in vesture, what aridity of conversation! It's not to be endured, it's not to be countenanced! What's more, I noticed that their neckcloths are not made by the right furnisher, and that their galligaskins are a good half-foot too narrow.

GORGIBUS: I think they're both crazy, and I can't understand anything of this gibberish. Cathos, and you, Magdelon—

MAGDELON: Please, Father, divest yourself of these strange appellations, and address us otherwise.

GORGIBUS: What strange appellations? Aren't they your christened names?

MAGDELON: Good heavens, how vulgar you are! One thing that amazes me is that you could have fathered a girl of my intelligence. Has anyone ever spoken in literary style of Cathos or of Magdelon? Won't you admit that one of those names would be enough to ruin the finest novel on earth?

CATHOS: It is true, Uncle, that a somewhat sensitive ear suffers furiously on hearing the utterance of those vocables; and the name of Polyxena, which my cousin has chosen, and that of Aminta, which I have adopted, have a certain grace, you will surely grant.

GORGIBUS: Listen; one word will be enough. I don't intend that you shall have any other names than those which were given to you by your godfathers and godmothers. And as for those gentlemen in question, I know their families and their finances, and it is my firm desire that you dispose yourselves to receive them as husbands. I'm getting tired of having you on my hands. Taking care of two girls is coming to be too much of a job for a man of my age.

CATHOS: As for me, Uncle, all I can tell you is that I find marriage a very shocking performance. How can one endure the idea of sleeping beside a man who is absolutely nude?

MAGDELON: Permit us only to breathe a bit in the fine society of Paris, where we have so recently arrived. Let us have time to weave the plot of our romance, and don't force the conclusion so fast.

GORGIBUS (*aside*): No doubt about it, they're completely mad. (*Aloud*) Once more, I don't understand anything of all this balderdash. I am going to be the master here; and to put an end to this sort of talk, either you'll both be married very soon, or, faith, you'll go into a nunnery. I take my oath on that.

(*Exit* GORGIBUS.)

CATHOS: Good heavens, my dear, how your father's spiritual substance is buried in gross matter! How coarse his intelligence is! What darkness in his soul!

MAGDELON: What do you expect, my dear? I am ashamed for him. I can hardly persuade myself that I am really his daughter, and I think that some day an adventure will occur which will reveal that I had a more illustrious origin.

CATHOS: I can well believe it. Yes, all the evidence points that way. And as for me, when I look at myself—

(*Enter* MAROTTE.)

MAROTTE: There's a lackey here asking if you're at home. He says his master wants to come and see you.

MAGDELON: Learn, idiot, to pronounce yourself less vulgarly. Say: "Here is a necessary evil, asking if your visibility is accessible."

MAROTTE: Well, I don't understand Latin, and I haven't had your chance to learn philosophy in *The Great Cyrus.*

MAGDELON: Impudent! Really, you're insufferable. Who is the master of this lackey?

MAROTTE: He says he's the Marquis de Mascarille.

MAGDELON: Oh, my dear, a marquis! Yes, go and tell him that he can see us. (*To* CATHOS) No doubt he's one of the wits who has heard about us.

CATHOS: Oh, assuredly, my dear.

MAGDELON: We'd better receive him in this parlor, and not in our bedroom as the great ladies do. Let's just arrange our hair a little, and support our reputation. (*To* MAROTTE) Quick, come into the other room and display before us the counselor of the graces.

MAROTTE: Good land, I don't know what kind of a creature that is. You've got to talk Christian, if you want me to understand.

CATHOS: Bring us the mirror, you ignorant fool, and take care not to sully the glass by the communication of your image.

    •(*Exit* CATHOS, MAGDELON, *and* MAROTTE. *Enter* MASCARILLE *in a sedan chair, carried by two* BEARERS.)

MASCARILLE: Hey, bearers, hey, hey, hey! Now, now, now, now, now, now! I think these scoundrels want to destroy me by crashing against the walls and the floors.

FIRST BEARER: Well, after all, it was a narrow door. And nothing would do but we should bring you right in here.

MASCARILLE: Naturally, indeed! Would you wish, menials, that I should expose the prolixity of my plumes to the inclemencies of the pluvious season, and that I should inscribe my shoe prints in mud? Come, get your chair out of here.

SECOND BEARER: Pay us, then, please sir.

MASCARILLE: Huh?

SECOND BEARER: I say, sir, that you should give us our money, if you please.

MASCARILLE (*giving him a slap on the face*):   What, rascal, ask money of a person of my quality?

SECOND BEARER: Is that the way you pay poor men? And does your quality give us anything to eat?

MASCARILLE: Ah ha! I will teach you your place! This riffraff wants to swindle me!

FIRST BEARER (*removing one of the poles from the sedan chair*): Come on, pay us—and quickly!

MASCARILLE: How's that?

FIRST BEARER: I say that I want my money right away.

MASCARILLE: He's a reasonable man.

FIRST BEARER: Hurry up!

MASCARILLE: Oh, yes, indeed. You talk very sensibly; but the other man is a knave who doesn't know what he's saying. Here. Are you satisfied?

FIRST BEARER: No, I'm not satisfied. You slapped my friend's face, and if—

MASCARILLE: Now, just take it easy. Here is for the slap. One can get anything from me if one goes about it properly. Now go, and come back for me soon to take me to the Louvre, for the King's retirement.

(*Exit* BEARERS. *Enter* MAROTTE.)

MAROTTE: Monsieur, my mistresses are coming in right away.

MASCARILLE: No need for haste; I am comfortably established here to await them.

MAROTTE: Here they are.

(*Enter* MAGDELON *and* CATHOS. *Exit* MAROTTE.)

MASCARILLE: Mesdames, you may no doubt be surprised by the audacity of my visit; but your merit brings this distress upon you, and merit has for me such a puissant charm that I speed everywhere in its pursuit.

MAGDELON: If you are in pursuit of merit, it is not upon our domains that you should hunt.

CATHOS: If merit is to be found here, you must necessarily have brought it with you.

MASCARILLE: Ah! I file objection against your statements. Renown speaks justly in reporting your worth; you will make a grand siam of the gallant world of Paris.

MAGDELON: Your amiability excites a little too far the liberality of its praises; and my cousin and I take good care not to confide our serious trust to the dulcet sound of your flattery.

CATHOS: My dear, we should have chairs set.

MAGDELON: Here, Almanzor!˙

(*Enter* ALMANZOR.)

ALMANZOR: Madame?

MAGDELON: Quick, propel hither the commodities of conversation.

(ALMANZOR *arranges chairs and exits.*)

MASCARILLE: But at least, is there security here for me?

CATHOS: What are you afraid of?

MASCARILLE: Some larceny of my heart, some assassination of my liberty. I see here some eyes which have the look of very naughty fellows, insulters of a man's freedom; they would treat a soul as a Barbary galley slave. What the devil is this? As one approaches them, they put themselves murderously upon their guard! Faith, I distrust them, I shall fly, or I demand a solid guarantee that they will do me no harm.

MAGDELON (*to* CATHOS):   My dear, he has the frolic character.

CATHOS: I see that he is Amilcar, out of the novel *Clélie.*

MAGDELON (*to* MASCARILLE):   Have no fear; our eyes have no evil designs, and your heart may sleep in assurance of their integrity.

CATHOS: But have mercy, monsieur; do not be inexorable toward this chair which has been holding out its arms to you for a good quarter-hour; content a little its desire to embrace you.

MASCARILLE (*after seating himself, combing his hair, adjusting his stockings*):   Well, ladies, and how do you find Paris?

MAGDELON: Dear me, what is there to say? It would be the very antipodes of reason not to confess that Paris is the great central office of marvels, the clearing-house of good taste, wit, and gallantry.

MASCARILLE: As for me, I insist that outside of Paris there is

CATHOS: That is an incontestable truth.

MASCARILLE: It's a little muddy, of course; but we have the sedan chair.

MAGDELON: It is true that the sedan chair is a sweet sanctuary against the insults of the mud and bad weather.

MASCARILLE: You receive many visits; what celebrated wit belongs to your circle?

MAGDELON: Alas! We are hardly known as yet; but we are becoming so, and we have a special friend who has promised to bring here all the gentlemen who write for the *Recueil des pièces choisies.*[2]

CATHOS: And certain others who have been indicated to us as the final authorities on gracious living.

MASCARILLE: I am the person to arrange that. They all come to see me, and I may say that I never rise in the morning without a half-dozen of the wits in attendance.

MAGDELON: Heavens, we shall be obliged to you, with a really perfervid obligation, if you will do us that kindness. For after all, one must be acquainted with all those gentlemen, if one wants to belong to the world of elegance. They are the ones who make and break reputations in Paris, and you know well that there is a certain individual whom you merely have to know personally to acquire the reputation of being an insider, even if you have no other qualifications. But personally, what I regard as most important is that by means of these feasts of wit and soul one learns hundreds of things which are absolutely essential, the very quintessence of smartness. Thus one finds out every day the chitchat of the gallant world, and all the quips and verses that are being passed around. We learn at just the right moment that so-and-so has composed the neatest little thing on such-and-such a subject; and a certain lady has supplied the words for a new tune; and a gentleman has written a madrigal on gaining a lady's favors; and another has com-

---

In an acting version any highbrow magazine may be substituted; or, to keep the seventeenth-century mood, *The Wits' Intelligencer.*

posed some stanzas on an infidelity; Monsieur Blank wrote last night an epigram in verse to Mademoiselle Dash, and she sent him the reply this morning about eight; an author has a certain plot for a new book; another has reached Part Three in his new novel; and another's works have just gone to press. That is what brings you regard in society; and if you don't know that sort of thing, I wouldn't give a penny for all the wit you might have.

CATHOS: In fact, I think anyone who makes the slightest claim to smartness is quite too ridiculous if he doesn't know the most trifling little quatrain which has just been written, and for my part, I should be abominably ashamed if someone should chance to ask me if I had seen something new, and I hadn't seen it.

MASCARILLE: It is certainly shaming not to have the first sight of everything which is being turned out. But don't distress yourselves. I am thinking of establishing in your house an Academy of the Wits, and I promise you that not a scrap of verse will turn up in all Paris without your knowing it by heart before anyone else. Why, for myself, not to boast, I toss them off when I'm in the mood. You will hear quoted in the most exclusive coteries of Paris two hundred songs of mine, and the same number of sonnets, four hundred epigrams and more than a thousand limericks, not counting the enigmas and the portraits.

MAGDELON: I will admit that I'm stupendously fond of portraits; I can't think of anything smarter.

MASCARILLE: Portraits are hard; they require depth, depth. You will see some of mine which won't displease you.

CATHOS: As for me, I love enigmas definitely monstrously.

MASCARILLE: A good exercise for the brains. I popped off four this morning, which I'll give you to guess.

MAGDELON: Limericks are agreeable, when they're deftly done.

MASCARILLE: They're my specialty! I'm busy now putting the whole of Roman history into limerick form.

MAGDELON: Oh, certainly that's immoderately lovely! Reserve a copy for me, if you have it printed.

MASCARILLE: I promise you each a copy, very handsomely bound. Publication is beneath my rank; I only do it to help out the booksellers, who simply persecute me.

MAGDELON: I should think it would be a great pleasure to see oneself in print.

MASCARILLE: Yes, rather. But while I think of it, I must tell you an impromptu I did yesterday when I was visiting a friend of mine, a duchess. I'm devilishly good at impromptus.

CATHOS: The impromptu is the absolute touchstone of wit.

MASCARILLE: Then listen.

MAGDELON: We are all ears.

MASCARILLE: Oh, oh! I was so carefree and imprudent!
I was just gazing at you, as who wouldn't?
You stole my heart, engulfing me in grief;
Stop thief! Stop thief! Stop thief! Stop thief! Stop thief!

CATHOS: Dear heaven! That's the last word in the gallant style!

MASCARILLE: Everything I do has a certain dash; there's nothing pedantic about it.

MAGDELON: Oh, it's a thousand leagues from the pedantic!

MASCARILLE: Did you notice the beginning: "Oh, oh"? In the sense of: "How extraordinary!—Oh, oh!" Like a man who suddenly becomes aware of something—"Oh, oh!" Surprise, you see—"Oh, oh!"

MAGDELON: Yes, I think that "Oh, oh!" is really prodigious.

MASCARILLE: But it seems like nothing at all.

CATHOS: Sweet heaven, what are you saying! That is the sort of thing that is completely priceless.

MAGDELON: Certainly. I would rather have written that "Oh, oh!" than a whole epic poem.

MASCARILLE: Your taste is good, egad.

MAGDELON: Well, it's not precisely bad.

MASCARILLE: Don't you rather like: "I was so carefree and imprudent"? Carefree and imprudent, taken off my guard, so to speak; a perfectly everyday turn of speech; carefree and imprudent. "I was just gazing at you," that is, innocently, respectfully, like an unhappy little sheep. "As who wouldn't?" That is, the most natural thing in the world, I observe you, I contemplate you, I gaze upon you, as who wouldn't? "You stole my heart, engulfing me in grief." How do you like "engulfing me in grief"?

CATHOS: Superb!

MASCARILLE: The two hard g's together give a suggestion of surprise and terror. "Engulf in grief." Like a poor little mousie suddenly engulfed by a dreadful cat. "Engulfing me in grief."

MAGDELON: Nothing could possibly be finer.

MASCARILLE: "You stole my heart," that is, you robbed me, you carried it away. "Stop thief! Stop thief! Stop thief! Stop thief! Stop thief!" Wouldn't you say it was a man shouting and running after a robber to try to catch him? "Stop thief! Stop thief! Stop thief! Stop thief! Stop thief!" (*He rises, runs around stage, and collapses in his chair.*)

MAGDELON: One must admit that that is extremely witty and gallant.

MASCARILLE: I must sing you the tune I've composed for it.

CATHOS: You've studied music?

MASCARILLE: What, me? Not at all.

CATHOS: How is it possible, then—

MASCARILLE: People of quality know everything without ever having learned anything.

MAGDELON: He's perfectly right, my dear.

MASCARILLE: See if the tune suits your taste. (*Clears his throat*) La, la, la, la, la. The brutality of the season has furiously outraged the delicacy of my voice. But no matter; it's just an offhand performance. (*Sings.*)

CATHOS: Oh, what passion in that tune! I don't know why I don't die of it.

MAGDELON: There is chromatic in that.

MASCARILLE: Don't you find that the thought is well rendered in the music? "Stop thief!" And then, as if you were shouting very loud: "Stop, stop, stop, stop thief!" And then finally, as if you were completely out of breath: "Stop thief!"

MAGDELON: It's the positive cream of art, the cream of the cream, or even the cream of the cream of the cream. I assure you, it's marvelous; I am enchanted with both words and music.

CATHOS: I've never heard anything quite so powerful.

MASCARILLE: Everything I do comes to me naturally; I've never studied.

MAGDELON: Nature has been your doting mother and you are her spoiled child.

MASCARILLE: Tell me, how do you pass your time?

CATHOS: Ah, we barely do.

MAGDELON: Till now, we have been enduring a ghastly starvation of amusement.

MASCARILLE: I shall be happy to take you to the theatre one of these days, if you like. As it happens, they are about to put on a new play which I should be happy to have you attend with me.

MAGDELON: That's an offer not to be refused.

MASCARILLE: But I must ask you to applaud properly, when we are there, for I have promised to help put the play over; the author came to request it just this morning. It's the custom here for the authors to come and read their new plays to us gentlemen of quality, to persuade us to approve them and give them some advance reputation. You may well suppose that when we say something, the commoners in the pit won't dare to contradict us. For my part, I am very scrupulous about it; and when I've promised some playwright, I always shout: "Beautiful! Beautiful!" before they've lit the footlights.

MAGDELON: No doubt about it, Paris is a wonderful place.

Hundreds of things go on here that one doesn't know in the provinces, however intelligent one may be.

CATHOS: You needn't say another word. Now that you've informed us, we shall make it a point to cry out properly at every speech.

MASCARILLE (*to* MAGDELON):   Possibly I'm mistaken, but you look to me like the kind of person who has written some little comedy.

MAGDELON: Oh, there might be something in what you say.

MASCARILLE: Aha! On my word, we must have a look at it. Just between us, I have scribbled one which I want to put on.

MAGDELON: Oho! Which troupe will you give it to?

MASCARILLE: A fine question! To the Hôtel de Bourgogne,[3] of course. They are the only ones who can bring out what's in a text; the others are ignoramuses who read their lines the way people speak. They don't know how to thunder out a good line of verse, and stop at the right place; and how can you tell which is the fine passage, if the actor doesn't pause at it, and thus indicate that it's time to applaud?

CATHOS: In fact, there is a way of communicating the beauties of a work to the audience; and nothing has any more value than what the performer puts into it.

MASCARILLE: How do you like my ribbons and galloons? Do you find them harmonious to my accouterments?

CATHOS: Oh, quite.

MASCARILLE: The ribbon is well chosen?

MAGDELON: Furiously well. It's pure Perdrigeon.[4]

MASCARILLE: What do you say to my knee ruffles?

MAGDELON: They strike the absolutely right note.

MASCARILLE: I can at least claim that they are a good foot wider than the common ones.

---

[3] The official troupe, Molière's rivals.
[4] The furnisher à la mode. In an acting version, an exclusive local merchant may be substituted.

MAGDELON: I must admit that I have never seen the elegance of the habiliments carried to such a fever pitch.

MASCARILLE: Apply a moment to these gloves the approbation of your olfactory organ.

MAGDELON: They smell petrifyingly good.

CATHOS: I have never inhaled a more harmonious aroma.

MASCARILLE (*presenting his powdered wig*): And how about this?

MAGDELON: It has real character; one's sense of sublimity is deliciously moved.

MASCARILLE: You don't mention my plumes. How do you find them?

CATHOS: Terrifyingly beautiful.

MASCARILLE: Do you know that each feather costs me a golden louis? But it's my weakness; I can't resist buying the very finest there is.

MAGDELON: I assure you that we utterly sympathize with you. I am furiously delicate about everything I wear; and even down to my stockings, I can't bear anything which doesn't come from the right shop.

MASCARILLE (*shouts suddenly*): Ow, ow, ow! Damme, ladies, you're treating me very badly! I have good cause to complain of your actions: this is not kind of you.

CATHOS: What is it? What's the matter?

MASCARILLE: What? When you both assault my heart at the same time? To attack me from right and left? Ha, that's contrary to all the rights of man. It isn't fair; I am going to shout: "Murder! Murder!"

CATHOS (*to* MAGDELON): One must admit that he says things in a most individual style.

MAGDELON: He has a very remarkable wit.

CATHOS (*to* MASCARILLE): You're more frightened than hurt; your heart cries out before it's wounded.

MASCARILLE: The devil it does! It's wounded from head to foot.

(*Enter* MAROTTE.)

MAROTTE: Madame, there's a gentleman to see you.

MAGDELON: Who is it?

MAROTTE: The Vicomte de Jodelet.

MASCARILLE: The Vicomte de Jodelet?

MAROTTE: Yes, sir.

CATHOS: Do you know him?

MASCARILLE: Why, he's my best friend!

MAGDELON: Have him come in immediately.

(*Exit* MAROTTE.)

MASCARILLE: We haven't seen each other for some time; I'm delighted by this happy chance.

CATHOS: Here he is.

(*Enter* ALMANZOR, *introducing* JODELET.)

MASCARILLE: Ah! Vicomte!

JODELET (*embracing* MASCARILLE):   Ah! Marquis!

MASCARILLE: How happy I am to see you again!

JODELET: How joyful I am to find you here!

MASCARILLE: Kiss me again, please. (*They embrace.*)

MAGDELON (*to* CATHOS):   Darling, we're beginning to be known; the world of fashion is finding the way to our door.

MASCARILLE: Ladies, permit me to present this gentleman to you. Upon my word, he is worthy of your acquaintance.

JODELET: It is only just that I should come to render to you what is your due; your charms exercise their seignorial rights on all sorts of people.

MAGDELON: You are carrying your civilities to the uttermost confines of flattery.

CATHOS: This day must be marked in our diaries by a red letter.

MAGDELON (*to* ALMANZOR):   Come, boy, must I always tell you what to do? Don't you see that we need the augmentation of a chair?

MASCARILLE: Don't be surprised at the Vicomte's looks. He

has just got out of bed from an illness which left him so pale.[5]

JODELET: That's the result of staying up so late at Court, and of all the sufferings of war service.

MASCARILLE: Do you realize, ladies, that you see in the Vicomte one of the most valiant men of our century? He is a champion soldier, a nonpareil nonesuch.

JODELET: You don't owe me any compliments, Marquis; your record is well known also.

MASCARILLE: It is true that we have met in the right spots.

JODELET: And in some pretty hot spots too.

MASCARILLE (*looking at the ladies*): Yes, but not so hot as this spot! Ha, ha, ha!

JODELET: We became acquainted in the army. The first time we saw each other, he was in command of a cavalry regiment on the Maltese galleys.

MASCARILLE: That's true. But you were in the army before I was; and I remember that I was still only a minor officer when you were in command of two thousand horses.

JODELET: War is a fine thing. but egad, the Court now rewards very poorly old servicemen like us.

MASCARILLE: That's why I'm going to hang up my sword on the hook.

CATHOS: As for me, I have an appalling weakness for men of war.

MAGDELON: I am fond of them too; but I like to have their valor seasoned with wit.

MASCARILLE: Vicomte, do you remember that half-moon fortification we took by storm at the siege of Arras?

JODELET: Half-moon? What do you mean? It was a good full moon.

MASCARILLE: I think you're right.

JODELET: Good gad, I ought to remember it. I was wounded

---

[5] Following the traditions of the *commedia dell' arte*, Jodelet played his part in white-face, like a modern clown or Pierrot.

there in the leg by a grenade; I still have the scars. (*To* CATHOS) Just feel a little there, please; you'll recognize where I got smacked.

CATHOS: It's true, it's a dreadful bump.

MASCARILLE (*to* MAGDELON):   Give me your hand a minute. Feel right there, at the back of my head. Have you got it?

MAGDELON: Yes, I feel something.

MASCARILLE: That's a musket shot I caught in my last campaign.

JODELET (*unbuttoning his shirt*):   And here's where a sword went right through me at the attack on Gravelines.

MASCARILLE (*putting his hand on his top breeches button*):   I'm going to show you a frightful wound.

MAGDELON: It's not necessary; we can believe it without seeing it.

MASCARILLE: They are honorable wounds, which show what kind of people we are.

CATHOS: We don't doubt at all what kind of people you are.

MASCARILLE: Vicomte, have you got your carriage here?

JODELET: Why?

MASCARILLE: We could take the ladies for a ride outside the gates, and give them an entertainment.

MAGDELON: Oh, we can't go out today.

MASCARILLE: Then let's have some music in and dance.

JODELET: A noble thought!

MAGDELON: Well, we'd agree to that. But we ought to have some more people.

MASCARILLE: Holà! Champagne, Picard, Bourguignon, Cascaret, Basque, La Verdure, Lorrain, Provençal, La Violette! Where the devil are all my lackeys? I don't think there's a gentleman in all France who is worse served than I am. Those rascals are always leaving me alone.

MAGDELON: Almanzor, tell the gentleman's servants to fetch some musicians; and bring in the ladies from next door, to people the solitude of our dance.

(*Exit* ALMANZOR.)

MASCARILLE: Vicomte, what's your opinion of those eyes there?

JODELET: Well, Marquis, what do *you* think?

MASCARILLE: Why, I say that our liberty will have some trouble in getting out of here with a whole skin. At least, to speak for myself, I'm all of aquiver, and my heart hangs only by a single thread.

MAGDELON (*to* CATHOS): How natural is everything he says! He puts things so agreeably!

CATHOS: It's true that he makes a furious expenditure of wit.

MASCARILLE: To show that I'm sincere, I'm going to make an impromptu on that theme. (*He meditates.*)

CATHOS: Oh, I implore you with all my heart's devotion, let us have something done especially for us.

JODELET: I should like to do the same, but I'm a little incommoded in the poetic vein, because of all the literary bleedings I've suffered in the last few days.

MASCARILLE: Now, what the devil is this? I can always do the first line very nicely, but I have a lot of trouble with the others. Gad, I'm being hurried too much. I'll make you an impromptu at my leisure, and I think you'll find it very fine indeed.

JODELET: He really has a devilish wit.

MAGDELON: And so gallant, and so neatly put!

MASCARILLE: Vicomte, tell me, will you, is it long since you've seen the Countess?[6]

JODELET: It's more than three weeks since I paid her a visit.

MASCARILLE: Do you know that the Duke came to see me this morning? He wanted to take me to the country to go stag hunting.

MAGDELON: Here are our friends now. (*Enter* LUCILE, CÉLI-

6 No doubt this phrase had some ephemeral double meaning, now forgotten.

MÈNE, ALMANZOR, FIDDLERS) Bless me, my dears, we must ask your pardon for disturbing you. These gentlemen had the fancy to give life and soul to the feet. So we sent for you to fill the void of our gathering.

LUCILE: We are much obliged to you, certainly.

MASCARILLE: This is just an improvised affair; but one of these days we'll give you a proper ball. Are the fiddlers here?

ALMANZOR: Yes, sir; here they are.

CATHOS: Come, my dears; take your places.

MASCARILLE (*dancing alone*):   La, la, la, la, la, la, la.

MAGDELON (*to* CATHOS):   He has really an elegant figure.

CATHOS: He's just the dancing type.

MASCARILLE (*taking* MAGDELON's *arm*):   My freedom takes a chance, by venturing to dance. Aha, the coranto! Keep the time, musicians, keep the time! Oh, what ignorant fools! No one can dance with them. Can't you play in time? La, la, la, la, la, la, la, la. Steady, you village fiddlers!

JODELET (*dancing*):   Hey there, don't play so fast; I'm just out of a sickbed.

(*Enter* DU CROISY *and* LA GRANGE.)

LA GRANGE: Aha, you scoundrels, what are you doing here? We've been looking for you for three hours. (*He beats* MASCARILLE *with his cane.*)

MASCARILLE: Ow, ow, ow! You didn't tell me there would be a stick in it.

JODELET (*beaten by* DU CROISY):   Ow, ow, ow!

LA GRANGE (*to* MASCARILLE):   It's a fine thing for you, you blackguard, to try to play the man of importance.

DU CROISY: This will teach you to know your place.

(*Exit* DU CROISY *and* LA GRANGE.)

MAGDELON: What does this mean?

JODELET: It's a wager.

CATHOS: What! To let yourself be beaten that way?

MASCARILLE: Egad, I didn't want to let myself go. I have a very violent character, and I might have got really angry.

MAGDELON: To endure such an insult in our presence!

MASCARILLE: A trifle, a trifle! Let's finish the dance. We've known each other for a long time. With old friends you don't let a little thing like that upset you.

(*Enter* DU CROISY *and* LA GRANGE.)

LA GRANGE: On my word, you rogues, you won't make fools of us, I assure you. Come in, you men.

(*Enter two sturdy* BULLIES.)[7]

MAGDELON: What kind of impudence is this, to come and disturb us in our house?

DU CROISY: What, ladies, we shall permit our lackeys to be better received than we were? We shall allow them to court you at our cost, and even offer you a dance?

MAGDELON: Your lackeys?

LA GRANGE: Yes, our lackeys. And it isn't honest and decent for you to spoil them the way you're doing.

MAGDELON: Oh, heaven! What insolence!

LA GRANGE: But they won't have the advantage of using our garments to bedazzle you. If you want to love them, it will have to be for their native charms. Come on, strip them, and be quick.

JODELET: Farewell to our finery!

MASCARILLE: Now the marquisate and the viscounty are humbled in the dust.

DU CROISY: Aha, you rascals, you wanted to follow in our footsteps! You'll have to go somewhere else for the equipment to charm your beauties. I can assure you.

LA GRANGE: It's too much, to try to take our places, and especially with our own clothes.

MASCARILLE: Ah, Fortune, what is thy inconstancy!

---

[7] These characters are usually omitted in stage presentation.

DU CROISY: Come on, take everything off them.[8]

LA GRANGE: Take away all those clothes; hurry. (*Exit the* BUL-LIES) Now, ladies, in their present state, you can continue your love passages with them as much as you please. We will leave you full liberty to do so, and my friend and I protest that we shall not be jealous at all.

(*Exit* LA GRANGE *and* DU CROISY.)

CATHOS: Oh, what a horror!

MAGDELON: I'm sick with shame!

FIDDLER (*to* MASCARILLE):   What's all this, anyhow? Who's going to pay us?

MASCARILLE: Ask Monsieur le Vicomte.

FIDDLER (*to* JODELET):   Who's going to give us our money?

JODELET: Ask Monsieur le Marquis.

(*Enter* GORGIBUS.)

GORGIBUS: Why, you little hussies, you've got us into a lovely mess, apparently! I've just heard some fine things about you from those gentlemen who have just gone out!

MAGDELON: Oh, Father, they've played us a cruel and ugly trick!

GORGIBUS: Yes, it's cruel and ugly, but it's the result of your impertinence, you shameful girls! They resented the way you treated them; and now, to my misfortune, I have to swallow their insult.

MAGDELON: Oh, I swear that we shall have our revenge, or I'll die of mortification! (*To* MASCARILLE *and* JODELET, *who are kneeling in supplication*) And you, you villains, do you dare to stay here after your insolent actions?

MASCARILLE: What a way to treat a marquis! What society has come to! The slightest little misadventure makes our dear ones scorn us! Come on, old comrade, let's seek our fortune some-

---

[8] The traditional stage business requires a slow, reluctant disrobing. Jodelet removes a series of waistcoats, and appears, wigless, in a cook's white cap and apron. Mascarille wears a lackey's smock.

where else. I see clearly that here only the vain appearances are prized, and there is no esteem for naked virtue.

(*Exit* MASCARILLE *and* JODELET.)

FIDDLER: Monsieur, we expect you to pay us for our music, since they didn't.

GORGIBUS: Yes, yes, I'll pay you; and this is how. (*Beats them*) And you, you rascally wenches, I don't know what keeps me from doing the same to you. We'll be a laughingstock to everybody; that's what you've brought on us by your fantasticalities. Go hide your faces, wenches; hide them for good. And you who are the cause of their follies, you crack-brained fancies, pernicious amusements of idle minds, novels, verses, songs and sonnets, may the devil take the lot of you!

The School for Wives

L'École des femmes was staged on December 26, 1662, and scored an immediate and lasting success. Molière played Arnolphe; Armande, his bride of less than a year, was Agnès. While we are repeatedly warned today against reading private meanings into Molière's plays, we may at least note that the situation, the problem of the ardent middle-aged lover and the bride he has trained from babyhood, was Molière's own.

The School for Wives was Molière's first five-act comedy in verse, hence the first play which his contemporary critics might accept as a comedy by definition. The tone is that of realism; the farcical note is permitted only to the servants. In modern terms, we should call The School for Wives a comedy of character, with some admixture of the comedy of manners; or perhaps simply we should call it a drama, or a play.

The theme is the old and welcome one that love conquers all, that youth cleaves to youth, that nature has decreed that the heart shall know itself and recognize the heart destined for it. The subsidiary theme, or thesis, is that a young woman has a right to a decent education, fitting to her intelligence and curiosities, and that the effort to keep her in ignorance is blamable and self-defeating.

The modern reader is likely to be disturbed and irritated by the lack of action. The play consists of interminable speeches; we do not see the action, we hear about it. This seems to us shocking; we did not expect a play to be a mere story in dialogue.

However, the French of 1662, like the ancient Greeks, did

have that expectation. A play in verse was a long poem, subject to certain rules of decorum. All violent action was banned from the stage. The audience found its pleasure in watching the opposition of attitudes and emotions, stated in rhythmical language, and in supplying the action from its imagination. There is something to be said for this dramatic system. One may find a radio announcer's description of a football game more thrilling than the actual hurly-burly.

There were also excellent material reasons for the absence of action. The stage was small—less than thirty feet in width. And at the sides and rear of the stage were set benches for wealthy patrons. Thus such episodes as the attempted abduction of Agnès, with Horace's fall from the ladder, could hardly have been shown in actuality.

Nevertheless, the static quality of the play is a defect, which was criticized by Molière's contemporaries. There were other criticisms, which will appear in *The Critique of the School for Wives*.

The Characters

ARNOLPHE, also known as Monsieur Delafield

AGNÈS, Arnolphe's ward

HORACE

ALAIN, peasant, Arnolphe's servant

GEORGETTE, Alain's wife

CHRYSALDE, friend of Arnolphe

ENRIQUE, Chrysalde's brother-in-law

ORONTE, father of Horace

A NOTARY

> The scene is a quiet street in a residential section of a provincial city. At the rear, the façade of a house, with practicable second-story casement windows. In front of the house, a small garden with a grilled gate. Outside the low enclosure, an arbor, with garden seats and a table.

ACT I

CHRYSALDE *and* ARNOLPHE *are discovered.*

CHRYSALDE: And so you say you've come to marry her?
ARNOLPHE: I want to get it over by tomorrow.
CHRYSALDE: We are alone; we can't be overheard;
So let's discuss the matter somewhat frankly.
Perhaps you'd care to have a friend's opinion?
Your project is alarming—for your sake.

And any way you look at it, I think
It's a rash act for you to take a wife.

ARNOLPHE: It may well be, Chrysalde, that you have reason
To find that marriage is a chancy state;
And one who feels the horns upon his brow
May well believe that they're inevitable.

CHRYSALDE: Fate plants the horns according to its whim;
All one's precautions are a waste of time.
But you're in special danger, from your habit
Of making fun of every hapless husband.
And you know well no cuckold, high or lowly,
Escapes the malice of your mockery.
My dear Arnolphe, your greatest pleasure is
To bring to light invisible intrigues—

ARNOLPHE: Why, very well; is there another town
Where husbands are so patient and enduring?
We have examples here of every sort
Who get their just deserts within the home.
One piles up wealth; his wife distributes it
To those who undertake to make him cuckold.
Another, somewhat happier, I admit,
Allows his wife to pocket handsome presents,
And never thinks of showing jealousy,
Because, she says, they're tributes to her virtue.
There's one who shouts and storms, without effect;
Another calmly lets things take their course,
And when he sees a gallant come to call,
He decently takes his hat and overcoat.
One cunning lady tells her faithful spouse
About the foul proposals of her friend,
And so she lulls him, and he smiles and pities
The gallant for his pains—which are not wasted.
Another lady, all too prosperous,
Ascribes her purchases to luck at gaming.

Her husband doesn't know what game she plays,
And renders thanks to heaven for her winnings.
So, with such themes for comedy around,
May I not, as a witness, be amused?
And not—

CHRYSALDE: Why, yes; but he who laughs at others
Must fear that others will have their laugh at him.
Now, I hear gossip, when the gossipers
Recount the current scandals of the town;
And yet, whatever juicy tales I learn,
No one has ever heard me gloat about them.
I keep my counsel; even though I may
Condemn some manifestations heartily,
And though I've no intention of enduring
What certain husbands placidly accept,
I don't proclaim my purpose openly;
For after all, the tables may be turned.
It's dangerous to swear what one will do,
Or what one won't, in such a circumstance.
For if, by some fatality, the horns
Of cuckoldry should sprout upon my brow,
I think that my behavior will ensure
That any mockery will be well hidden.
Even, perhaps, some kindly folk will say
That my affliction is regrettable.
But you, Arnolphe, would find it otherwise;
The risk you run is devilishly great.
Since you have always joked most savagely
About your comrades' marital misfortunes,
Since you have chosen to be merciless,
You must beware lest others take the challenge;
And any hint of infidelity
Will be the joy of every tattletale.
And if—

ARNOLPHE: My good Chrysalde, you needn't worry.

No one is going to make a fool of *me:*
For I know all the tricks, all the devices
That ladies use to victimize their husbands,
And I know how they work their sleight-of-hand,
And so I've taken adequate precautions.
The girl I'll marry is an innocent,
And her simplicity is my protection.

CHRYSALDE: And you imagine that simplicity—

ARNOLPHE: One isn't simple to take a simple wife.
Of course I know your wife is virtuous,
But an intelligent woman isn't safe.
I know what certain friends of mine have suffered
For marrying women with too many talents.
I'll hardly pick an intellectual,
Whose talk is all of literary clubs,
Who writes seductively in prose and verse,
While I am just the lovely lady's husband,
A saint, of course, but one without worshipers.
No, I don't care for the blue-stocking type;
If she writes books, she knows a lot too much.
I want her so sublimely ignorant
That she won't even know that words can rhyme.
Why, if one plays the crambo-game,[1] you know—
"What goes in?" you ask, and expect a rhyme-word—
I'd gladly have her answer: "A cream tart!"
Let her have no accomplishments at all.
I shall be satisfied if she knows how
To say her prayers, and sew and spin, and love me.

CHRYSALDE: So it's your whim to have a stupid wife?

ARNOLPHE: Exactly. I'd rather have an ugly fool
Than a beautiful woman with intelligence.

CHRYSALDE: Beauty and charm—

ARNOLPHE: Morality's enough.

1 *Corbillon*, a parlor game in which one side asks a question demanding a rhyming response.

CHRYSALDE: But how do you expect a simpleton
Will ever understand morality?
I needn't mention what a dreadful bore
One's life would be beside a witless wife;
But do you think your principle is sound,
That it's a guarantee against disaster?
A clever woman may betray her faith;
At least, she has to do so consciously.
The fool is often false without intention,
Hardly aware of what it is she does.

ARNOLPHE: Let me reply by quoting Rabelais.
Pantagruel answered his friend Panurge:
"Offer me any woman but a fool,
And preach and pound from now to Pentecost,
And you will be astounded to discover
You will not have convinced me an iota."

CHRYSALDE: All right; enough.

ARNOLPHE: Everyone has his method.
I have my own; and it applies to marriage.
I'm rich enough to do without a dowry;
My wife will be dependent upon me.
She'll be in no position to allege
Her property rights, or her superior birth.
I noticed her when she was four years old,
And I was taken by her modest air.
Her mother was destitute, and so I had
The idea of asking for her guardianship.
And the good peasant woman was delighted
To make provision for her daughter's welfare.
In a small convent, off the beaten track,
I had her educated by my system.
That is, I furnished them a set of rules
To cultivate her simple-mindedness.
And God be praised, the process was successful.
Now she is grown; and she's so innocent

That I bless heaven which has favored me,
Making a bride to fit my specifications.
She's out of the convent now; but since my house
Is always open to all sorts of people,
And since one always should foresee the worst,
I have installed her in that small house yonder.
And to preserve unspoiled her natural goodness,
I've chosen servants simple as herself.
You wonder why I tell you this long story?
Simply to show how carefully I work.
And since you're one of my best and oldest friends,
I'd like to have you sup with me tonight.
You'll have a chance to examine her a little;
We'll see if you will criticize my choice.

CHRYSALDE: I shall be happy to.

ARNOLPHE: You will be able
To judge her person and her innocence.

CHRYSALDE: Well, as for that, all that you've just related
Certainly proves—

ARNOLPHE: I have been understating.
Why, her naïve remarks are my delight.
Some of them make me nearly die with laughing.
The other day—and this you'll hardly credit—
She was much troubled, and she came to ask me,
In absolute and perfect innocence,
If children are begotten through the ear!

CHRYSALDE: I'm very glad, Seigneur Arnolphe—

ARNOLPHE: Now look!
Why must you always call me by that name?

CHRYSALDE: It's automatic; and despite myself
I never think of Monsieur Delafield.
Anyway, what possessed you, at the age
Of forty-two, to unbaptize yourself,
And give yourself an aristocratic name
After a stony field on your country place?

ARNOLPHE: The name not only goes with the property,
            But Delafield sounds better than Arnolphe.
CHRYSALDE: But why should you renounce your father's name,
            To take one which is only fanciful?
            The process, to be sure, is all the rage.
            I am reminded—not by comparison—
            Of a poor countryman named Peterkin,
            Who owned a wretched acre or two of land;
            He dug a muddy ditch around the field,
            And proudly called himself Monsieur de l'Isle.[2]
ARNOLPHE: Such an example has no application.
            Remember that my name is Delafield.
            It's legally warranted; besides, I like it.
            To call me anything else is disobliging.
CHRYSALDE: It's hard for people to get used to it.
            Your mail comes mostly to Seigneur Arnolphe.
ARNOLPHE: I can accept Arnolphe from the uninformed.
            But you—
CHRYSALDE: All right. I shan't insist upon it.
            I shall do violence to my ancient habit,
            And call you only Monsieur Delafield.
ARNOLPHE: Good-by. I'll merely knock by way of greeting,
            So that they'll know that I am home again.
CHRYSALDE   (*aside*): Really, poor old Arnolphe is off his head!
            (*Exit* CHRYSALDE.)
ARNOLPHE: On certain subjects he's a little cracked.
            It's always curious to see how people
            So desperately cling to their opinions.
            (*Knocking at gate*)
            Holà!
            (*The head of* ALAIN *appears at upper window.* **He**
            does not at first see ARNOLPHE.)
ALAIN: Who's there?

[2] Thomas Corneille, writer of tragedies and brother of the great Pierre Corneille, similarly took the name of Corneille de l'Isle. Molière's mocking reference caused a break between him and the Corneilles.

ARNOLPHE: Open! (*To himself*) They will be pleased,
I think, to see me after ten days' absence.

ALAIN: Who is it?

ARNOLPHE: Me.

ALAIN   (*without looking at* ARNOLPHE, *calls to a lower window*):

                  Georgette!

GEORGETTE   (*putting her head out of lower window and looking up at* ALAIN):

                          What?

ALAIN: Open the door!

GEORGETTE: You do it!

ALAIN: No, you do it!

GEORGETTE: Faith, I won't!
(*Slams window shut.*)

ALAIN: And I won't neither!
(*Slams his window shut.*)

ARNOLPHE: What's this hocus-pocus?
To leave me here outside! (*Pounds knocker*) Holà
there! Ho!

GEORGETTE   (*opening window*):
Who's there?

ARNOLPHE: Your master!

GEORGETTE   (*frightened*):   Alain!

ALAIN   (*opening window*):   What?

GEORGETTE: It's Master!
Open the door!

ALAIN: You do it!

GEORGETTE: I'm blowing the fire.

ALAIN: I'm keeping the cat from catching the canary.
(*Both windows slam shut.*)

ARNOLPHE: Whoever doesn't open the door for me
Will get no food during four days at least.
(ALAIN *and* GEORGETTE *appear, blocking each other in doorway.*)

GEORGETTE   (*to* ALAIN): Why do you come when I am almost
                there?

ALAIN: Why you, not me? A trick! A strodagem!

GEORGETTE: Get out of here!

ALAIN: Get out of here yourself!
             (*They emerge from doorway and run to gate.*)

GEORGETTE: I want to open the gate!

ALAIN: I want to, too!
             (*They struggle.*)

GEORGETTE: You won't!

ALAIN: Well, you won't neither!

GEORGETTE: Neither will you!

ARNOLPHE   (*to himself*): Surely I have a very patient spirit!
             (ALAIN *and* GEORGETTE *open the gate together.*)

ALAIN: I opened it!

GEORGETTE: Like fun you did! 'Twas me!

ALAIN: Saving the presence of our master here,
             I'd—
             (ALAIN *throws himself on* GEORGETTE, *who dodges
             behind* ARNOLPHE. ARNOLPHE *receives* ALAIN's *blow.*)

ARNOLPHE: Curses!

ALAIN: I beg your pardon.

ARNOLPHE: You clumsy fool!

ALAIN: It's her fault, sir!

ARNOLPHE: Now both of you be quiet.
             Answer my questions; let's have no more nonsense.
             Now, Alain, how have things been going here?

ALAIN: Why, things, sir—
             (ARNOLPHE *removes* ALAIN's *hat from his head;*
             ALAIN, *uncomprehending, replaces it*)
                        Everything—
             (*Same business*)
                               Thanks be to God,
             We've been—

ARNOLPHE (*removes* ALAIN's *hat and throws it on ground*):
Where did you learn, you impudent rogue.
To wear your hat while speaking to your master?

ALAIN: You're right.

ARNOLPHE: Now ask Miss Agnes to come down.
(*Exit* ALAIN)
Was she unhappy when I went away?

GEORGETTE: Unhappy? No.

ARNOLPHE: No?

GEORGETTE: Yes, she was!

ARNOLPHE: And how?

GEORGETTE: Why, she kept thinking you'd be coming back.
We didn't hear a horse or mule or ass
Pass by, without she thought it might be you.
(*Enter* AGNÈS, *carrying needlework, and* ALAIN.)

ARNOLPHE: She has her work in hand; that's a good sign.
Well, Agnes, here I am back from my journey.
And are you pleased?

AGNÈS: Oh yes, sir, God be praised.

ARNOLPHE: And I am very pleased to see you too.
You've been as well, I hope, as you appear?

AGNÈS: Why yes; though the fleas bothered me last night.

ARNOLPHE: You'll soon have someone who will drive them off.

AGNÈS: That will be nice.

ARNOLPHE: Yes; I imagine so.
What's that you're making?

AGNÈS: A linen cap for me.
Your nightshirts and your nightcaps are all done.

ARNOLPHE: That's excellent. Now go upstairs again.
Keep yourself busy. I shall come back soon.
I'll have important things to talk about.
(*Exit* ALAIN, GEORGETTE, AGNÈS)
Heroines of our time, and learned ladies,
Partisans of the simpering, love-sick mode,

I defy you and all your prose and poems,
Your novels and your billets-doux, to equal
This decent, modest, honest ignorance.
(*Enter* HORACE)
In marriage, money's not the important thing.
If honor's there— Who's this? It can't be— Yes!
Or maybe not. It is, though! Yes, it's Horace!

HORACE: My dear Ar—

ARNOLPHE: Horace!

HORACE: Arnolphe!

ARNOLPHE: What a surprise!
How long have you been in town?

HORACE: Just eight days.

ARNOLPHE: Really!

HORACE: I called first at your house, but you weren't there.

ARNOLPHE: I'd gone to the country.

HORACE: Yes; two days before.

ARNOLPHE: Well, how young people grow in a few short years!
It's really amazing to see you as you are,
When I remember you no bigger than that!

HORACE: You see—

ARNOLPHE: Enough of that. Your father Oronte,
My excellent friend, whom I esteem and honor,
What is he up to? He's still gay and hearty?
He knows I'm interested in all his news.
We haven't seen each other for four years;
In fact, we haven't written in all that time.

HORACE: Seigneur Arnolphe, he's gayer than you and I are!
He gave me a letter to present to you.
But now a later message has informed me
He's coming in person; he hasn't told me why.
Do you perhaps know of a local man
Who's coming home soon with a lot of money
He's made in fourteen years in America?

ARNOLPHE:	No; no. You wouldn't know his name?
HORACE:	Enrique.
ARNOLPHE:	No; no.
HORACE:	Well, father speaks of his return

As if I ought to be acquainted with him.
And they expect, he says, to travel together
To treat an important matter; he doesn't say what.
(*He hands letter to* ARNOLPHE.)

ARNOLPHE: I'll certainly be glad to see him again,
And I shall give him a proper welcome here.
(*Reads letter, and pockets it*)
Old friends hardly require such protestations;
He needn't waste his time in mere politeness.
Without a word from him, I would have offered
To let you draw on me, if you need cash.

HORACE: Since you're so cordial, I'll take you at your word.
I do in fact need some pistoles. A hundred.

ARNOLPHE: Why, it's a pleasure to have you act so frankly;
And by a fortunate chance I have them on me.
(*Hands a fat purse to* HORACE, *who starts to empty it*)
Keep the purse, too.

HORACE: But I must give you—

ARNOLPHE: Nonsense!
Tell me, Horace, how do you find our city?

HORACE: Busy; and with some very handsome buildings.
And I suspect that people enjoy themselves.

ARNOLPHE: Everyone seeks for pleasures to his taste.
And those they call the gay Lotharios
Find plenty of opportunity in this town.
Our women know the tricks of coquetry,
And both brunettes and blondes are—very kind.
And husbands are uncommonly indulgent.
Why, it's a happy hunting ground! I often

Get much amusement from the goings-on.
Perhaps you've smitten some tender heart already?
Some gallant enterprise among the ladies?
Good looks like yours get more than money will;
You are the type that manufactures cuckolds.

HORACE: Why, there's no reason I should hide the truth.
In fact, I've landed in a little adventure.
I'll gladly tell you, if you'd be amused.

ARNOLPHE: Good! I can see a spicy story coming,
An item I can add to my collection.

HORACE: But please, it must be absolutely secret.

ARNOLPHE: Of course!

HORACE: You're well aware that in these matters,
If anything leaks out, the affair is ended.
I will admit to you in utter frankness
That I've been captured by a lovely lady.
And my attentions have been so successful
That I have taken the first important steps.
I mustn't boast, or do her any wrong,
But I can say that things look promising.

ARNOLPHE   (*laughing*): Who is she?

HORACE   (*pointing to* AGNÈS' *house*):
                    She's a beautiful girl who lives
In this very house, with the red vines on the walls.
She is naïve; but that's the fault of a man
Who hides her away from contact with the world.
Although he tries to keep her ignorant,
She shows the most entrancing qualities:
A sweet, engaging air, with something tender
About her, which is utterly captivating.
But possibly you've seen her, that young star
Of love, so radiant with every charm
Her name is Agnes.

ARNOLPHE   (*aside*):   Hellfire!

HORACE: The man's name

Is Delavan or Delaware or something.
I wasn't much concerned about his name.
Rich, so they say, but not intelligent.
In fact, they say he's rather ridiculous.
You wouldn't know him?

ARNOLPHE   (*aside*):   This is too much to take!

HORACE: You didn't speak?

ARNOLPHE: What? Oh yes, yes, I know him.

HORACE: He's crazy, isn't he?

ARNOLPHE: Well—

HORACE: Is that your answer?

"Well—" That means yes. Also absurdly jealous?
A fool? I see my information's good.
In short, the charming Agnes fascinates me.
She is a lovely and alluring creature.
It would be sinful if so rare a creature
Should stay in the clutches of that nincompoop.
So I shall bend all my most earnest efforts
To winning her heart, despite the jealous ogre.
The money that I borrowed so brazenly
Will serve in bringing my enterprise to pass.
For you know well that labor's not enough,
And money is the key to victory.
That pleasant metal has the power to smite
And to make conquests, in both war and love.
You're looking very solemn. Can it be
That you do not in fact approve my purpose?

ARNOLPHE: No; I was thinking—

HORACE: I am boring you.

Good-by. I'll call at your house to state my thanks.
(*Starts to leave.*)

ARNOLPHE   (*to himself*): Oh, it must be—

HORACE   (*returning*):   Again, please be discreet.

Kindly don't tell my secret to a soul.
(*Starts to leave.*)

ARNOLPHE   (*to himself*) : That I must suffer—
HORACE   (*returning*) :   Especially to my **father.**
             This is the kind of thing that makes him angry.
ARNOLPHE: Yes.

             (*Exit* HORACE; ARNOLPHE, *after a false presentiment
             that* HORACE *is again returning, sinks down on a
             bench*)

             Oh, how I suffered during that interview!
             Was anyone ever so disturbed in mind!
             How recklessly, and how imprudently,
             He came and told me all about his dealings!
             Though my new name was strange to him, **no fool**
             Ever ran quite so eagerly into folly!
             In spite of my pain, I should have led him **on,**
             To learn exactly what I have to fear.
             I should have pushed his indiscretion **further,**
             To find the purport of their conversations.
             I'll catch him up. He isn't far, I think.
             I need complete disclosure of the facts.
             I tremble at my possible misfortunes;
             Often we seek more than we wish to find.

ACT II

Enter ARNOLPHE.

ARNOLPHE: Perhaps it was a good thing after all
             I lost his track and couldn't run him down.
             For I might well have given him a hint
             Of my obsessing agony of mind;
             I might not have contained my secret grief.
             It's best he should remain in ignorance.
             But I'm not one to take things lying down,
             And leave the way wide open to that gosling.

I'll spoke his wheels! I'll find out right away
How much of an understanding he's obtained.
I take a notable interest in my honor,
And I regard her as my wife already,
So any fault of hers is shame to me,
And I am chargeable for what she's done.
Curses! Why did I ever go away?
(*He knocks at gate. The door flies open. Enter*
ALAIN *and* GEORGETTE.)

ALAIN: Ah, sir, this time—

ARNOLPHE: Silence! Come here, you two.
This way, this way. Come here, come here, I tell you
    you.

GEORGETTE (*falling on her knees*):
You frighten me, sir. Faith, you curdle my blood.

ARNOLPHE: So, this is how you obey me in my absence!
So, you have plotted together to betray me!

GEORGETTE: Don't eat me alive, monsieur, I beg of you!

ALAIN (*aside*): I vow, a mad dog must have bitten him!

ARNOLPHE (*aside*):
Ouf! I can't speak, I have such premonitions!
My blood's aboil; I'd like to pull my clothes off.
(*Aloud*) And so, you dirty dogs, you have permitted
A man to come here!
(ALAIN *starts to run away*)
                              Ha! You would escape!
(*To* GEORGETTE) You must immediately— Don't
    move! (*To* ALAIN) I want
To have you tell me— Uh! I want you both—
(ALAIN *and* GEORGETTE *rise and try to flee*)
If anyone moves, I swear to God I'll kill him!
How did that fellow get into the house?
Come on, speak up! Hurry! Quick! Right away!
Without delay!

ALAIN *and* GEORGETTE (*on their knees*):

Oh! Oh!

GEORGETTE: My heart has stopped!

ALAIN: I'm dead!

ARNOLPHE   (*aside*): I'm sweating so, I must cool off.
I must calm down, and take a little walk.
Could I have guessed, when he was just a boy,
That he would grow—to this? God, how I suffer!
I think it would be best if I could get
From her own lips the truth about the matter.
I must attempt to hide my bitterness.
Be still, my heart; softly, my heart; go softly.
(*Aloud*) Get up, and ask your mistress to descend.
No. Stop. (*Aside*) I'd lose the advantage of surprise.
They would inform her of my troubled state.
I'll go and ask her to come down myself.
(*Aloud*) Wait for me here.
(*Exit* ARNOLPHE.)

GEORGETTE: Oh, isn't he terrible!
He scared me with his looks, he scared me so!
I never saw such a hideous Christian man!

ALAIN: The other gentleman made him mad; I told you.

GEORGETTE: But why does he make such an almighty fuss
About our keeping the lady shut in the house?
Why does he want to hide her from everyone,
And not let anybody at all come near her?

ALAIN: Because such things arouse his jealousy.

GEORGETTE: But how does it come that he has that idea?

ALAIN: That comes from the fact—from the fact that he is
           jealous.

GEORGETTE: But why is he jealous? And why does he get so angry?

ALAIN: Why, jealousy—now get this well, Georgette—
Jealousy's something which upsets a man,
And makes him chase all other men away.

I'm going to give you a comparison
To help you understand the matter better.
Isn't it true that when you've got your stew,
If a hungry man should come and try to eat it,
You would get mad, and poke him on the nose?

GEORGETTE: I understand that.

ALAIN: Well, it's just the same.
The woman is in fact the stew of man;
And sometimes when a man sees other men
Trying to dip their fingers in his stew,
Right away he displays a terrible anger.

GEORGETTE: But why don't everybody act the same?
Why do some husbands look so very pleased
To have their wives out with fine gentlemen?

ALAIN: It isn't every man who is so greedy
He wants it all for himself.

GEORGETTE: Unless I'm blind,
He's coming back.

ALAIN: Your eyes are good; it's him.

GEORGETTE: Isn't he sulky!

ALAIN: Well, he has his troubles.
(*Enter* ARNOLPHE.)

ARNOLPHE (*aside*): A Greek once gave to Emperor Augustus
A piece of useful, sensible advice.
He said that when we're overcome by anger,
We should at once recite the alphabet,
To give our fury a chance to spend itself,
And to prevent our doing something foolish.
That's what I've done, with reference to Agnes.
I've asked her to come down and join me here,
Under the pretext of a promenade,
So that the sick suspicions of my mind
May bring her to the subject casually.
Thus I may probe her heart and learn the truth.

(*Calls*) Agnes, come out. (*To* ALAIN *and* GEORGETTE)
   Go in.
   (*Exit* ALAIN *and* GEORGETTE. *Enter* AGNÈS. *The two
   stroll in silence*)
            It's nice to walk.

AGNÈS: Very.
ARNOLPHE: The day is fine.
AGNÈS: Very.
ARNOLPHE: What news?
AGNÈS: The kitten's dead.
ARNOLPHE: Why, that's too bad. But still,
   We are all mortal; we must take our chances.
   Didn't it rain while I was in the country?
AGNÈS: Oh, no.
ARNOLPHE: And were you bored?
AGNÈS: I'm never bored.
ARNOLPHE: What have you done during the past ten days?
AGNÈS: Six shirts, I think, and half a dozen coifs.
ARNOLPHE   (*after a meditative pause*):
   The world, dear Agnes, is a funny place,
   For people talk, and often slanderously.
   Some neighbors say that while I was away
   A strange young man has visited the house,
   And you received him, listening to his talk.
   I put no credit in this ugly gossip,
   And I would wager it's entirely false—
AGNÈS: You'd better not, for you would certainly lose.
ARNOLPHE: What! It is true that a man—
AGNÈS: Oh, absolutely!
   I vow, he hardly left the house at all!
ARNOLPHE   (*aside*): At least, the admission made with sincerity
   Indicates the simplicity of her mind.
   (*Aloud*) But if my memory is good, I think
   I had forbidden you to see anyone.

AGNÈS: Yes, but although I saw him, you don't know why.
You would have done the same thing in my place.

ARNOLPHE: Perhaps. But tell me the story anyway.

AGNÈS: It's really astonishing, and hard to believe.
I'd taken my work to the cool of the balcony,
And then I saw, under the nearby trees,
A very fine young man. He caught my eye,
And he saluted me with a humble bow.
And since I didn't wish to be impolite,
I made a proper bow in acknowledgment.
All of a sudden he makes another bow,
And so immediately I make one too.
And then he makes another one, his third,
So I return a third one of my own.
He passes by, comes back; and every time
He makes a new and lower reverence.
I watched him closely, and to each salute
I answered, bowing very civilly.
In fact, if the dark of night had not come down,
I think I would have been right there forever.
I didn't want to yield, and let him think
That I could be less courteous than he.

ARNOLPHE: Why, fine.

AGNÈS: Next day, when I was at the door,
There came an elderly woman, and she said:
"My dear, God bless you most abundantly,
And keep you ever beautiful and blooming!
He did not make you such a pretty person
In order to ill use his kindly gifts;
And you must know you have severely wounded
A heart which must protest its suffering!"

ARNOLPHE (*aside*): Oh, cursèd agent of the devil himself!

AGNÈS: "What, I have wounded someone?" I exclaimed.
"Yes," she said. "Wounded! Wounded grievously

The man you saw from your balcony yesterday."
"Now what," I said, "could be the cause of that?
Did I let something drop on him carelessly?"
"No, it's your eyes," she said, "that did the deed.
It's from their glance that all his trouble comes."
"Why, I'm amazed!" I answered. "Do my eyes
Have some contagious trouble which he's caught?"
"Yes, yes," she said; "your eyes have deadly power;
They're filled with poison which you're not aware of.
In short, he's languishing, the poor dear boy.
And if—" the charitable lady said,
"If you're so cruel as to refuse all aid,
He'll certainly be buried in two days."
"Good heavens!" I cried. "I should be very sorry!
But what assistance can I give to him?"
"My child," she said, "he only wants to gain
The privilege of seeing and speaking to you.
Your eyes alone can save him from destruction;
They have the medicine for the hurt they've done."
"Why, gladly!" I replied. "If that's the case,
He can come here as often as he likes."

ARNOLPHE	(*aside*): Oh, cursèd witch and poisoner of souls!
	May hell reward your charitable plots!
AGNÈS:	That's how he came to see me, and was cured.
	Don't you agree I did the proper thing?
	Could I have had the weight upon my conscience
	Of letting him die for lack of a little aid,
	I who can't bear to see poor people suffer,
	And can't help crying, to see a chicken die?
ARNOLPHE	(*aside*): This proceeds only from an innocent soul,
	And I must blame my absence, so imprudent,
	Which left, without a guide, her natural goodness
	Exposed to the wiles of cunning reprobates.
	But I'm afraid the enterprising rogue

	Has carried matters past the joking stage.
AGNÈS:	What is the matter? You seem to be displeased.
	Was there anything wrong in what I told you about?
ARNOLPHE:	Why, no, indeed. But tell what happened then,
	And how the young man occupied his visits.
AGNÈS:	Oh, dear, if you could see how happy he was,
	How he immediately lost his affliction,
	And the beautiful jewel box he presented me,
	And the money he gave to Alain and Georgette,
	You'd love him too, you'd join with us in saying—
ARNOLPHE:	Yes, yes. But what did he do, alone with you?
AGNÈS:	He swore he loved me, with unparalleled love,
	And said the sweetest things you can imagine,
	Things like things no one ever heard before.
	They kind of tickled me inside, and stirred
	Something which makes me sort of excited still.
ARNOLPHE	(*aside*): Oh, cruel probing of a mysterious evil,
	Wherein the surgeon suffers all the pain!
	(*Aloud*) Now, in addition to all these lovely words,
	Didn't he also give you some—caresses?
AGNÈS:	Oh, lots! He took my hands, he took my arms;
	He never seemed to tire of kissing them.
ARNOLPHE:	And, Agnes, didn't he take something else?
	(AGNÈS *seems taken aback*)
	Ouf!
AGNÈS:	Well, he—
ARNOLPHE:	What?
AGNÈS:	Took—
ARNOLPHE:	Uh!
AGNÈS:	My—
ARNOLPHE:	Well?
AGNÈS:	I daren't!
	I am afraid you may be angry with me.
ARNOLPHE:	No.

AGNÈS:	Yes, you will!
ARNOLPHE:	No, no!
AGNÈS:	Then give me your word.
ARNOLPHE:	All right, then.
AGNÈS:	Well, he took my—you'll be mad!
ARNOLPHE:	No.
AGNÈS:	Yes.
ARNOLPHE:	No, no! What's all the mystery?

ARNOLPHE: No, no! What's all the mystery?
What did he take?

AGNÈS: Well, he—

ARNOLPHE (*aside*):   God, how I suffer!

AGNÈS: He took my ribbon, the ribbon that you gave me.
To tell you the actual truth, I couldn't stop him.

ARNOLPHE (*subsiding*):
We'll let the ribbon go. I wanted to know
If he did anything else than kiss your arms.

AGNÈS: Why, are there other things to do?

ARNOLPHE: No; no.
But to cure the pains afflicting him—he says!—
Didn't he ask some other remedy?

AGNÈS: No. But you can be sure, if he had asked it,
I would have granted everything, to cure him.

ARNOLPHE (*aside*): Thanks be to heaven, I have got off cheap;
And I'll deserve the worst, if I slip again.
Enough! (*Aloud*) Your innocence, Agnes, is at fault.
I don't reprove you, and what's done is done.
I know that by his flatteries the gallant
Wants to deceive you, and after, laugh at you.

AGNÈS: Oh, not at all! He's told me a dozen times.

ARNOLPHE: Ah, you don't know how little you can trust him!
But learn this: that to accept a jewel box,
To listen to the wheedling of young dandies,
And out of mere passivity, to let them
Thus kiss your hands and tickle your insides
Is a mortal sin, and one of the very biggest!

	Has carried matters past the joking stage.
AGNÈS:	What is the matter? You seem to be displeased.
	Was there anything wrong in what I told you about?
ARNOLPHE:	Why, no, indeed. But tell what happened then,
	And how the young man occupied his visits.
AGNÈS:	Oh, dear, if you could see how happy he was,

AGNÈS: Oh, dear, if you could see how happy he was,
How he immediately lost his affliction,
And the beautiful jewel box he presented me,
And the money he gave to Alain and Georgette,
You'd love him too, you'd join with us in saying—

ARNOLPHE: Yes, yes. But what did he do, alone with you?

AGNÈS: He swore he loved me, with unparalleled love,
And said the sweetest things you can imagine,
Things like things no one ever heard before.
They kind of tickled me inside, and stirred
Something which makes me sort of excited still.

ARNOLPHE (*aside*): Oh, cruel probing of a mysterious evil,
Wherein the surgeon suffers all the pain!
(*Aloud*) Now, in addition to all these lovely words,
Didn't he also give you some—caresses?

AGNÈS: Oh, lots! He took my hands, he took my arms;
He never seemed to tire of kissing them.

ARNOLPHE: And, Agnes, didn't he take something else?
(AGNÈS *seems taken aback*)
Ouf!

AGNÈS: Well, he—

ARNOLPHE: What?

AGNÈS: Took—

ARNOLPHE: Uh!

AGNÈS: My—

ARNOLPHE: Well?

AGNÈS: I daren't!
I am afraid you may be angry with me.

ARNOLPHE: No.

AGNÈS: Yes, you will!

ARNOLPHE: No, no!

AGNÈS: Then give me your word.

ARNOLPHE: All right, then.

AGNÈS: Well, he took my—you'll be mad!

ARNOLPHE: No.

AGNÈS: Yes.

ARNOLPHE: No, no! What's all the mystery?
What did he take?

AGNÈS: Well, he—

ARNOLPHE (*aside*):   God, how I suffer!

AGNÈS: He took my ribbon, the ribbon that you gave me.
To tell you the actual truth, I couldn't stop him.

ARNOLPHE (*subsiding*):
We'll let the ribbon go. I wanted to know
If he did anything else than kiss your arms.

AGNÈS: Why, are there other things to do?

ARNOLPHE: No; no.
But to cure the pains afflicting him—he says!—
Didn't he ask some other remedy?

AGNÈS: No. But you can be sure, if he had asked it,
I would have granted everything, to cure him.

ARNOLPHE (*aside*): Thanks be to heaven, I have got off cheap;
And I'll deserve the worst, if I slip again.
Enough! (*Aloud*) Your innocence, Agnes, is at fault.
I don't reprove you, and what's done is done.
I know that by his flatteries the gallant
Wants to deceive you, and after, laugh at you.

AGNÈS: Oh, not at all! He's told me a dozen times.

ARNOLPHE: Ah, you don't know how little you can trust him!
But learn this: that to accept a jewel box,
To listen to the wheedling of young dandies,
And out of mere passivity, to let them
Thus kiss your hands and tickle your insides
Is a mortal sin, and one of the very biggest!

AGNÈS: A sin, you say! And what's the reason, please?

ARNOLPHE: The reason? It's the sanctified pronouncement
That by such actions heaven is offended.

AGNÈS: Offended? Why should heaven be offended?
Oh, dear! It was all so pleasant and so nice!
It's wonderful how one enjoys all that!
I didn't know about those things at all.

ARNOLPHE: Yes, they're enjoyable, all those endearments,
Those melting words, those softening caresses;
But they must be enjoyed in righteousness;
Their wickedness must be removed by marriage.

AGNÈS: And when you're married, it's a sin no more?

ARNOLPHE: Quite so.

AGNÈS: Then let me get married right away.

ARNOLPHE: If that's what you desire, why, I do too.
I have come back to see about your marriage.

AGNÈS: Can it be possible!

ARNOLPHE: Yes.

AGNÈS: How happy you'll make me!

ARNOLPHE: Yes, I don't doubt that you'll be happy in marriage.

AGNÈS: You want to have the two of us—

ARNOLPHE: Exactly.

AGNÈS: If that takes place, how I will love and kiss you!

ARNOLPHE: Aha! And I, my dear, shall reciprocate.

AGNÈS: I never can tell when people are making jokes.
You're speaking seriously?

ARNOLPHE: Oh, yes; you'll see.

AGNÈS: We shall be married?

ARNOLPHE: Yes.

AGNÈS: But when?

ARNOLPHE: This evening.

AGNÈS (*laughing*): This evening?

ARNOLPHE: This evening. So it makes you laugh?

AGNÈS: Oh, yes.

ARNOLPHE: My one desire is to see you happy.

AGNÈS: I am so mightily indebted to you!
How happy I am going to be with him!

ARNOLPHE: With whom?

AGNÈS: Why, him.

ARNOLPHE: Not him. No, that's a mistake.
You are a little hasty in picking a husband.
No, it's another I have in mind for you.
And as for that fellow—*him*—it's my idea
That though his famous illness should carry him off,
You must break off all dealings with him, now.
And if he comes to the house, you will salute him
By slamming the door politely in his face,
And if he knocks, you'll drop a brick from the window,
And thus oblige him to forgo his visits.
You understand me, Agnes? I'll be hidden
In a corner, where I'll watch all that you do.

AGNÈS: Oh, dear! He's so good-looking!

ARNOLPHE: No more talk!

AGNÈS: I shall not have the heart—

ARNOLPHE: And no more noise!
Now go upstairs.

AGN᷒ . But what! You want—

ARNOLPHE: Enough.
I'm master here. I order; you obey.

ACT III

ARNOLPHE, AGNÈS, *with some sewing or other work in hand,* ALAIN, GEORGETTE.

ARNOLPHE: Yes, everything went well, and I'm delighted.
You have obeyed my orders most exactly,
And put to rout the villainous seducer.
That shows the importance of good management.

Your innocence, dear Agnes, was abused.
Just see how you were thoughtlessly involved!
Had I not intervened, you would have taken
The highroad leading to hell and to perdition.
We know too well the ways of those young dandies,
Their ribbons, plumes, and ruffles at the knee.
They have long hair, fine teeth, and ready speech;
But as I tell you, the claws are sheathed beneath.
They are real Satans, whose insatiable jaws
Seek ever to devour the honor of women.
But after all, thanks to my care and foresight,
You have escaped their hellish wiles unscathed.
Your attitude, in throwing the brick at him
And thus demolishing his hopeful projects,
Convinces me that we should not defer
The wedding I have had in mind for you.
But first, I think it proper I should give you
A little serious talk, for your improvement.
(*To* ALAIN) A chair, out here in the cool. (*To*
　　GEORGETTE) And you, if ever—

GEORGETTE: Oh, we'll remember all your lessons well.
That other gentleman, he took us in;
But—

ALAIN: 　　　　　If he gets in, I'll never drink again.
He's a fool anyhow; the other time
He gave us two gold crowns—light weight; no good.

ARNOLPHE: Get what I ordered, then, for supper tonight.
And as I told you, when you're coming back,
You'll bring along the notary who lives
At the corner, to draw up the marriage contract.
(*Exit* ALAIN *and* GEORGETTE; ARNOLPHE *sits*)
Agnes, let your work go and listen to me.
Lift up your head a little. Turn your face.
(*He puts his finger on his forehead*)
There; look at me there, while I am talking to you.

And fix well in your mind my slightest word.
Agnes, I'm wedding you. And every moment
You ought to bless your happy destiny.
Reflect upon your original low estate,
And realize my own benevolence
In raising you from the humble rank of peasant
To that of the honorable bourgeoisie,
To share the bed, to enjoy the love of one
Who has always fled the yoke and bonds of marriage,
Who has refused, to eligible partners,
The honor which he now confers on you.
You should, I say, keep ever before your eyes
Your insignificance without this union,
So that this thought may ever the more inspire you
To merit the state of life to which I call you,
And know yourself, and so act that I may
Congratulate myself on my decision.
Marriage, my dear, is not a laughing matter.
The status of wife binds one to solemn duties,
And you will not ascend to that position
In order to live a free and easy life.
Agnes, your sex is made to be dependent;
The beard is the symbol of authority.
Although mankind's divided in two halves,
Nevertheless these halves are far from equal.
One is the major half, the other minor;
One is the governing half, the other subject.
And what obedience the well-instructed
Soldier displays to his appointed captain,
The servant to his lord, the child to his father,
The least lay brother to his Superior,
Is nothing at all, to the docility,
And the obedience, and the humility,
And the profound respect that a wife should show
To her husband, who is her master, chief, and king.

When he confers on her a serious glance,
Her duty is forthwith to lower her eyes,
And never to dare to look him in the face
Till he vouchsafes to her a pleasant look.
The women today don't understand this well,
But don't be led astray by others' example,
Don't imitate those horrible coquettes
Whose escapades the entire city rings with,
And don't be caught by the wiles of the Evil One—
That is, by listening to some young dandy.
Reflect that when I make you half of me,
It is my honor I entrust to you.
This honor is tender; it is easily hurt.
On such a subject there can be no trifling,
And down in hell there are some boiling caldrons
In which are plunged women of evil life.
What I am saying is not just idle talk;
You should lay up these lessons in your heart.
If you regard them, fleeing coquettishness,
Your soul will be like a lily, white and pure.
But if you take a step away from honor,
Your soul will turn a dreadful black, like coal;
You will look horrible to everyone,
And one day you will be the devil's prey;
You'll roast in hell to all eternity.
But may God's mercy guard you from that fate!
Drop me a curtsy. Now, as in a convent
A novice ought to know by heart her office,
A bride, entering marriage, should do the same.
(*Rising*) I have in my pocket a valuable book
Which will instruct you in the office of wife.
The writer I don't know; he's some good soul.
I want this booklet to be all your study.
Here it is. Let me see how well you read it.

AGNÈS   (*reading*): "Marriage Maxims; or, The Duties of

the Married Woman; with daily exercises. First
Maxim:

A woman who's admitted
To a matrimonial bed
Will be much benefited
To get it in her head
That when a husband takes her for his own,
He does so for his interest alone."

ARNOLPHE: I will explain the meaning of all that.
But for the present, simply read the text.

AGNÈS: "Second Maxim:

She should adorn her face,
And seek for personal grace
Only as much as her master may decree:
He judges if she's comely;
That others find her homely
Is a matter of complete irrelevancy.

Third Maxim:

Let her eschew the ogling glance magnetic,
And every face cream, powder, and cosmetic
Designed the casual passer-by to strike.
Such vanities are foes to honor and duty.
Let her refrain from worrying about beauty:
Good husbands do not care what their wives look
like.

Fourth Maxim:

Under her coif, whenever she leaves the house,
She must suppress that look which lures and
melts.
If she would give full pleasure to a spouse,
She must give none to anybody else.

Fifth Maxim:

Except for those who pay a business call,
She should receive no visitors at all.
They'll try all artifices,

With offers to assist her;
But what's good for the missis
Is no good for the mister.
Sixth Maxim:
Men's gifts she will always refuse,
Unless she would pass for a dumb thing;
According to present-day views,
Men always want something for something.
Seventh Maxim:
She'll have no paper, pencil, pen, or ink,
But have no incommodities, despite it.
Her husband's obligation is to think;
If anything needs writing, he will write it.
Eighth Maxim:
The gatherings one calls
Dances, parties, balls,
Often of all corruptions are the den.
They ought to be suppressed,
For all too many a guest
Is plotting there against poor married men.
Ninth Maxim:
A woman who is virtuous regards
Nothing more evil than to play at cards;
For runs of ill luck often make
Her lose more than she counted on,
And she is then inclined to stake
What's left when all her money's gone.
Tenth Maxim:
When one receives a tempting invitation
To an entertainment in some fine resort,
Or to a lavish country celebration,
One always should decline to join the sport:
For in the end, come what come may,
The husbands are the ones who pay."

ARNOLPHE: You'll finish them alone, and I'll explain

These matters properly and in detail.
I have a little business to attend to.
It isn't serious; I won't be long.
Go in now; guard the booklet preciously.
And if the notary comes, tell him to wait.
(*Exit* AGNÈS)
The best thing I can do is to marry her.
I'll mold her spirit according to my will.
She's like a piece of wax I hold in my hand,
And I can give her whatever form I wish.
During my absence I was nearly caught,
It's true, by her excessive innocence;
And yet it's better that a wife should err
In that direction, if she errs at all.
For such mistakes the remedy's at hand.
The simple soul is readily teachable;
And if she leaves the straight and narrow path,
A word of censure brings her back to it.
But the shrewd woman is quite different;
Our lot in life depends upon her whim.
Nothing can turn her from her purposes;
Our admonitions get lip service only.
She uses her wits to mock our principles,
And, often, she makes virtues of her crimes,
And, to attain her culpable purposes,
She finds devices to trick the cleverest man;
There is no way to block her enterprises.
There's no intriguer like an intelligent woman.
If she makes up her mind to repudiate
A husband's honor, he might as well surrender.
Plenty of worthy men can tell you that.
But that young fool will have no cause to boast;
He has undone himself by talking too much—
And that's the Frenchmen's ordinary fault.
When they are lucky in a love affair,

They can do everything but keep it secret.
Their silly vanity has such a power
They'd rather be hung than not tell anyone.
A woman must be tempted by the devil,
When she puts confidence in these scatterbrains.
—But here he is. I must conceal my thoughts,
And find out how he's taking his defeat.
(*Enter* HORACE.)

HORACE: I've just come from your house. It's clearly fated
That I should never find you when I call.
But I'll continue to pay my formal visits—

ARNOLPHE: Now, now, you needn't be punctilious.
Our social ceremonies are a bore;
I should be glad to see them done away with.
Most of us waste three quarters of our time
In these nonsensical formalities.
Put on your hat, please. Now, your love affairs—
Good Horace, may I learn how they're progressing?
I'm sorry I was sulky when I left you;
I was distracted. Now my mind is clear.
You took the first steps with amazing speed;
I'd like to know how you are getting on.

HORACE: The fact is, since I made you my report,
There's been a setback to my enterprise.

ARNOLPHE: Oho! And how is that?

HORACE: A cruel fate
Brought back my lady's master from the country.

ARNOLPHE: Bad luck!

HORACE: Besides, to my very great regret,
He's learned about our secret interviews.

ARNOLPHE: And how the devil did he find that out?

HORACE: I couldn't say; but anyway, it's certain.
I thought that I would pay, at the usual time,
A little visit to my charming lady;
And all of a sudden, changing their attitude,

The pair of servants wouldn't let me in;
And saying: "Go away, you troublemaker!"
They very rudely shut the door in my face.

ARNOLPHE: The door in your face!

HORACE: In my face.

ARNOLPHE: That's going far.

HORACE: I tried to argue with them, in the doorway;
To all I said they only had one answer:
"You won't come in; the master has forbid it."

ARNOLPHE: So they didn't open?

HORACE: No. And from the window
Agnes confirmed that her master had returned
By driving me off, with a very haughty tone,
Accompanied by a brick she threw at me.

ARNOLPHE: A brick, you say?

HORACE: A brick of the larger size.
A most discouraging present for a caller.

ARNOLPHE: The devil! That's hardly much ado about nothing!
The situation's bad, it seems to me.

HORACE: It's true, the fellow's return has thrown me off.

ARNOLPHE: It makes me sorry for you, I protest.

HORACE: He upsets everything.

ARNOLPHE: Why, never mind.
You'll find some way to come back into favor.

HORACE: I must get inside information somehow
To trick the vigilance of the jealous man.

ARNOLPHE: That should be easy. After all, the girl
Loves you?

HORACE: Oh, yes.

ARNOLPHE: Well then, you'll find a way.

HORACE: I hope so.

ARNOLPHE: You were routed by the brick;
You shouldn't let that stun you.

HORACE: Certainly not.
I understood the goodman was at home,

Secretly organizing the defense.
But what surprised me—it'll surprise you, too—
Was another incident I'll tell you about,
A bold contrivance of my little beauty.
You wouldn't expect it, from her simple air.
You have to admit, love is a splendid teacher,
Telling us how to be what we never were.
Love often gives us accurate instructions
How we can change our character in a jiffy.
It breaks down all the obstacles of nature;
Its transformations seem like miracles.
In a moment it makes a miser generous,
A coward valiant, and a boor polite.
It makes the dullest sluggard enterprising,
And gives sagacity to the innocent girl.
That miracle has taken place in Agnes.
She broke off with me outwardly, by saying:
"Sir, go away. I do not want your visits.
I know all you will say, and here's my answer!"
And then this brickbat, which surprised you so,
Fell at my feet, together with a letter.
And I'm amazed to see how the letter fits
With her uttered words, and the symbolic brick.
Now don't you find this action very surprising?
Isn't love wonderful in sharpening wits?
Can you deny love's power to inspire
The most amazing things in human hearts?
What do you think of the trick and the little letter?
Don't you admire her readiness of wit?
And don't you find it comic to think of the role
Our jealous fellow plays in the comedy?
Tell me.

ARNOLPHE: Oh, very comic.

HORACE: Well, then, laugh.

(ARNOLPHE *laughs painfully*)

That man, the enemy of my amour,
Entrenches himself, with bricks for ammunition,
As if I threatened to scale the walls of his house!
And then, in his fantastic fear, he rouses
All of his household troops, to repel the assailant!
And the girl he tries to keep in ignorance
Befools him, in plain sight, with his own contrivance!
Why, I admit, although his coming back
Has put a nasty obstacle in my path,
It's one of the funniest things I've ever heard of!
I cannot even think of it without laughing . . .
It doesn't seem to me you're laughing much.

ARNOLPHE: Forgive me, I'm laughing at it as much as I can.

HORACE: For friendship's sake, I'll have to show you the letter.
She's found the way to express what her heart feels
In touching terms, displaying all her virtue,
Her artless, frank, and innocent affection,
In short, in such a way as nature itself
Reveals the earliest troubling sting of love.

ARNOLPHE (*aside*):
So that's what comes of knowing how to write!
It was against my orders that she learned to.

HORACE (*reading*): "I want to write to you, but I have a lot
of trouble knowing how to start. I have some
thoughts that I wish you could know about; but
I don't know exactly how to tell them to you, and
I don't really trust my own words. As I'm beginning to realize that I've always been kept in a
state of ignorance, I'm afraid of putting down
something wrong, and of saying more than I
ought to. To tell the truth, I don't know what is
the terrible thing you've done to me, but I feel
dreadfully unhappy about what they are making
me do to you, and it will cause me great distress
not to see you, and I would be very glad to be

yours. Perhaps there is something wrong in saying
that; but anyway I can't help saying it, and I wish
I could be yours without doing anything wrong.
People tell me all the time that young men are
deceivers, and that one mustn't listen to them, and
that everything you tell me is only to trick me;
but I assure you that I haven't yet been able to
conceive that of you; and I am so touched by
your words that I can hardly believe they are lies.
Tell me frankly the truth about it; for after all,
as I have no evil intentions, you would act very
wrongly in deceiving me, and I think I would die
of sorrow."

ARNOLPHE   (*aside*):
The snake!

HORACE: What's wrong?

ARNOLPHE: What? Nothing. I was just coughing.

HORACE: Have you ever heard a sweeter utterance?
In spite of all that tyranny could do,
Can a lovelier nature thus reveal itself?
Isn't it surely a punishable crime
To corrupt the innate quality of that soul,
To try to stifle her natural endowments
With a cloak of ignorance and stupidity?
Love has begun to tear away the veil,
And if, by the aid of favorable fate,
I may, as I hope, repay that animal,
That traitor, hangman, scoundrel, villainous brute—

ARNOLPHE: Good-by.

HORACE: What? Leaving so soon?

ARNOLPHE: I've just remembered
I must attend to a very urgent matter.

HORACE: Wait! Since they keep her shut in, wouldn't you
know
Someone who might have access to the house?

Maybe it's an unreasonable request,
But friends may be asked to give such services.
The occupants of the house are hostile to me,
And the two servants, when I run across them,
Will not abandon their mistrustful manner,
No matter what the blandishments I try.
I did have a useful agent, an old woman,
Whose genius, in some ways, was superhuman.
In the beginning she served me very well,
But just four days ago the poor thing died.
Wouldn't you know some intermediary?

ARNOLPHE: No, really. You will do all right without me.
HORACE: Good-by, then. I give you all my confidence.
(*Exit* HORACE.)

ARNOLPHE: How I am forced to suffer in his presence!
How I must struggle to conceal my pain!
How can an innocent girl conceive such tricks?
Either her innocence is all pretended,
Or the devil whispers cunning in her soul.
I thought that fatal letter was going to kill me!
That scoundrel has taken possession of her mind,
He's forced his way in, and supplanted me.
It's anguish to me; it drives me to despair.
The theft of her heart inflicts a double wound,
For my love suffers, and my honor too.
I'm furious to be ousted from my place,
And furious that my pains have gone for nothing.
I know that I can punish her guilty love
By letting her evil destiny take its course,
That I'll be avenged on her by her own actions;
But it's distressing to lose the one we love.
Good God! I picked a wife on policy;
Why must I now be so obsessed by her?
She has no parents, protectors, property,
And she betrays my kindness, pains—and love!

I love her still, after this evil trick,
So that I cannot do without her love!
Have you no shame, fool? Oh, it drives me mad!
Oh, I could cudgel myself a thousand times! . . .
I will go in a while, but only to see
The face she shows, after her foul behavior.
God grant my honor may remain unsullied,
Or if it's written that that is not to be,
Grant that in my misfortune I may show
The constancy I see in some about me.

ACT IV

Enter ARNOLPHE *from the house.*

ARNOLPHE: I find it very hard to stay in place.
My mind is troubled by necessary cares,
Planning defenses, in the house and out,
To cross the purposes of that young coxcomb.
How unconcernedly she welcomed me!
She's not disturbed by all her evil acts!
And though she brings me to the edge of death,
It seems to be no business of hers!
The more I watched her sitting, cool and calm,
The more I felt a fury rise in me;
And the upsurging transports of my heart
Seemed to redouble all my amorous ardor.
I was embittered, angry, desperate;
And yet she never looked so beautiful.
Her eyes had never seemed so bright and searching,
And never they roused such sharp desire in me.
I feel in my heart that I must burst asunder
If the calamity should fall on me.
So! I have supervised her education
With such precaution and with such affection,

I've had her in my house from babyhood,
On her I've built my tenderest hopes and dreams,
I've fondly watched her grow to be a woman,
For thirteen years I've trained her character,
So that a silly youth may catch her fancy,
And carry her off, under my very eyes,
When she's already almost married to me!
No, no! Good God, no, no! My dear young fool,
Play all your little games, but I'll be bound,
I will annihilate your happy hopes,
And you will find you cannot laugh at me!
(*Enter* NOTARY.)

NOTARY: Why, there you are! I was on my way to see you
To draw the contract which you want to make.

ARNOLPHE   (*oblivious*): How shall I do it?

NOTARY: In the regular form.

ARNOLPHE   (*oblivious*): I must take every vigilant precaution.

NOTARY: I shall write nothing against your interests.

ARNOLPHE   (*oblivious*): I must protect myself against surprise.

NOTARY: If things are in my hands, you needn't worry.
You'll just remember never to endorse
The contract till the money has been paid.

ARNOLPHE   (*oblivious*): But if I act too openly, I fear
There will be cau•e for gossip in the town.

NOTARY: It's easy to prevent publicity;
The contract can be kept entirely secret.

ARNOLPHE   (*oblivious*): But how I shall stand with her, that is
the question.

NOTARY: Her dowry is proportionate to yours.

ARNOLPHE   (*oblivious*):
I love her; it's my love that makes the trouble.

NOTARY: In that case, she'll expect a little more.

ARNOLPHE   (*oblivious*):
How shall I treat her, in the circumstances?

NOTARY: The husband pays a sum equivalent to
              One third of the dowry; but the rule's not fixed.
              He can go further, if he wishes to.

ARNOLPHE   (*oblivious*):
              If— (*He catches sight of* NOTARY.)

NOTARY: One may provide for a surviving spouse.
              In short, the husband can endow the wife
              Just as he pleases.

ARNOLPHE: Eh?

NOTARY: He can well serve her,
              If he loves her much and wishes to benefit her,
              Either by jointure, or a settlement
              Which is annulled on occasion of her death,
              With or without reversion to named heirs;
              Or according to common law, as specified,
              Or deed of gift, as stated in the contract,
              Which may be unilateral or mutual.
              Why do you make a face? I don't make sense?
              You think I don't know how a contract's drawn?
              Then who is going to teach me? No one alive!
              Don't I know well that consorts hold in common
              Property, chattels, goods, appurtenances,
              Unless this right is formally renounced?
              And don't I know that a third of the bride's posses·
                sions
              Enter the joint estate—

ARNOLPHE: Yes, yes, of course
              You know all that. Who said a word about it?

NOTARY: You did; you're trying to make me pass for a fool,
              Shrugging your shoulders, making faces at me.

ARNOLPHE: The devil take the man and his ugly face!
              Good-by, good-by; we'll have no more of this.

NOTARY: But didn't you send for me to draw a contract?

ARNOLPHE: Why, yes, I did; but the matter has been postponed.

You will be summoned when the time is fixed.
You make me sick with your gabble-gabble-gabble.
(*Exit* ARNOLPHE.)

NOTARY: I think he's mad; I think I'm right to think so.
(*Enter* ALAIN *and* GEORGETTE)
You've come to fetch me at your master's order?

ALAIN: Yes, sir.

NOTARY: I don't know what you think of him,
But kindly give him this important message:
That he's a blockhead.

GEORGETTE: We won't fail to do so.
(*Exit* NOTARY. *Enter* ARNOLPHE.)

ALAIN: Monsieur—

ARNOLPHE: Come here. You are my faithful servants,
My good, true friends. I've had a report of you.

ALAIN: The notary—

ARNOLPHE: Don't bother with him now.
Some enemies are plotting against my honor.
And what an outrage it would be to you,
My friends, to have your master lose his honor!
You'd never dare to appear again in public,
For everyone would point at you and jeer!
Since it is your affair as much as mine,
You must be sure to keep such careful guard
That that young gallant can't in any way—

GEORGETTE: We have already learned our lesson well.

ARNOLPHE: You mustn't let his fine words take you in.

ALAIN: Really, sir—

GEORGETTE: We know how to protect ourselves.

ARNOLPHE (*to* ALAIN):
Supposing he says, "Alain, my excellent fellow,
Help me a little to assuage my grief—"

ALAIN: "You are a fool!"

ARNOLPHE: Splendid! (*To* GEORGETTE) "My
sweet Georgette,

You are so darling and so good by nature—"

GEORGETTE: "You are a booby!"

ARNOLPHE: Good! (*To* ALAIN) "What harm is there
In my honest, upright, virtuous purposes?"

ALAIN: "You are a rascal!"

ARNOLPHE: Good! (*To* GEORGETTE) "My death is certain
Unless you pity the agony I endure!"

GEORGETTE: "You are an impudent lummox!"

ARNOLPHE: Excellent!
"Of course, I don't expect something for nothing;
When people serve me well, I don't forget it.
So, Alain, here's a little present for you;
And Georgette, go and buy yourself a dress.
(*He holds out money, which the servants take*)
That's just a sample of my liberal nature.
The only favor that I ask of you
Is a moment's conversation with your lady."

GEORGETTE (*pushing him*):
"You think I'm crazy?"

ARNOLPHE: Good!

ALAIN (*pushing him*):   "Get out!"

ARNOLPHE: Good!

GEORGETTE (*pushing him*):   "Now!"

ARNOLPHE: Good—but that's plenty.

GEORGETTE: Didn't I do it right?

ALAIN: That is the way you mean it, isn't it?

ARNOLPHE: Except for the money, which you shouldn't have taken.

GEORGETTE: I guess we didn't remember that part right.

ALAIN: Do you want to have us do it over?

ARNOLPHE: No.
Enough. Go back in the house.

ALAIN: You've only to say so.

ARNOLPHE: No, no; go back in the house, those are my orders.
You can keep the money. I'll join you presently.
Keep your eyes peeled, and lend a hand at need.
(*Exit* ALAIN *and* GEORGETTE)
I think that I'll engage the worthy cobbler
At the corner of our street to be my spy.
And Agnes will be well shut up in the house.
I'll keep good guard. Especially I'll banish
All ribbon sellers, and female notion dealers,
Hairdressers, glovers, peddlers of handkerchiefs,
All those who make a business on the side
Of encouraging the mysteries of love.
I've been around, I know their little tricks.
My man will have to be extremely clever
To get a note or message past my guard.
(*Enter* HORACE.)
HORACE: I have great luck in meeting you in this quarter.
Well, I've just had a very narrow escape!
Just now, when I left you, what should I happen to
see
But Agnes, appearing alone on her balcony,
Enjoying the cool of the overhanging trees!
She made me a signal; then she was bright enough
To come downstairs and open the garden gate.
We went up to her room; but a moment after
She heard her jealous guardian mount the stairs.
In the face of danger she found the expedient
Of shutting me up in a wardrobe, with her dresses.
He entered right away. I couldn't see him,
But I heard him striding to and fro, unspeaking,
But uttering pitiful sighs from time to time,
And sometimes smiting the table with his fist,
And kicking a little dog who was sorry for him,
And throwing Agnes' garments on the floor.
He even broke, with a furious hand, some vases

With which my lady adorned her mantelpiece.
So certainly this man, this hornèd goat,
Must have some inkling of his situation.
After a time, when he had thus discharged
His anger on these uncomplaining objects,
In agitation, but without a word,
He left the room, and I my hiding place.
Naturally, in fear of the gentleman,
We couldn't hazard staying together longer.
It was too dangerous. However, tonight,
Late, I am due to slip into her room.
I shall announce myself by coughing thrice,
And she will open her window at the signal.
Then, with a ladder and with Agnes' aid,
Love will attempt to wing me to her side.
I'm glad to tell it to you, my only friend.
The heart's delight increases with the telling;
No matter how perfect a person's bliss may be,
He's hardly satisfied if nobody knows it.
You will be happy to learn how things are going.
Good-by. I have to attend to my preparations.
(*Exit* HORACE.)

ARNOLPHE: And so the hostile fate which has decreed
My agony, gives me hardly time to breathe!
I am to see my prudent vigilance
Forever undone by their conspiracies!
I, in my ripeness, am to be the dupe
Of a simple girl and a rattleheaded youth!
For twenty years, a sage philosopher,
I've watched the unhappy destiny of husbands,
I've counted up the various accidents
Which bring the most sagacious to their doom;
I've profited by their calamities,
And when I chose a wife, I sought for ways
To guard myself against all interlopers,

And guarantee that I would be no cuckold.
And, to my ends, I thought I had employed
The ultimate in human artfulness!
But fate no doubt has issued a decree
That never a husband is to be exempt;
For after all my study, after all
The experience I've gained upon the matter,
After some twenty years of meditation
On the precautions I proposed to take
To distinguish myself from all the other husbands,
I'm caught with them in the universal trap!
No, no! That cursèd fate shall not be mine!
I hold her still secure in my possession.
Though the young fop has robbed me of her heart,
I shall make sure that that is all he'll win.
The night appointed for their tender triumph
Will not pass so delightfully as they think.
And, in my griefs, it is some satisfaction
To be informed of the snare that's laid for me.
It's nice that this ambitious idiot
Should take his rival for his confidant.
(*Enter* CHRYSALDE.)

CHRYSALDE: Good evening. Shall we dine, as we agreed?
ARNOLPHE: No, not this evening.
CHRYSALDE: What is this, a joke?
ARNOLPHE: Excuse me, please. Some troubles have arisen.
CHRYSALDE: Something has happened to your marriage plans?
ARNOLPHE: You needn't be concerned with my affairs.
CHRYSALDE: My, what a temper! You're in trouble, then?
          Has some mischance occurred, to interrupt
          The happy progress of your love addresses?
          Indeed, from your appearance, I would guess it.
ARNOLPHE: Whatever happens, at least I'll have the advantage
          Of not resembling certain friends of mine
          Who calmly admit supplanters to their homes.

CHRYSALDE: It's strange that you, with all your understanding,
Should be so sensitive upon this subject,
Equating happiness with security,
And making honor lie in one point only!
Cruelty, greed, baseness and double-dealing
Are unimportant, in comparison;
Regardless of one's life and character,
Honor consists in dodging cuckoldry!
Why, in all logic, should a man's good name
Depend upon this casual circumstance?
Why should a sensible man reproach himself
For a misfortune which he can't prevent?
Why should the actions of a wife determine
If a man is worthy of honor or of blame?
And if she's false to her trust, why should we make
A frightful monster of her falsity?
A gentleman should properly regard
Cuckoldry in a reasonable way.
Since no one can ward off the blows of chance,
This accident should not be taken to heart.
For after all, the trouble comes entirely
From the way in which you choose to treat the
    matter.
To guide oneself among such difficulties
One should avoid excess in everything.
Don't imitate those too broad-minded people
Who seem complacent with their situation,
And proudly name the lovers of their wives,
Extolling their talents and their excellence,
Avowing a warm affection for the gallants,
Attending all their little dinner parties,
So that society most justly finds
That tolerance can turn to effrontery.
Such conduct, certainly, we ought to blame,
But the other extreme is equally indecent.

If I decry the lovers of wives' lovers,
I likewise disapprove the turbulent husbands
Whose noisy and imprudent lamentations
Arouse the general curiosity.
Their outbursts are apparently intended
To leave no man in ignorance of their state.
Between these courses is a middle way
Which the prudent man, if need be, should adopt.
Taking this course, he will not have to blush
At the worst a faithless wife can do to him.
And thus, in short, the state of cuckoldry
Need not be so appalling, after all.
The thing to do is to make the best of it;
And the best, as I insist, is not so bad.

ARNOLPHE: After this speech, the fellowship of cuckolds
Should give a vote of thanks to your noble worship;
And anyone who listens to your discourse
Would be delighted to join the fraternity.

CHRYSALDE: I don't say that, for that's what I condemn.
But since it's fate that designates our wives,
One should take marriage as a game of dice;
When you don't get the numbers that you want,
Play with the utmost caution, take no chances,
And change your luck by prudence and delay.

ARNOLPHE: In other words, sleep sound and eat your fill,
And say unfaithfulness is no great matter.

CHRYSALDE: You are sarcastic; but quite seriously,
I can see many things more terrifying,
More potent of calamity, than this
Particular accident which scares you so.
If I were given a choice of alternatives,
I'd so much rather be—what you're talking of—
Than spouse of one of those immaculate wives
Whose spleen makes life a constant inquisition,

Dragons of virtue, spotless female devils,
Entrenched behind their bulwarks of decorum,
Who, on the strength of one fault uncommitted,
Assume the right to vilify the world,
And who, on the grounds that they are always faith-
    ful,
Make us endure unnumbered miseries!
No, no, my excellent friend; in actual fact
The state of cuckoldry is what we make it.
It may be welcomed, in some circumstances;
It has its compensations, like the rest.

ARNOLPHE: You may well choose to make the best of it,
But I am in no mood to try it out.
And rather than accept that lot, I swear—

CHRYSALDE: Don't swear; an oath might lead to perjury.
If fate has willed it, you will struggle in vain.
You will not be consulted on the subject.

ARNOLPHE: I'd be a cuckold, then?

CHRYSALDE: Don't take it to heart,
Or be offended. Plenty of people are,
Who have much less than your advantages
Of person, character, and property.

ARNOLPHE: Don't compare me to such contemptible persons.
But anyway, I'm sick of your mockeries.
We'll have no more of this, if you please.

CHRYSALDE: You're angry.
I can't imagine why. Good-by. Remember,
Whatever your touchy honor may suggest,
That when you swear you'll never do a thing,
You've come already halfway toward the goal.
(*Exit* CHRYSALDE.)

ARNOLPHE: I swear it once again. Immediately
I'll take my measures against that accident.
(*Enter* ALAIN *and* GEORGETTE)

My friends, I want to beg your kind assistance.
I am most happy to know of your affection,
And now it must be clearly demonstrated.
And if you properly repay my trust,
You can be certain of a good reward.
The man you know about—but keep this quiet—
Expects to try his enterprise tonight,
And scale the wall, to force Miss Agnes' room.
But we will ambush him, the three of us!
I want to have you each take a good stick,
And when he reaches the top rung of his ladder
—I will take care to open the window shutters—
Both of you land your best blows on this traitor,
And leave his back well marked for a souvenir,
And teach him not to try such tricks again.
However, be sure you do not utter my name,
Or indicate that I am standing behind you.
You think you'll have the wits to pay him off?

ALAIN: When it comes to beating, sir, we're really good!
I hit, when I hit, with a very noble hit.

GEORGETTE: My hit, perhaps, doesn't look quite so hard,
But everybody says it hurts like fury.

ARNOLPHE: Go in, then. Not a word to anyone.
(*Exit* ALAIN *and* GEORGETTE)
The young man will receive a useful lesson.
If all the husbands of our little city
Should welcome thus the gallants of their wives,
The list of cuckolds would be much reduced.

ACT V

Early morning; the stage is nearly dark. Enter ALAIN
and GEORGETTE; *then* ARNOLPHE.

ARNOLPHE: You rogues, what made you act so violently?
ALAIN: Why, sir, we were only doing what you said.

ARNOLPHE: There's no use trying to give me that excuse.

My order was to beat him, not to kill him;

And on the back, I said, not on the head,

You were to land the blows which I commanded.

Good God! What accident has fate contrived!

How can I bear to go and find him dead!

Go back into the house. Don't breathe a word

Of a certain innocent order I may have given.

(*Exit* ALAIN *and* GEORGETTE)

It's nearly dawn. I'll have to lay my plans

How I shall act, in the face of this disaster.

Oh, what will become of me? And the boy's father,

What will he say, when he learns of this affair?

(*Enter* HORACE.)

HORACE: I'd better find out who this fellow is.

ARNOLPHE: No one could have predicted— (*Recognizes presence of* HORACE) What! Who's there?

HORACE: Seigneur Arnolphe, it's you?

ARNOLPHE: Yes; you—

HORACE: It's Horace.

I was just going to ask a favor of you!

You get up early.

ARNOLPHE   (*aside*):   I don't understand!

Is it a ghost? An optical illusion?

HORACE: In fact, I was in quite a predicament,

And I am grateful for heaven's kindly act

In placing you right here, just when I need you.

I'm glad to tell you everything turned out well,

Better indeed than I had dared to hope,

And by an incident that threatened ruin.

Suspicion was aroused, I don't know how,

About the meeting which had been arranged.

When I had climbed up almost to the window,

All of a sudden I saw some people appear,

Well armed, and raising clubs to smite me down.

They made me lose my footing and fall to the
    ground;
And though I suffered some bumps and scratches,
    still
My tumble saved me from a mighty clubbing.
These people—I think my jealous friend was with
    them—
Supposed my fall resulted from their blows.
As I was stunned and startled, and my pains
Made me lie motionless for quite a time,
They thought that they had actually killed me,
And the idea filled them with alarm.
I lay in silence, listening to their noise;
They were accusing each other of violence;
They cursed their fate; and then, without a light,
They came and felt me, to find if I were dead.
You can imagine that, in the night's darkness,
I did my best to imitate a corpse.
Then they retreated, frightened out of their wits.
I was considering retreating too,
When little Agnes, moved by the tragedy,
Came running to my side, in desperation.
For all the talk among them, naturally,
Was overheard by her attentive ear;
And, unobserved in the midst of all the tumult,
She had escaped quite easily from the house.
And when she found that I was safe and sound,
She fell into an ecstasy of joy.
To put it briefly, that delightful creature
Is yielding to the dictates of her love.
She has rebelled against returning home,
And she's entrusted all her fate to me.
Strange how her idiot keeper's tyranny
Has forced her innocence to desperate courses!

What are the perils which she would encounter,
If I did not adore her as I do!
But I love Agnes honorably and purely;
I'd rather die than cheat her confidence.
She is the one girl in the world for me;
Nothing but death will ever separate us.
I can foresee my father will make trouble,
But we'll be cautious, and appease his anger.
She has completely carried me away,
And a man must try to get what he wants in life.
Now what I ask of you—you'll be discreet—
Is to let me put my lady in your hands;
Favor my love by giving her retreat
In your own house, at least for a day or two.
I have to hide the fact of her escape;
No doubt there'll be a terrible hue and cry;
And naturally a girl of her appearance,
With a young man, arouses dark suspicions.
And so, sure as I am of your good will,
I've given to you my total confidence.
Also to you alone, my generous friend,
Can I entrust the partner of my love.

ARNOLPHE: Of course, I'm at your service. Yes, of course.

HORACE: You're willing to do me this momentous favor?

ARNOLPHE: Why, very gladly, I say. I am delighted
By the opportunity to help you out.
Oh, I thank heaven for its gracious gift!
I've never been so glad to do anything!

HORACE: I'm very grateful to you for your kindness.
I was afraid you might make difficulties.
But you're a man of the world; you understand
And sympathize with the ardor of the young.
I have a man who's guarding her at the corner.

ARNOLPHE: How shall we manage it? It's getting light.

                    If I meet her here, I may perhaps be seen.
                    And if you two should turn up at my house,
                    We'll have the servants talking. The best thing is
                    To bring her to me in a secluded place.
                    That garden's handy. I shall wait for her there.

HORACE: All these precautions are most sensible.
                    So I shall merely hand her over to you,
                    And then I'll go back quietly to my lodgings.
                    (*Exit* HORACE.)

ARNOLPHE: Ah, fortune! Here's a favorable shift
                    To make up for the evils you have done me!
                    (*He muffles his face in his cloak, and retreats to
                    the garden entrance. Enter* HORACE *and* AGNÈS)

HORACE   (*to* AGNÈS):
                    Don't worry about the place I'm taking you to.
                    I've found a refuge where you'll be secure.
                    You wouldn't be safe a moment in my lodgings.
                    Just go in there, and you'll be taken care of.
                    (ARNOLPHE, *in the garden entrance, takes her hand.*)

AGNÈS   (*to* HORACE):
                    Why are you leaving me?

HORACE: My dear, I have to.

AGNÈS: Well, then, come back as soon as possible.

HORACE: That is exactly what my love suggests.

AGNÈS: Whenever I don't see you, I'm not happy.

HORACE: And when you're absent, I'm unhappy too.

AGNÈS: If that were true, you would stay here with me.

HORACE: You don't suspect my love's not genuine?

AGNÈS: You don't love me as much as I love you.
                    (ARNOLPHE *tugs at her hand*)
                    Someone is pulling me.

HORACE: It's dangerous
                    For us to be seen together in this place.
                    The man beside you is my trusty friend,

And he's entirely in our interest.

AGNÈS: But I don't know him, and—

HORACE: Don't be afraid.

Nothing can happen when you're in his hands.

AGNÈS: But I would rather be in the hands of Horace!

And I'd— (*To* ARNOLPHE, *who is pulling her*)

You wait!

HORACE: Good-by. It's getting light.

AGNÈS: When will I see you?

HORACE: Certainly very soon.

AGNÈS: But I shall be in torture until then!

HORACE (*departing*):

Thank heaven, there's now no obstacle to my bliss;

I can repose in full security!

(*Exit* HORACE.)

ARNOLPHE (*disguising his voice*):

Come with me. This is not your lodging place.

I have prepared a refuge for you elsewhere.

There you will be secure—and solitary.

(*He throws back his cape, and resumes his normal voice*)

You recognize me?

AGNÈS: Oh!

ARNOLPHE: My face, you rogue,

Startles and terrifies you, obviously.

You are distressed and pained to see me here;

I'm the impediment to your love affair.

(AGNÈS *looks wildly about*)

You needn't look for help from your paramour;

He's now too far away to bring you aid.

Aha! So young! Already a double-dealer!

In your apparent innocence, you ask

If children are begotten through the ear,

And you appoint a midnight assignation,

And plan elopement with your cavalier!
'Odsbody! How your tongue runs on with him!
Where did you get your schooling? Who the devil
Taught you so much, and in so short a time?
Haven't you any fear of ghosts and goblins?
The visitor in the night has given you courage?
Oh, wicked girl, to plot such perfidy!
What a reward for all my kindnesses!
Serpent, whom I have cherished in my bosom,
Who came to consciousness, only to try
To poison me in pay for my caresses!

AGNÈS: Why are you shouting at me?

ARNOLPHE: And why not?

AGNÈS: I don't see anything wrong in what I've done.

ARNOLPHE: Isn't it wrong to follow a paramour?

AGNÈS: He tells me that he wants me for his wife.
I learned your lessons. You had preached to me
That one must marry to remove the sin.

ARNOLPHE: But I expected to take you for my wife.
I thought that I had made that perfectly clear.

AGNÈS: Yes, but to tell you frankly how I think,
He somehow seems to suit me better than you.
With you, marriage is very grim and tiresome,
And you describe it as a terrible thing.
But he—oh, dear!—he makes it so delightful,
He really makes me anxious to get married.

ARNOLPHE: You love him, then, you traitor?

AGNÈS: Yes, I love him.

ARNOLPHE: And you're so brazen as to tell me that!

AGNÈS: Why shouldn't I tell it to you, if it's true?

ARNOLPHE: You had the right to love him, minx?

AGNÈS: Oh, dear!
I couldn't help it! He's responsible!
I didn't really intend to, when it happened.

ARNOLPHE: You ought to have suppressed that amorous impulse.

AGNÈS: But how can one suppress something so nice?

ARNOLPHE: Didn't you know that I would disapprove?

AGNÈS: Oh, not at all! How could it injure you?

ARNOLPHE: Why, certainly, I ought to be delighted.
So you don't love me, then?

AGNÈS: Love you?

ARNOLPHE: Yes, me.

AGNÈS: Oh, no.

ARNOLPHE: What, no?

AGNÈS: You wouldn't have me lie?

ARNOLPHE: And why not love me, impudent, saucy girl?

AGNÈS: Oh, dear! It isn't me you ought to blame.
Why didn't you make me love you, as he did?
I don't think I prevented you at all.

ARNOLPHE: I did my best; I tried to do my best.
But all my efforts clearly came to nothing.

AGNÈS: He just knows how, assuredly, better than you.
He had no trouble at all in making me love him.

ARNOLPHE: Look how this peasant argues and replies!
One of the lady wits could do no better!
Oh, I misjudged her; or, upon this theme,
A silly girl knows more than a clever man.
Since you've become so keen in disputation,
Tell me, is it for him that I so long
Have fed and lodged and educated you?

AGNÈS: Oh, no. He'll pay you back with interest.

ARNOLPHE (*aside*):
Ouch! How she hits on painful turns of phrase!
(*Aloud*) But will he pay me back in full, you jade,
The obligations that you owe to me?

AGNÈS: Maybe the obligations aren't so great.

ARNOLPHE: It's nothing, then, to rear you from a child?

AGNÈS: You certainly did it in a funny way;

It was a pretty kind of education!
You think I like it? I don't realize
That I am trained to be a simpleton?
I am ashamed, myself; and at my age
I've had enough of passing for a fool.

ARNOLPHE: So, to escape from ignorance, you want
To have this dandy's lessons?

AGNÈS: Certainly.
He has revealed that I could know so much!
I think I owe him more than I do you.

ARNOLPHE: I don't know what restrains me from rewarding
This insolent speech with a good dressing-down!
I'm driven wild by her offensive calm!
It would do me good to give her a slap in the face.

AGNÈS: Why, you can slap me, if it gives you pleasure.

ARNOLPHE   (*aside*): Somehow she makes my anger disappear,
And all my old affection surges back
To obliterate the thought of her wickedness.
What a strange thing it is to love! How weak
A man can be, knowing he is betrayed!
Well we know women's faults and imperfections,
Their skittish humors and their lack of logic.
Their minds are evil, and their souls are frail;
There's nothing weaker, nothing sillier,
Nothing more faithless; and in spite of all,
Man will do everything for those animals.
(*Aloud*)
Well, let's make peace. And so, my little traitor,
I'll pardon you everything, and love you again.
Thus you can realize how much I love you;
Repay my charity by loving me.

AGNÈS: I'd most devoutly like to give you pleasure.
But if I could, it would be terribly hard.

ARNOLPHE: You can, my dainty darling, if you wish.

(*Sighs*) Why, I am sighing! That was a lover's sigh.
Look at me; see the torture in my face;
Give up that puppy and his puppy love.
He must have cast some evil spell upon you.
You will be so much happier with me!
You have a passion for fine clothes and gear;
You'll have them always, that I promise you.
And night and day I'll pet you and caress you,
Cuddle and coddle you; I'll eat you up!
And you can do exactly what you please.
. . . I won't explain my meaning. That's enough.
(*Aside*) To what extremities can passion drive us!
(*Aloud*) In short, no love can match the love I offer.
Ingrate, what is the proof you ask of me?
You want to see me weep? And beat my breast?
You want to have me tear out half my hair?
Or shall I kill myself? Is that what you want?
Oh, cruel girl, I'm ready to prove it so.

AGNÈS: Why, all your speeches don't engage my feelings.
Horace could do much more with a couple of words.

ARNOLPHE: You've flouted and provoked me long enough!
I have my plans for you, you saucy minx.
You scorn my wooing, and you drive me mad;
A convent cell will serve for my revenge.
(*Enter* ALAIN.)

ALAIN: Excuse me, sir. It's funny, but I think
Miss Agnes must have gone off with the corpse.

ARNOLPHE: No, here she is. Go put her in my room.
He certainly won't go looking for her there.
It's only for a half-hour, anyway.
I'm off to fetch a carriage, to convey her
To a securer place. Go, lock up well;
Don't let her out of your sight for a single moment.
(*Exit* ALAIN *and* AGNÈS)

Perhaps the change of circumstances may
Shake her out of her mad infatuation.
(*Enter* HORACE.)

HORACE: Arnolphe! You see a man in agony!
Heaven has put the crown on my misfortune!
There is a project, cruel and unjust,
To separate me from the one I love!
My father's chosen this morning to arrive.
I met him, just descending from the coach,
And no one could be more surprised than I was.
The reason for his visit is that he
Has made a marriage for me, without warning,
And he's come here to put it in effect!
Imagine—you will sympathize, I know—
Whether a worse disaster could occur!
I told you yesterday about Enrique;
He is the one who causes my misfortune.
He has arrived with father to destroy me;
His only daughter is the bride in question!
Hearing them talk, I thought that I would faint.
When father spoke of paying you a call,
I took no further heed, I hurried here
In panic fear, to be the first to warn you.
So please, for heaven's sake, don't breathe a word
Of my attachment; it would madden him.
And since he has such great regard for you,
Try to dissuade him from that other match.

ARNOLPHE: Why, yes, indeed.

HORACE: Tell him to put things off;
Render this friendly service to my love.

ARNOLPHE: Certainly.

HORACE: All my hope resides in you.

ARNOLPHE: Splendid!

HORACE: You are the truest father to me.

Tell him that at my age—I see him coming.
Listen; here are some arguments to use.

(HORACE *pulls* ARNOLPHE *to a corner of the stage,*
where they speak confidentially. Enter CHRYSALDE,
ORONTE, *and* ENRIQUE.)

ENRIQUE   (*to* CHRYSALDE):
The moment that I laid my eyes on you,
Without a word I would have recognized you.
You have the features of your lovely sister,
Whom I was privileged to call my wife.
How happy I would be, if the cruel fates
Had granted that she might return with me
To see again her home and relatives
After our sufferings in a foreign land.
But since the fatal power of destiny
Has robbed us of her presence, and forever,
We must resign ourselves, and give our thought
To the one surviving evidence of our love.
You are concerned; I should not venture to
Settle her fate without your warm approval.
The son of Oronte's an honorable choice,
But it must please you as it pleases me.

CHRYSALDE: You have a poor opinion of my judgment
If you can doubt that I approve of Horace.

ARNOLPHE   (*to* HORACE): Yes, I will properly defend your cause.

HORACE   (*to* ARNOLPHE):
And keep my secret—

ARNOLPHE   (*to* HORACE):   Oh, depend on that!

(ARNOLPHE *leaves* HORACE, *joins the others, and em-*
braces ORONTE.)

ORONTE: What a warm greeting from my good old friend!
ARNOLPHE: I'm filled with happiness to see you again!
ORONTE: I have come here—
ARNOLPHE: You needn't say a word.

I know what brings you.

ORONTE: You've been told already?

ARNOLPHE: Yes.

ORONTE: Very good.

ARNOLPHE: Your son resists this marriage.
He's prejudiced; he finds it most displeasing.
He even begged me to dissuade you from it.
But as for me, I give you this advice:
Do not allow the match to be postponed;
Exercise the authority of a father.
You ought to keep the young in strict control;
Indulgence injures their own interests.

HORACE   (*aside*):
Traitor!

CHRYSALDE: But if he finds the match distasteful,
I hold he ought not to be driven to it.
I think my brother will agree with that.

ARNOLPHE: He'll let himself be governed by his son?
You think a father ought to be so weak
As not to exact obedience from his children?
A fine thing, if our parents let themselves
Be guided by the ones they ought to guide!
No, no; my old friend's acts concern me deeply.
He's given his word; of course he has to keep it.
So let him show the firmness of his nature,
And make his son obey his wise decisions.

ORONTE: I quite agree; and in this marriage business
I can assure you he'll obey my orders.

CHRYSALDE   (*to* ARNOLPHE):
Really, I'm puzzled by the enthusiasm
You show in favor of this marriage bond.
I can't imagine what your motive is.

ARNOLPHE: Never you mind; I know what I am doing.

ORONTE: Yes, yes, Seigneur Arnolphe—

CHRYSALDE: That name annoys him.

	You have to call him Monsieur Delafield.
ARNOLPHE:	No matter.
HORACE:	What's all this?
ARNOLPHE (*to* HORACE):	Yes, that's the answer.
	And now you understand why I acted so.
HORACE:	I am bewildered—
	(*Enter* GEORGETTE.)
GEORGETTE (*to* ARNOLPHE):	Sir, if you don't come,
	We'll have a time holding Miss Agnes back.
	She's bound she's going to escape; perhaps
	She'll throw herself headfirst out of the window.
ARNOLPHE:	Bring her to me. (*Exit* GEORGETTE) Anyway, I intend
	To take her away. (*To* HORACE) You needn't be upset.
	Too much good luck leads to self-confidence.
	Every dog has his day, the proverb says.
HORACE:	Oh, heaven, was ever a man so miserable,
	Or plunged in such a bottomless pit of woe!
ARNOLPHE (*to* ORONTE):	Do not delay the day of the ceremony.
	I am concerned; I'm anxious to be present.
ORONTE:	That's my intention.
	(*Enter* AGNÈS, ALAIN, GEORGETTE.)
ARNOLPHE:	Come, my beauty, come;
	You troublemaker, whom we couldn't hold!
	Here is your gallant; give him his reward
	By dropping him a nice, respectful curtsy!
	(*To* HORACE)
	Good-by. You find the outcome disappointing;
	You see, love does not always conquer all.
AGNÈS:	Oh, Horace, will you let him carry me off?
HORACE:	I'm in such pain, I don't know what I'm doing.
ARNOLPHE (*pulling* AGNÈS' *arm*):	
	Come, chatterbox.
AGNÈS:	I want to stay right here.

ORONTE: Tell us the answer to the mystery.
            None of us understands what it's about.

ARNOLPHE: I'll tell you all when I have a little time.
            Now I must say good-by.

ORONTE: But where are you off to?
            You do not treat us very courteously.

ARNOLPHE: Well, I advised you not to heed his protests,
            And make the marriage.

ORONTE: Certainly; but to make it,
            If you've been fully informed, were you not told
            That the intended bride is in your house,
            The long-lost daughter of Seigneur Enrique
            And Angélique, born of a secret marriage?
            So what's the reason for this talk of yours?

CHRYSALDE: I too was most astonished by his actions.

ARNOLPHE: What's this?

CHRYSALDE: My sister made a runaway match;
            Her daughter's fate was hidden from us all.

ORONTE: For secrecy, the father put the child
            To nurse in the country, under fictitious names.

CHRYSALDE: And then unkindly circumstances forced him
            To take departure from his native land—

ORONTE: And brave the perils of adventurous life,
            To seek his fortune far beyond the seas.

CHRYSALDE: And there his industry has won again
            What envy and deceit had stolen here.

ORONTE: And back in France, he sought the woman out
            Whom he had charged with the care of his baby
                daughter—

CHRYSALDE: And this good peasant woman told him frankly
            That she had put the infant in your charge.

ORONTE: Because of your charitable reputation;
            Also because of her desperate poverty.

CHRYSALDE: And so Enrique, delighted beyond measure,

Has brought the woman here to be a witness.

ORONTE: You'll see her arriving in a minute or two
To publicly resolve the mystery.

CHRYSALDE: I can appreciate your own distress;
Fate is not kind to you in this affair.
Since you're so terrified of cuckoldry,
The wisest policy is—not to marry.

ARNOLPHE: (*overcome*):
Oh!

(*Exit* ARNOLPHE.)

ORONTE: Why does he leave without a word?

HORACE: Ah, father,
You will be told the clue to the mystery.
Fate had already executed here
The plan which you so wisely had designed.
For I was bound, by my own plighted word,
To the engagements of requited love.
She is the person whom you came to seek,
The person I rejected, all unknowing.

ENRIQUE: When I first saw her I was deeply stirred.
My heart bears witness, it is she indeed.
My daughter dear, I yield to my impulses.
(*Embraces* AGNÈS.)

CHRYSALDE: Happily, brother, I would do the same,
But this is not the place for intimacies.
Let us go in, review this strange adventure,
And thank our friend Arnolphe for his helpfulness—
And Providence, which does all for the best!

The Critique of The School for Wives

The success of *The School for Wives,* its innovations, merits, and faults, evoked much comment and criticism, of the sort that would today be expressed in letters to the drama section of the metropolitan Sunday newspapers. Molière was moved to reply; but since he knew much about writing dialogue and little about polemic pamphlets, he put his defense in a one-act discussion piece. He killed another bird with this stone; he provided a novel afterpiece, to be played on the same bill with *The School for Wives,* when the points at issue were alive in every hearer's mind. It was first produced on June 1, 1663.

The idea of adding a critique to his play was a brilliant one, reminding the modern reader of the epilogue of the critics in Shaw's *Fanny's First Play.* Its technique is Shavian also, in that it consists frankly of talk, with no pretense of action. It is included in this volume partly because of its technical novelty, but chiefly because it contains Molière's clearest statement of his purposes and methods.

Each character is distinct, representing a point of view. Dorante speaks for the author; Lysidas states the literary criticisms of the play; Climène expresses the moral criticisms.

I shall not attempt to judge the judgments. Molière expects every spectator, or reader, to do this for himself. I shall merely notice that some of Lysidas' criticisms, as of the lack of action, are very well taken; and that Molière's defense of the notorious *le*—, or *my*—,[1] is to say the least disingenuous.

[1] See Act II of *The School for Wives.* pages 53–54.

96

The Characters

URANIE

ÉLISE, cousin of Uranie

CLIMÈNE

GALOPIN, a lackey

THE MARQUIS

DORANTE, a chevalier

LYSIDAS, a dramatic author

The scene is Uranie's drawing room, in Paris.

ÉLISE *is discovered. Enter* URANIE.

URANIE: How's this, my dear cousin? No one has come to call?

ÉLISE: Not a soul.

URANIE: Really, it's surprising that we've both been alone all day.

ÉLISE: I'm surprised too, cousin Uranie. This is hardly our custom. Your house, thank God, is the ordinary refuge of all the loafers of the court.

URANIE: The fact is, the afternoon has seemed very long.

ÉLISE: As for me, I have found it very short.

URANIE: Well, cousin Élise, intellectuals love solitude.

ÉLISE: Thanks for the compliment; but you know I'm hardly an intellectual.

URANIE: I like people around, I admit.

ÉLISE: So do I; but I like certain people. And we have to endure so many tiresome callers that I enjoy being alone.

97

URANIE: You're too fussy, if you can only bear the chosen few.

ÉLISE: And others are far too undiscriminating, if they can bear all sorts of people without distinction.

URANIE: I like the sensible ones, and the idiots amuse me.

ÉLISE: Well, bless me, it doesn't take an idiot long to become a bore; and most of that lot aren't very amusing after the second visit. But speaking of idiots, can't you get rid of that troublesome marquis for me? Are you going to leave him on my hands forever? I can't stand his everlasting puns much longer.

URANIE: Well, that's the fashionable way to talk; they seem to like it at court.

ÉLISE: I'm sorry for those who like it, and who wear themselves out concocting that mysterious gibberish. Really, it's a nice thing, to bring into conversations at the Louvre Palace all the old double meanings picked up in the mud of the markets! What a pretty kind of badinage for courtiers! How witty it is for a man to say to you: "Madame, here you are in the Place Royale, and yet you are visible from three leagues away, for everyone looks at you *de bon œil!*"[2] Because Bonneuil is a village three leagues away. Isn't that elegant and sparkling! And those who can invent such plays on words, haven't they reason to be proud of them?

URANIE: In fact, they don't claim that such things are really witty. Most of those who affect that kind of talk know very well it's ridiculous.

ÉLISE: It's too bad, if they take the trouble to talk nonsense, and make bad jokes deliberately. I think they're all the less excusable for that reason; and if I were a judge, I know how I'd punish all those fashionable wags.

URANIE: Let's drop the subject. It gets you too excited. Let's remark on the fact that Dorante is late for the supper we've invited him to.

ÉLISE: Perhaps he's forgotten it. Or perhaps—

[2] *De bon œil:* amiably. The pun defiies the translator.

(*Enter* GALOPIN.)

GALOPIN: Madame, Madame Climène has come to call on you.

URANIE: Good heavens! What a visit!

ÉLISE: You were just complaining about being left alone. Heaven is punishing you.

URANIE (*to* GALOPIN):   Hurry; tell her I'm not home.

GALOPIN: She has already been informed that you are at home.

URANIE: Who is the idiot who told her that?

GALOPIN: Me, madame.

URANIE: The devil take the little rascal! I will teach you not to make up your own answers.

GALOPIN: I will tell her, madame, that you have decided to be out.

URANIE: Stop, you fool! Have her come up, since the damage is done.

GALOPIN: She is still talking to a gentleman in the street.

(*Exit* GALOPIN.)

URANIE: Oh, Élise, what an awkward thing to happen right now!

ÉLISE: It is true that the lady has a gift for being embarrassing. I never could stand her, myself; and with all due respect to her high rank, she's the stupidest creature who ever undertook to have opinions.

URANIE: That's rather a superlative.

ÉLISE: No, no, she deserves it, and even something stronger, if justice were done. Could anyone be a more perfect example of the precious type, to take the word in its worst meaning?

URANIE: However, she objects to having that name given her.

ÉLISE: That's true. She objects to the name, and not to the thing. She is precious from head to foot; she's the most affected person on earth. Her whole body seems to be loose-jointed; her hips and shoulders and head all seem to be moved by springs. She always affects a languishing, simpering tone of voice, and she pouts to show her little mouth, and she rolls her eyes to make them look big.

URANIE: Careful; if she should hear you—

ÉLISE: Oh, no, she hasn't come upstairs yet. I still remember the evening she wanted to see Damon,[3] because of his reputation and the things he has published. You know what he's like, and how he's too lazy to keep a conversation going. She had invited him to supper to play the wit, and he never seemed so dull, among half a dozen people whom she'd asked to hear him perform; they were staring at him wide-eyed, as if he weren't an ordinary human being. They all thought he was there in order to amuse the company, and every word he uttered was bound to be extraordinary, and he was going to make impromptu verses on any subject of conversation, and he couldn't ask for a drink without some whimsical conceit. But he fooled them all by keeping silent, and the lady was as displeased with him as I was with her.

URANIE: Be quiet. I am going to the door to receive her now.

ÉLISE: Just one more word. I'd like to see her married to the marquis we were talking about. It would be a fine match—a précieuse and a buffoon!

URANIE: Will you be quiet? Here she is. (*Enter* GALOPIN, *ushering in* CLIMÈNE) Really, you're coming late—

CLIMÈNE: Oh, please, darling, have a chair brought for me, quickly!

URANIE (*to* GALOPIN):   A chair here, quick!
            (GALOPIN *brings a chair, and exits.*)

CLIMÈNE: Ah, dear God!

URANIE: What's the matter?

CLIMÈNE: I'm ready to drop!

URANIE: But what's wrong?

CLIMÈNE: My heart fails me!

URANIE: Is it the vapors?

CLIMÈNE: No.

URANIE: Do you want to have your stays unlaced?

[3] Supposed to be Molière.

CLIMÈNE: Oh, dear, no. Oh!

URANIE: What's your trouble, then? And when did it strike you?

CLIMÈNE: More than three hours ago. I caught it in the Palais-Royal Theatre.

URANIE: How's that?

CLIMÈNE: I've just seen, for my sins, that wretched travesty, *The School for Wives.* It made me so sick at my stomach, I'm still weak. I don't think I'll get over it for a fortnight.

ÉLISE: It's amazing how one can fall sick without a moment's warning.

URANIE: My cousin and I, I don't know what we're made of. We saw the play day before yesterday, and we both came back sound and healthy.

CLIMÈNE: What? You saw it?

URANIE: Yes; and we listened from one end to the other.

CLIMÈNE: And it didn't drive you almost into convulsions, darling?

URANIE: I'm not so delicate, thank God. Personally, I think the play would be more likely to cure people than to make them sick.

CLIMÈNE: Good heavens, what are you saying? Can such a proposition be advanced by a person with a pittance of common sense? Can one with impunity bite one's thumb at reason, as you are doing? And in the last analysis, can there be a spirit so starved of wit that it can relish the insipidities which season that comedy? As for me, I admit that I found in it no smallest grain of the true Attic salt. The "children begotten through the ear" seemed to me in the most detestable taste; the "cream tart" made me positively sick at my stomach; and at "the husband's stew" I almost vomited!

ÉLISE: Bless me, how neatly you put it! I would have said that the play was a good one; but your eloquence is so persuasive, you phrase things in such an agreeable way, that I have to accept your judgment, in spite of myself.

URANIE: For my part, I'm not so ready to yield; and, to give my honest opinion, I think this play is one of the most amusing the author has done.

CLIMÈNE: Really, such talk makes me sorry for you! I cannot endure such obscurity of discernment in you. Can a virtuous person find any charm in a play which forever keeps modesty in a state of alarm, and constantly befouls the imagination?

ÉLISE: Oh, I like the way you put things! How sharp you are in criticism, madame! How I pity poor Molière to have you for an enemy!

CLIMÈNE (*to* URANIE):   Believe me, my dear, you must positively revise your judgment. For the sake of your reputation, don't go telling people that you liked the play.

URANIE: I don't really know what you found in it that wounds modesty.

CLIMÈNE: Alas, everything! I maintain that a decent woman couldn't see it without confusion, so many were the filthy, dirty things I noticed.

URANIE: You must have special gifts for discovering obscenities, for I didn't observe any myself.

CLIMÈNE: You just won't admit noticing them, assuredly; for all the obscenities are there, please God, and perfectly bare-faced. There isn't the slightest veil to disguise them, and the boldest eyes are appalled by their nudity.

ÉLISE (*admiringly*):   Ah!

CLIMÈNE (*simpering*):   He, he, he!

URANIE: But anyway, please point out one of those obscenities.

CLIMÈNE: Oh, dear! Is it necessary to point them out?

URANIE: Yes. I'm just asking for one passage which shocked you so much.

CLIMÈNE: Do I need any other than the scene with that Agnes, when she says what the young man has taken?

URANIE: Well, what's dirty about that?

CLIMÈNE: Ah!

URANIE: But, please—

CLIMÈNE: Oh, fie!

URANIE: Still, what—

CLIMÈNE: I have nothing to say.

URANIE: As for me, I see nothing wrong in it.

CLIMÈNE: All the worse for you.

URANIE: All the better for me, I should say. I look at the side of things that is shown to me; I don't turn them over to look for what one isn't supposed to see.

CLIMÈNE: A woman's virtue—

URANIE: A woman's virtue doesn't consist in pretenses. It's improper to try to be purer than the pure. Affectation in this matter is worse than in any other; I think nothing is so ridiculous as that delicacy of honor which takes everything amiss, and gives a criminal meaning to the most innocent words, and takes offense at mere shadows. Believe me, women who are so squeamish aren't regarded as the more high-principled just for that. On the contrary, their suggestive primness and their affected airs make people the more censorious toward their actions. Everyone is delighted to discover some subject for criticism in them. To give you an example, the other day at the play there were some ladies across from our box, and by their silly behavior during the whole play, by the way they would turn their heads aside and hide their faces, they provoked a lot of foolish remarks which otherwise wouldn't have been made. One of the lackeys even shouted out that their ears were chaster than all the rest of their bodies.

CLIMÈNE: Well, the fact is, when you see that play you have to be blind, and pretend not to see what it means.

URANIE: You mustn't try to see meanings which aren't there.

CLIMÈNE: Oh, I insist the smut is there; you can't dodge it.

URANIE: And I just don't agree.

CLIMÈNE: What! Decency is not clearly offended by what Agnes says in the part we were speaking of?

URANIE: No, really. She doesn't say a word which isn't perfectly decent; and if you want to imagine that something else is understood, you are the one who is indecent, not she, because she is just speaking of a ribbon which has been taken from her.

CLIMÈNE: Oh, ribbon, ribbon all you like; but that "my—" where she stops isn't put in for nothing. That "my—" gives you some strange thoughts. That "my—" is furiously scandalizing. No matter what you say, you can't defend the impudence of that "my—."

ÉLISE: It's true, cousin Uranie; I am on madame's side against that "my—." That "my—" is impudent to the highest degree. You're quite wrong to defend that "my—."

CLIMÈNE: It has a most intolerable lubricity.

ÉLISE: What was that word, madame?

CLIMÈNE: Lubricity, madame.

ÉLISE: Oh, bless me, lubricity! I don't exactly know what it means, but I think it is perfectly lovely.

CLIMÈNE (*to* URANIE): Anyway, you see how your own cousin takes my side.

URANIE: Oh, she just likes to talk, and she doesn't always say what she thinks. If you take my advice, you won't trust her too much.

ÉLISE (*to* URANIE): Oh, you're very naughty, to try to make madame distrust me! What a position I would be in, if she should actually believe what you are saying! (*To* CLIMÈNE) Could I be so unfortunate, madame, as to provoke this opinion of me?

CLIMÈNE (*to* ÉLISE): No, no. I don't take her words seriously. I think you are more serious than she suggests.

ÉLISE: Oh, how right you are, madame! You will do me only justice, if you believe that I find you most convincing, I share in your sentiments, and I am fascinated by every word you utter.

CLIMÈNE: Ah well, I'm merely saying what I think.

ÉLISE: That's very clear, madame; you are speaking from the heart. Your words, and your tone of voice, and your expression, and your walk and gestures, and your dress, all have a certain enchanting air of distinction. I am studying you closely; I'm so impressed by you that I try to imitate you, to ape you in everything.

CLIMÈNE: You're making fun of me, madame.

ÉLISE: I beg your pardon, madame. Who would want to make fun of you?

CLIMÈNE: I am not a good model, madame.

ÉLISE: Oh, I disagree, madame.

CLIMÈNE: You flatter me, madame.

ÉLISE: Not at all, madame.

CLIMÈNE: Please spare me, madame.

ÉLISE: I am sparing you as it is, madame. I am not saying half of what I really think, madame.

CLIMÈNE: My word, let's have no more, for pity's sake. You would plunge me into a really appalling embarrassment. (*To* URANIE) Anyway, both of us are against you; and it is so unfitting for intelligent people to be obstinate—

(GALOPIN *appears at the door, with the* MARQUIS *crowding him.*)

GALOPIN: Stop, sir, please!

MARQUIS: You don't know me, evidently.

GALOPIN: Oh, yes, I know you; but you can't come in!

MARQUIS: What a lot of noise, little lackey!

GALOPIN: It isn't proper to try to come in in spite of people.

MARQUIS: I want to see your mistress.

GALOPIN: She's not at home, I tell you.

MARQUIS: There she is in the room!

GALOPIN: That's true, there she is; but she's not at home.

URANIE: What's all this?

MARQUIS: It's your lackey, madame, who is playing the fool.

GALOPIN: I tell him you're not at home, madame, and he keeps on trying to come in.

URANIE: And why do you tell the gentleman I'm not at home?

GALOPIN: You scolded me the other day for telling him you were at home.

URANIE: What insolence! I beg you, sir, not to believe a word of it. He's a little imbecile, who took you for someone else.

MARQUIS: I saw that clearly, madame; and were it not for the respect I owe you, I would have taught him to recognize people of quality.

ÉLISE: My cousin is much obliged to you for your respectful behavior.

URANIE: A chair, impertinent puppy.

GALOPIN: Isn't that a chair behind him?

URANIE: Push it closer.

(GALOPIN *pushes the chair rudely, and exits.*)

MARQUIS: Your little lackey, madame, is scornful of my person.

ÉLISE: He's very wrong, surely.

MARQUIS: Perhaps I am paying for my ill demeanor, which is getting de meaner and de meaner! Ha, ha, ha, ha!

ÉLISE: With time, he will learn to recognize the right people.

MARQUIS: What were you discussing, ladies, when I interrupted you?

URANIE: The new play, *The School for Wives.*

MARQUIS: I've just left the theatre!

CLIMÈNE: Well, monsieur, please tell us how you found it.

MARQUIS: Absolutely intolerable.

CLIMÈNE: Oh, I'm delighted to hear it!

MARQUIS: It's the most wretched thing ever seen. Why, what the devil! I could hardly get a seat. I was nearly smothered at the entrance, and I never had my feet so stepped on. Look at the state of my knee ruffles and ribbons!

ÉLISE: Clearly, *The School for Wives* is quite impossible. You are quite right in condemning it.

MARQUIS: I don't think there's ever been such a bad play.

(*Enter* DORANTE.)

URANIE: Oh, here is Dorante! We were waiting for him.

DORANTE: Don't stir, please; don't interrupt your conversation. You're discussing a subject which has been the principal theme in all the houses in Paris for the last four days; and nothing is more amusing than the variety of opinions expressed. For in short I have heard some people condemn the play for the same things that others esteem the most.

URANIE: Monsieur le Marquis has just been speaking very harshly of it.

MARQUIS: That's true. I find it detestable; *morbleu,* detestable as detestable can be; what you might call detestable.

DORANTE: And for my part, my dear Marquis, I find the judgment detestable.

MARQUIS: What, Chevalier, you wouldn't propose to defend that play?

DORANTE: Yes, I propose to defend it.

MARQUIS: *Parbleu!* I guarantee it's detestable.

DORANTE: The guarantee is not absolutely iron-clad. Tell me, please, Marquis, why the play is—what you say?

MARQUIS: Why it's detestable?

DORANTE: Yes.

MARQUIS: It's detestable, because it's detestable.

DORANTE: After that, there's no more to be said; the case is settled. But still, inform us; tell us the faults of the play.

MARQUIS: How do I know? I didn't even take the trouble to listen. But anyway, damme sir, I know I've never seen anything so bad. And Dorilas, who was next me, agreed with me.

DORANTE: There's an authority; you are well seconded.

MARQUIS: All you needed was to listen to the continual roars of laughter from the pit. I don't need any other proof that the play is worthless.

DORANTE: So, Marquis, you are one of the gentlemen of fashion who won't admit that the pit has any common sense, and who would be sorry to join in its laughter, even at the best joke on earth? At the theatre the other day I saw one of our friends making himself ridiculous in that way. He listened to the whole play with a very serious and somber expression; and whatever amused the others made him scowl. At every burst of laughter he would shrug his shoulders and look pityingly at the groundlings in the pit. And sometimes with an air of disgust he would say loudly: "Laugh, pit; go ahead and laugh!" His peevishness made a comedy in itself; he was courteous enough to perform it free to the whole audience, and everyone agreed that no one could play it better than he did. I tell you, Marquis, and the others too, that good sense has no reserved seats at the play; the difference between a gold half-louis and a fifteen-sou piece does not at all affect good taste. One can deliver a poor judgment either standing or sitting down. And in general I would be inclined to trust the approval of the pit; for in that audience there are some few who are able to judge a play according to the rules, and the others judge it according to the right method, which is to let oneself be captured by the play, without blind prejudice, or an affectation of favor, or exaggerated delicacy.

MARQUIS: So, Chevalier, now you're the defender of the pit! *Parbleu*, I'm delighted, and I shan't fail to inform it that you're one of its friends! Ha, ha, ha, ha, ha, ha!

DORANTE: Laugh all you like. I'm in favor of good sense, and I can't bear the cranks and crotchets of all our Marquises de Mascarille.[4] It makes me furious to see those people who deliberately make themselves ridiculous in spite of their rank; who boldly decide everything and talk about everything, without knowledge; who cry out in delight at the bad parts of a play, without stirring at the good parts; who, similarly, when they see a painting or hear a concert, blame and praise everything wrongly; who pick up somewhere the technical terms of the art they're criticizing, and always mispronounce and misuse them. Eh, *morbleu!* My good sirs, when God hasn't given you knowledge about something, keep quiet; don't make your

---

4 Reference to type created in *The Precious Damsels.*

hearers laugh; and reflect that if you don't say a word, maybe people will think you're profound.

MARQUIS: *Parbleu*, Chevalier, you're taking it in a way—

DORANTE: Good heavens, Marquis, I'm not addressing you! I'm referring to a dozen gentlemen who dishonor court society by their extravagant manners, and make the commoners think we're all alike. For my part, I want to escape this reproach as far as possible; and I'll belabor them at every opportunity until they decide to be sensible.

MARQUIS: Just tell me, Chevalier, do you think Lysandre is an intelligent man?

DORANTE: Certainly; very intelligent.

URANIE: You can't deny his intelligence.

MARQUIS: Ask him his opinion of *The School for Wives;* he will tell you he doesn't like it.

DORANTE: Well, there are many people who suffer by being too intelligent, and who are bedazzled by their own illumination, and who can't bear to agree with anyone else, so that they may have the distinction of uttering final decisions.

URANIE: That's true. Our friend is certainly one of those people. He wants to be the first to state an opinion, and he wants others to await his judgment out of respect. Any approval which is expressed in advance of his is an offense, which he avenges publicly by taking the opposite side. He wants to be consulted about all artistic productions; I am sure that if the author had shown him the play before producing it, he would have found it admirable.

MARQUIS: And what will you say of the Marquise Araminte, who proclaims everywhere the play's appalling, and says she couldn't endure the filth it's full of?

DORANTE: I shall say that the remark is worthy of the character she has assumed; and that there are people who become ridiculous through trying to be too high-principled. Although she's intelligent enough, she has followed the bad example of the women who reach a certain age and look for something to replace what they're losing, and assume that a show of very scrupulous prudery will be a substitute for youth and beauty. Araminte carries this system to its limits; her scruples are so scrupulous that she finds dirty suggestions where no one else had ever perceived them; I understand that her scrupulosity goes so far as to disfigure our language; that the lady is so censorious that she wants to lop off the head or tail of many words, because of the indecent syllables they contain.

URANIE: Chevalier, you're too absurd!

MARQUIS: In short, Chevalier, you think you're defending the play by making fun of those who criticize it.

DORANTE: Not at all; but I insist the lady has no reason to be scandalized—

ÉLISE: Careful, Monsieur le Chevalier; there might be others beside her who have the same feeling.

DORANTE: I know it wouldn't be you, at least; when you saw the performance—

ÉLISE: That's true; but I've changed my opinion. Madame Climène has supported her view by such convincing reasons that she has brought me over to her side.

DORANTE (*to* CLIMÈNE):   Madame, I ask your pardon. And if you wish, I will retract everything I've said, for love of you.

CLIMÈNE: I don't want you to do so for the love of me, but for the love of good sense; for after all, this play is totally indefensible, if you look at it closely; and I can hardly imagine—

URANIE: Ah, here is the celebrated author, Monsieur Lysidas! Just at the right moment! (*Enter* LYSIDAS) Monsieur Lysidas, take a chair, and sit down there.

LYSIDAS: Madame, I've come a little late; but I had to read my play at the home of Madame la Marquise—you know, I told you about her. And the applause was such that I was kept an hour longer than I expected.

ÉLISE: Applause has a magical power to detain an author.

URANIE: Do sit down, Monsieur Lysidas; we shall read your play after supper.

LYSIDAS: Everyone who was present there is coming to the première; they all promised to do their duty properly.

URANIE: I can well believe it. But do sit down, please. We were just dealing with a subject which I should like to see carried further.

LYSIDAS: I hope, madame, that you will take a box for the opening.

URANIE: We shall see. So please, let's continue our discussion.

LYSIDAS: I warn you, madame, that they're nearly all taken.

URANIE: All right, all right. Anyway, when you came in, I needed you. Everyone here was against me.

ÉLISE (*indicating* DORANTE):   At first he was on your side; but now that he knows that Madame Climène is in the opposition, I think you'll have to get help somewhere else.

CLIMÈNE (*to* ÉLISE):   No, no; I shouldn't want him to be ungallant to your charming cousin, and I permit his mind to be on the same side as his heart.

DORANTE: With this permission, madame, I shall venture to defend myself.

URANIE: But first let's learn the opinion of Monsieur Lysidas.

LYSIDAS: On what subject, madame?

URANIE: On *The School for Wives.*

LYSIDAS: Ha, ha!

DORANTE: What do you think of it?

LYSIDAS: I have nothing to say. You know that among us authors, we must speak of one another's works with great circumspection.

DORANTE: Yes, but just among us here, what do you think of the play?

LYSIDAS: I, sir?

URANIE: Yes, give us your honest opinion.

LYSIDAS: I think it's very fine.

DORANTE: Positively?

LYSIDAS: Positively. Why not? Isn't it in fact very fine indeed?

DORANTE: Umm. You're a sly devil, Monsieur Lysidas. You don't say what you think.

LYSIDAS: I beg your pardon!

DORANTE: Good Lord, I know you! Don't pretend to me!

LYSIDAS: I, sir?

DORANTE: I can see clearly that your praise of the play is only out of courtesy; at the bottom of your heart, you agree with many people who think it's very bad.

LYSIDAS: He, he, he!

DORANTE: Come, admit that the play is really terrible.

LYSIDAS: It is true that it is not much approved by the connoisseurs.

MARQUIS: 'Pon my soul, Chevalier, you're caught! You're paid off for your mockeries! Ha, ha, ha, ha, ha!

DORANTE: Go right ahead, my dear Marquis.

MARQUIS: You see we have the scholars on our side.

DORANTE: It is true, Monsieur Lysidas' judgment carries weight. But Monsieur Lysidas will permit me not to surrender, even for that; and since I have been so bold as to defend myself against the opinions of Madame Élise, he cannot take it ill if I oppose his views.

ÉLISE: What! You see Madame Climène, Monsieur le Marquis, and Monsieur Lysidas against you, and you still dare to resist? Oh, fie! What wrong-headedness!

CLIMÈNE: Really, it's beyond me, how reasonable people can take it into their heads to defend the offensive absurdities of that play.

MARQUIS: Damme, madame, it's wretched from beginning to end.

DORANTE: That's a pretty sweeping judgment, Marquis. Nothing is easier than to settle a matter that way; and nothing can be proof against such absolute decisions.

MARQUIS: Gad, sir, all the other actors who went to see it said nothing but bad about it.

DORANTE: Ah, that's final! You are right, Marquis. Since all the other actors speak ill of it, we have to believe them, assuredly. They are very enlightened people, and unprejudiced. So there's no more to say; I surrender.

CLIMÈNE: Whether you surrender or not, I know very well that you won't persuade me to endure the immodesties of that play, or the very offensive satire against women in it.

URANIE: For me, I shall be careful not to take offense at anything, or assume it regards me personally. That sort of satire hits at manners and customs, and only indirectly at individuals. So let's not apply these general criticisms to ourselves; and let's profit by the lesson, if we can, without suggesting that we are the objects of it. All these ridiculous exaggerations we see on the stage ought not to be taken to heart. They are public mirrors, and we should never admit that we see ourselves in them; and if we take offense at reproof, we are making a public confession of our faults.

CLIMÈNE: As for me, I'm not talking of these things on the ground that I may have any connection with them; I think my way of life is such that no one would identify me in those representations of ill-behaved women.

ÉLISE: Assuredly, madame, no one would think of identifying you with them. Your conduct is perfectly well known; certainly no one would argue about it.

URANIE: And besides, madame, I said nothing which could have reference to you. My words, like the satires of the theatre, develop only a general thesis.

CLIMÈNE: I don't doubt it, madame. But let's not dwell further on this theme. I don't know how you accept the insults offered our sex at one point in the play; for me, I admit that it makes me frightfully angry that this impertinent author should call us *animals*.

URANIE: Don't you see that he puts that in the mouth of a ridiculous character?

DORANTE: And besides, madame, don't you know that lovers' insults never cause offense? That there are passionate loves as well as sweet and dainty ones? And in such circumstances the strangest words—and even worse—are often taken as marks of affection by the very women who receive them?

ÉLISE: Say all you please, I can't bear them, any more than the "husband's stew" and the "cream tart," which Madame was just speaking of.

MARQUIS: Oh, my word, yes, cream tart! That's what I had noticed myself: cream tart! How much I am obliged to you, madame, for reminding me of cream tart! Are there enough apples in Normandy to throw at actors who say "cream tart"? Cream tart, *morbleu*, cream tart!

DORANTE: What do you mean, "cream tart"?

MARQUIS: *Parbleu!* Cream tart, Chevalier!

DORANTE: Well, what of it?

MARQUIS: Cream tart!

DORANTE: But tell us your reasons.

MARQUIS: Cream tart!

URANIE: But you must explain your idea, it seems to me.

MARQUIS: Cream tart, madame!

URANIE: What objection do you have to that?

MARQUIS: Oh, nothing, nothing. Cream tart!

URANIE: I give up.

ÉLISE: Monsieur le Marquis certainly pitches into you, and he doesn't leave you a leg to stand on. But I should like to hear Monsieur Lysidas settle the matter with a few of his characteristic critical shafts.

LYSIDAS: It isn't my custom to condemn anything, and I am disposed to be indulgent toward other men's works. But still, with due regard for Monsieur le Chevalier's evident friendship for the author, it will be granted that this kind of comedy is not properly a comedy, in the traditional meaning, and there is a great difference between these trifling amusements and the beauty of a serious drama. Nevertheless, everyone is going in for that sort of thing nowadays; that's the only thing that draws crowds; and there is an appalling void in theatres that show the great works, while nonsense captures all Paris. I admit to you that this fact sometimes makes my heart sick; it is shameful for France.

CLIMÈNE: It is true that general taste has become woefully corrupt, and that our times are putrescifying monstrously.

ÉLISE: That's pretty, putrescifying! Did you invent that, madame?

CLIMÈNE: He, he!

ÉLISE: I suspected it.

DORANTE: So you think, Monsieur Lysidas, that all intelligence and beauty are in the serious drama, and all the comic plays are tomfooleries which deserve no praise at all?

URANIE: That isn't my opinion, if I may speak up. Certainly the tragedy has its beauty when it's well done; but comedy too has its charms, and I think that one is no less difficult to do than the other.

DORANTE: Assuredly, madame; and when you say difficult, if you should assert that a comedy is the more so, perhaps you wouldn't be mistaken. For in short, I think it is much easier to float on a cloud of noble maxims, to defy the fates in rhyme, to accuse destiny, and to challenge the gods, than it is to recognize human follies, and to present the errors of average men acceptably on the stage. When you portray heroes, you can do just what you please. These are fanciful portraits; no one looks for lifelike resemblances in them. You merely have to follow the suggestions of your roving imagination, which often abandons the true in order to pursue the marvelous. But when you are painting men, you must paint from nature. Everyone insists that the likenesses resemble reality; and you haven't accomplished anything, unless you make your audience recognize the men of our own time. In a word, in serious plays, all you need to do, to escape criticism, is to say reasonable things in good style. But in the lighter plays that isn't enough; you have to amuse. And it's a strange enterprise, to make honest folk laugh.

CLIMÈNE: I think I can number myself among the honest folk; and yet I didn't find a thing to laugh at in all I heard.

MARQUIS: My word, neither did I.

DORANTE: As for you, Marquis, I'm not surprised; there weren't any puns in it.

LYSIDAS: Faith, sir, what there was in it was hardly better; all the witticisms were rather flat, in my opinion.

DORANTE: That was not the court's judgment.

LYSIDAS: Ah, sir, the court!

DORANTE: Go ahead, finish your thought, Monsieur Lysidas. You mean, clearly, that the court is no judge of these matters. It is the ordinary refuge of you authors, when your works are failures, to accuse the injustice of our times and the ignorance of the courtiers. Remember, please, Monsieur Lysidas, that the courtiers have just as good eyes as anyone else; that a man can be intelligent with a lace collar and feather plumes, as well as with a short wig and a plain neckcloth; that the great test of all plays is the court's judgment; that it's the court's taste one must study if one wants to succeed; that nowhere else does one get such fair decisions; and not to mention the scholars established there, remember that what with natural good sense and social contacts, there is developed at court a special kind of intelligence, which judges things with incomparably greater finesse than does all the rusty scholarship of the pedants.

URANIE: It's true that if you live at court, you see constantly so many things happening that you do acquire the habit of judging them, especially in the matter of true and false wit.

DORANTE: The court has its follies, I agree; and as you see, I am the first to attack them. But God's truth, there are plenty of them also among the professional wits; and if the plays burlesque a few marquises, I think there is much better reason to burlesque the authors. It would be funny to put on the stage their scholarly affectations and their absurd refinement, their vicious custom of assassinating real people in their works, their lust for applause, their cautious reticences, their deals for gaining reputation, their offensive and defensive leagues, as well as their wars of wit, and their battles of prose and verse.

LYSIDAS: Molière is very fortunate, monsieur, to have so warm a defender. But to come to the point, the question is whether or not the play is a good one; and I am ready to indicate a hundred evident faults in it.

URANIE: It's a funny thing about you playwrights, that you always condemn the big successes, and you say nothing but good about the plays no one goes to. You show an invincible hatred for the first lot, and a hardly conceivable affection for the second.

DORANTE: It is very noble to take the part of the afflicted.

URANIE: Please, Monsieur Lysidas, point out these faults, which I didn't notice.

LYSIDAS: Those who know their Aristotle and their Horace immediately recognize that this play sins against all the rules of the art.

URANIE: I must admit that I am not familiar with those gentlemen, and I don't know the rules of the art.

DORANTE: You make me laugh with your rules, which you are always blasting in our ears, to confound the ignorant. To hear you talk, one would think that these rules of art are the greatest mysteries in the world; and yet they are only a few obvious observations that common sense has made, regarding what can diminish one's pleasure in such productions. And the same common sense which made these observations long ago readily makes them over again every day, without any help from Horace and Aristotle. I should like to know if the great rule of all rules is not merely to give pleasure, and if a play which has attained this end has not taken the right course. Do you think that the entire public is mistaken about these matters, and that every man is not a judge of his own pleasure?

URANIE: I have noticed one thing about those gentlemen; those who talk the most about the rules and know them better than anybody write plays that no one admires.

DORANTE: That shows, madame, how little one should be concerned about their endless involved disputes. For in short, if people don't like the plays which observe the rules and if they do like the plays which don't observe the rules, then necessarily there must be something wrong with the rules. So let's not worry about those quibbling regulations which they want to impose on public taste, and when we see a play let's consult only the effect it makes on us. Let us confidently enjoy those works which actually grip us and touch our hearts, and let's not seek out arguments to prevent our finding pleasure in them.

URANIE: As for me, when I see a play, I only want to know if I am touched and moved. And when I have been really amused, I don't begin wondering if I was wrong, and if Aristotle's rules forbade me to laugh.

DORANTE: That's like a man who might find a sauce delicious, and who would then try to find out if it was good by looking it up in *Le Cuisinier français*.

URANIE: That's true; and I wonder at some people's hairsplitting about things which we ought to feel for ourselves.

DORANTE: You are right, madame, to find those mysterious distinctions peculiar. For if they are justified, we are forced not to believe ourselves; our own senses must be slaves of authority. And even to our food and drink, we can no longer dare to call anything good without the approval of the experts.

LYSIDAS: In short, sir, your only argument is that *The School for Wives* is a success; you don't care at all whether it follows the rules, provided—

DORANTE: Wait a minute, Monsieur Lysidas; I don't grant you that. I do say that the great art is to please, and that since this play has pleased those for whom it was written, I think that's sufficient, and there's not much reason to bother about the rest. But even so, I maintain that it does not offend against any of the rules you're talking of. I have read about them, please God, as well as the next man; and I could readily demonstrate that perhaps we have no play in the theatre more regular than that one is.

ÉLISE: Courage, Monsieur Lysidas! If you draw back, we are lost!

LYSIDAS: What, sir! The protasis, the epitasis, and the peripetia—

DORANTE: Oh, Monsieur Lysidas, don't smite us with your big words! Please don't be quite so scholarly. Humanize your speech, and speak so as to be understood. Do you think that a Greek name gives more weight to your argument? And don't you think it would be just as effective to say the exposition as the protasis, the plot development as the epitasis, and the resolution as the peripetia?

LYSIDAS: They are artistic terms which it is quite permissible to use. But since the words offend your ear, I shall explain myself otherwise, and I shall ask you to reply categorically to three or four remarks I shall make. Can one endure a play which sins against the very definition of a play? For in short the word "drama" comes from a Greek word meaning "to act," indicating that the essential of this sort of poetic composition lies in action. And in this particular play there is no action; everything consists in the recitals which either Agnes or Horace makes.

MARQUIS: Aha, Chevalier!

CLIMÈNE: That is very keenly observed; he has put his finger on the weak spot.

LYSIDAS: Is there anything so unhumorous, or, to say it outright, anything more vulgar, than some of the phrases at which everyone laughs; especially the "children through the ear"?

CLIMÈNE: Very good.

ÉLISE: Ah!

LYSIDAS: The scene where the two servants in the house delay in opening the door, isn't it tiresomely long, and entirely out of place?

MARQUIS: That's true.

CLIMÈNE: Certainly.

ÉLISE: He's right.

LYSIDAS: Doesn't Arnolphe give his money too readily to Horace? And since he is the ridiculous character, should he be given the action of a worthy man?

MARQUIS: Good. Excellent point.

CLIMÈNE: Admirable!

ÉLISE: Marvelous!

LYSIDAS: The sermon to Agnes and the maxims she reads, aren't they grotesque, and thus shocking to the respect we owe to the holy mysteries?

MARQUIS: Well said!

CLIMÈNE: That's the way to talk!

ÉLISE: Nothing could be better!

LYSIDAS: And that Monsieur Delafield, who is presented to us as an intelligent man, and who seems so serious in many places, doesn't he descend to an excessively low level of comedy in the fifth act, when he explains to Agnes the violence of his love, with that extravagant rolling of the eyes, those absurd sighs, and those idiotic tears which make everyone laugh?

MARQUIS: Egad! It's marvelous!

CLIMÈNE: A miracle!

ÉLISE: *Vive* Monsieur Lysidas!

LYSIDAS: I leave out a thousand other things for fear of boring you.

MARQUIS: *Parbleu,* Chevalier, now you're in a nice fix!

DORANTE: Well, let's see.

MARQUIS: You've found your match, faith!

DORANTE: Perhaps.

MARQUIS: Answer, answer, answer, answer!

DORANTE: Gladly. He—

MARQUIS: Go on and answer, I beg you.

DORANTE: Then let me alone. If—

MARQUIS: By Jove, I defy you to answer!

DORANTE: Of course, if you talk all the time.

CLIMÈNE: Please, let's hear his arguments.

DORANTE: Firstly, it is hardly true to say that the whole play consists of recitals. Many actions do take place on the stage, and the recitals themselves are actions, in accordance with the nature of the subject; all the more since these recitals are made innocently to the person concerned, who thus falls constantly into a confusion of mind which amuses the spectators, and who, at each new revelation, takes all the measures he can to ward off the calamity he fears.

URANIE: To me, the beautiful thing about *The School for Wives* is just those perpetual confidences of Horace. And what seems to me very funny is that an intelligent man, who is warned of everything by the simple girl he loves and by an infatuated rival, can't for all that avoid what happens to him.

MARQUIS: Mere bagatelle, mere bagatelle.

CLIMÈNE: Weak reply.

ÉLISE: Poor argument.

DORANTE: As for the "children through the ear," that is only funny as echoed by Arnolphe; and the author did not put that in as a joke in itself, but only as a means of characterizing the man. The phrase points up his mental twist, since he reports a silly little triviality of Agnes' as the funniest thing in the world, which gives him almost inconceivable joy.

MARQUIS: Not much of an answer.

CLIMÈNE: Hardly satisfactory.

ÉLISE: Nothing at all.

DORANTE: As for the money he gives so freely, not to mention that the letter from his best friend is a sufficient guarantee, there's nothing incompatible in a man's being ridiculous in certain things and a worthy man in others. And as for the scene with Alain and Georgette in the house, which some have found too long and too forced, there is certainly good reason for it. Just as Arnolphe has been caught, during his absence, by the naïveté of his beloved, when he returns he is kept at his own door for a long time by the simplicity of his servants, so that he may be punished constantly by the very precautions which he thought would save him.

MARQUIS: As reasons, they don't amount to much.

CLIMÈNE: Just whitewash.

ÉLISE: Really pitiful.

DORANTE: And as for the moral admonitions which you call a sermon, it is certain that really religious people who heard them didn't find that they profaned our holy mysteries. And clearly the words "hell" and "boiling caldrons" are well justified by Arnolphe's monomania and by the simplicity of the girl he's talking to. And as for the amorous transport of the fifth act, which is accused of being too excessive and too farcical, I should like to know if that isn't a proper satire of lovers, and if the most serious and sober gentlemen, on such occasions, don't do things—

MARQUIS: 'Pon my word, Chevalier, you would do better to say nothing.

DORANTE: Very well. But still, if we should look at our own selves, when we are very much in love—

MARQUIS: I won't even listen to you.

DORANTE: Please do listen to me. In moments of violent passion—

MARQUIS (*sings*):   La, la, la, la, lare; la, la la, la, la la.

DORANTE: What—

MARQUIS: La, la, la. la, lare; la, la la. la, la, la.

DORANTE: I don't know if—

MARQUIS: La, la. la. la, lare; la, la, la, la, la, la.

DORANTE: It seems to me that—

MARQUIS: La, la, la, la, lare; la, la, la, la, la, la.

URANIE: Our dispute is really funny. I think someone could make a little play of it. That wouldn't be bad as an afterpiece to *The School for Wives.*

DORANTE: You're right.

MARQUIS: Jove, Chevalier, you'd play a part in it which wouldn't do you much credit!

DORANTE: That's true, Marquis.

CLIMÈNTE: I should really like to have it done, provided everything was treated just as it took place.

ÉLISE: I should gladly contribute my own character.

LYSIDAS: I shouldn't refuse mine, I'm sure.

URANIE: Since everyone would be so pleased, Chevalier, do make notes on everything, and give them to your friend Molière, to make a play out of them.

CLIMÈNE: He'd certainly have nothing to do with it; it would hardly be a paean of praise.

URANIE: I disagree. I know what he's like; he doesn't care whether people criticize his plays, provided they come to see them.

DORANTE: Yes; but what ending could he find to it? For there can hardly be a marriage, or the discovery of a long-lost daughter. I don't know how one could finish off the dispute.

URANIE: We would have to think up some startling incident.

(*Enter* GALOPIN.)

GALOPIN: Madame, supper is on the table.

DORANTE: Why, that's just what we need for the dénouement! We couldn't find anything more natural! We'll argue long and hotly, on both sides, as we have just done; and no one will give in. Then a little lackey will come to say supper is ready; we'll all stand up; and we will have supper.

URANIE: There couldn't be a better ending for a play. We will do well to stop right here.

The Versailles Impromptu

A CRITICAL DISQUISITION IN ONE ACT

In October 1663, Molière was commanded by the King, at a week's notice, to bring his troupe to Versailles. He presented his unfortunate tragicomedy, *Don Garcie de Navarre,* and as an afterpiece a novelty, the surprising *Impromptu,* since known as *L'Impromptu de Versailles.*

Here was Molière's opportunity to smite his enemies, before the highest and mightiest of spectators. The production of the *Critique,* four months before, had provoked some angry rejoinders, promoted by the rival acting company of the Hôtel de Bourgogne. Molière was accused of many literary shortcomings, of plagiarism, of indecency, of irreligion, and of disrespect toward nobility. Such criticisms appear in Boursault's insipid *Le Portrait du peintre, ou la contre-critique de l'École des femmes,* a parody of Molière's *Critique de l'École des femmes.*

The critics did not confine themselves to literary strictures. A printed pamphlet hinted broadly that Molière was a complaisant husband, wearing his horns without discomfort. The son of the actor Montfleury, who is burlesqued in the *Impromptu,* responded by presenting to the King a violent denunciation of Molière, even, it would seem, accusing Molière of marrying his own daughter. The King's reply was to act as godfather to Molière's newborn son.

Molière, having once stated his position in the *Impromptu*, took no further part in this *guerre comique*.

The idea of showing on the stage actors in rehearsal was not absolutely new, nor has it failed to occur to later playwrights. (We think, of course, of *A Midsummer Night's Dream*, of *The Critic*, of *Six Characters in Search of an Author*.) Molière's device is none the less strikingly original. By its means he was enabled to play tricks with the principle of stage illusion, in a Pirandellian or Thornton Wilderish manner. He could also delight his audience by his famous imitations of other actors, and then impose on his hearers, warmed by laughter, a definition of his artistic purpose and a ringing protest against the intrusion of his enemies into his private life. The playlet is thus a critical document of the greatest interest to anyone who is curious about Molière the writer and actor, or indeed about dramatic writing and acting in general.

The acting style of the Hôtel de Bourgogne was one of bellowing bombast. Heart attacks on stage carried off several actors, including the very Montfleury whose excesses Molière imitates. By contrast, Molière insists on "the natural," fidelity to the habits of everyday speech. The trouble is that, as Émile Faguet said, the natural of one period seems conventional and affected to the next. We may therefore not know exactly what Molière meant by "the natural"; but with his aspiration to attain it we must certainly agree.

The Characters

MOLIÈRE, a comic marquis

BRÉCOURT, a gentleman of rank

LA GRANGE, a comic marquis

DU CROISY, a playwright

LA THORILLIÈRE, an importunate marquis

BÉJART, a busybody

MADEMOISELLE[1] DU PARC, an affected marquise

MADEMOISELLE BÉJART, a prude

MADEMOISELLE DE BRIE, a prudent coquette

MADEMOISELLE MOLIÈRE, a satiric mocker

MADEMOISELLE DU CROISY, a sugary nuisance

MADEMOISELLE HERVÉ, a *précieuse* ladies' maid

FOUR BUSYBODIES

The scene is the stage of the Royal Theatre at Versailles. It is bare of scenery.

MOLIÈRE *is discovered, alone on the stage.*

MOLIÈRE: Come, come, ladies and gentlemen! What's all this delay? Where are you, for heaven's sake? The devil take the lot of them! Holà ho! Monsieur de Brécourt!
(*Enter* BRÉCOURT.)

[1] A woman of the bourgeoisie was called mademoiselle, whether or not she was married.

126

BRÉCOURT: What's the matter?

MOLIÈRE: Monsieur de la Grange!

(*Enter* LA GRANGE.)

LA GRANGE: What's all the fuss about?

MOLIÈRE: Monsieur du Croisy!

(*Enter* DU CROISY.)

DU CROISY: All right, all right.

MOLIÈRE: Mademoiselle du Parc!

(*Enter* MLLE DU PARC.)

MLLE DU PARC: Were you calling me?

MOLIÈRE: Mademoiselle Béjart!

(*Enter* MLLE BÉJART.)

MLLE BÉJART: What's up, anyway?

MOLIÈRE: Mademoiselle de Brie!

(*Enter* MLLE DE BRIE.)

MLLE DE BRIE: What do you want?

MOLIÈRE: Mademoiselle du Croisy!

(*Enter* MLLE DU CROISY.)

MLLE DU CROISY: I hear you.

MOLIÈRE: Mademoiselle Hervé!

(*Enter* MLLE HERVÉ.)

MLLE HERVÉ: Coming, coming.

MOLIÈRE: Mademoiselle Molière!

(*Enter* MLLE MOLIÈRE.)

MLLE MOLIÈRE: Calm down, Molière!

MOLIÈRE: This gang will be the death of me! Hell's delight! Ladies and gentlemen, do you want to drive me insane today?

BRÉCOURT: What do you expect? We don't know our lines. We're the ones who will go insane, if you try to make us play this way.

MOLIÈRE: My God, actors are peculiar creatures to manage!

MLLE BÉJART: Well, here we all are. Now what do you want us to do?

MLLE DU PARC: What's your idea?

MLLE DE BRIE: What's it all about, anyway?

MOLIÈRE: Please, let's take our places. And since we're all in costume, and the King won't come for two hours, let's use the time in rehearsing and figuring how to put the show on.

LA GRANGE: How can we play something we don't know?

MLLE DU PARC: As for me, I tell you frankly I don't remember a word of my part.

MLLE DE BRIE: I'll have to be prompted from one end to the other.

MLLE BÉJART: My idea is to hold my lines in my hand.

MLLE MOLIÈRE: So will I.

MLLE HERVÉ: Anyhow, I haven't got much to say.

MLLE DU CROISY: Neither have I. But even so, I can't be sure of getting it right.

DU CROISY: I'd give ten pistoles to get out of the whole business.

BRÉCOURT: I'd take twenty lashes for the same privilege.

MOLIÈRE: So you're scared to death, just to have a miserable little part to play! What would you do if you were in my place?

MLLE BÉJART: You? There's no reason to be sorry for you. You wrote the thing; you can't go wrong.

MOLIÈRE: So the only thing I have to fear is forgetting my lines? You don't count my anxiety about the success of a performance which I'm entirely responsible for? You think it's a trifle to put on a comedy before this court audience, and to try to get a laugh from people of importance, who only laugh when they feel like it? Is there any author who isn't bound to tremble when he's put to such a test? I'm the one who can properly say that I'd give anything on earth to get out of it.

MLLE BÉJART: Well, if you were really bound to tremble, you'd have been more prudent, and you wouldn't have undertaken to put the show on in a week.

MOLIÈRE: And how could I get out of it, when a king ordered me?

MLLE BÉJART: How? Why, a nice respectful excuse, on the grounds that the thing is impossible in the time you're allowed.

Anyone else in your place would have had more concern for his reputation, and would have taken care not to get into such a dangerous position. Let me ask you, what will happen to you if the whole thing goes off badly? And what a windfall it will be for all your enemies!

MLLE DE BRIE: That's right. You should have excused yourself from doing it, with all due respect to the King; or else you should have asked for more time.

MOLIÈRE: Good heavens, mademoiselle, what kings like is prompt obedience; they aren't pleased at meeting obstacles. They want things at the time they want them; if they see their amusements postponed, they no longer find them amusing. They like pleasures they don't have to wait for; and the ones they like best are the ones which aren't too elaborately prepared. We shouldn't consult our own convenience in the things they ask us to do. We are here only to please them. When they order us to do something, it's our business to profit immediately by the desire they express. It's much better to do badly what they ask than not to do it on time; and if we have the distress of not succeeding as we should like, we have at least the merit of obeying their commands quickly. But please, let's get at our rehearsal.

MLLE BÉJART: And how do you expect us to rehearse, if we don't know our parts?

MOLIÈRE: You will know them, I tell you. And even if you aren't letter-perfect, haven't you wits enough to ad-lib, since it's prose, and you know the general idea?

MLLE BÉJART: How simple! Prose is even worse than poetry.

MLLE MOLIÈRE: You want to know what I think? You should have done a play in which you'd act all by yourself.

MOLIÈRE: Shut up, my good wife; you're a fool.

MLLE MOLIÈRE: Thank you very kindly, dear husband. That's the way it is; marriage certainly changes people. You wouldn't have said that to me a year and a half ago.

MOLIÈRE: Will you be so kind as to shut up?

MLLE MOLIÈRE: It is certainly strange that a little ceremony is capable of suppressing all a man's fine qualities, and that a husband and a suitor look at the same person so differently.

MOLIÈRE: What a lot of nonsense!

MLLE MOLIÈRE: Faith, if I were to write a play, I'd do it on that subject. I would justify women against a lot of accusations that men make; and I'd warn husbands about the difference between their rude manners and the compliments of lovers.

MOLIÈRE: Ouch! Let's drop it. This is no time for conversation; we have something else to do.

MLLE BÉJART: But since you've been ordered to deal with the published criticisms of your work, why didn't you do that *Comedy of the Players,* which you've been telling us about for so long? It was all ready to your hand, and fitted the circumstances perfectly. Especially since the critics had tried to take you off, and so they gave you the opportunity to take them off. The result could have been called their portrait much more appropriately than their effort can be called your portrait.[2] For when they try to give a burlesque description of an actor in a comic role, they don't present his own personality, they imitate his conception of the character he is playing, and they use the same tricks and devices which he uses, necessarily, in representing the eccentricities which he imitates from nature. But if you imitate an actor in a serious part, you pin down the faults which are really his own, since the serious roles don't admit the special tricks and mannerisms which are, in a way, his trademark.

MOLIÈRE: That's true. But I have my reasons for not doing so. Just among ourselves, I decided that the project wasn't worth the trouble; and then it would take too much time to carry it out. Since they play on the same days that we do, I've hardly been to see them three or four times since we've been in Paris,

---

[2] Reference to Boursault's *Le Portrait du peintre,* which had just been acted at the rival theatre, the Hôtel de Bourgogne.

so I have only a superficial impression of their acting style. I would need to study them longer in order to make really faithful portraits.

MLLE DU PARC: As for me, I have recognized some of them by your imitations.

MLLE DE BRIE: Imitations? I hadn't heard about that.

MOLIÈRE: Oh, it was just a stray idea, but I dropped it, as a mere whimsicality which might not have roused much of a laugh.

MLLE DE BRIE: Tell me about it, since you've told the others.

MOLIÈRE: We haven't the time now.

MLLE DE BRIE: Just in a couple of words!

MOLIÈRE: Well, I had thought of a play in which there would be a playwright—I would have played him myself. He would come to offer a play to a theatrical troupe just arrived from the country. He'd say: "Have you got any actors and actresses who can really bring out a play's quality? For my play—well, it's a play . . .!" And the actors would reply: "Why, sir, we have some men and women who have been found adequate everywhere we've gone." "Who does the kings for you?" "There's an actor who takes them on occasionally." "What! That young, handsome man? You're crazy! You have to have a king as big and fat as four people, a king, *morbleu*, magnificently potbellied, a king of vast circumference, who can properly fill a noble throne.[3] A nice business, to have a king with an elegant figure! That's a serious drawback. But let me hear him recite a few lines." Then the player would render, for instance, a few lines of the king's part in *Nicomède:*[4]

> *Te le dirai-je, Araspe? Il m'a trop bien servi;*
> *Augmentant mon pouvoir . . .*

He would read the lines in the most natural manner possible.

---

[3] Reference to Montfleury, famous actor of the Hôtel de Bourgogne.
[4] A tragedy by Corneille. On the stage Molière recited the whole speech, as he did the other speeches later indicated.

And the playwright would say: "What! You call that delivery! You're joking! You must say things with pomp and circumstance. Listen to me!" (*He gives an imitation of Montfleury, bombastically declaiming the same lines*) "Notice the way I stand?" says the playwright. "Observe that closely. And bellow the last line properly. That's what brings out the applause, that's what makes them roar." And the actor would reply: "But, sir, it seems to me that a king who is talking in private to the captain of his guards might speak in a more human manner; his tone of voice wouldn't be quite so—demoniac." "You don't know what you're talking about," says the playwright. "Deliver it the way you're doing, and see if you get a single 'Oho! Aha!' Now let's have a scene between two lovers." Then an actor and an actress would do a scene together, perhaps the one between Camille and Curiace:[5]

> *Iras-tu, ma chère âme, et ce funeste honneur*
> *Te plaît-il aux dépens de tout notre bonheur?*
> *—Hélas, je vois trop bien,* etc.

They would do it like the other speech, that is, as naturally as they could. Then the playwright would say: "You're crazy! Absolutely impossible! Let me show you how to do that part." (*He imitates Mlle Beauchâteau of the Hôtel de Bourgogne*)

> *Iras-tu, ma chère âme,* etc.

The playwright would go on: "You see how natural, how passionate that is? See how wonderfully she keeps a smiling face in the midst of the most terrible afflictions!" . . . In short, that was my idea. And the playwright could have run through all the actors and actresses in the same way.

MLLE BE BRIE: I think it's a charming idea. I recognized the speakers immediately. Won't you go on?

MOLIÈRE (*imitates Beauchâteau, of the Hôtel de Bourgogne, delivering the famous poetic monologue of Corneille's* Le Cid):
> *Percé jusques au fond du coeur,* etc.

---

5 From Corneille's *Horace.*

And do you recognize this person, playing Pompey in Corneille's *Sertorius?* (*He imitates Hauteroche*)

L'inimitié qui règne entre les deux partis
N'y rend pas de l'honneur, etc.

MLLE DE BRIE: I certainly do recognize him.

MOLIÈRE: How about this one? (*He imitates Villiers*)

Seigneur, Polybe est mort, etc.[6]

MLLE DE BRIE: Yes, I know who that is. But I think there are some of them you'd have trouble in taking off.

MOLIÈRE: Oh, there aren't any I couldn't catch in some way or other, if I had studied them well. But you're making me lose precious time! Please, let's get down to business, and not get distracted by idle talk. (*To* LA GRANGE) You, take good care to play properly, along with me, your role as a marquis.

MLLE MOLIÈRE: What, more marquises!

MOLIÈRE: Yes, more marquises. Who the devil do you expect us to take as the comic character in a play? Today the marquis has become the stage buffoon. Just as in the old plays there was always a comic servant to make the audience laugh, so nowadays we always have to have a ridiculous marquis as the funny man.

MLLE BÉJART: True enough, we couldn't do without them.

MOLIÈRE (*to* MLLE DU PARC): As for you, mademoiselle—

MLLE DU PARC: As for me, I will do my part very badly. I don't know why you gave me the role of the affected, simpering lady.

MOLIÈRE: Good Lord, mademoiselle, that's what you said when I gave you the same character in the *Critique of The School for Wives;*[7] and you did it splendidly; everybody agreed that no one could do it better. Believe me, this will be just the same. You will play it better than you think.

MLLE DU PARC: How can that be? There's no one on earth less affected than I am.

[6] From Corneille's *Oedipe.*
[7] Mlle du Parc played Climène.

MOLIÈRE: Quite true. That's how you demonstrate that you're an excellent actress, by playing so well a character who is entirely the contrary of yourself. So all of you, try to get well inside the parts you're playing, and imagine that you are really what you are representing.

(*To* DU CROISY) You're the playwright. You must put yourself totally into the character, and bring out his pedantic air, which he keeps in the midst of frivolous society, and his sententious tone of voice, and his ex-act-ness of pro-nun-ci-ation, which gives full value to every syllable, so that no one could misspell a word he utters.

(*To* BRÉCOURT) You're a worthy and sensible courtier, as you were in the *Critique of The School for Wives;*[8] that is, you keep a calm demeanor and a natural tone of voice, and you use as few gestures as possible.

(*To* LA GRANGE) And as for you, I have nothing to tell you.

(*To* MLLE BÉJART) You represent one of those women who think that if only they don't make love, everything else is permissible; one of those women who entrench themselves proudly behind their prim virtue, look down on everyone, and are convinced that all the good qualities others may possess count for nothing in comparison with their own sorry honor—which no one else has any interest in. So keep that character well in mind, and show it in your face and manner.

(*To* MLLE DE BRIE) You play one of those women who think they are perfectly virtuous if they preserve appearances; they think that sin consists only in being found out; they try to disguise their amorous adventures as blameless attachments, and call those people friends whom others call their lovers. Get well inside that character.

(*To* MLLE MOLIÈRE) You play the same type as in the *Critique;*[9] and I have nothing to say to you, or to Mademoiselle du Parc either.[10]

---

[8] Brécourt had played Dorante.
[9] Mme Molière had played Élise in the *Critique.*
[10] See footnote 7.

(*To* MLLE DU CROISY) And you play one of those ladies who sweetly bestow a dose of malice on everyone, who always have some casual, cutting remark to make, and who can't bear to hear anything good about their neighbors. I think you will put that over very nicely.

(*To* MLLE HERVÉ) And you're the pert servant of the *Précieuses*, the soubrette. You join in the conversation from time to time, and you pick up your mistress' phrases as well as you can.

I'm telling you all about your characters, so that you will have a real sense of them. And now let's get the rehearsal started, and see how it goes. Oh, here's another interferer! This is the last straw!

(*Enter* LA THORILLIÈRE.)

LA THORILLIÈRE: Good day, Monsieur Molière!

MOLIÈRE: At your service, sir. (*Aside*) The devil take him!

LA THORILLIÈRE: How are things going with you?

MOLIÈRE: Very well, thank you. (*To the actresses*) Mesdemoiselles, don't—

LA THORILLIÈRE: I've just been in a place where I said some very nice things about you.

MOLIÈRE: I am deeply obliged to you. (*To the troupe*) Now pay close attention—

LA THORILLIÈRE: You're putting on a new play today?

MOLIÈRE: Yes, monsieur. (*To the troupe*) Now, don't forget—

LA THORILLIÈRE: It's by the King's order?

MOLIÈRE: Yes, monsieur. (*To the troupe*) For heaven's sake, remember—

LA THORILLIÈRE: What's its name?

MOLIÈRE: Yes, monsieur.

LA THORILLIÈRE: I'm asking you the name of the play.

MOLIÈRE: My word, I don't know. (*To the troupe*) Now, please, you'll have to—

LA THORILLIÈRE: How will you be costumed?

MOLIÈRE: Just as you see us. (*To the troupe*) I beg you—

LA THORILLIÈRE: When will you begin?

MOLIÈRE: When the King comes. (*Aside*) To hell with him and his questions!

LA THORILLIÈRE: When do you think he'll come?

MOLIÈRE: May the plague carry me off if I know!

LA THORILLIÈRE: You don't know—

MOLIÈRE: Look here, sir, I am the most ignorant man on earth. I don't know anything about anything you may ask me, I swear to you. (*Aside*) He'll drive me mad! This hangbird comes and calmly asks his questions, and never worries about all I have to do!

LA THORILLIÈRE (*to the actresses*):   Mesdemoiselles, I am your humble servant.

MOLIÈRE: Good! He's taking on someone else.

LA THORILLIÈRE (*to* MLLE DU CROISY):   You're as beautiful as a sweet little angel. (*With a glance at* MLLE HERVÉ) And you're both playing today?

MLLE DU CROISY: Yes, monsieur.

LA THORILLIÈRE: Without you two, the play wouldn't amount to much.[11]

MOLIÈRE (*to the actresses*):   Aren't you going to get rid of that fellow?

MLLE DE BRIE (*to* LA THORILLIÈRE):   Monsieur, we have something to rehearse together.

LA THORILLIÈRE: Ah, *parbleu,* I won't stop you. Go right ahead.

MLLE DE BRIE: But—

LA THORILLIÈRE: No, no, I should be sorry to discommode anyone. Do what you have to do quite freely.

MLLE DE BRIE: Yes, but—

LA THORILLIÈRE: I don't stand on ceremony, I tell you. You can rehearse anything you like.

MOLIÈRE: Monsieur, these ladies have some trouble in telling

[11] In fact, Mlles du Croisy and Hervé were regarded as the weakest in the troupe.

you that they would much prefer to have no visitors here during the rehearsal.

LA THORILLIÈRE: Why? There's no danger for me.

MOLIÈRE: Monsieur, it's just the custom in the theatre. You will
have more pleasure if the play comes as a surprise.

LA THORILLIÈRE: Very well. I'll go and report that you're ready.

MOLIÈRE: Not at all, sir. Don't hurry, I beg you. (*Exit* LA
THORILLIÈRE) What a lot of meddlers there are in the world!
Now come on, let's get started. You're to realize first that the
scene is the King's antechamber; for that's a place where a lot
of amusing things happen every day. It's easy to bring in there
any characters we may want, and we can even find good pre-
texts for presenting our women characters. The play opens with
the meeting of the two marquises. (*To* LA GRANGE) You, remember to come in there, as I told you, with the air of the
stylish dandy, combing your wig, and humming a little song.
La, la, la, la, la, la. You others stand back, for the marquises
need a lot of room; they aren't the kind of people who can be
confined in a small space. Now go ahead; speak your lines.

LA GRANGE: Good day, Marquis!

MOLIÈRE: Wait a minute. That's not the tone of a marquis. You
must pitch your voice higher. And most of these gentlemen
affect a special style of speech, to distinguish themselves from
the common sort. "Good day, Marquis!" Now begin again.

LA GRANGE: Good day, Marquis!

MOLIÈRE: Ah, Marquis, I am your humble servant!

LA GRANGE: What are you doing here?

MOLIÈRE: Egad, you see! I am waiting for all those gentlemen
to disencumber the door, so that I may proffer my visage.

LA GRANGE: Gadzooks, what a hurly-burly! I do not desiderate
their noisome contact; I prefer to enter with the last comers.

MOLIÈRE: There are still a score who may be assured of having
no entrance; but they crowd and push none the less, and occupy
every avenue to the King's door.

LA GRANGE: Let us shout our names to the usher, and he will summon us to enter.

MOLIÈRE: That's well enough for you, my dear; but as for me, I don't want Molière to make fun of me.

LA GRANGE: And yet, Marquis, I think it's you he takes off in the *Critique*.

MOLIÈRE: Me? Oh, with all due respect, you're his model in person.

LA GRANGE: Ah! I vow, it's nice of you to fasten your own character on me.

MOLIÈRE: *Parbleu,* I think you're very funny to give me what belongs to you.

LA GRANGE: Ha, ha, ha! Very droll, very droll!

MOLIÈRE: Ha, ha, ha! I am amused.

LA GRANGE: What! You maintain that the original of the marquis in the *Critique* is not you?

MOLIÈRE: Oh, true enough, it's me! "Detestable, *morbleu!* Detestable! Cream tart!" That's me, that's me, assuredly that's me!

LA GRANGE: Yes, 'pon my soul, that's you! You can't put me off by joking. If you like, we'll wager on it, and we'll see who's right.

MOLIÈRE: And what do you want to wager?

LA GRANGE: I'll bet a hundred pistoles it's you.

MOLIÈRE: And I'll bet a hundred it's you.

LA GRANGE: A hundred pistoles down?

MOLIÈRE: Down. Or practically down. Ninety pistoles that Amyntas owes me, and ten in cash.

LA GRANGE: All right.

MOLIÈRE: Done!

LA GRANGE: Your money is in great danger.

MOLIÈRE: And yours is running a frightful hazard.

LA GRANGE: But who will be the judge?
         (*Enter* BRÉCOURT.)

MOLIÈRE: There's a man we'll take for umpire. Chevalier!

BRÉCOURT: What is it?

MOLIÈRE (*dropping his role*):   That's nice! Now the other man is taking on the marquis' tone of voice! (*To* BRÉCOURT) Didn't I tell you that in your part you must speak naturally?

BRÉCOURT: That's right.

MOLIÈRE: All right. Let's go on . . . Chevalier!

BRÉCOURT: What is it?

MOLIÈRE: Please settle a wager we've made.

BRÉCOURT: What wager is that?

MOLIÈRE: We're arguing who is the marquis in Molière's *Critique*. He bets it's me, and I bet he's the one.

BRÉCOURT: And for me, I decide that it's neither one nor the other. You're both crazy, to try to apply that kind of thing to yourselves. That's just what I heard Molière complaining about the other day; he was talking to some people who were making the same accusation that you are. He said that nothing annoyed him so much as to be accused of aiming at some person in his types. His purpose, he said, was to depict manners in general without touching particular individuals, and all his characters, he said, are fanciful, phantoms, you might say, whom he clothes with his imagination, in order to amuse the audience. He'd be very sorry, he said, ever to suggest any real person at all; and the one thing which could disgust him forever with writing plays was people's constant eagerness to find likenesses of real individuals; and his enemies were maliciously trying to build up that idea, in order to get him into trouble with certain people he'd never even thought of. And in fact I think Molière is right; for why, I ask you, should we try to find particular models for all his gestures and words, and stir up a hornet's nest by proclaiming: "He's taking off so-and-so!" when the role can fit a hundred people? As the function of a comedy is to represent in general all men's failings, and principally those of our contemporaries, it's impossible for Molière to create any character which doesn't suggest someone in our society; and if he is to be accused of having in mind all the people who may have the failings he indicates, he'll certainly have to give up writing plays.

MOLIÈRE: On my word, Chevalier, you want to justify Molière, and spare the feelings of our friend here.

LA GRANGE: Not at all. (*To* MOLIÈRE) It's your feelings he's sparing. We'll find some other umpires.

MOLIÈRE: Good. But tell me, Chevalier, don't you think your Molière has written himself out, and he won't find any further subject matter—

BRÉCOURT: No further subject matter? Ah, my good Marquis, we will always furnish him with plenty of subject matter; and we will hardly be persuaded to reform ourselves by all he says and writes.

MOLIÈRE (*resuming his own character*):   Wait a minute. You must emphasize that whole passage more. Listen to me do it. "He won't find any further subject matter . . . No further subject matter? Ah, my good Marquis, we will always furnish him with plenty of subject matter; and we will hardly be persuaded to reform ourselves by all he says and writes. Do you think he has exhausted all human follies in his plays? Even staying in court circles, hasn't he a score of characters he hasn't touched on? Hasn't he, for example, those who protest the warmest friendship on earth, and then, as soon as their backs are turned, follow fashion by tearing each other to ribbons? Hasn't he the excessive praisers and applauders, those insipid flatterers who lay on their commendation with a trowel, and whose compliments have a sickly sweetness which revolts the listeners?[12] Hasn't he those mean courtiers of favor, those faithless adorers of success, who praise you to the skies in your prosperity and who kick you when you're down? Hasn't he those who are always dissatisfied with the court, those useless hangers-on, those indefatigable misfits, those people, I say, whose only services are their everlasting solicitations, and who want

---

[12] Molière later developed this character in the role of Oronte in *The Misanthrope*.

to be rewarded for badgering the Prince for ten years without stopping?[13] And hasn't he those who caress everyone alike, who bestow their civilities equally on all sides, and who greet everyone they see with the same embraces and protestations of friendship: 'Monsieur, I am your very humble servant. —Monsieur, I am utterly at your service. —Consider me your most devoted, dear boy. —Esteem me, sir, the very warmest of your friends. —Monsieur, I am overjoyed to be able to embrace you. —Ah, monsieur, I didn't see you! Do, please, ask me any service! Be assured that I am totally given to your interests. You are the man I revere most on earth. There are none whom I honor as I do you; I adjure you to believe it. I beg you not to have the slightest doubt of it. —I am your servant, sir. —And I am your most humble and obedient.'[14] No, no, Marquis, Molière will always have more subjects than he can use; and what he has treated so far is trifling in comparison with his opportunities.". . . Now that's about how the speech should be delivered.

BRÉCOURT: That's all I need.

MOLIÈRE: Now go ahead.

BRÉCOURT (*assuming his role*):   Why, here are Climène and Élise![15]

MOLIÈRE (*in his natural tone, to* MLLE DU PARC *and* MLLE MOLIÈRE):   Now you two come in. (*To* MLLE DU PARC) You be sure to wiggle your hips properly, and put on lots of affectation. You'll have to strain yourself a little, but what of it? Sometimes one has to do violence to one's own character.

MLLE MOLIÈRE (*assuming her role*):   Indeed, madame, I recognized you when you were still far off, and I realized from your manner it could be no one else.

MLLE DU PARC: Well, you see, I have come to meet here a certain man, when he leaves the King's chamber; I have some business with him.

---

13 Molière never treated this type.
14 See the opening scene of *The Misanthrope*.
15 Characters from *The Critique*.

MLLE MOLIÈRE: My case exactly.

MOLIÈRE (*in his natural voice*):   Ladies, there are a couple of boxes you can use for chairs.

MLLE DU PARC (*in her role*):   Come, madame, won't you sit down?

MLLE MOLIÈRE: After you, madame.

MOLIÈRE (*in his natural voice*):   Good. After this little business, everyone will sit down and speak seated, except the two marquises, who will keep standing up and sitting down, according to their natural fidgetiness. (*Assuming his role*) Parbleu, Chevalier, you should give your knee ruffles a dose of medicine.

BRÉCOURT: How is that?

MOLIÈRE: They aren't looking well.

BRÉCOURT: My compliments on the joke.

MLLE MOLIÈRE (*to* MLLE DU PARC):   Good heavens, madame, your complexion is simply dazzling; your lips are amazingly rosy!

MLLE DU PARC: What do you mean, madame? Don't look at me; I'm ugly as sin today.

MLLE MOLIÈRE: Ah, madame, do lift your veil a little.

MLLE DU PARC: Oh, fie! I'm perfectly appalling, I tell you; I even frighten myself.

MLLE MOLIÈRE: You're lovely!

MLLE DU PARC: Not at all, not at all.

MLLE MOLIÈRE: Do show your face.

MLLE DU PARC: Oh, fie, fie, I beg of you.

MLLE MOLIÈRE: Oh, please!

MLLE DU PARC: Dear heaven, no.

MLLE MOLIÈRE: Yes, do.

MLLE DU PARC: You'll drive me to despair!

MLLE MOLIÈRE: Just for a moment.

MLLE DU PARC: Oh, alas!

MLLE MOLIÈRE: Absolutely, you will have to uncover. We mustn't be deprived of the sight of you.

MLLE DU PARC: Dear me, what a strange person you are! You want so frightfully what you want!

MLLE MOLIÈRE: Ah, madame, you have nothing to fear from showing yourself in broad daylight, I swear to you. How wicked are those people who say you make yourself up! Now I am ready to prove they are liars.

MLLE DU PARC: Oh, dear, I don't even know what it means, to make oneself up. But where are those ladies going?

(*Enter* MLLE DE BRIE, MLLE HERVÉ, MLLE DU CROISY, MLLE BÉJART; *also* DU CROISY.)

MLLE DE BRIE (*to* MLLE MOLIÈRE *and* MLLE DU PARC):   Ladies, let us give you, in passing, a delightful bit of news. Here is Monsieur Lysidas,[16] who has just informed us that a play has been written against Molière, and the Hôtel de Bourgogne is going to put it on!

MOLIÈRE: That's true; I have heard it read. The author's name is Br—Brou—Brossaut.[17]

DU CROISY: Monsieur, the play is announced under the name of Boursault. But to tell you the facts, many people have taken a hand in the play; one may expect great things of it. As all the authors and the players regard Molière as their greatest enemy, we have united to pay him off. Each of us added a few brush strokes to this portrait; but we took good care not to sign our names to it. It would have been too glorious for him to succumb in public to the attacks of the whole of Parnassus. So to make his downfall the more ignominious, we chose a totally unconsidered author to be our champion.

MLLE DU PARC: Personally, I grant that I am unimaginably delighted.

MOLIÈRE: And I too! Zounds and zooks! The mocker will be mocked! He'll catch it properly!

MLLE DU PARC: This will teach him to make fun of everything!

---

[16] Du Croisy had played Lysidas in *The Critique*.
[17] Boursault. The play is *Le Portrait du peintre*.

What! This upstart won't admit that women may be intelligent! He condemns all our refined expressions, and wants us to talk the vulgar, earthy language!

MLLE DE BRIE: The language doesn't matter; but he censures all our friendships, however innocent they may be. According to him, it's criminal to have meritorious qualities.

MLLE DU CROISY: It's unendurable! A woman can no longer do anything at all! Why doesn't he leave our husbands at peace, instead of opening their eyes and making them take notice of things they would never have observed?

MLLE BÉJART: That's of no consequence. But he even satirizes virtuous women. This sorry jester gives them the name of spotless female devils![18]

MLLE MOLIÈRE: He's an insolent rogue. He must get his comeuppance.

DU CROISY: The production of this comedy, madame, will need plenty of support; the actors of the Hôtel de Bourgogne—

MLLE DU PARC: Good Lord, they needn't be alarmed. I absolutely guarantee the success of their play.

MLLE MOLIÈRE: You are right, madame. So many people have an interest in approving it. Obviously all those who think they are satirized by Molière will seize the opportunity for revenge by applauding the comedy.

BRÉCOURT: Surely; and for me, I'll answer for twelve marquises, six précieuses, twenty coquettes and thirty cuckolds, who will certainly come and beat their hands to a blister.

MLLE MOLIÈRE: Naturally. Why should he go and offend all those people? Especially the cuckolds, who are the finest fellows on earth?

MOLIÈRE: Zounds and zooks! I hear that they're going to smite him hip and thigh, him and his comedies! And that all the players and authors, from the topmost to the bottommost, are devilishly up in arms against him.

[18] See *The School for Wives,* Act IV.

MLLE MOLIÈRE: Just what he deserves! Why does he write those nasty plays which all Paris goes to see—plays in which he puts such lifelike characters that everyone recognizes himself in them? Why doesn't he write plays like those of Monsieur Lysidas? He wouldn't rouse up people against him, and all the authors would speak well of them. It is true that such plays don't draw very big crowds, but on the other hand they are always very well written, no one attacks them, and everyone who sees them simply yearns to find them beautiful.

DU CROISY: It is true that I have the merit of not making enemies, and all my works are warmly approved by the scholarly critics.

MLLE MOLIÈRE: You have every reason for self-satisfaction. And that is much better than all the public applause and all the money that Molière's plays may receive. What difference does it make whether people come to your productions, since they are approved by your learned colleagues?

LA GRANGE: But when will they play *The Portrait of the Painter?*

DU CROISY: I don't know; but I am ready to put myself at the head of the list, to shout "Beautiful! Beautiful!"

MOLIÈRE: And so will I, *parbleu!*

LA GRANGE: And I too, God save me!

MLLE DU PARC: And as for me, I won't spare myself. I guarantee you a salvo of applause which will put all hostile opinions to rout. The least we can do is to lend a helping hand to the defender of our interests.

MLLE MOLIÈRE: Very well said.

MLLE DE BRIE: That's what we must all do.

MLLE BÉJART: Assuredly.

MLLE DU CROISY: Certainly.

MLLE HERVÉ: No quarter to that mimicker of nice people!

MOLIÈRE: Faith, my dear Chevalier, your Molière will have to go into hiding!

BRÉCOURT: Who, Molière? I warrant you, Marquis, that he intends to see the performance, and laugh with the rest at the portrait of himself.[19]

MOLIÈRE: *Parbleu!* It'll be a pretty forced laugh!

BRÉCOURT: Come now, perhaps he'll find more to laugh at than you think. I've seen the text of the play; and as the only amusing passages in fact are the ideas which are taken from Molière,[20] he certainly won't be offended by any success it may have. As for the part where the author tries to blacken the character of Molière,[21] I shall be very much surprised if anyone approves of it; and as for all the people whom the author has tried to stir up against Molière, on the ground that his portraits are too lifelike, not only is the criticism in very bad taste, but it is ridiculous and misapplied. I had never realized that an author should be criticized for depicting men too truthfully.

LA GRANGE: The players told me that they were ready and waiting for his answer, and—

BRÉCOURT: His answer? Faith, I would call him an idiot, if he should go to the trouble of answering their abuse. Everyone knows perfectly well their motives; and the best answer he could make would be another play which would succeed like the rest. That's the right way to avenge himself properly. And judging by their character, I am convinced that a new play which will take away their audiences will annoy them much more than all the satires he might make of their persons.

MOLIÈRE: But, Chevalier—

MLLE BÉJART (*resuming her own character*):   May I interrupt the rehearsal a moment? You know what I think? If I had been in your place, I would have put the case differently. Everyone expects a good stiff reply from you; and after the treatment you apparently had in that comedy, you had the right to say every-

---

[19] In fact, Molière did attend a performance of *Le Portrait du peintre*. His enemies asserted that he was mortified; his friends insisted that he laughed loudly.

[20] In fact, *Le Portrait du peintre* is a mere witless reversal of the theme of the *Critique*.

[21] Boursault had hinted that Molière was dangerously irreligious.

thing you pleased against those actors. You shouldn't have
spared one of them.

MOLIÈRE: That kind of talk makes me sick. You women always
go off half-cocked. You would like to have me take fire immediately, and burst out with insults and abuse, following their
example. Much honor that would be for me, and much pain I
would cause them! Aren't they eager to receive such treatment?
And when they discussed whether or not to play *The Portrait
of the Painter,* for fear of a counterattack, didn't some of them
reply: "Let him insult us all he pleases, provided we make
money"? That shows how sensitive to shame they are. Wouldn't
it be a nice revenge, to give them just what they want?

MLLE DE BRIE: Still, the players made a lot of complaint about
three or four phrases you used about them in the *Critique*[22] and
in *The Precious Damsels.*[23]

MOLIÈRE: All right then, those three or four phrases are very offensive, and they are within their rights to quote them. But no,
be honest, that's not the heart of the matter. The greatest injury
I've done them is my good luck in succeeding more than they
liked; and everything they've done since we arrived in Paris
has shown only too well what hurts them. But let them do whatever they please; I shouldn't be upset by anything they undertake. They criticize my plays; good! Heaven preserve me from
ever putting on one they approve of! That would be a disaster
for me.

MLLE DE BRIE: Well, it can't be much of a pleasure to have your
works torn to pieces.

MOLIÈRE: What do I care? Haven't I got from my play all I
wanted to get, since it had the good fortune to please the august
personages whom I am especially trying to please? So haven't
I good reason to be satisfied with its outcome? And don't all
these criticisms come too late? Am I the one, I ask you, who is

22 See the *Critique,* page 113.
23 See *The Precious Damsels,* page 20.

now chiefly concerned? When people attack a successful play, aren't they really attacking the judgment of those who have approved it, more than the art of the playwright?

MLLE DE BRIE: Anyhow, I would have poked some fun at that insignificant author, who takes it on himself to criticize people who never even thought of him.

MOLIÈRE: You're crazy! What a fine theme that would be for the court's amusement—Monsieur Boursault! I'd like to know how one could dress him up to make him amusing! And if one should burlesque him on the stage, how happy he would be to make people laugh! He would be too much honored, to be taken off before a distinguished audience; there's nothing he'd like better. He attacks me so irresponsibly, just to get into the limelight by any means at all. He's a man who has nothing to lose; the players have launched him against me only to get me entangled in a silly war, and thus to distract me from doing the other plays I have still to write. And yet you are simple enough to fall into the trap! But anyway, I will make my declaration publicly. I don't intend to make any reply to all their blasts and counterblasts. Let them say all the ugly things they like about my plays; all right, I agree. Let them pick them up after we've done them, and turn them inside out like a coat to stage them in their own theatre, and let them try to profit by any qualities they can find in them, and by any originality I've had the luck to hit upon—good; I consent. They need help, and I shall be very glad to contribute to their support—provided that they content themselves with what I can decently grant them. But courtesy has its limits. There are some things which don't amuse either the audience or the person who is being travestied on the stage. I gladly surrender to them my writings, my face, my gestures, my words, my tone of voice, my mannerisms, and they can do and say all they like about them, if they can get any profit from them. I don't oppose their use of all that; I shall be delighted if such things raise a laugh. But since I surrender all that, they should do me the favor of leaving the rest to me, and of refraining from touching on such subjects as, I hear, they are using to attack me.[24] That is the civil request I make of the honorable gentleman who has undertaken to write for them; and that is the only reply they will get from me.

MLLE BÉJART: But nevertheless—

MOLIÈRE: But nevertheless, you will drive me crazy. Let's say no more about that; we are wasting time making speeches, instead of rehearsing our play. Where were we? I've forgotten.

MLLE DE BRIE: We were at the place—

MOLIÈRE: Good God! I hear a noise! It's the King coming, for certain. I see very well that we won't have time to go on. That's what comes of dawdling! Well, you'll just have to do the best you can with the rest of it.

MLLE BÉJART: Oh, dear, I'm scared to death! I can never play my part, unless I rehearse it right through.

MOLIÈRE: What, you can't play out your part?

MLLE BÉJART: No.

MLLE DU PARC: I can't do mine either.

MLLE DE BRIE: Neither can I.

MLLE MOLIÈRE: Nor I.

MLLE HERVÉ: Nor I.

MLLE DU CROISY: Nor I.

MOLIÈRE: Then what do you expect to do? Are you going to make a fool out of me?

(*Enter* BÉJART.)

BÉJART: Ladies and gentlemen, I have come to announce that the King has arrived, and he is waiting for you to begin.

MOLIÈRE: Ah, sir, you see me in agony! You see a desperate man! These women are all frightened to death; they say they have to rehearse their parts before beginning. For pity's sake, we beg a few minutes more. The King is full of kindness and

24 Molière's enemies were not only accusing him of irreligion, but were dropping scurrilous hints about his marital relations.

bounty; he knows how hurried we've been. (*To the actors*) Now for heaven's sake, try to calm down. Pull yourselves together, please.

MLLE DU PARC: You should go and make an excuse.

MOLIÈRE: And how can I make an excuse?

(*Enter* A BUSYBODY.)

BUSYBODY: Gentlemen, begin, please.

MOLIÈRE: Just a moment, sir. I think this business will drive me raving mad, and—

(*Enter* ANOTHER BUSYBODY.)

SECOND BUSYBODY: Gentlemen, begin, please.

MOLIÈRE: Right away, sir. (*To the actors*) What! Do you want me to make a public failure—

(*Enter* ANOTHER BUSYBODY.)

THIRD BUSYBODY: Gentlemen, begin, please.

MOLIÈRE: Yes, sir, we're just about to do so. (*To the actors*) What a lot of people who don't mind their own business, and come and say: "Gentlemen, begin, please!" without any order from the King!

(*Enter* ANOTHER BUSYBODY.)

FOURTH BUSYBODY: Gentlemen, begin, please.

MOLIÈRE: At once, sir! What! Must I be so confounded— (*Enter* BÉJART) Monsieur, you are coming to tell us to begin, but—

BÉJART: No, gentlemen; I have come to tell you that the King has been informed of your difficulties, and by a very special bounty he has put off your new play until later, and for today he will be satisfied with any play in your repertory.

MOLIÈRE: Ah, monsieur, you bring me back to life! The King has granted us the greatest boon possible, in giving us time to fulfill his desires; and now we shall all thank him for the measureless kindness he has manifested to us.

Tartuffe

Tartuffe was first presented, in a three-act form, on May 12, 1664, as a part of a sumptuous festival at Versailles. The King liked it, but, under pressure from the Church, forbade Molière to produce it in public. Then for five years Molière strove to bring his play to life, revising and rewriting, presenting appeals to authority, pulling every string. At length, for reasons not entirely clear, Louis revoked his ban. *Tartuffe* was publicly performed on February 5, 1669. Its success was sensational and lasting. Over the centuries it has totaled more performances than any other Molière play.

Molière had suffered at the hands of religious zealots. The French hierarchy, in a Puritan phase, condemned out of hand the theatre, professional players, offensive passages in *The School for Wives,* and Molière's person. A clerical writer termed Molière (in August 1664) "a demon in the flesh, dressed in men's clothing, the most impious, libertine spirit of all time, who should be burned alive." The *Compagnie du Saint-Sacrement,* a secret society of laymen concerned with improving morals by interfering in private lives, organized the opposition to *Tartuffe.* Molière's play is in some part at least a counterattack against the excesses of pious rigor.

We classify it as a comedy of character, in that its interest is concentrated on the picture of a religious hypocrite. It contains elements of the thesis play, showing the social danger of the perversion of faith; of the comedy of manners; and of course of farce. Or one may call the play a *drame bourgeois,* according to the term invented by Diderot a century later.

151

Its construction has been much criticized; but perhaps the successive reworkings did it no good. The central character does not appear until the third act; the lovers' quarrel in Act II stalls the action and chills the modern reader; the introduction of the strongbox at the end of Act IV is unprepared; the dénouement is hardly admirable. However, the dénouement is Molière's way of expressing his gratitude to the King for lifting the ban; it may well have replaced another, possibly more logical, conclusion.

The import of *Tartuffe* has been endlessly discussed. Was Molière really attacking professional confidence men, who use religion as a cloak? Or did he criticize by implication a group, the *Compagnie du Saint-Sacrement,* the Jansenists, the Jesuits? Or, despite all his disclaimers, was he mocking the practice of Catholicism, of all religion?

Certainly every spokesman for the Church in the seventeenth century condemned the play as dangerous to true religion. Certainly today's playgoer, seeing the practice of religion represented by a hypocrite, a dupe, and a fool, and hearing the laughter at the actors' burlesques of piety, is likely to agree. One difficulty resides in the nature of hypocrisy. The more competent a hypocrite is, the less can his visible behavior be distinguished from the real thing. And is Tartuffe really a hypocrite? In his attempt to seduce Elmire, who is by no means a fanatic, he employs the language of mystical devotion, which would be better calculated to repel than to win her. No words of his own, even to the play's end, reveal his hypocrisy. To the spectator he looks like a bigoted, avaricious sensualist—which is a very different thing from a hypocrite.

Some modern critics beg the whole question by saying that there is no problem. The character Tartuffe is just an actor's part; the moment he leaves the stage he ceases to exist. The play is just a play, a super-farce, designed to make an audience laugh. But it seems strange that Molière would have worked so hard, risking the most savage reprisals, in order to produce a meaningless play.

The Characters

MADAME PERNELLE, mother of Orgon

ORGON

ELMIRE, Orgon's wife

DAMIS, son of Orgon, stepson of Elmire

MARIANE, daughter of Orgon and stepdaughter of Elmire

VALÈRE

CLÉANTE, brother-in-law of Orgon, brother of Elmire

TARTUFFE

DORINE, companion of Mariane

MONSIEUR LOYAL, bailiff

A POLICE OFFICER

FLIPOTE, Madame Pernelle's servant

The setting throughout is the salon of Orgon's house, in Paris. The furnishings are those of a well-to-do bourgeois.

ACT I

MADAME PERNELLE, FLIPOTE, ELMIRE, MARIANE, DORINE, DAMIS, CLÉANTE.

MME PERN.: Come on, Flipote, come on; I've had enough.
ELMIRE: Mother, you walk so fast I can't keep up.
MME PERN.: Don't try to keep up, then. Ha! Daughter-in-law!
Little I care if you're polite with me.

153

ELMIRE:	I want to be so with my husband's mother.
	Why must you go? I hope you're not offended.
MME PERN.:	Why? I can't stand the way that things are going!
	In my son's house they pay no heed to me.
	I am not edified; not edified.
	I give you good advice. Who pays attention?
	Everyone speaks his mind, none shows respect.
	This place is Bedlam; everyone is king here.
DORINE:	If—
MME PERN.:	You, my dear, you're just a paid companion,
	A forward hussy, who talks a lot too much.
	You have to give your views on everything.
DAMIS:	But—
MME PERN.:	You are a fool. F-O-O-L spells fool.
	Your grandmother, she ought to know a fool.
	And I have told your father a hundred times
	You're impudent, your character is bad;
	And what he'll get from you, my boy, is trouble.
MARIANE:	I think—
MME PERN.:	You think! The fool's little sister thinks!
	Butter won't melt in that prim mouth of yours.
	Still waters, they are deep—and dangerous.
	And something hides behind that mousy manner.
ELMIRE:	But, Mother—
MME PERN.:	Dear Elmire, I will be frank.
	I find your attitude unfortunate.
	Your task should be to set a good example.
	Their own dead mother did so, better than you.
	I disapprove of your extravagance;
	You get yourself all rigged up like a princess.
	A wife, my dear, needs no such finery,
	If she would please her husband's eyes alone.
CLÉANTE:	But, madame, after all—
MME PERN.:	You are her brother.

You have my reverence, esteem, and love.
But if I were my son, her happy husband,
I'd beg of you never to call again.
The principles I hear you recommend
Are not the sort that decent folk observe.
I'm speaking frankly; that's the way I am;
And when I feel a thing, I cannot hide it.

DAMIS: There's nothing wrong about Monsieur Tartuffe?

MME PERN.: He is a worthy man with principles;
And I admit that I am irritated
To hear him criticized by fools like you.

DAMIS: You want me to permit a canting critic
To come and play the tyrant in our home?
We can't indulge in innocent amusement
Unless that gentleman gives his consent?

DORINE: If one believes him and his principles,
Everything that we do becomes a crime.
He checks on everything, he's so sincere.

MME PERN.: And what he checks on is most properly checked.
He wants to lead you on the road to heaven.
My son is well inspired to make you love him.

DAMIS: Grandmother, look; Father can do his utmost;
Nothing on earth can make me love the fellow.
Anything else I'd say would be a lie.
I simply cannot stand him and his actions.
I can see trouble coming; I can see
I'll have a set-to with that holy fraud.

DORINE: It seems to me perfectly scandalous
That this outsider should take over things.
He came to us a beggar, with no shoes,
And all his clothes were worth about a dollar.
But that's forgotten, now he's found his place;
He has the final veto; he's the boss.

MME PERN.: Mercy upon us! Things would be much better

If all his pious rules were put in force.

DORINE: He is a saint in your imagination.

In fact, he's nothing but a hypocrite.

MME PERN.: What silly talk is this!

DORINE: I wouldn't trust him

Out of my sight; his servant Laurent either.

MME PERN.: The servant I don't know; but for the master,

I guarantee that he's a man of virtue.

And you dislike him, you cold-shoulder him

Merely because he tells the truth about you.

The one thing that he really hates is sin,

And heaven's advantage is his only motive.

DORINE: Yes, but why is it that for some time now

He won't allow us any visitors?

What is so shocking in a friendly call,

That he should make a frightful fuss about it?

And shall I tell you what I really think?

I think that he is jealous of Madame.

(*She indicates* ELMIRE.)

MME PERN.: Be quiet, you! Be careful what you say!

He's not the only one who blames these visits.

All the commotion that these callers make,

Their carriages forever at the door,

The noisy gangs of lackeys, hanging around,

Have caused a lot of comment from the neighbors.

Oh, I will grant that nothing serious happens,

But people talk, and people shouldn't talk.

CLÉANTE: You want to put a stop to conversation?

Wouldn't it be somewhat regrettable

If we should have to give up our best friends,

Just because fools may say some foolish things?

Even supposing we should bar the door,

Do you think people then would cease to talk?

There is no wall so high it shuts out slander.

So let's not give a thought to silly gossip,
And let us try to live in innocence,
And let the talkers talk just as they please.

DORINE: Our neighbor Daphne and her little husband
Are doubtless those who speak so ill of us.
Those whose behavior is ridiculous
Always are first to see the faults of others.
They never fail to catch the faintest hint
That mutual attachments may exist.
And then how glad they are to spread the news,
Suggesting—oh, what horrors they suggest!
And others' acts, colored to suit their tastes,
They put to use to authorize their own.
They think that some resemblance will appear
To mask their own intrigues with innocence;
They hope thus to confuse the public censure
And make it fall on good and ill alike.

MME PERN.: All these fine words do not affect the case.
Orante, for instance, leads a model life.
She works for heaven alone; and people say
That she condemns the customs of this house.

DORINE: There is a fine example! That good woman!
She lives austerely now, that's true enough;
But age has put this ardor in her soul,
And makes her play the prude, despite herself.
As long as men would pay their court to her,
She made her graces work for her advantage.
But her allurements ceasing to allure,
She quits society, which quitted her,
And with a veil of virtue tries to hide
The dimming of her antiquated charms.
That is the classic fate of old coquettes;
They hate to see their gallants disappear.
Unhappy and abandoned, they can see

No other recourse than the trade of prude.
And these good women with severity
Make universal censure, pardon nothing.
Loudly they blame the lives of everyone,
Not out of charity, but out of envy,
Which can't endure that any woman share
In pleasures time has thieved away from them.

MME PERN.   (*to* ELMIRE):

That is the kind of nonsense that you like;
Thus in your house we have to hold our tongues
So that my lady here can hold the floor.
But I've a little speech to make myself,
And here it is: My son did very wisely
In welcoming that pious gentleman;
And heaven sent him here advisedly
To guide your spirits, strayed from the true path.
And you should heed him, for your souls' salvation.
What he reproves has needed his reproof.
These parties and these balls, these conversations,
Are all inventions of the Evil One.
There one may hear no edifying speeches,
But only idle words and songs and chatter,
Often at some poor fellow man's expense.
There you find masters in the art of slander.
Even the man of sense may be upset
By the loose talk one hears in such assemblies,
All a great buzz of gossip and of rumor.
As a great preacher said the other day,
These gatherings are towers of Babylon,
For people merely babble on, he said.
And then in illustration of his point—
(*Points to* CLÉANTE)
And now Monsieur is snickering already!
Go join the funny men who make you laugh!

My dear Elmire, good-by; I've said enough.
This household has come down in my opinion.
'Twill be a blue moon ere I come again.
(*Giving* FLIPOTE *a box on the ear*)
Wake up, woolgatherer! Wake up, rattlehead!
God's mercy! I will beat those brains of yours!
On your way, trollop!
(*Exit all except* CLÉANTE *and* DORINE.)

CLÉANTE: I wouldn't see her out
For fear I'd get another dressing-down.
For really, that good woman—

DORINE: It's too bad
The lady didn't hear you call her good.
She'd tell you you are kind to term her good,
But she's not old enough yet to be good.

CLÉANTE: Didn't she get excited about nothing!
And isn't she crazy about her Tartuffe!

DORINE: In fact, that son of hers is twice as bad.
If you could see him, you'd be really shocked.
He played a fine part in the civil wars,
Was faithful to the King through thick and thin;
But now he acts as if he'd lost his wits,
Since he has been bewitched by his Tartuffe.
He calls him brother, actually loves him
More than his mother, son, daughter, and wife,
Confides his secrets to Tartuffe alone,
And makes him sole director of his actions;
Hugs him and pats him tenderly; he couldn't
Show more affection for a darling bride;
Gives him the place of honor at his table,
And beams to see him eat enough for six.
He saves the best bits for Tartuffe alone,
And cries "God bless you!" when the fellow belches.
He's mad about the man, his pet, his hero,

And quotes him, apropos of everything,
And makes a miracle of every action,
An oracle of every slightest word.
And Tartuffe knows a good thing when he sees it,
Puts on an act, the better to fool his dupe;
His holy manner pays him off in cash,
While he makes bold to criticize us all.
Even that boy who serves him as a lackey
Takes it upon himself to give us lessons,
And lectures us with angry, popping eyes,
And throws away our ribbons, rouge, and patches.
The rascal tore to bits a neckerchief
We'd put to press in some big holy book,
Saying we made a criminal connection
Between the devil's toys and holiness!
(*Enter* ELMIRE, MARIANE, DAMIS.)

ELMIRE: Lucky for you you didn't come and hear
The speech she made us, standing in the doorway.
I saw my husband, but he didn't see me.
I think I'll wait for him in the upstairs parlor.
(*Exit* ELMIRE *and* MARIANE.)

CLÉANTE: Not to waste time, I'll wait to see him here.
I merely want to greet him and be gone.

DAMIS: Bring up the question of my sister's marriage.
I've an idea Tartuffe is against it.
He's swaying Father, making difficulties.
You know I'm personally interested.
As Valère and my sister are in love,
I'm more than fond myself of Valère's sister.
And if I had to—

DORINE: He's coming.
(*Exit* DAMIS. *Enter* ORGON.)

ORGON: Good morning, brother.

CLÉANTE: I was just leaving. I'm glad to see you back.
And did you find the country all in bloom?

ORGON: Dorine . . . Just wait a minute, please, **Cléante,**
            Until I have a chance to inform myself
            About the household news during my absence.
            (*To* DORINE)
            Everything's been all right, the past few days?
            How's everyone? What has been going on?

DORINE: Two days ago, your lady had a fever,
            And a bad headache, really terrible.

ORGON: And Tartuffe?

DORINE: Tartuffe? Oh, he's doing fine,
            So fat and red-faced, such a healthy color.

ORGON: Poor fellow!

DORINE: She had some nausea in the evening,
            And couldn't touch a single thing at supper.
            Her headache still was a real torture to her.

ORGON: And Tartuffe?

DORINE: Ate his supper in her presence,
            And piously devoured two partridges,
            Also a hash of half a leg of mutton.

ORGON: Poor fellow!

DORINE: During all the following night
            She did not shut her eyes a single moment.
            It was so very warm she could not sleep;
            We had to sit beside her until morning.

ORGON: And Tartuffe?

DORINE: Oh, Tartuffe was sleepy enough.
            He went right after dinner to his room,
            Immediately he got in his warm bed,
            And peacefully slept until the following day.

ORGON: Poor fellow!

DORINE: She listened to our arguments,
            And had the doctor give her a good bleeding,
            And after that she felt a great deal better.

ORGON: And Tartuffe?

DORINE: Why, he cheered up very nicely.

To fortify his spirit against trouble
And to make up for Madame's loss of blood,
He took at lunch four glasses full of wine.

ORGON: Poor fellow!

DORINE: Now both are doing very well.
I'll tell Madame the sympathetic interest
You've taken in the news of her recovery.
(*Exit* DORINE.)

CLÉANTE: She's laughing in your face, my dear Orgon;
And while I wouldn't want to make you angry,
I'm frank to say she has good reason to.
I can't conceive such an infatuation.
This fellow must cast some uncanny spell
Which paralyzes all your common sense.
After you've rescued him from poverty,
To think you've gone so far—

ORGON: Enough, Cléante.
You do not know the man you're talking of.

CLÉANTE: Well, I don't know him personally, it's true,
But I know well what kind of man he is.

ORGON: Brother-in-law, you would be charmed to know him.
You would be simply overwhelmed with pleasure.
He's a man who . . . a man who . . . well, he's a
    man!
Follow his teachings, you gain peace of mind,
You learn to see the world as so much filth.
My talks with him have changed me utterly;
He's taught me to despise worldly attachments,
He frees my soul from earthly love and friendship;
If brother and children, mother and wife should die,
It wouldn't bother me as much as that!
(*Snaps his fingers.*)

CLÉANTE: These sentiments are what I call humane.

ORGON: If you'd been present when we made acquaintance,
You'd have become his friend, the same as I.

He used to come to our church every day,
And kneel near me, with such a gentle air!
And everyone in church would notice him
Because of the fervent way in which he prayed.
He sighed so deep, he made such cries of transport!
And every now and then he'd kiss the floor!
When I was going out, he'd run ahead
To offer me holy water at the door.
His servant lad, no less devout than he,
Told me about his life, his poverty.
I made him presents; but with modesty,
He always tried to give me back a part.
"This is too much!" he'd tell me. "Twice too much!
I don't deserve to have you pity me!"
And when I would refuse to take them back,
He'd give them to the poor! I saw him do it!
'Twas heaven that made me bring him to my house;
And since that time, everything prospers here.
He censures everything, and for my honor
He takes an active interest in my wife,
Warns me when people look too kindly at her—
He's twice as jealous of her as I could be.
You can't imagine his religious scruples!
The merest trifle is a sin to him;
Nothing's too insignificant to shock him.
Why, he accused himself the other day
Of capturing a flea while he was praying,
And pinching it to death with too much anger!

CLÉANTE: Good Lord, my dear Orgon, I think you're crazy!
Or are you trying to make a fool of me?
What do you think that all this nonsense means?

ORGON: Cléante, this sounds to me like irreligion!
You've had some tendency to that already;
And as I've warned you a good dozen times,
You'll get yourself in trouble some fine day.

CLÉANTE: I've heard that kind of talk from others like you.
They want to make the whole world blind like them.
It's irreligion just to have open eyes!
If you're not taken in by mummery,
They say you've no respect for sacred things.
You cannot scare me with that sort of language.
I know what I say, and heaven can see my heart.
We aren't befooled by such performances;
There's false devotion like false bravery.
And as you see upon the field of honor
The really brave are not the noisiest ones,
The truly pious, whom we should imitate,
Are not the ones who show off their devotion.
Isn't there some distinction to be made
Between hypocrisy and piety?
It seems you want to treat them both alike,
Honor the mask as much as the true face,
Make artifice equal sincerity,
Confuse the outward semblance with the truth,
Esteem the phantom equally with the person,
Take counterfeit money on a par with gold.
Really, humanity is most peculiar!
Men won't remain in the mean middle way;
The boundaries of reason are too narrow.
They force their character beyond its limits,
And often spoil even most noble aims
By exaggeration, carrying things too far.
All this, Orgon, is only said in passing.

ORGON: Cléante, you are no doubt a reverend doctor.
All of man's wisdom has been lodged in you.
You are the world's one wise, enlightened sage,
The oracle, the Cato of our times,
And all mankind, compared with you, are fools.

CLÉANTE: No, Orgon, I am not a reverend doctor,
And the world's wisdom is not lodged in me.

But there is one thing that I do well know:
To tell the difference between true and false.
And as I see no kind of character
More honorable than true devotion is,
Nothing more noble and more beautiful
Than fervent, genuine, holy piety,
So I find nothing on earth more odious
Than the false show of whited sepulchres,
These charlatans, these public pietists
Whose sacrilegious and perfidious manners
Deliberately betray and parody
All that men hold most hallowed and most sacred.
These are the people who for mean advantage
Make piety their trade and merchandise,
And try to buy credit and offices,
Rolling their eyes and mouthing holy words.
Their pilgrim's progress takes the road to heaven
As a short, easy way to worldly fortune.
We see them pray with one hand out for alms;
They preach of solitude, but stay at court.
And with their holy zeal they keep their vices;
They're vengeful, faithless, treacherous, and tricky,
And to destroy an enemy, they cover
Their savage hate with heaven's interest.
And when they hate, they're the more dangerous,
Because they take up weapons we revere,
Because their fury, to general applause,
Takes an anointed sword to stab our backs.
The type that I describe is all too common.
But the true pietists can be recognized.
Take Ariston, for instance, Périandre,
Oronte, Alcidamas, or Polydore.
No one's suspicious of their genuineness.
Such people don't go trumpeting their virtue,
They don't put on a nauseating show,

For their devotion's human, reasonable.
They do not censure all the acts of men—
There's too much pride in taking on that role.
They leave the high talk to their imitators,
And by their actions set us an example.
They don't see evil everywhere abounding;
Indeed, they're lenient toward their fellow men.
They don't form pressure groups to push intrigues;
To lead a good life is their only aim.
They don't pursue the sinner with their hate;
The sin and not the sinner is their target.
They don't espouse the interests of heaven
With greater zeal than heaven does itself.
That is the kind of people I admire;
They are the models we should imitate;
And, to be frank, your man's not one of them.
Although I know you praise him in good faith,
I think you're taken in by false appearance.

ORGON: Cléante, you've now entirely finished?

CLÉANTE: Yes.

ORGON: I am your humble servant.

    (*Starts to leave.*)

CLÉANTE: Just a moment.
Let's deal with something else. You have consented
That young Valère should have your daughter's
    hand.

ORGON: Yes.

CLÉANTE: And what's more, you'd even set the day.

ORGON: That is correct.

CLÉANTE: Then why is it postponed?

ORGON: I don't know why.

CLÉANTE: You have another idea?

ORGON: Perhaps.

CLÉANTE: You hint you'd go back on your word.

ORGON: I won't say that.

CLÉANTE: There is some obstacle
To keep you from fulfilling your engagement?

ORGON: Maybe.

CLÉANTE: Why must you beat around the bush?
Valère has asked me to inquire about it.

ORGON: How fortunate!

CLÉANTE: What shall I tell him, then?

ORGON: Whatever you like.

CLÉANTE: But it is necessary
To know your plans. So what are they?

ORGON: To follow
The will of heaven.

CLÉANTE: I want to get this clear.
You've given Valère your word. You'll keep your
word?

ORGON: Good-by.
(*Exit* ORGON.)

CLÉANTE: I fear that courtship's in for trouble;
And I must tell Valère the look of things.

ACT II

ORGON, MARIANE.

ORGON: Mariane!

MARIANE: Father?

ORGON: Come here. I want to speak
In confidence.
(*He peers into a cupboard.*)

MARIANE: What are you looking for?

ORGON: I want to see if there's an eavesdropper there,
For that's the kind of place they choose to hide in.
No, it's all right. Now, Mariane, my dear,

You've always had a gentle character,
And I have always been most fond of you.

MARIANE: I have been very grateful for your love.

ORGON: Excellent, daughter. To deserve my affection
You should be ready to accept my judgments.

MARIANE: I've always done so, and I'm proud of it.

ORGON: Splendid. Now tell me, what do you think of Tartuffe?

MARIANE: What do I think?

ORGON: Yes. Don't speak hastily.

MARIANE: Dear me! I think whatever you think I should.
(DORINE *enters unnoticed.*)

ORGON: Well said. Now this is what you ought to think.
He is a man of most unusual merit;
He moves your heart, and you'd be overjoyed
To have me pick him out to be your husband.
Eh?
(MARIANE *starts back in surprise.*)

MARIANE: Eh?

ORGON: What?

MARIANE: What did you say?

ORGON: What?

MARIANE: Did I hear rightly?

ORGON: What's this?

MARIANE: Who is it you say that moves my heart?
Who is it that it would make me overjoyed
To have you fix upon to be my husband?

ORGON: Tartuffe.

MARIANE: Oh, no, no, no, it's impossible.
Why do you want to make me say what's false?

ORGON: I say it because I want to make it true.
I have decided on it, that's enough.

MARIANE: Father, you really mean—

ORGON: Yes, it's my purpose
To make Tartuffe a member of our family.

He'll be your husband, I'm resolved on that.
And your desires—
(*He turns, and perceives* DORINE)
                              What are you doing here?
Your curiosity is certainly excessive
To make you listen to our private talk.

DORINE: I'd heard the story—I suppose it started
Out of pure guesswork or some chance remark—
That this peculiar marriage was afoot;
But I've been saying it's all poppycock.

ORGON: You mean you find it unbelievable?

DORINE: So much so that I don't believe you now.

ORGON: I know how I can bring you to believe it.

DORINE: Yes, you're just being funny. I know *you*.

ORGON: I'm telling you exactly what will happen.

DORINE: Rubbish!

ORGON: My good girl, it's not rubbish at all.

DORINE (*to* MARIANE):
Do not believe a word your father says.
He's joking.

ORGON: I tell you—

DORINE: No, whatever you do,
Nobody can believe it.

ORGON: I can't hold in—

DORINE: All right, then, I'll believe you, if I must.
But how a sensible-looking man like you,
With a big beard in the middle of his face,
Can be so simple-minded—

ORGON: Listen to me.
You have been taking certain liberties here
Which I don't like at all, I tell you frankly.

DORINE: Now, let's not get excited, sir, I beg you.
Is your idea just to look absurd?
A bigot has no business with your daughter;

He has a lot of other things to think of.
What good does such a marriage do to you?
How comes it that you, with your property,
Should choose a beggar son-in-law—

ORGON: Be quiet!
That's just the reason why we should revere him!
His poverty's a worthy poverty,
Which properly sets him above rank and wealth.
He's let his worldly goods all slip away,
Because he'd no concern for temporal things,
Because he loved eternal goods alone.
But my financial aid will help him rise
Out of his troubles, regain his property,
Estates well known in his home territory.
He is a landed squire, a gentleman.

DORINE: Yes, so he says. His vanity about it
Is unbecoming with his piety.
When you take up a holy, innocent life,
You shouldn't boast about your name and rank.
Devotion should imply humility,
Which doesn't fit with smugness and ambition.
Why be so proud? . . . But you don't like this talk.
Let's treat his person, not his noble blood.
Doesn't it trouble you that a man like him
Should be possessor of a girl like her?
Shouldn't you think about the decencies,
Foresee the consequence of such a union?
You're putting a girl's virtue to the test
By forcing her to a distasteful marriage;
And her desire to be a faithful wife
Depends upon the qualities of the husband.
The men who wear the horns are just the ones
Who force their wives to be—what they become.
It's hard indeed for a woman to be faithful
To certain husbands cast in a certain mold.

	A father who gives a girl to a man she hates

A father who gives a girl to a man she hates
Must be responsible for her missteps.
So think how dangerous your project is!

ORGON: And so you want to teach me about life!

DORINE: You could do worse than follow my advice.

ORGON: Daughter, we'll waste no time with all this nonsense.
I know what's best for you; I am your father.
It's true that I had pledged you to Valère,
But now I hear that he plays cards for money;
Further, I fear he's somewhat a freethinker.
I do not see him frequently in church.

DORINE: You think he ought to go there just when you do,
Like those who only want to catch your attention?

ORGON: I didn't ask your views upon the matter.
(*To* MARIANE)
The other man has made his peace with heaven.
And that's the greatest wealth a man can have.
This marriage will be rich in every blessing,
And filled with pleasures and with satisfactions.
You will be faithful, in your mutual joys,
Just like a pair of little turtle doves.
There'll never be an argument between you;
You'll make of him whatever you want to make.

DORINE: All that she'll make of him is a horned monster.

ORGON: What talk is this?

DORINE: I say he has the build for it.
The stars have doomed him, and his natural fate
Will be more powerful than your daughter's virtue.

ORGON: Stop interrupting me, and hold your tongue,
And don't go meddling in what's none of your business.

DORINE: I'm only speaking, sir, for your own good.
(*She interrupts* ORGON *whenever he turns to speak to his daughter.*)

ORGON: That's all too kind of you; and so, be silent.

DORINE: If I didn't love you—

ORGON: I don't want to be loved.

DORINE: I want to love you, sir, in spite of yourself.

ORGON: Ha!

DORINE: Cherishing your honor, I can't bear
The mockeries you'd lay yourself open to.

ORGON: You won't shut up?

DORINE: My conscientious duty
Is not to permit you to make such an alliance.

ORGON: Will you shut up, you snake! Your impudence—

DORINE: Why, you're so holy, and you fly in a rage!

ORGON: You drive me crazy with your balderdash,
And so I order you to keep your mouth shut.

DORINE: All right. But even when silent, I can think.

ORGON: Think if you like; but take good care you don't
Utter a word, or else—
(*Threatens* DORINE *with a gesture. Turns to* MARI-
ANE)
                          As a sensible man,
I've thought the matter out.

DORINE: It drives me mad
Not to be able to speak.
(ORGON *turns to her; she falls silent.*)

ORGON: Although no dandy,
Tartuffe has looks—

DORINE: All right, if you like them hard.

ORGON: And even if you had no sympathy
For his other gifts—

DORINE: Oh, what a lucky girl!
If I were she, I would make sure no man
Would marry me by force and escape scot-free;
And I would prove, soon after the ceremony,
That a woman always has her vengeance ready.

ORGON   (*to* DORINE):

So, you won't pay attention to my orders?

DORINE: What's your objection? I'm not talking to you.

ORGON: Then what are you doing?

DORINE: Talking to myself.

ORGON: Excellent. So, to punish her insolence,
I'll have to give her a good slap in the face.
(*Raises his hand and poises it for a blow, but when-
ever he looks at* DORINE, *she stands still and mute*)
Daughter, you ought to think well of my project . . .
Believe the husband . . . whom I've chosen for
you . . .
(*To* DORINE)
Why don't you talk to yourself?

DORINE: I've nothing to say.

ORGON: Just say one little word!

DORINE: I don't feel like it.

ORGON: I was all ready for you.

DORINE: I'm not so dumb.

ORGON (*turns to* MARIANE):
In short, Mariane, you owe obedience,
And you must show respect for my opinion.

DORINE (*fleeing*):
You'd never make me agree to such a husband.
(ORGON *tries to slap her; she escapes, and exits.*)

ORGON: That forward girl of yours, Mariane, is a pest,
And she provokes me to the sin of anger.
I'm in no state to carry on our talk;
Her insolent speech has got me all excited,
And I must take a walk to calm myself.
(*Exit* ORGON. DORINE *re-enters cautiously.*)

DORINE: What, Mariane, you've lost your power of speech?
And do I have to play your part for you?
You'll let him make this asinine proposal,
And not combat it with a single word?

MARIANE:	What can I do against his absolute power?
DORINE:	Anything, in the face of such a threat.
MARIANE:	And what?
DORINE:	Tell him a heart can't love by proxy;
	The marriage is for your sake, not for his;
	And since you are the person who's concerned,
	The husband ought to please you and not him;
	And since he finds Tartuffe so fascinating,
	He is the one who ought to marry him.
MARIANE:	I know; but Father is so masterful
	I've never had the courage to oppose him.
DORINE:	Look here; Valère has made his formal suit;
	Now let me ask you: Do you love him, or don't you?
MARIANE:	Oh, you're unjust, Dorine! You know I love him!
	You have no reason even to ask the question!
	Haven't I poured it out a hundred times,
	And don't you know the greatness of my love?
DORINE:	I never know if one is quite sincere,
	If your great love is really genuine.
MARIANE:	You do me a great wrong in doubting it.
	I thought my feelings were sufficiently clear.
DORINE:	In short, you love him?
MARIANE:	Yes, and passionately.
DORINE:	And it would seem that he loves you no less?
MARIANE:	I think so.
DORINE:	And you both are equally eager
	To be united in marriage?
MARIANE:	Certainly.
DORINE:	About this other proposal, what's your plan?
MARIANE:	To kill myself, if I am driven to it.
DORINE:	Splendid! I hadn't thought of that way out.
	To escape from trouble, you only have to die.
	A marvelous remedy . . . It makes me furious,
	Whenever I listen to that kind of talk.

MARIANE:	Good heavens, what a temper you get into!
	You don't much sympathize with others' sorrows.
DORINE:	I don't much sympathize with those who drivel,
	And then go limp, like you, when the test comes.
MARIANE:	What can I do? I'm naturally timid—
DORINE:	But love demands a firm, courageous heart.
MARIANE:	I have been constant, answering Valère's love.
	But he must ask, and gain, Father's consent.
DORINE:	But if your father is a perfect crank,
	Who's so infatuated with Tartuffe
	He disavows the marriage he agreed to,
	Is that a thing to blame your suitor for?
MARIANE:	If I refuse Tartuffe with open scorn,
	Won't I reveal how deeply I'm in love?
	Brilliant though Valère is, shall I abandon
	For him my modesty, my daughterly duty?
	Do you want me to display my love to the world?
DORINE:	No, I want nothing at all. I see you wish
	To be Madame Tartuffe; and now I think of it,
	I'm wrong in weaning you from this alliance.
	Why should I argue against your inclinations?
	The match would seem an advantageous one.
	Monsieur Tartuffe! He's not a nobody!
	Monsieur Tartuffe is not the kind who needs
	To stand on his head to get applause and money.
	One would be lucky indeed to be his wife.
	Why, everyone is glorifying him!
	He's noble—in his own home town! And handsome!
	His ears are rosy red, like his complexion!
	You will be all too happy with such a husband.
MARIANE:	Yes, but—
DORINE:	What ecstasy will fill your soul,
	When you are wife to that good-looking man!
MARIANE:	Stop, if you please, this agonizing talk,

	And give me counsel how to escape the marriage.
	I've made my mind up; I'll do anything.
DORINE:	No, a good daughter should obey her father,
	Though he should choose a monkey for her mate.
	You've a fine future; what are you grumbling for?
	You'll have a coach to perambulate his city,
	Which you'll find rich in uncles, aunts, and cousins
	Whom you will be delighted to entertain.
	You'll be received in high society,
	You'll call upon the Lord High Mayoress,
	And on the Lord High Tax-Collectoress,
	Who'll seat you honorably on a kitchen chair.
	And you can hope for a ball at carnival time,
	An orchestra consisting of two bagpipes,
	And sometimes a marionette show—with a monkey!
	However, if your huband—
MARIANE:	You're killing me!
	Stop it, and help me with some good advice.
DORINE:	You must excuse me.
MARIANE:	Oh, dear Dorine, please!
DORINE:	To punish you, the marriage must go through.
MARIANE:	Dorine!
DORINE:	No!
MARIANE:	If I state my opposition—
DORINE:	Tartuffe's your man. You must put up with him.
MARIANE:	I have confided everything to you.
	So now—
DORINE:	No. You will be tartufficated.
MARIANE:	Since my unhappy destiny can't move you,
	I must surrender now to my despair.
	And from despair my heart will take advice.
	I know the infallible remedy for my woes.
DORINE:	Here, here, come back. I'll put aside my anger.
	I must take pity upon you after all.

MARIANE:	If they insist on making a martyr of me,
	I tell you, Dorine, that I shall simply die.
DORINE:	Don't worry. If we're clever enough, we can
	Prevent it . . . But here's your lover, your Valère.
	(*Enter* VALÈRE. *He speaks at first jestingly.*)
VALÈRE:	Mademoiselle, a story's going round
	That's new to me. Very fine news, no doubt.
MARIANE:	What's that?
VALÈRE:	That you're to marry Tartuffe.
MARIANE:	Truly,
	My father has this idea in his head.
VALÈRE:	Your father, mademoiselle—
MARIANE:	Has changed his purpose.
	And he has just been making this proposal.
VALÈRE:	Seriously?
MARIANE:	Yes, seriously indeed.
	He has come out in favor of this marriage.
VALÈRE:	And what is your opinion on the matter,
	Mademoiselle?
MARIANE:	I don't know.
VALÈRE:	Frank, at least.
	You don't know?
MARIANE:	No.
VALÈRE:	No?
MARIANE:	What is your advice?
VALÈRE:	Why, my advice is to accept this husband.
MARIANE:	That's your advice?
VALÈRE:	Yes.
MARIANE:	Really?
VALÈRE:	Certainly.
	It is an opportunity not to be scorned.
MARIANE:	Well, I am very glad to have your counsel.
VALÈRE:	I think you'll follow it without much trouble.
MARIANE:	With no more trouble than you had in giving it.

VALÈRE:	I gave the advice only to give you pleasure.
MARIANE:	And I shall follow it to give *you* pleasure.
DORINE	(*aside*): We'll soon find out how this is going to end.
VALÈRE:	So this is how you love me? You deceived me
	When you—
MARIANE:	I beg you not to talk of that.
	You told me outright that I ought to accept
	The man who is designated for my husband;
	And I say that's what I intend to do,
	Since now you give me that excellent advice.
VALÈRE:	Don't try to excuse yourself by quoting me;
	You had already formed your resolution,
	And now you're seizing on a frivolous pretext
	To authorize yourself to break your word.
MARIANE:	Well said; it's true.
VALÈRE:	Certainly. And your heart
	Has never felt any real love for me.
MARIANE:	Oh, dear! Why, you may think so, if you wish.
VALÈRE:	Yes, if I wish! You think you've wounded me,
	But maybe I have other plans in mind.
	I know where I can get a better welcome.
MARIANE:	I don't doubt that. Anyone would admire
	Your character.
VALÈRE:	Let's leave my character out.
	It's not so wonderful; indeed, you prove it.
	But there's another girl who may be kinder;
	She won't be ashamed to take me on the rebound,
	And gladly she'll console me for losing you.
MARIANE:	The loss is not so great. The consolation
	Ought to come easily in this shift of partners.
VALÈRE:	I'll do my very best, you may be sure.
	Nobody likes to know he's been forgotten.
	In such a case, the best is to forget,
	And if you can't forget, pretend to do so.
	It is unpardonably weak, I think,

	To display love for one who abandons us.
MARIANE:	That is a very lofty sentiment.
VALÈRE:	You're right. It should be generally approved.
	What! You would like to have me keep forever
	My love for you unchanging in my heart,
	See you go happily to another's arms,
	And seek no solace for my cast-off love?
MARIANE:	Why, not at all! That's just what I desire!
	I wish that it were all arranged already!
VALÈRE:	You'd like that?
MARIANE:	Yes.
VALÈRE:	I've borne insults enough!
	I'll try immediately to satisfy you.
	(*Starts to leave and returns, as in succeeding speeches.*)
MARIANE:	Good.
VALÈRE:	Remember at least that you're the one
	Who is driving me to this expedient.
MARIANE:	Yes.
VALÈRE:	And remember that my purpose is
	To follow your example.
MARIANE:	If you like.
VALÈRE:	Enough. Your wishes will be carried out.
MARIANE:	Fine!
VALÈRE:	So this is the last time that you'll see me.
MARIANE:	Excellent!
VALÈRE:	(*starts to exit; at the door, turns*):
	Uh?
MARIANE:	What?
VALÈRE:	Did I hear you call me?
MARIANE:	You must be dreaming.
VALÈRE:	Well, I'm on my way.
	I bid you farewell.
MARIANE:	Adieu, sir.
DORINE:	As for me,

I think you both are addled in the brain.
I've let you squabble to your heart's content
To find out where you'd land yourselves at last.
Monsieur Valère!
(DORINE *tries to take* VALÈRE *by the arm, but he*
makes a show of resistance.)

VALÈRE: What do you want, Dorine?

DORINE: Come here!

VALÈRE: No, no, she's put me in a fury.
I'm doing what she wanted, don't restrain me.

DORINE: Stop!

VALÈRE: No, the matter's settled, you can see.

DORINE: Aha!

MARIANE: My presence seems to irritate him;
The best thing is for me to leave him alone.
(DORINE *leaves* VALÈRE *and runs to* MARIANE.)

DORINE: Where are you going?

MARIANE: Let me alone!

DORINE: Come back!

MARIANE: There's no use trying to hold me back, Dorine.

VALÈRE: Clearly it tortures her to look at me.
I'd better free her from that painful sight.

DORINE   (*leaving* MARIANE *and running to* VALÈRE):
What the deuce! You'll do nothing of the sort!
Stop all this nonsense! Both of you come here!
(*She pulls at them, one with each hand.*)

VALÈRE: What's your idea?

MARIANE: What do you want to do?

DORINE: Make peace between you and get you out of trouble.
(*To* VALÈRE)
You must be crazy to get in such a quarrel.

VALÈRE: Didn't you hear the way she talked to me?

DORINE   (*to* MARIANE):
You must be crazy too, to get so angry.

MARIANE:	Didn't you see the way he treated me?
DORINE	(*to* VALÈRE):
	You're crazy, both of you. I can bear witness
	The only thing she wants is to be yours.
	(*To* MARIANE)
	He loves you only, and his one desire
	Is marriage with you, I'll stake my life on that.
MARIANE	(*to* VALÈRE):
	Then why did you give me your horrible advice?
VALÈRE	(*to* MARIANE):
	And why ask my advice on such a subject?
DORINE:	I said you were both crazy. Give me your hands.
	(*To* VALÈRE)
	Yours, now.
VALÈRE	(*giving* DORINE *his hand*):
	Why give you my hand?
DORINE	(*to* MARIANE):
	Now give me yours.
MARIANE	(*giving* DORINE *her hand*):
	What is the sense of this?
DORINE:	Come on, step forward.
	You're both in love more than you realize.
VALÈRE	(*to* MARIANE):
	Yes, but don't do things so reluctantly,
	And give a man at least a friendly look.
	(MARIANE *looks at* VALÈRE, *and smiles feebly*.)
DORINE:	The fact is, lovers are extremely crazy!
VALÈRE	(*to* MARIANE): Haven't I reason to complain of you?
	Tell me sincerely, wasn't it unkind
	To amuse yourself by hurting me so much?
MARIANE:	But you yourself, aren't you the most ungrateful—
DORINE:	Let's leave this argument to another time,
	And think of fending off that fatal marriage.
MARIANE:	But have you any idea how to do so?

DORINE: There are a lot of things that we can do.
            Your father's talking nonsense, he's not serious.
            But the best thing for you is to pretend
            To gently yield to his fantasticality
            So that, in case of crisis, you can easily
            Keep on postponing the wedding ceremony.
            You can cure many things by gaining time.
            First you will take as your excuse some illness,
            Which will strike suddenly and cause delays;
            And then you'll meet an omen of misfortune.
            You'll pass, perhaps, a funeral in the street,
            Or break a mirror, or dream of muddy water.
            The great thing is that nobody can bind you
            To anyone without your saying yes.
            But out of prudence, it would be advisable
            That you two shouldn't be caught talking together.
            (*To* VALÈRE)
            Now go, and use the influence of your friends
            To help you get the girl who was promised you.
            And we shall make her brother work for us;
            And her stepmother, she'll be on our side.
            Good-by.

VALÈRE   (*to* MARIANE): Though we'll all do the most we can,
            My greatest hope and confidence lie in you.

MARIANE: I can't be sure what Father may decide,
            But I shall never be anyone's bride but yours.

VALÈRE: You make me very happy! In spite of all—

DORINE: Lovers are never tired; they talk forever.
            Come on; get going.

VALÈRE   (*takes a step toward exit, and returns*):
            Finally—

DORINE: Talk, talk, talk!
            (*Pushes each of them by the shoulder*)
            You go out this way; you go out the other.

ACT III

DAMIS, DORINE.

DAMIS: Now let a bolt of lightning strike me dead,
             Call me a scoundrel, anything you please,
             If any talk of duty will hold me back,
             If I don't take some action to settle things.
DORINE: Just take it easy, calm yourself a little.
             Your father has merely talked about the matter.
             People don't execute all they propose;
             There's many a slip between the cup and the lip.
DAMIS: I've got to stop that swine's conspiracies;
             I've got to tell him a few simple facts.
DORINE: I tell you, take it easy; let your stepmother
             Handle the fellow, as she does your father.
             She has some influence on Tartuffe's mind.
             He acts in a very obliging way to her;
             Maybe he has a kind of weakness for her.
             Lord knows I hope so! That would be convenient!
             For your sake she will have to interview him,
             Learn what his feelings are, point out to him
             What dreadful troubles he will bring about
             If he encourages Orgon in his purpose.
             His valet says he's praying; I couldn't see him.
             But he'll be coming down in a moment or two.
             So go out, please; let me arrange the matter.
DAMIS: I can be present during the interview.
DORINE: No, they must be alone.
DAMIS: I will keep quiet.
DORINE: Nonsense! I know how you can get excited,
             And that's the way to ruin everything.
             Go on!
DAMIS: I want to see, and I won't get angry.

DORINE: Oh, what a nuisance you are! He's coming! Get out!
           (DORINE *pushes* DAMIS *out. Enter* TARTUFFE. *He ob-*
           serves DORINE *and calls off-stage.*)

TARTUFFE: Put my hair shirt away and my flagellator,
           Laurent; and pray for heaven's continual grace.
           If anyone wants me, say I'm off to the prison
           To give away the charity given me.

DORINE   (*aside*): Eyewash and affectation, if you ask me!

TARTUFFE: What do you want?

DORINE: To tell you—

TARTUFFE   (*drawing out a handkerchief*):   Oh, dear heaven!
           Before you speak, please take this handkerchief.

DORINE: What?

TARTUFFE: Cover that bosom which I must not see.
           Such sights as that are hurtful to the spirit,
           And they may well awaken guilty thoughts.

DORINE: You must be very sensitive to temptation.
           Flesh makes a great impression on your senses!
           Of course, I don't know how you're stimulated,
           But I am not so readily aroused.
           If I should see you naked from head to foot,
           I wouldn't be tempted by all the skin you've got.

TARTUFFE: Please be a little modest in your speech,
           Or I must leave the room immediately.

DORINE: No, no, it's I who will go and leave you in peace.
           But there is something that I have to tell you.
           Madame Elmire is coming to the parlor,
           And she would like to have a word with you.

TARTUFFE: Oh, very gladly.

DORINE   (*aside*):   How he softens down!
           Bless me, I think that I was right about him.

TARTUFFE: She's coming soon?

DORINE: I think I hear her now.
           Yes, here she is. I'll leave you two together.

(*Exit* DORINE. *Enter* ELMIRE.)

TARTUFFE: May heaven, by its high, omnipotent mercy,
Forever grant you health of soul and body,
And bless your days according to the desire
Of one who is humblest of heaven's worshipers!

ELMIRE: I'm deeply grateful for your pious wish.
Let us sit down, to be more comfortable.

TARTUFFE: I hope you have recovered from your illness?

ELMIRE: It's better, thank you; the fever left me soon.

TARTUFFE: My prayers are all too insignificant
To have brought this grace upon you from on high;
But every supplication I have made
Has had as object your recovery.

ELMIRE: Your pious zeal took all too much upon it.

TARTUFFE: Your precious health concerned me very deeply,
And to restore it gladly I'd give my own.

ELMIRE: You're carrying Christian charity too far;
But I'm indebted to you for your kindness.

TARTUFFE: What I have done is less than you deserve.

(*Enter* DAMIS *cautiously, behind backs of* TARTUFFE
and ELMIRE; *he hides in the cupboard previously
mentioned.*)

ELMIRE: I wanted to speak privately to you.
I'm glad we have this chance to be unobserved.

TARTUFFE: I am glad too. It's very sweet to me,
Madame, to find myself alone with you.
It is an opportunity I've prayed for
Without success, until this happy moment.

ELMIRE: I too have wished a chance for intimate talk,
When you might speak from the heart, without disguise.

TARTUFFE: And what I wish is, as a singular grace,
To lay my soul utterly bare before you,
And vow to you that all of my objections

To the visitors who come to pay you homage
Do not arise from any hostility,
But rather from the extravagance of my zeal,
From my emotion—

ELMIRE: I gladly take it so.
I'm sure my welfare gives you this concern.

TARTUFFE   (*squeezing her fingertips*):
Indeed, madame, indeed; such is my ardor—

ELMIRE: Ouch! You are hurting me!

TARTUFFE: Excess of zeal!
I'd no idea of hurting you at all.
I'd rather . . .
(*Puts his hand on her knee.*)

ELMIRE: Your hand—what, pray, is it doing there?

TARTUFFE: Just feeling the material; so soft!

ELMIRE: Well, please stop feeling it. I'm very ticklish.
(*She pushes her chair aside;* TARTUFFE *brings his
chair close.*)

TARTUFFE: Really, this lace is marvelously done!
The modern needlework is truly astounding.
There's never before been anything to match it.

ELMIRE: Quite so. But let us talk about our business.
I hear my husband wants to break his word
And marry to you his daughter. Is that true?

TARTUFFE: He's hinted at it. But to tell the truth,
That's not the happiness I languish for.
It's elsewhere that I see the alluring charms
Of the felicity that I desire.

ELMIRE: I see; you do not love the things of earth.

TARTUFFE: The heart in my bosom is not made of stone.

ELMIRE: I think that all your longings turn to heaven,
That nothing upon this earth tempts your desires.

TARTUFFE: The love which draws us to eternal beauty
Does not exclude the love of temporal things.

And easily our senses may be charmed
By the perfect vessels heaven has fabricated.
Its glory is reflected in such creatures
As you, who show its rarest marvels forth.
Upon your face are heavenly beauties lavished
To dazzle the eyes, to fill the heart with transport.
O perfect beauty! I could not look upon you
Without admiring in you Nature's author,
And without feeling ardent love in my heart
For this fair portrait of divinity!
At first I trembled, lest my secret flame
Should be a stratagem of the Evil One;
Even, I was resolved to flee your presence,
A possible obstacle to my salvation.
But finally I realized, my fair one,
That there need be no guilt in such a passion,
That I can make it chime with modesty;
And so I let my heart follow its bent.
I know it is a great audacity
For me to dare to offer you this heart;
But my affection seeks all from your bounty,
And nothing from my own weak enterprise.
In you is all my hope, my good, my peace;
On you depends my punishment or my bliss;
By your decree alone may I be happy,
If you are willing; unhappy, if that's your will.

ELMIRE: This is a gallant declaration indeed,
But I must say I find it rather surprising.
I think you should have steeled your emotions bet-
ter,
Considering what such a purpose means.
A pious man like you, so widely known—

TARTUFFE: Ah, pious though I be, I'm still a man.
And when one glimpses your celestial beauties,

The heart is captured, and it cannot argue.
I know such words from me may seem surprising,
But after all, madame, I'm not an angel.
If you condemn the avowal I make to you,
You must accuse your own bewitching charms.
Since I first saw their more than earthly splendor,
You were the sovereign of my secret soul,
And the ineffable sweetness of your glance
Broke the resistance of my struggling heart.
You conquered all, my fasting, prayers, and tears;
And all my vows were made to you alone.
My eyes have told you this, so have my sighs;
And now, for greater clarity, my words.
And if you look with a compassionate spirit
Upon the woes of your unworthy slave,
If you consent to bring me consolation,
To condescend to my unworthiness,
I'll vow to you, O lovely miracle,
Immeasurable worship and devotion.
And in my hands your honor runs no risk,
Nor need it fear any disgrace or scandal.
These young court gallants women dote upon
Are careless in their acts and vain of speech.
They like to boast about their amorous triumphs;
There are no favors that they don't divulge;
Their inconsiderate tongues betray their trust,
Dishonoring the altar where they worship.
Men of my stamp, however, are discreet;
With us one is always sure of secrecy.
The care we take of our own reputations
Is a guarantee to the person we adore.
She who accepts our heart acquires in us
Love without scandal, pleasure without fear.

ELMIRE: I'm fascinated; and your rhetoric

Explains itself in very lucid terms.
Aren't you afraid that I may be in the mood
To tell my husband about your gallant longings,
And that this information may disturb
The warm affection that he holds for you?

TARTUFFE: I know that you are far too merciful,
That you will pardon my temerity;
Pity for human weakness will excuse
The violence of a love which may offend you.
Look in your mirror, you will recognize
A man's not blind, he's only flesh and blood.

ELMIRE: Another woman might take it otherwise,
But I will show that I can be discreet.
I'll not repeat the matter to my husband,
But in return I want one thing of you:
That's to urge openly, with no quibbling talk,
The marriage of Valère and Mariane,
And to renounce the unreasonable claim
By which you'd win her who is pledged to another.
And—

DAMIS (*emerging from the cupboard*):
No, madame, no! This news must be reported!
I was concealed there, I could hear everything!
And heaven's favor must have led me there
To confound the pride of a treacherous evildoer,
To open a way for me to avenge myself
On his hypocrisy and insolence,
To undeceive my father, and lay bare
The soul of a scoundrel who talks to you of love!

ELMIRE: No, Damis; it's enough if he mends his ways,
Deserving the pardon which I offer him.
I've promised it; don't make me break my word.
It's not my character to make a scene.
A woman laughs at such absurdities,

And doesn't trouble her husband's ears about them.

DAMIS: You have your reasons to take matters thus,
And I've my reasons to do otherwise.
It is ridiculous to try to spare him.
His sanctimonious impudence too long
Has got the better of my just resentment;
Too long he's roused up trouble in our home;
And far too long the rogue has ruled my father,
And blocked my courtship as he has Valère's.
It's time that Father should be told the truth,
And heaven has given me the means to do so.
To heaven I owe this opportunity;
It's far too favorable to be neglected.
Why, I'd deserve to have it snatched away,
If I held it in my hand and didn't use it.

ELMIRE: Damis—

DAMIS: Please, I must do what I think best.
I've never been so happy as I am now!
There's no use trying to force me to surrender
The pleasure of holding vengeance in my hand!
I'm going to settle things immediately—
And here's my opportunity in person.
(*Enter* ORGON)
Father, we're going to celebrate your coming
With a tasty bit of news which will surprise you.
You are well paid for all your kindnesses!
Monsieur has a special form of gratitude.
He's just revealed his zeal for your well-being,
Which aims at nothing less than your dishonor.
I have surprised him making to Madame
The insulting avowal of a guilty love.
Her character is gentle; generously
She earnestly desired to keep it secret.
But I cannot condone such impudence.
To keep you in the dark would be an outrage.

ELMIRE: I think a wife ought never to disturb.
               A husband's peace with silly tales like these;
               They have no application to her honor,
               And it's enough that we defend ourselves.
               That's what I think. Damis, you'd have said nothing,
               If I had had some influence over you.
               (*Exit* ELMIRE.)

ORGON: Oh, heavens, is this strange story credible?

TARTUFFE: Yes, brother; I am a wicked, guilty man,
               A wretched sinner full of iniquity,
               The greatest scoundrel who has ever lived.
               Each moment of my life has been polluted,
               It is a mass of crime and filthiness.
               I see that heaven, for my punishment,
               Chooses this circumstance to mortify me.
               However great the misdeed I am charged with,
               I will not pridefully defend myself.
               Believe their words, and give your anger rein,
               And drive me from the house like a criminal.
               No matter what may be my portion of shame,
               I have deserved to suffer far, far more.

ORGON   (*to* DAMIS):
               Traitor! And do you dare, by lying words,
               To try to tarnish his virtue's purity?

DAMIS: What! All this hypocritic blubbering
               Will make you disbelieve —

ORGON: Silence, you pest!

TARTUFFE: Ah, let him speak! How wrongly you accuse him!
               You would do better to believe his words.
               Why, in this case, be favorable to me?
               How do you know of what I am capable?
               How can you trust, dear brother, my appearance?
               Does my behavior prove me better in fact?
               No, no, you let my outward semblance cheat you.
               Alas, I am far from being what men think!

I'm taken commonly for an upright man,
But the truth is that I am nothing worth.
(*To* DAMIS)
Speak, my dear boy, and call me infamous,
Perfidious, worthless, thief and murderer,
Load me with names still more detestable;
I do not contradict, for I have deserved them.
(*Kneels*)
I long to suffer their shame upon my knees,
As retribution for my criminal life.

ORGON   (*to* TARTUFFE): Dear brother, it's too much. (*To*
     DAMIS) Your heart's not moved,
     Traitor?

DAMIS: His talk can fool you to this point?

ORGON: Silence, scoundrel! (*To* TARTUFFE) Brother, I beg
     you, stand.
     (*To* DAMIS) Rascal!

DAMIS: He can—

ORGON: Silence!

DAMIS: I will go mad!

ORGON: Just say a word, and I will break your head!

TARTUFFE: Be not enangered, brother, in God's name.
     For I would rather bear most grievous pain
     Than have him suffer the slightest scratch for me.

ORGON   (*to* DAMIS):
     Ingrate!

TARTUFFE: Leave him in peace. If I must kneel
     To ask you for his pardon—

ORGON   (*to* TARTUFFE):   Alas, you're joking!
     (*To* DAMIS)
     Observe his goodness!

DAMIS: Then—

ORGON: Peace!

DAMIS: What, I—

ORGON: Enough!

I can see well the motive of your attack.
You hate him, all of you; I see my wife,
Children, and servants baying after him.
You're using every impudent device
To oust this holy person from my home.
But the more efforts you make to banish him,
The greater efforts I'll make to keep him here.
And now I'll hasten to give him my daughter's hand
To abase the pride of the entire family.

DAMIS: You think that you will force her to marry him?

ORGON: Yes, and to spite you, on this very evening.
Oh, I defy you all! And I will teach you
You'll have to obey me! I'm the master here.
Now, take your words back, ruffian! On the spot
Cast yourself at his feet to ask his pardon!

DAMIS: What! From this scoundrel, by whose trickeries—

ORGON: Ah, you resist, you knave! And you insult him!
Give me a stick, a stick! (*To* TARTUFFE) Don't hold
    me back!
(*To* DAMIS) Now you get out of this house this very
    minute,
And never dare to enter it again!

DAMIS: All right, I'll go, but—

ORGON: Quick, get out of here!
Reptile, I'll take your name out of my will,
And for good measure you can have my curse!
(*Exit* DAMIS)
Think of offending so a holy man!

TARTUFFE: May heaven pardon him the pain he gives me!
(*To* ORGON) Ah, could you know how grievous it
    is to see
My character blackened in my brother's eyes—

ORGON: Alas!

TARTUFFE: The thought of this ingratitude
Makes my soul suffer such a cruel torture . . .

	The horror it inspires . . . My heart is **torn**
	So that I cannot speak! I'll die of it!
ORGON	(*runs weeping to the door whence he has driven*
	DAMIS): Villain! I'm sorry I withheld my hand,
	And didn't knock you down upon the spot!
	Brother, compose yourself; don't be distressed.
TARTUFFE:	Let's have no more of these afflicting quarrels.
	I see I bring dissensions to your home;
	I think it best, dear brother, that I leave it.
ORGON:	You're joking!
TARTUFFE:	Here I'm hated, and I see
	That one would bring my rectitude in question.
ORGON:	What of it? Do you think I listen to them?
TARTUFFE:	Ah, they'll continue surely their campaign.
	These stories you repudiate today
	Perhaps another time will be believed.
ORGON:	Oh, never, brother, never.
TARTUFFE:	Brother, a wife
	Can easily beguile a husband's mind.
ORGON:	No, No!
TARTUFFE:	I'll leave the house upon the instant,
	And thus remove all reason to attack me.
ORGON:	No, you'll remain; my life depends upon it.
TARTUFFE:	Well, I'll remain, to mortify my spirit.
	Still, if you wished it—
ORGON:	Oh!
TARTUFFE:	We'll say no more.
	I see how I must now conduct myself.
	Honor is delicate, and as your friend
	I'll avoid cause for gossip and suspicion,
	And flee the presence of your wife; I'll never—
ORGON:	No, you'll attend her, to defy them all.
	My greatest pleasure is to spite the world.
	I want you to be seen with her constantly.

And that's not all; the better to affront them
I want to have no other heir than you.
And so I'll take immediately the steps
To make you sole inheritor of my wealth.
A good friend, whom I make my son-in-law,
Is dearer to me than my wife and children.
Will you accept what I propose to you?

TARTUFFE: May heaven's will be done in everything!

ORGON: Poor fellow! Let's draw up the document,
And let the jealous drown in their own bile!

ACT IV

CLÉANTE, TARTUFFE.

CLÉANTE: The matter's common talk. You may believe me,
The scandalous tale is not to your advantage.
And I am glad I chanced to find you, sir,
To tell you my opinion in a word.
I won't attempt to weigh the rights and wrongs,
I will assume the unpleasant story's true.
Granted that Damis acted badly toward you,
And that his accusation was unfounded,
Should not a Christian pardon the offense,
Extinguishing thus Damis' desire for vengeance?
And should you let this quarrel be the cause
Of the exile of a son from his father's house?
Let me repeat to you, in perfect frankness,
That everybody's scandalized about it.
And if you take my advice, you will make peace
And not let things be carried to extremes;
You'll sacrifice your bitterness to God,
And bring the son back to his father's favor.

TARTUFFE: Alas, for my part, I would happily do so.

I harbor no resentment, sir, against him.
I pardon him freely, blame him not at all;
I long with all my heart to do him good.
But this is not in heaven's interest.
If he returns here, I must leave the house.
After his unimaginable action
We can't associate without disgrace.
God knows what people would conclude about it;
They would accuse me of sheer calculation.
Knowing my guilt, they'd say, I was pretending
Feelings of charity for my accuser.
They'd say I fear him and want to humor him
In order to persuade him to keep silence.

CLÉANTE: You try to give me plausible excuses,
But all your arguments are too far-fetched.
Why take heaven's interest upon yourself?
Does heaven need you to punish malefactors?
No, no; let God take care of his own vengeance;
He has prescribed forgiveness for offenses.
Don't be concerned about the world's reactions
When you are following heaven's almighty orders.
Will you let worry about what people say
Wipe out the credit of doing a good deed?
No, no; let's rather do what God commands,
And let's not trouble with other considerations.

TARTUFFE: I've told you that I pardon him in my heart;
Thus I obey God's holy ordinances.
But after the scandalous insults of today,
God does not order me to live with him.

CLÉANTE: And does God order you to lend yourself
To the father's act, prompted by pure caprice,
And to accept the gift of property
To which you have no legal right at all?

TARTUFFE: No one who knows me well can have the thought
That I am prompted by self-interest.

All this world's goods have little charm for me,
I am not dazzled by their deceptive glitter.
If I decide to accept from the father's hands
This gift of his benevolence, the reason
Is only, I tell you truly, that I fear
That all this wealth may fall in wicked hands,
That its possessors may be men who make
A criminal usage of it in the world,
Who will not use it, as my purpose is,
For heaven's glory and for my neighbor's good.

CLÉANTE: Your fears, my good sir, are sophistical.
They may give rise to suits by legal heirs.
Let Damis be inheritor of his wealth
At his own risk, without your interference.
Reflect, it's better that he should misuse it
Than that you be accused of cheating him.
I am astounded that you could have heard
This proposition made without being shocked.
For are there any maxims of true piety
Which teach the robbing of legitimate heirs?
If God has put in your heart an adamant
Objection to your living with Damis,
Would not the best thing be for you to leave
Decently and with honor, and not permit
The son of the house to be forbidden the door,
Against all common sense, and for your sake?
Believe me, sir, your character would look
Extremely strange—

TARTUFFE: Sir, it is half-past three;
And it is time for my pious exercises.
You will excuse me if I leave you now.
(*Exit* TARTUFFE.)

CLÉANTE: Oh!
(*Enter* ELMIRE, MARIANE, DORINE.)

DORINE: Sir, I beg you, won't you help to save her?

For she is suffering from a cruel grief.
The pledge of marriage that her father has made
Plunges her in continual despair.
He's coming now; please, let's unite our efforts
And try to upset, either by force or trick,
That fatal project which undoes us all.
(*Enter* ORGON.)

ORGON: Ah! I'm delighted to see you all assembled!
(*To* MARIANE) There's something nice for you in
  this contract here!
And certainly you know what that implies.

MARIANE   (*kneeling*): Father, I call on heaven, which knows
  my grief!
By everything that can affect your heart,
Relax a little the rights of fatherhood,
And set me free from this obedience.
Do not reduce me, by your harsh command,
To cry to heaven against my bounden duty.
Alas, don't make a long calamity
Of the life which you, Father, have given me.
Though you forbid me to wed the one I love,
In spite of all the fond hopes I had cherished,
At least—I beg your mercy on my knees—
Spare me the anguish of wedding one I hate,
And do not force me to some desperate act
By using all your powers upon my person.

ORGON   (*aside*): Courage, my heart! Down with this human
  weakness!

MARIANE: I'm not distressed by your affection for him;
Openly show it; give him your property;
And if that's not enough, give him mine too.
I'm perfectly willing; I'll hand it over to you.
But do not give him, pray, my self, my person!
And let me in the austerity of a convent

ORGON:
    Consume the unhappy days allotted me.

ORGON:
    Aha! You're one of those who seek a convent
    As soon as a father crosses them in love!
    Get up! The more your heart recoils from him,
    All the more meritorious is the yielding.
    So mortify your senses by this marriage,
    And let's have no more nonsense out of you!

DORINE:
    But what—

ORGON:
              Be silent! Speak when you're spoken to!
    I won't allow you to utter a single word!

CLÉANTE:
    If you'll permit me to offer some advice—

ORGON:
    Cléante, your advice is perfectly marvelous,
    So sensible I prize it very highly;
    But it's my privilege not to follow it.

ELMIRE
    (*to* ORGON): Seeing what's happening, I'm almost
        speechless.
    I am amazed by your infatuation.
    You must be totally bewitched by him
    To doubt our word about today's occurrence.

ORGON:
    My precious, I believe the evidence.
    I know how fond you are of my rascal son.
    Clearly you were afraid to disavow
    The scheme he tried to work on that poor fellow.
    You were too calm, in short, to be quite convincing.
    You'd have looked otherwise if really moved.

ELMIRE:
    And should a woman's honor be so stirred
    If someone makes an amorous proposal?
    And does the mere suggestion then require
    A fiery glance and fierce, abusive words?
    Why, all I do is laugh at such advances,
    And I don't like to bring them into notice.
    I think that we should show our virtue calmly;
    I don't agree with those excited prudes
    Whose honor is equipped with teeth and claws,

Ready to scratch your face at the slightest word.
Heaven preserve me from such purity!
For Virtue needs no diabolic look;
I've noticed that a haughty, chilly No
As a rebuff is mightily effective.

ORGON: You needn't try to throw me off the track.

ELMIRE: Your gullibility amazes me!
I wonder if your blind faith would be shaken
If I could make you witness of the truth.

ORGON: Witness?

ELMIRE: Yes.

ORGON: Nonsense!

ELMIRE: What if I found a way
To show you the fact under your very eyes?

ORGON: Fairy tales!

ELMIRE: What a man! I wish you'd answer.
I don't suggest that you believe our words.
But let's suppose that we could hide you here
Where you could clearly see and hear everything,
Then what would you say about your worthy friend?

ORGON: I'd say in that case . . . I'd say nothing at all,
For it can't be.

ELMIRE: You've been too long in error,
And you've accused me far too long of falsehood.
Now for my satisfaction, on the spot
I'll make you witness that we tell the truth.

ORGON: I'll take you up on that. We'll see your tricks;
We'll see what you can do to keep your promise.

ELMIRE (*to* DORINE): Send him in here.

DORINE: He's clever as a fox;
Perhaps it won't be easy to decoy him.

ELMIRE: No, one is easily fooled by one's belovèd,
And self-conceit will end in self-deception.
Have him come down. (*To* CLÉANTE *and* MARIANE)

And you two, please go out.

(*Exit* DORINE, CLÉANTE, *and* MARIANE)

(*To* ORGON) Pull up this table. Now get under it.

ORGON: What?

ELMIRE: You will have to be concealed, of course.

ORGON: But why beneath this table?

ELMIRE: Good heavens, don't argue!

I have my plan; you'll see how it comes out.

Under the table, I say; and when you're there,

Make sure that nobody can see or hear you.

ORGON: I'm very indulgent to you, I confess.

I want to see how you get out of this.

(*Crawls under table, which is draped with a cloth hanging nearly to floor.*)

ELMIRE: I doubt if you'll have any reproach to make.

But I am going to deal with a ticklish subject,

So please don't let yourself be scandalized.

Whatever I say must be permissible;

It's only to convince you, as I promised.

Since I am forced to it, I'll have to use

Blandishing words to tempt him to unmask,

And smile upon his impudent desires,

And let him be audacious as he likes.

As it's for your sake, and for his confusion,

That I'll pretend to yield to his appeals,

I'll stop as soon as you are quite convinced;

Things will go only so far as you may wish.

Your task will be to check his bold advances

When you think matters have gone far enough,

And you must spare your wife, and not expose her

To more than you need to disillusion you.

Your interests are concerned; you are the master—

He's coming! Keep quiet! Don't let yourself be seen!

(*Enter* TARTUFFE.)

TARTUFFE: I understand you wished to speak to me.

ELMIRE: Yes, I've a secret to reveal to you.
            But first, please shut that door before I speak;
            And take a look around for fear of surprise.
            (TARTUFFE *shuts door and looks in cupboard*)
            We certainly don't want a repetition
            Of what took place a little while ago.
            That was a disagreeable surprise,
            And Damis put me into a panic for you.
            You saw that I did everything I could
            To cross his purpose and to calm him down.
            It's true that I was thrown in such confusion
            It didn't occur to me to deny his words.
            But heaven be praised, the result was all the better,
            And everything is on a surer footing.
            Your reputation is proof against all storms;
            And now my husband cannot be suspicious.
            In order to show a confident face to slander,
            He wants us to be constantly together.
            So now I'm able, without fear of blame,
            To be alone with you here—and with the door shut.
            And so I am at liberty to reveal
            My feelings—but perhaps I go too far.

TARTUFFE: This talk is somewhat hard to understand,
            Madame. You seem to have changed considerably.

ELMIRE: Why, if you're angry that I once rebuffed you,
            Little you understand a woman's heart!
            You don't know what it's trying to convey,
            When it defends itself so languidly!
            Our modesty must always make a struggle
            Against the emotions which may rise in us.
            Even though overmastered by our feelings,
            We always find it shameful to admit them.
            At first we fight against them; but our manner

Ought to make evident the heart's surrender.
For honor's sake we must oppose our longings,
And our denials promise everything.
I am afraid I'm speaking all too frankly,
And showing small regard for modesty;
But since I've come into the open, tell me,
Would I have struggled to hold Damis back?
And would I, please, so graciously, so long,
Have listened to the offer of your heart?
Would I have taken the matter as I did,
If I had not found pleasure in your offer?
And when I tried on my own part to force you
To refuse the marriage which had been announced,
What was the import of my urgency,
If not my personal interest in you,
And my distress for fear the projected union
Would divide a heart I wanted to keep entire?

TARTUFFE: Surely, madame, it gives me joy extreme
To hear such words from the belovèd lips!
Their honey pours into my senses, makes
Undreamed-of sweetness flood through all my veins!
My highest aim is that of pleasing you;
My heart finds its beatitude in your love;
And yet this heart now begs the liberty
To dare to doubt its own felicity.
For I could think your words a mere device
To force me to break off a marriage arranged.
And to explain myself with perfect clearness,
I shall not put my trust in your sweet words,
Until the tangible favors which I long for
Will guarantee your words' sincerity,
And in my soul implant a constant faith
In the dear bounties which you would bestow.

ELMIRE   (*coughs to warn her husband*) : What do you mean?
              You want to go so fast
              And push love to its climax all in a moment?
              I've forced myself to make a fond admission;
              However, that is not enough for you.
              You won't be satisfied unless you gain
              The final favors at the very beginning?

TARTUFFE: The less one merits, the less one dares to hope;
              And talk gives little assurance to our longing.
              One easily mistrusts a promise of bliss;
              One has to enjoy it before one can believe it.
              Knowing how little I deserve your bounty,
              I doubt the happiness I dare aspire to.
              And I shall not believe a word, madame,
              Until you crown my ardent love with facts.

ELMIRE: Dear me! Your love is acting like a tyrant!
              It puts me in an awkward situation!
              It seems to set a fury in men's hearts,
              With such a violence it seeks its goal!
              Can I not raise my hands against your onslaught?
              Will you not give me even time to breathe?
              And is it decent to be so exacting,
              To give no quarter when you ask surrender?
              And thus, by your insistence, to abuse
              The inclination a person may have for you?

TARTUFFE: If you receive my homage with compassion,
              Why, pray, withhold the tangible testimony?

ELMIRE: But how can I consent, without offending
              Heaven, according to your constant theme?

TARTUFFE: If it is only heaven that stands in the way,
              It's easy for me to remove such obstacles,
              And that need not restrain your heart's desire.

ELMIRE: And yet they frighten us so with heaven's decrees!

TARTUFFE: I can soon banish such ridiculous fear,

Madame; there is an art of removing scruples.
It's true that heaven forbids some satisfactions,
But there are possible ways to understandings.
To suit our various needs, there is a science
Of loosening the bonds of human conscience,
And rectifying the evil of an action
By means of the purity of our intention.
Madame, I shall instruct you in these secrets,
If you will put your confidence in me.
Content my longings, do not be afraid;
All the responsibility is mine . . .
(ELMIRE *coughs*)
You have a nasty cough.

ELMIRE: It tortures me.

TARTUFFE: Perhaps you'd care to accept a licorice cough drop?

ELMIRE: It's a persistent cold, and I'm afraid
That all the cough drops in the world won't help it.

TARTUFFE: Very distressing.

ELMIRE: More than I can say.

TARTUFFE: Well, anyway, I can dispel your scruples.
You are assured that I will keep the secret.
Evil does not exist until it's published;
It's worldly scandal that creates the offense;
And sin in silence is not sin at all.

ELMIRE   (*coughs*):   In short, I see that I shall have to yield,
Make up my mind to grant you everything.
Otherwise, I suppose, I can't convince
One who is asking irrefutable proof.
Certainly I dislike to go so far,
I take the step against my better judgment;
But since I'm mercilessly driven to it,
Since no one listens to my arguments,
Since absolute conviction is demanded,
I must decide to satisfy all doubts.

And if there's any offense in my consenting,
The one who forces me must take the blame;
Certainly I am not responsible.

TARTUFFE: I take it on myself, madame. The matter—

ELMIRE: But first, open the door a little, please;
See if my husband isn't in the hall.

TARTUFFE: What sense is there in worrying about him?
He is the type that you can lead by the nose,
The type to glory in our intimacies.
He can see anything now and not believe it.

ELMIRE: It makes no difference. Please, I'd feel much safer
If you would take a careful look around.
(*Exit* TARTUFFE. ORGON *emerges from under the table.*)

ORGON: Oh, what a bad, abominable man!
I am astounded! I just can't understand it.

ELMIRE: What, coming out so soon? Don't be absurd!
Crawl in again, nothing has happened yet!
Why don't you wait till the end to make quite sure,
So you won't have to trust to mere conjectures?

ORGON: Nothing more wicked has ever come out of hell!

ELMIRE: You shouldn't be in a hurry to believe things,
So why not let yourself be quite convinced?
Just take your time; maybe you're still mistaken . . .
(*As* TARTUFFE *returns,* ELMIRE *makes* ORGON *crouch behind her.*)

TARTUFFE: Everything's working out, madame, for the best.
I've had a look into the neighboring rooms.
There's no one there. And now, to my delight—

ORGON   (*springing forth*):
Hold on a minute! Don't get so excited,
And let your passions run away with you!
Aha! You holy man, you wanted to fool me!
How rapidly you yielded to temptation!

Wedding my daughter and lusting for my wife!
I've long suspected things were not aboveboard;
I always thought that you would change your style.
But now the proof is carried far enough.
I'm satisfied, and this is all I need.

ELMIRE   (*to* TARTUFFE): It's not my nature to have done
                  all this,
              But I've been forced to treat you in this manner.

TARTUFFE   (*to* ORGON):
              What, you can think—

ORGON: Come on, don't make a fuss.
              Get out of here without another word.

TARTUFFE: I only wanted—

ORGON: There's no time for talk.
              But now, this very second, leave the house!

TARTUFFE: You are the one to leave! Don't be so proud!
              I will remind you, the house belongs to me!
              I'll show you that it's useless to resort
              To such poor shifts to pick a quarrel with me!
              You're in a bad position to insult me,
              For I have means to break and punish imposture,
              To avenge offended heaven, and make repent
              Those who dare say that I must leave the house!
              (*Exit* TARTUFFE.)

ELMIRE: What is he talking about? What can he mean?

ORGON: Faith, I am worried. It's no laughing matter.

ELMIRE: What is it?

ORGON: His talk has shown me my mistake.
              I am disturbed about that deed of gift.

ELMIRE: A deed of gift?

ORGON: Yes; it's been signed already.
              But there's another thing which bothers me.

ELMIRE: What's that?

ORGON: I'll tell you; but first I want to see
              If there's a certain strongbox still upstairs.

ACT V

Enter ORGON *and* CLÉANTE.

CLÉANTE: Where are you hurrying to?

ORGON: How do I know?

CLÉANTE: I think we ought to have a consultation
To see what can be done about the affair.

ORGON: It is the strongbox that alarms me most,
More than the other matters all together.

CLÉANTE: So the mysterious strongbox is important?

ORGON: My poor friend Argas gave it me in trust,
Pledging me to the utmost secrecy.
When he was exiled, he came first to me;
He said his life and all his property
May hang upon the contents of these papers.

CLÉANTE: Then why did you entrust them to another?

ORGON: My motive was to keep my conscience easy.
I told that scoundrel all about the matter,
And then his arguments persuaded me
To let him keep the strongbox in his hands,
So that, in case of any investigation,
I'd have a pretext to deny the facts,
And thus my conscience, in security,
Could take an oath contrary to the truth.

CLÉANTE: It looks to me as if you're in for it.
The deed of gift, the transfer of the strongbox—
I have to tell you frankly what I think—
Were inconsiderate, to say the least.
With these as evidence, he can involve you deeply.
Since he has such a weapon in his hands,
You were imprudent to push him to extremes;
You should have looked for some more subtle
method.

ORGON: What! Under all his outward show of fervor,
           To hide a treacherous heart, an evil soul!
           To think I picked him up, a penniless beggar!
           All right, I now renounce all worthy men.
           Henceforth I'll have a terrible horror of them;
           I'm going to be a devil to them all!

CLÉANTE: Now there you go again, getting excited!
           You can't be moderate in anything.
           You never seem to find the sensible course;
           From one excess you fall into the other.
           You see your error, and you recognize
           That you were taken in by pious fraud;
           But now, to correct yourself, what reason is there
           That you should fall into a greater error,
           And lump the character of all worthy men
           With the character of a perfidious rascal?
           Because a blackguard boldly takes you in,
           Impersonating an austere believer,
           You would conclude that everyone's like him,
           And that no true believer now exists?
           Let the freethinkers draw those false conclusions.
           Distinguish virtue from its outward seeming,
           Never give your esteem too hastily,
           Keep to the reasonable middle way.
           Try not to give your honor to impostors,
           But don't insult genuine piety.
           And if you must choose one extreme or the other,
           Let your fault be excessive leniency.
           (*Enter* DAMIS.)

DAMIS: Is it true, father, that a rogue threatens you,
           Forgetting all the favors he's received,
           And that he's now presumptuous enough
           To use your benefits as arms against you?

ORGON: I'm deeply grieved to say, my son, it's true.

DAMIS: Give me the word, I'll go and cut his ears off!
           One shouldn't waver before his insolence.
           I'll undertake to set you free of him;
           I'll fix him so he'll never bother us!

CLÉANTE: That's a young man's solution, certainly.
           Compose yourself and don't get so excited.
           Under the government we have today,
           Violence is no way to settle matters.
           (*Enter* MME PERNELLE, MARIANE, ELMIRE, DORINE.)

MME PERN.: What are these goings-on I hear about?

ORGON: Strange things indeed I've seen with my own eyes,
           And a strange reward for all my kindnesses!
           I rescue a man out of his poverty,
           Give him a home, treat him like my own brother,
           And every day I load him with benefits,
           I give him my daughter and all my property;
           At the same time, the faithless, infamous scoundrel
           Foully proposes to seduce my wife!
           And still not satisfied with this base purpose,
           He dares to use against me my own favors,
           And tries to ruin me by using the hold
           I've given him, out of my foolish kindness,
           To throw me out of my own property,
           And bring me down to the state in which I found
           him!

DORINE: Poor fellow!

MME PERN.:   My son, I can't believe
           He could have wished to do such an evil thing.

ORGON: What!

MME PERN.:   Men of principle are always envied.

ORGON: Mother, please tell me exactly what you mean.

MME PERN.: I mean that people here are very peculiar,
           And I know well how everybody hates him.

ORGON: And what has hatred got to do with it?

MME PERN.: When you were a boy, I told you a thousand times

Virtue is always unpopular in this world;
The envious, they will die, but envy won't.

ORGON: What has all that to do with the present case?

MME PERN.: Surely, people have made up stories about him.

ORGON: I told you that I saw everything myself!

MME PERN.: The malice of slanderers is most excessive.

ORGON: You'll make me sin through anger, Mother! I tell you
I saw his attempt at crime with my own eyes!

MME PERN.: Many a tongue is ready to spread slander,
And nothing in this world is proof against it.

ORGON: What you are saying makes no sense at all.
I saw him, I say, with my own eyes I saw him!
I saw him try to do it! Now do I have to
Yell in your ears a hundred times: "I saw him"?

MME PERN.: Mercy! Appearances are often deceptive;
You cannot always judge by what you see.

ORGON: You'll drive me crazy!

MME PERN.: False suspicions are common,
And good is often ill interpreted.

ORGON: I should interpret then as a charity
The attempt to kiss my wife?

MME PERN.: To accuse a man,
You have to have a full and sufficient reason;
You ought to wait until you're sure of things.

ORGON: And how the devil can I be any surer?
I should have waited until, before my eyes,
He'd . . . No, you pretty nearly made me say it.

MME PERN.: His soul is filled with a too holy zeal.
I simply can't conceive the possibility
He could have attempted the things that people say.

ORGON: Good heavens, you put me into such a fury,
I don't know what I'd say, if you weren't my mother!

DORINE: It's only fair, good sir; you wouldn't believe us,
           And now you find they won't believe you either.
CLÉANTE: We're losing precious time in idle talk.
           We ought to plan our actions, and not sleep
           In view of the threats that scoundrel has expressed.
DAMIS: What! Do you really think he'd have the nerve—
ELMIRE: Oh, I don't think that he'd take legal action,
           For his ingratitude would be all too clear.
CLÉANTE: Don't be too sure. No doubt he has devices
           To get a show of reason on his side.
           For less than this a powerful organization
           Has got men into a very nasty mess.
           And I repeat that since he holds such weapons,
           You never ought to have driven him so far.
ORGON: All right, but what could I do? At his insolence
           I simply couldn't hold my anger in.
CLÉANTE: I wish with all my heart we could patch up
           Some kind of outward peace between you two.
ELMIRE: If I had known he held such trumps in hand,
           I wouldn't have given him such provocation.
           (MONSIEUR LOYAL *appears at door.* DORINE *goes to
           meet him.*)
ORGON   (*to* DORINE): What does that fellow want? Find out
               and tell me.
           I'm in no state to deal with callers now.
M. LOYAL: How do you do, dear sister? Will you arrange
           For me to speak to the gentleman?
DORINE: He's engaged.
           I doubt if he can talk to anyone now.
M. LOYAL: I shouldn't like to intrude upon him here,
           But I don't think my business will upset him.
           I'm sure he'll find my news most interesting.
DORINE: Your name?
M. LOYAL: Just tell him that Monsieur Tartuffe

Has sent me, with a most obliging message.

DORINE   (*to* ORGON): He is a messenger—and quite soft-
                  spoken—
                  From our Tartuffe. He says he has some news
                  That you'll be glad to hear.

CLÉANTE: You'd better see
                  Who this man is and what he has to say.

ORGON: Maybe he's coming to patch the business up.
                  How do you think I ought to act to him?

CLÉANTE: You mustn't show how deeply you're offended;
                  And if he offers peace, you'd better heed him.

M. LOYAL: Greetings, good sir! May heaven smite your foes,
                  And shower its blessings on you in abundance!

ORGON   (*to* CLÉANTE): A civil opening! As I foresaw,
                  This is a hint of reconciliation.

M. LOYAL: Your family was always dear to me,
                  And frequently I served your honored father.

ORGON: I am ashamed, sir, and I ask your pardon;
                  I cannot place you or recall your name.

M. LOYAL: My name is Loyal; I'm from Normandy[1]
                  And I'm a process server by profession.
                  For forty years I've had the happiness
                  Praise God, to hold that honorable office.
                  And so I come, sir, with your kind permission,
                  To serve upon you this judicial writ.

ORGON: What! You came here—

M. LOYAL: Now, no excitement, please.
                  It's just a little notice of eviction.
                  You and your family must quit the house,
                  Remove your furniture, make place for others,
                  Without delay, deferment, or reprieve.

ORGON: What, leave this house!

M. LOYAL: If you will be so good.

1 A byword for pettifoggery.

The house belongs, as you are well aware,
To good Monsieur Tartuffe, beyond dispute.
He is possessed of all your property
By virtue of a contract which I bear.
It's in due form, it cannot be protested.

DAMIS: I am amazed to hear such impudence!

M. LOYAL: Young sir, I have no business here with you,
But with your father, a reasonable man,
Who knows the duties of a court officer,
And wouldn't think of contravening justice.

ORGON: But—

M. LOYAL: Yes, I know that not for a million francs
Would you propose to defy authority,
And that, like a gentleman, you will permit
The execution of my orders here.

DAMIS: You might well get a sound and wholesome caning
On your black jacket, Monsieur Process Server.

M. LOYAL   (*to* ORGON): Sir, bid your son be silent or retire.
I should regret to put in my report
Menaces of assault and battery.

DORINE   (*aside*): His name is Loyal? I should say Disloyal.

M. LOYAL: I have a great respect for upright men,
And I agreed to serve this writ on you
Just to oblige you and to give you pleasure,
To keep the service from the hands of others
Who would not feel my admiration for you,
And would not act with my consideration.

ORGON: What could be worse than ordering a man
To quit his home?

M. LOYAL: But I am giving you time.
I will suspend, monsieur, until tomorrow
The execution of the legal writ.
I'll merely come with a dozen of my men
To spend the night, without publicity.

And for form's sake I'll ask you, please, to bring me
The keys of the house before you go to bed.
We'll take care not to trouble your repose,
Nor suffer any impropriety.
Tomorrow morning early you'll remove
Your personal possessions from the house.
My men will help you; I picked sturdy ones
To serve you in putting everything outside.
No one, I think, could act more fairly with you.
And as I'm treating you with great indulgence,
I'll ask you for your kind co-operation
In not impeding my duties' execution.

ORGON   (*aside*): How happily I'd give this very moment
My last remaining hundred golden louis
For the pleasure of landing on that ugly snout
The most enormous punch in history!

CLÉANTE   (*aside to* ORGON):
Easy, don't spoil things.

DAMIS: At his insolence
I can't hold in; I've got an itching fist.

DORINE: That noble back of yours, Monsieur Loyal,
Seems to demand a few good cudgel blows.

M. LOYAL: Such words, my dear, may call for penal action.
The law makes no distinction as to sex.

CLÉANTE: Let's have no more of this, sir. That's enough.
Give us that paper, please, and leave the house.

M. LOYAL: *Au revoir*, gentlemen. God keep you in joy!

ORGON: May he confound you, and the man who sent you!
(*Exit* M. LOYAL)
Well, Mother, you see if I was right or not;
And by this summons you can judge of the rest.

MME PERN.:   I'm flabbergasted, I'm struck all of a heap!

DORINE: Oh, really! Aren't you doing wrong to blame him?
Clearly his purposes are for your good!

He's showing how he loves his fellow man;
He knows that often wealth corrupts the soul.
Out of pure charity, he would remove
The slightest obstacle to your salvation.

ORGON: Shut up, shut up! How often must I say it?

CLÉANTE: Let's think about the proper course to take.

ELMIRE: Go tell the world of his audacity!
His action makes the contract null and void.
Public opinion will be so aroused
By his black treason that he can't succeed.

(*Enter* VALÈRE.)

VALÈRE: I'm sorry, sir, to bring you any distress,
But I'm obliged to by the pressing danger.
An old and excellent friend of mine, who knows
How I'm affected by all that touches you,
Out of regard for me has violated
The secrecy he owes to state affairs.
The news he sends me makes it very clear
That you can save yourself only by flight.
The scoundrel who befooled you for so long
Has made an accusation to the King,
And to support his charges has delivered
The strongbox of an outlaw of the state,
Which you, he says, have criminally hidden,
Flouting the duty of a loyal subject.
I don't know much about the crime alleged,
But orders to arrest you have been issued.
Tartuffe himself is charged to accompany
The officer who is to take you prisoner.

CLÉANTE: Thus he gets armed support, to aid his purpose
To take possession of your property.

ORGON: Oh what a wicked creature that man is!

VALÈRE: Any delay is fatal; so I've brought
My carriage to the door to whisk you off,

And a thousand louis for the emergency.
So don't lose time; this is a knock-down blow;
The only way to dodge it is to flee.
I'll guarantee you a sure hiding place,
And I'll accompany you until the end.

ORGON: Oh, I owe everything to your kindly actions!
I'll leave my thanks until a better time;
I pray that heaven may grant me the occasion
Some day, to recognize your generous service.
Good-by, my friends; be sure to—

CLÉANTE: Hurry, hurry!
Dear brother, we will take care of everything.
(ORGON *and* VALÈRE *start to run off. Enter* POLICE
OFFICER *and* TARTUFFE.)

TARTUFFE: Here, here, good sir! Don't run away so fast!
A lodging's ready for you close at hand.
By the King's orders you're a prisoner!

ORGON: Scoundrel, you kept this wicked deed till last!
And thus, you rascal, you complete my ruin!
This is the crown of all your villainies!

TARTUFFE: I shall not be embittered by your insults.
I have been taught by heaven to suffer all.

CLÉANTE: So this is holy moderation, is it?

DAMIS: Shameful to make of heaven his accomplice!

TARTUFFE: You cannot move me by a show of anger,
For all I think of is to do my duty.

MARIANE: Much glory you will draw from this affair,
And surely you'll derive much honor from it.

TARTUFFE: An action can be only glorious
When it's commanded by the royal power.

ORGON: Have you remembered that my helping hand
Was all that rescued you from beggary?

TARTUFFE: True, I may be beholden for some aid,
But my first duty is to serve the King.

This sacred, just, and all-compelling duty
Extinguishes all gratitude in my heart.
To its compulsion I would sacrifice
My friends, my relatives, my wife—myself!

ELMIRE: Impostor!

DORINE: How he treacherously makes
A cloak and shield of all that we revere!

CLÉANTE: But if this noble zeal which animates you
Is quite as perfect as you say it is,
How comes it that it waited to appear
Till you were caught addressing Orgon's wife?
And why did you denounce him only when,
For honor's sake, he had to throw you out?
I won't allege—though it might have held you
    back—
His gift to you of all his property;
But since you treat him now as a guilty man,
Why did you stoop to accepting all his money?

TARTUFFE   (*to* POLICE OFFICER): Deliver me, sir, from all
    these railing words,
And execute your orders, if you please.

OFFICER: Yes, I've delayed too long in doing so.
Aptly enough, you ask for it yourself.
So here's the execution: follow me
To the prison cell that's ready for your lodging.

TARTUFFE: What, me, sir?

OFFICER: You, sir, yes.

TARTUFFE: But why to prison?

OFFICER: It's not to you I owe an explanation.
(*To* ORGON) You've had a nasty scare; but calm
    yourself.
Our present King is enemy of fraud,
His eyes can penetrate his subjects' hearts;
The art of charlatans cannot delude him.

And his great spirit, wise in the ways of men,
Watches his kingdom with discerning eyes.
No one can take him easily by surprise,
And his firm reason yields to no excess.
To worthy men he gives immortal glory,
And yet his zeal for virtue is not blind.
His love for genuine faith does not eclipse
The horror one should feel for false devotion.
Tartuffe was not the sort to hoodwink him
Who has avoided many a subtler snare.
Immediately he saw in its true color
The base conniving of that evil mind.
This man, accusing you, betrayed himself;
And, by the retribution of high justice,
The King identified him as a rogue
Already famous under another name,
And with a criminal record to his credit
Lengthy enough to fill a score of volumes.
In short, His Majesty abhorred this man's
Mean and ungrateful treachery toward you.
With this crime added to the ample list,
The King commanded me to accompany him,
Only to see what impudence would dare,
And force Tartuffe to make you reparation.
Now in your presence I shall seize the papers
Of which the scoundrel has possessed himself.
The King declares the contract null and void
Which made Tartuffe a gift of all your wealth,
And finally he pardons that offense
In which the exile of a friend involved you.
Thus he rewards your past fidelity,
Which, in the civil wars, upheld his rights;
And thus he proves his heart ever remembers
To recompense a subject's worthy action.

He shows that merit's not unrecognized,
That he is mindful more of good than evil.

DORINE: May heaven be praised!

MME PERN.:   Now I can breathe again!

ELMIRE: All's well then!

MARIANE: Who would have dared foretell it!

ORGON   (*to* TARTUFFE):

So now we've got you, villain—

CLÉANTE: Brother, stop.

Don't stoop to any unworthy exultation,
But leave a wretched man to his wretched fate;
You need not add to the pangs of his remorse.
Hope rather that his heart may now be touched
To heed the call of virtue; that he may
Detest his vice and thus correct his life,
And move the justice of our King to mercy;
While you shall kneel before the royal bounty,
And pay its due to the King's clemency.

ORGON: Well said, indeed. So let us, at his feet,
Joyfully thank him for his heartfelt kindness.
And after this first duty has been done,
There is a second claiming our concern;
So by a happy marriage we shall crown
The noble-hearted ardor of Valère.

The Misanthrope

Le Misanthrope was presented on June 4, 1666, and had only a mild success. Audiences felt frustrated; they found too little to laugh at, too much to think about.

Molière had been meditating his play for years. In *The Versailles Impromptu* he had forecast some developments, and the theme: the falsity underlying social life.

While Molière's career was outwardly successful, he had private reasons for reflecting on misanthropy. The violent attacks on *The School for Wives, Tartuffe,* and *Don Juan,* his disappointment in marriage, the death of his first-born child, and particularly his exhaustion from overwork and the gathering of his fatal illness must have provoked many moods of black pessimism. The "romantic" critics, now in disfavor, saw in Alceste a transformation of Molière's distressed idealism; they heard Molière's voice in such lines as "Leave me here alone/In this dark corner with my gloomy heart." *Dans ce petit coin sombre, avec mon noir chagrin.* And to tell the truth, I do too.

The Misanthrope is a comedy of character and manners, a parlor comedy, in which the dramatic effect is gained by the revelation of emotion in stylized, courtly phrasing. It is therefore a psychological play, a considerable test both of actors and of readers. The plot is thin: at the beginning Alceste demands an explanation from Célimène; various obstacles prevent him from having this explanation until the end of the fifth act. Some of the devices, such as the everlasting purloined letters, seem to us clumsy. The dénouement is most unusual. Instead of assembling all his actors for the final curtain, Molière has them depart one by one, till only the faithful Éliante and Philinte are left. It is a diminuendo, a dying fall, and it is very sad.

The dramatic problem is: How shall a man behave in society? Should he be honest at all costs, like Alceste, or should he be reasonable, like Philinte? Should he defy the world on principle, or should he recognize the fallibilities of principle, and accept the world's sensible compromises? In another seventeenth-century context we may say: Should he be Jansenist or Jesuit?

To Molière's contemporaries the answer was obvious. Society was good and reasonable, and Alceste was a comic figure, mad as Quixote, who failed to overturn society, and was properly condemned by it. Molière clowned the part of Alceste, making him ridiculous, even grotesque.

In the mid-eighteenth century Rousseau posed the question anew. In his *Lettre à M. d'Alembert* he called *The Misanthrope* immoral and vicious, since the play makes virtue (Alceste, and his alter ego, Rousseau) ridiculous, and approves vice (Philinte, the kind of compromiser Rousseau hated). Rousseau's paradox is still hotly argued, according to the character of every reader. On the one hand, critics point out Alceste's unsympathetic character, his "helpless, puerile egocentricity, his constant escape into fits of sulks, his desire for solitude which hardly masks his distress at being too solitary, his excessive style of speech, which betrays more ill humor than virtue, his constant exhibitions of anger."[1] On the other hand, many insist that Alceste, despite all his faults, is right, right, right, and the world is wrong. In most modern performances the tone is relatively serious. Alceste is played straight, and the audience's sympathies are with him.

There is, then, a certain ambiguity in *The Misanthrope*. Today we feel kindly toward ambiguity, and indeed if a work of art can disengage successive and different meanings, it is all the richer for that. Molière's creation of a character which still puzzles and fascinates us is a great artistic achievement. Alceste continues to live and change in time. *The Misanthrope* is Molière's Hamlet.

---

[1] P. Bénichou: *Morales du grand siècle* (1948), page 213.

The Characters

ALCESTE
PHILINTE
ORONTE — Gentlemen of the Court
ACASTE
CLITANDRE

CÉLIMÈNE
ÉLIANTE, Célimène's cousin — Ladies of the Court
ARSINOÉ

BASQUE, Célimène's footman

An Officer of the Court of Honor

DU BOIS, Alceste's manservant

The scene throughout is a salon in the Paris house of Célimène.

ACT I

Enter ALCESTE *rapidly, followed by* PHILINTE.

PHILINTE: What is the matter with you?

ALCESTE: Let me alone!

PHILINTE: But wait! Tell me what crazy idea possessed you—

ALCESTE: Let me alone, I say! Go hide your face!

PHILINTE: But you can listen, at least, and not get angry?

ALCESTE: I want to be angry! I don't want to listen!

223

PHILINTE: I'm baffled by your sudden sulky fits.
              Good friends as we are, nevertheless I feel—
ALCESTE: Your friend, am I? Don't be so sure of that!
              Certainly I've declared it, up to now;
              But your behavior has enlightened me.
              I tell you frankly, I'm your friend no longer.
              I want no place in a corrupted heart.
PHILINTE: And so, Alceste, you judge me very guilty?
ALCESTE: Why, you should go and die out of pure shame!
              There can be no excuse for such an action!
              A man of honor should be scandalized!
              I watch you load a man with compliments,
              With protests of the tenderest affection;
              You put your arm around him, uttering vows
              Of aid and comfort and profound esteem;
              And when I ask you afterwards who he is,
              You're hardly able to recall his name—
              You tell me he's a man of no importance.
              Good God! I call it infamous, outrageous,
              To stoop to the betrayal of one's self;
              And if by some misfortune I had done so,
              I think remorse would make me hang myself.
PHILINTE: I hope that hanging's not imperative;
              And I will ask you for your kind indulgence
              To let me plead an appeal from your decision.
              Please don't insist that I go hang myself.
ALCESTE: I don't think the occasion calls for humor.
PHILINTE: But seriously, what should a person do?
ALCESTE: A man should be sincere; and in all honor
              He shouldn't say a word his heart disclaims.
PHILINTE: When a man greets you warmly, joyfully,
              You naturally respond in the same way.
              You meet his cordiality with your own,
              And match his offers and return his vows.

ALCESTE: No, I can't stand that mean, unworthy fashion
Which you society people now affect.
There's nothing I detest like the contortions
Of all these great dispensers of lip service,
Spreading their arms for insincere embraces,
Overflowing with useless courtesies,
Trying to win a war of compliments,
Treating alike the gentleman and the fool.
What does it mean if a man pats and pets you,
Swears to his friendship, constancy, regard,
Extols your shining merits to the skies,
Then does the same to the next nobody?
A man who has some self-respect despises
The expression of such prostituted homage.
One's vanity is easily satisfied
By having a share in universal honors.
But true esteem is based on preference;
Esteeming everyone, you esteem nothing.
Since you accept the vices of our time,
Morbleu, Philinte, you're not the man for me!
And I reject a love so comprehensive
That it can see no difference in merit.
I want a special love; to put it frankly,
The friend of the human race is not my friend.

PHILINTE: Well, in society you have to express
The usual formulas of polite behavior.

ALCESTE: But I say no! I say you should denounce
This shameful game of imitation friendship!
A man should be a man, and dare to show
The substance of his spirit in his words.
A man's true self should speak, and never mask
His genuine feelings in vain compliments.

PHILINTE: Still, there are many times when utter frankness
Would be ridiculous and out of place.

Sometimes, with all respect to your high honor,
It's a good thing to hide what's in one's heart.
Would it be suitable to tell to people
Everything that you really think about them?
Dealing with someone whom you much dislike
Or really hate, ought you to tell him so?

ALCESTE: Yes.

PHILINTE: What! And so you'd tell old Émilie
It's time to lay aside her claims to beauty,
Say her enameled face is really an outrage?

ALCESTE: Surely.

PHILINTE: Tell Dorilas that he's a bore,
That he has deafened every ear at court
With his nobility and gallant deeds?

ALCESTE: Assuredly.

PHILINTE: You're joking!

ALCESTE: Not at all.
I'm going to tell the truth, and spare no man.
I've seen enough. The life of court and town
Presents a picture which revolts my soul.
I'm filled with loathing, I am nauseated
To see how men behave with one another.
All I see everywhere is flattery,
Injustice, treason, selfishness, deceit.
It makes me furious; I cannot stand it;
I will defy the entire human race.

PHILINTE: Your spleen is philosophic, but excessive.
In fact, your evil humor makes me laugh.
We two, with the same background, make me think
Of the brothers in Molière's *The School for Husbands,*
Wherein—

ALCESTE: Oh, that comparison's too silly.

PHILINTE: Now seriously, give up these violent fits.

The world won't change for anything you do.
And since you think that frankness is so charming,
I will be frank, and say that your obsession
Amuses people, everywhere you go;
And your high fury against current customs
Makes you ridiculous in the eyes of many.

ALCESTE: Splendid, *morbleu!* Splendid! That's what I want!
An excellent sign! I am delighted at it!
Men have become so odious to me
I'd hate to have them think me sensible!

PHILINTE: You certainly have it in for human nature.

ALCESTE: Yes, I have learned to hate it thoroughly.

PHILINTE: And all poor mortal men, without exception,
Will be the objects of your disapproval?
I see a number, as I look about me—

ALCESTE: My hate is general; I detest all men;
Some because they are wicked and do evil,
Others because they tolerate the wicked,
Refusing them the active, vigorous scorn
Which vice should stimulate in virtuous minds.
Why, only see their toleration toward
The arrant rogue who's gone to law with me!
Behind his mask the scoundrel's visible.
Here everybody knows his character;
And his protesting eyes, his honeyed tongue,
Impose on no one but a casual stranger.
And that contemptible boor notoriously
Has made his way in the world by dirty means,
So that his present splendid situation
Makes merit grumble and makes virtue blush.
Whatever eminence he may have gained,
There's no one to respect his reputation.
Call him an infamous swindler, filthy sneak,
You hear no contradiction; all agree.

And yet his fawning face is widely welcomed,
He crawls in everywhere, he is accepted;
And if intrigue can gain some precedence,
You see him win, over the worthiest man.
Damnation! How it wounds me to the heart
To see how tactful people are with vice!
And sometimes I am seized by a wild impulse
To flee from human beings to some desert.

PHILINTE: Don't take so seriously our social habits,
And be more merciful to human nature.
Don't treat it with such rigorous principle,
And look a little kindly on its errors.
Virtue should be indulgent, in our world;
A man who is overwise may be at fault.
The soundest judgment flees extremities,
Urging that we be sober in our wisdom.
The rigid virtue of the ancient sages
Is out of key with present usages;
It asks too much perfection of mankind.
A man should bend to the prevailing mood;
And it's assuredly a signal folly
To try to reform and cure society.
Like you, I notice a hundred things a day
Which might be better if they were different;
But when these matters do present themselves,
I don't fly into a fury, as you do.
I just take men serenely as they are,
And train myself to suffer what they do.
I think that both at court and in the city
My calm is philosophic as your spleen.

ALCESTE: But, sir, this calm, which reasons so astutely,
Cannot this calm be stirred by anything?
And if it chances that a friend betrays you,
And baits a trap to get your property,

Or if he spreads slanderous tales about,
You'll see all that without becoming angry?

PHILINTE: Why, yes; I see these faults which you complain of
As vices which are part of human nature.
In short, my spirit is no more offended
To observe a selfish, unjust, rascally man
Than to see vultures upon their prey,
Or mischievous monkeys, or ferocious wolves.

ALCESTE: And I should see myself betrayed and robbed,
And I should not— *Morbleu!* I shan't reply.
Your argument is far too idiotic.

PHILINTE: In fact, you would do well to hold your peace.
Don't rage so much against your adversary,
And pay some more attention to your case.

ALCESTE: I won't pay any at all, and that is that.

PHILINTE: But who will make solicitation for you?

ALCESTE: Who? Reason, my just right, and equity.

PHILINTE: You won't have anyone call upon the judge?

ALCESTE: By no means. Is my case unjust or doubtful?

PHILINTE: Certainly not. But schemers can make trouble,
And—

ALCESTE: No, I've resolved I will not take a step.
I'm right or I'm wrong.

PHILINTE: I wouldn't trust to that.

ALCESTE: I will not move an inch.

PHILINTE: Your enemy's strong;
He has his gang—

ALCESTE: It makes no difference.

PHILINTE: You'll suffer for it.

ALCESTE: I want to see what happens.

PHILINTE: But—

ALCESTE: Then to lose the case will be my pleasure.

PHILINTE: However—

ALCESTE: In this lawsuit I will learn

If men will have enough effrontery,
If they'll be wicked and rascally enough
To do injustice in the sight of the world.

PHILINTE: What a man!

ALCESTE: Yes, no matter what it costs,
I'd like to lose the case, for the beauty of it.

PHILINTE: People would really laugh at you, Alceste,
If they should hear you talking in this way.

ALCESTE: Then let them laugh.

PHILINTE: But these high principles
Which you expect to be exactly followed,
And this uprightness of your character,
Can they be matched in the lady whom you love?
Frankly, I am surprised that you, who seem
To be the enemy of the human race,
Have chosen, from odious humanity,
A representative who charms your eyes.
And what astonishes me even more
Is that you've picked on this particular person.
Éliante the sincere has a liking for you,
The prim Arsinoé looks kindly on you,
And yet you seem unconscious of their fondness,
While Célimène holds you in servitude—
She whose coquettish humor and sharp tongue
Are so consistent with the current fashion.
And since you hate this fashion so intensely,
How can you bear the lady's pleasure in it?
Do the faults vanish in so sweet a creature?
Do you excuse the faults? Or don't you see them?

ALCESTE: The love I feel for the lady, widowed so young,
Can hardly blind me to her obvious faults.
I am the first to see them and condemn them,
Despite the affection she inspires in me.
Nevertheless, whatever I may do,

I grant my weakness, recognize her power.
And though I see her faults and blame them in her,
It is too much for me, she makes me love her.
Her charm subdues me; but certainly my love
Will cure her of these fashionable vices.

PHILINTE: If you do that, you will be doing something.
And so you're sure she loves you?

ALCESTE: Yes, *parbleu!*
I shouldn't love her if I didn't think so.

PHILINTE: But if her preference is evident,
Why are you so disturbed about your rivals?

ALCESTE: A total love demands a total love;
And I came here with only this in mind:
To tell her what I feel and what I ask.

PHILINTE: If I were free to follow my impulses,
Her cousin Éliante would be my choice.
She has an upright spirit, she esteems you;
She would be much more suitable for you.

ALCESTE: It's true, my reason often tells me so;
But reason's not the governor of love.

PHILINTE: I don't feel easy for you; and your hopes
Might well . . .

(*Enter* ORONTE. *During the following speech* AL-
CESTE, *dreaming, seems unaware that he is ad-
dressed.*)

ORONTE: I learned downstairs that Célimène
And her cousin Éliante have gone out shopping;
But when I was informed that you were here,
I came right up to tell you I've conceived
Almost incredible regard for you.
And my regard has stimulated me
To a passionate desire to be your friend.
I recognize true merit, I applaud it.
I long for brotherhood with its possessor.

                I think a true friend, of my noble rank,
                Is not to be too casually rejected.
                . . . It is to you, sir, that my words are addressed.

ALCESTE: To me, sir?

ORONTE: Yes. I hope you aren't offended.

ALCESTE: Oh, no, indeed; but I am much surprised.
                I didn't expect the honor that you do me.

ORONTE: You shouldn't be surprised by my regard;
                You might well claim it from the universe.

ALCESTE: Monsieur—

ORONTE: The country has no parallel
                For the lofty virtues I discern in you.

ALCESTE: Monsieur—

ORONTE: I hold that you're superior
                To the most eminent of all our nation.

ALCESTE: Monsieur—

ORONTE: May heaven blast me if I lie!
                In evidence of my sincerity,
                Permit me to embrace you lovingly,
                Asking to be admitted to your friendship.
                Your hand, sir, if you please. You'll promise me
                To be my friend?

ALCESTE: Monsieur—

ORONTE: What! You resist?

ALCESTE: Monsieur, it's too much honor that you do me.
                But friendship asks a little mystery;
                And we profane its name, assuredly,
                By making it too easy to attain.
                This union should be circumspectly formed,
                And first, we ought to know each other better.
                We might turn out to have such characters
                That we would both be sorry for our bargain.

ORONTE: *Parbleu!* You speak like the wise man that you are,
                And I esteem you all the more for it!

Let us then trust to time to do its work,
And meanwhile, let me offer my devotion.
If you should need some influence at court,
I'm on an excellent footing with the King.
He listens to my counsel; no one, in fact,
Could be more decent than His Majesty.
In short, consider me quite at your service.
And as I prize your judgment and your taste,
I'll make my first appeal to your good will
By showing you a sonnet I have written,
And asking whether I should make it public.

ALCESTE: Sir, I am ill equipped to be a judge,
              So please excuse me.

ORONTE: Why?

ALCESTE: I have the fault
Of being far too frank in such a case.

ORONTE: That's what I want! And I should be offended
If, when I ask for your sincere opinion,
You should betray me, holding something back.

ALCESTE: Well, I am willing, sir, since you insist.

ORONTE   (*at each pause, he looks at* ALCESTE):
"Sonnet." It is á sonnet. "Hope—" A lady
Had flattered my devotion, offering hope.
"Hope—" It is not your pompous, high-flown verse,
But rather gentle, tender, languorous.

ALCESTE: We'll soon see.

ORONTE: "Hope—" I don't know if the style
Will seem to you sufficiently clear and smooth,
If you'll be satisfied with the choice of words.

ALCESTE: We'll see, monsieur.

ORONTE: Anyway, you must know
I dashed it off in a quarter of an hour.

ALCESTE: The time one takes doesn't affect the product.

ORONTE: Hope, it is true, relieves us,

	By hope our woe's disguised;
	But, Phyllis, hope deceives us
	If never realized!
PHILINTE:	I am already charmed by the dainty verse.
ALCESTE	(*to* PHILINTE):
	You have the cheek to say that that is good?
ORONTE:	And hope you offered freely
	In pity for my moan;
	Ah, you were heartless, really,
	To offer hope alone!
PHILINTE:	An elegant and happy choice of words!
ALCESTE	(*to* PHILINTE):
	Morbleu, bootlicker, you can praise this nonsense?
ORONTE:	If I must wait forever,
	While torment quits me never,
	To Death I shall repair!
	Restrain me not! For clearly
	Perpetual hope is merely
	Perpetual despair!
PHILINTE:	Why, what a sweet, seductive dying fall!
ALCESTE	(*to* PHILINTE):
	The devil take the fall, you poisoner!
	I wish you'd take one which would break your skull!
PHILINTE:	I've never heard such deftly rendered lines.
ALCESTE:	*Morbleu!*
ORONTE:	You flatter me! Perhaps you think—
PHILINTE:	No, I'm not flattering.
ALCESTE	(*to* PHILINTE): What *are* you doing?
ORONTE	(*to* ALCESTE):
	But, sir, you know what our agreement is,
	So tell me, please, in all sincerity.
ALCESTE:	Sir, this affair is always delicate;
	We always like to hear our wit commended.
	But once a friend of mine, I won't say who,

Showed me some poetry he'd just composed.
I said a gentleman should never yield
Too readily to the itch of authorship;
He ought to hold in check his urgent wish
To publicly display his private pleasures.
I said our eagerness to show our works
Leads us to play an inadvisable role.

ORONTE: And are you trying to tell me by these words
That I am wrong to wish—

ALCESTE: I don't say that.
I told my friend to avoid all tepid writing,
Which is enough to bring a man discredit,
For though we have good qualities aplenty,
We're commonly judged according to our faults.

ORONTE: You have some criticism of my sonnet?

ALCESTE: I don't say that. But, to discourage him,
I hinted that this mania for writing
Has injured many well-considered men.

ORONTE: Do I write badly? I resemble them?

ALCESTE: I don't say that. But anyway, I asked him:
"What is your pressing need to rhyme? And why
For God's sake must you get yourself in print?
The only excuse for a bad book's publication
Is that some needy hack has written it.
Take my advice and fight against temptation,
And hide your occupations from the public,
And don't let folk persuade you to exchange
Your reputation as a man of sense
For that, conferred by a mercenary printer,
Of a ridiculous and wretched author."
That's what I tried to make him comprehend.

ORONTE: Oh, very good. I think I understand you.
But may I not discover how my sonnet—

ALCESTE: Frankly, it's only fit to be pigeonholed.

You've taken bad examples as your models,
And your expressions are not natural.
What do you mean—"By hope our woe's disguised"?
And did you moan for pity audibly?
And is your torment driving you to death?
Was Phyllis really heartless, offering hope?
Do you believe perpetual hope is merely
Perpetual despair? Is that a fact?
This sickly imagery that's now the rage
Is false to human nature and to truth;
It's only word play, it's pure affectation,
And that is not the way that Nature talks.
The bad taste of our time is terrifying;
That of our rude forefathers was much better.
I think much less of what is now admired
Than of an old song which I'll sing to you:
 If the King should offer me
  Paris, his great city,
 If he said the price would be
  That I'd leave my pretty,
 I would tell the King Henri:
 Keep your Paris, leave me be,
 I prefer my pretty sweet,
  I prefer my pretty.
The rhyme is obvious and the style is old,
But don't you see that that's a better poem
Than all these trumpery things that flout good sense,
For there emotion's talking her true language.
 If the King should offer me
  Paris, his great city,
 If he said the price would be
  That I'd leave my pretty,
 I would tell the King Henri:
 Keep your Paris, leave me be,

I prefer my pretty sweet,

I prefer my pretty.

That's what a man in love might really say.

(*To* PHILINTE)

Yes, you may laugh; despite your intellectuals,

I prize that more than all the affectation

Of the gimcrack poetry of the current mode.

ORONTE: And I maintain my poem's excellent.

ALCESTE: You have your reasons to esteem it so;

But you'll permit me to have other reasons

Which will dispense me from accepting yours.

ORONTE: Since others praise it, that's enough for me.

ALCESTE: They have the art of feigning; I have not.

ORONTE: You think then all the wit in the world is yours?

ALCESTE: I would need more, in order to praise your poem.

ORONTE: I can do very well without your approval.

ALCESTE: I fear that you will have to do without it.

ORONTE: I should just like to see you write a poem

On the same subject and in your own style.

ALCESTE: I could write one, unhappily, just as bad,

But I'd be certain not to show it around.

ORONTE: This is high talk! You're very sure of yourself—

ALCESTE: If you want incense, go find someone else.

ORONTE: My little man, don't take this lofty tone!

ALCESTE: Why, my big man, I take the tone I like.

PHILINTE (*interposing*):

Gentlemen, calm yourselves! Enough of this!

ORONTE: All my profound regrets. I take my leave.

I am, monsieur, your very humble servant.

ALCESTE: And I, sir, most obsequiously yours.

(*Exit* ORONTE.)

PHILINTE: Well, you can see; by being too sincere

You've got a nasty business on your hands.

Now clearly Oronte, in order to be flattered—

ALCESTE:	Don't talk to me!
PHILINTE:	But look—
ALCESTE:	And leave me alone.
PHILINTE:	Why, really—
ALCESTE:	On your way!
PHILINTE:	If I—
ALCESTE:	No talk!
PHILINTE:	What?
ALCESTE:	I won't listen.
PHILINTE:	But—
ALCESTE:	Enough!
PHILINTE:	Now wait—
ALCESTE:	This is too much, *parbleu!* Don't follow me!
PHILINTE:	Say what you please, I shall stay right beside you.

ACT II

Enter ALCESTE, *giving his hand to* CÉLIMÈNE.

ALCESTE: Madame, you wish me to speak all my thought?
I am offended by the way you act,
And your behavior wounds me to the heart.
I fear that we may come to an outright breach.
If I spoke otherwise I should deceive you;
Sooner or later we shall have to quarrel.
Though I should promise you the contrary
A thousand times, I could not keep my word.

CÉLIMÈNE: And so it was to scold me, evidently,
That you entreated so to bring me home?

ALCESTE: I am not scolding; but your attitude
Is far too cordial to the casual stranger.
You have too many suitors always about you,
And that's a thing I find it hard to stomach.

CÉLIMÈNE: Is it my fault if people choose to court me?

How can I help it if I seem attractive?
When people take some pains to visit me,
You want me to seize a stick and drive them out?

ALCESTE: No, madame, no; it's not a stick you need,
Rather a heart less welcoming to their vows.
I know that you are always beautiful;
Your charm attracts men, then your manner holds
   them.
Your gracious disposition toward your captives
Completes the work your loveliness began.
You kindle in them overconfidence,
Which makes them persevere in their attentions.
A somewhat less promiscuous affability
Would soon drive off this multitude of suitors.
Tell me at least, madame, by what enchantment
Clitandre is so fortunate as to please you?
Upon what fund of merit and of virtue
Do you bestow the honor of your regard?
Is it his lengthy little fingernail
That has established him in your esteem?
Have you surrendered, with society,
To the excellence of his bright yellow wig?
Is it his great knee ruffles which have won you?
Or the profusion of his dangling ribbons?
Did his wide German breeches cast a spell,
When he professed himself to be your slave?
Perhaps it is his high falsetto snigger
Which found the way to captivate your heart?

CÉLIMÈNE: You take offense at him too readily.
You must know, surely, why I humor him—
Because he's promised to engage his friends
To help me in the lawsuit on my hands.

ALCESTE: Then lose your case, madame, with fortitude,
Rather than humor my offensive rival.

CÉLIMÈNE: You're getting jealous of the entire world!
ALCESTE: Because you give the entire world your welcome.
CÉLIMÈNE: But this should reassure your sensitive soul:
            That I act pleasantly to all alike.
            You would have much more cause to be offended
            If I distinguished one particular man.
ALCESTE: But I, whom you accuse of jealousy,
            What do I have, madame, that they have not?
CÉLIMÈNE: The happiness of knowing that I love you.
ALCESTE: And what grounds do you give me to believe it?
CÉLIMÈNE: I think that since I venture to admit it,
            My statement should be quite enough for you.
ALCESTE: And what assures me that you are not making
            A similar statement to the other men?
CÉLIMÈNE: Now that's a pretty compliment from a lover!
            What a sweet character you give to me!
            I will relieve you, since you're so distressed,
            And take back everything I've just been saying.
            No one can now deceive you but yourself,
            And so be happy.
ALCESTE: God! Why must I love you!
            Why, if my heart is mine again, I'll bless
            Heaven for granting me its kindly favor!
            I won't disguise the fact, I do my best
            To kill the infatuation of my heart;
            But all my utmost efforts are in vain.
            It must be for my sins I love you so.
CÉLIMÈNE: Your love—it is remarkable, at least.
ALCESTE: Why, yes, it is indeed. It's like no other.
            It is beyond conception; and I grant
            No one has ever loved, madame, as I do.
CÉLIMÈNE: In fact, the manner has its novelty.
            You love a lady only to abuse her,
            Stating your passion with a string of insults.

	Such an ill-tempered love is something new.
ALCESTE:	But it is in your power to change its humor,
	So let us have no more disputes, I beg you.
	Let us speak frankly, find a way to check—
	(*Enter* BASQUE.)
BASQUE:	Monsieur Acaste is here.
CÉLIMÈNE:	Well, send him up.
	(*Exit* BASQUE.)
ALCESTE:	What! I can never speak to you alone?
	I always find you ready to welcome guests?
	You never can make up your mind to say
	To visitors that you cannot receive them?
CÉLIMÈNE:	So I should have a falling-out with him?
ALCESTE:	But your civilities I find excessive.
CÉLIMÈNE:	He is a man who never would forgive me
	If he should learn I did not welcome him.
ALCESTE:	And why should that disturb you in the least?
CÉLIMÈNE:	Why, the good will of men like him is useful.
	They have acquired at court, I don't know how,
	The privilege of being listened to.
	They have a share in every conversation.
	They may not help you, but they *can* do harm.
	No matter what protection one may have,
	One shouldn't quarrel with these windy ranters.
ALCESTE:	And so, whatever one may say or argue,
	You justify receiving everybody,
	And all your actions rest upon precaution—
	(*Enter* BASQUE.)
BASQUE:	Monsieur Clitandre's here, madame.
ALCESTE:	Exactly.
	(*Exit* BASQUE. ALCESTE *makes a move to leave.*)
CÉLIMÈNE:	Where are you going?
ALCESTE:	Away.
CÉLIMÈNE:	No, wait!
ALCESTE:	And why?

CÉLIMÈNE: Please wait!

ALCESTE: I can't.

CÉLIMÈNE: I want you to.

ALCESTE: No use.
These conversations merely bore me still,
And it's too much to try to make me bear them.

CÉLIMÈNE: I want you to.

ALCESTE: No, it's impossible.

CÉLIMÈNE: All right, then; go away. I won't prevent you.
(ALCESTE *retires. Enter* BASQUE, ÉLIANTE, PHILINTE.)

ÉLIANTE: The marquises were coming up with us.
Were they announced?

CÉLIMÈNE: Yes. Basque, some chairs!
(BASQUE *arranges chairs and exits;* ALCESTE *comes forward*)
(*To* ALCESTE)
Still here?

ALCESTE: Quite so. I want you to make clear
Whether your preference is for them or me.

CÉLIMÈNE: Be quiet!

ALCESTE: You will explain yourself today.

CÉLIMÈNE: You're crazy!

ALCESTE: No. You will declare yourself.

CÉLIMÈNE: Ah!

ALCESTE: You'll make up your mind.

CÉLIMÈNE: I think you're joking.

ALCESTE: No, you will choose. I've borne this long enough.
(*Enter* CLITANDRE *and* ACASTE. *Exaggerated salutations. All take seats.*)

CLITANDRE: Madame, I've just come from the King's levee—
And how ridiculous Cléonte appeared!
Has he no charitable friend who might
Give him some good advice about his manners?

CÉLIMÈNE: It's true he plays the fool in society,

And at first glimpse he strikes you as peculiar.
But after you've not seen him for a while,
You meet him again—he's even more peculiar.

ACASTE: *Parbleu!* And, speaking of peculiar people,
I've just escaped from one of the prime examples:
Damon the man of words. He kept me standing
An hour in the sun, with a foot in my sedan chair.

CÉLIMÈNE: He's perfect in his way. He has learned the art
Of saying all and signifying nothing.
Since he achieves a total lack of meaning,
His words are properly a social noise.

ÉLIANTE (*to* PHILINIE): A good beginning! And it promises
A nice annihilation of our neighbors.

CLITANDRE: And Timante too, madame, is a curious type.

CÉLIMÈNE: He's the embodiment of mystery.
He casts at you a frantic, furtive glance,
And he is always busy—about nothing.
How he contorts his face to tell you something,
And how he wearies you with his affectations!
He draws you out of a pleasant conversation
To tell you a secret—which you know already.
He makes a marvel of every commonplace,
And even "Good morning!" he whispers in your ear.

ACASTE: And how about Géralde?

CÉLIMÈNE: The snob reporter!
His single subject is the high nobility,
He has no intimates without a title,
And only quotes a princess, prince, or duke.
He's mad about gentility; all his talk
Is horses, hounds, and hunting ceremonies.
He always uses first names for the great;
"Monsieur" is dropped from his vocabulary.

CLITANDRE: They say he's very friendly with Bélise.

CÉLIMÈNE: Well, she is dull enough, poor thing, to match him.

It is a torture to receive her call.
You struggle for a theme within her grasp,
And then her helplessness in finding words
Keeps conversation at the point of death.
In vain, to rouse her from her sodden silence,
You try to startle her with platitudes.
But even rain and sunshine, cold and heat,
Are subjects soon exhausted in her presence.
And still her appalling visit lasts and lasts,
Until it seems to approach infinity.
You look at the clock, you yawn a dozen times,
But she's immovable as a block of wood.

ACASTE: How do you like Adraste?

CÉLIMÈNE: The man of pride,
Inflated with affection for himself!
His virtue's most dissatisfied with the court;
He rails against its actions every day.
Every appointment that the court announces
He takes as a personal insult to his merit.

CLITANDRE: And popular young Cléon, who receives
All the best people, what do you think of him?

CÉLIMÈNE: His most outstanding merit is his cook,
So people call upon his dinner table.

ÉLIANTE: It's true he serves very delicious food.

CÉLIMÈNE: But I could wish he did not serve himself.
His foolish person is unappetizing,
And spoils the savors of his splendid dinners.

PHILINTE: His uncle Damis is well spoken of.
How do you like him?

CÉLIMÈNE: He's a friend of mine.

PHILINTE: I find him a worthy man, intelligent.

CÉLIMÈNE: Yes, but he's too intelligent for me.

He tries too hard; and when he holds the floor,
You hear the grinding of his witticisms.
Since he's become an intellectual,
Nothing can please his taste, he's so refined.
He sees the faults in all our literature,
And thinks that clever men should never applaud,
That criticism shows your scholarship,
That only idiots admire and laugh,
And that one proves superiority
By disapproving all contemporaries.
He even looks askance at conversation;
He cannot stoop to deal with commonplaces.
Crossing his arms, he looks with pity down
From his intellectual summit on the babblers.

ACASTE: Damme if that is not his perfect portrait!

CLITANDRE: How marvelous your character sketches are!

ALCESTE: Now thrust and stab, my worthy courtly friends!
No one is spared, everyone has his turn.
And yet if one of them should show himself,
We'd see you all hurry to welcome him,
Hold out your hands and take him in your arms,
Swearing you are his very humble servants.

CLITANDRE: Why attack *us*? If you don't like this talk,
You should address your scoldings to Madame.

ALCESTE: No, no! To you, *morbleu!* Your fawning laughter
Impels her to produce these cynical slurs!
And you encourage her satiric humor
By the cajolement of your flatteries.
She would be less inclined to mock and sneer,
If she observed that you did not applaud her.
And so the flatterers are most to blame
For the common vices of humanity.

PHILINTE: Why do you take such interest in the victims?

	You would condemn in them what she condemns.
CÉLIMÈNE:	The gentleman is forced to contradict.
	You don't expect that he would condescend
	To common judgments, failing to display
	His native character of opposition?
	He never likes what other people like,
	And his opinion's always the contrary.
	He thinks he'd seem an ordinary man,
	If he should ever agree with anyone.
	He likes so much the honor of contradicting,
	He often starts an argument with himself.
	He battles against his own sincere convictions
	As soon as he hears another man express them.
ALCESTE:	Madame, you have the laughers on your side,
	And you can satirize me as you please.
PHILINTE:	Still, it's a fact that you are always ready
	To shout defiance to every utterance.
	The peevish humor you yourself confess
	Takes issue with both praise and criticism.
ALCESTE:	*Morbleu!* The fact is, men are always wrong,
	And peevishness against them's always proper.
	I note in every circumstance they're either
	Untimely applauders or unblushing critics.
CÉLIMÈNE:	But—
ALCESTE:	No, madame, I'll say it though it kills me.
	You have amusements which I can't endure;
	And one does wrong to encourage an inclination
	For the very faults which privately one condemns.
CLITANDRE:	Well, I can testify I've always thought
	That Célimène possessed no fault at all.
ACASTE:	And I can well discern her charms and graces;
	But faults? They are invisible to me.
ALCESTE:	They're visible to me; I don't disguise them;
	And she knows well how I reproach her for them.

The more you love, the less you ought to flatter;
And true love is incapable of pardon.
If I were she, I'd banish all admirers
Submissive to my slightest sentiment,
Fawning upon me with their cheap applause
For even my most extreme extravagances.

CÉLIMÈNE: In short, according to your laws for lovers,
You would forbid all pretty compliments;
And the supreme ideal of perfect love
Is to insult and vilify one's darling.

ÉLIANTE: Love doesn't fit with such high principles.
Lovers are always sure they've chosen well.
They can't see qualities to criticize,
For in the loved one all is lovable.
And so defects take on the air of virtues,
And love provides its own vocabulary.
The pale girl is as pure and white as jasmine,
The swarthy one's a smoldering brunette,
The thin young lady's willowy and svelte,
The fat girl has a fine majestic carriage,
The sloppy and untidy miss becomes
A wild and carefree harum-scarum beauty:
The giantess takes on a goddess air,
The dwarf is dainty and too cute for words,
The vain girl has a dignity serene,
The sly girl's smart, the dull girl's sweet and simple,
The chatterbox has an engaging humor,
The silent one has dark, mysterious depths.
And thus a truly smitten lover loves
Even the faults of his inamorata.

ALCESTE: For my part, I maintain—

CÉLIMÈNE: Enough of this.
Come, let us take a walk in the gallery.

	. . . Gentlemen, you're not going?	
CLITANDRE *and* ACASTE:		No, madame.
ALCESTE	(*to* CÉLIMÈNE):	
	You are obsessed with fear of their departure.	
	. . . Leave when you like, messieurs! I give you warning	
	That I won't go till after you have left!	
ACASTE:	Unless Madame should find my call excessive,	
	I have no reason to leave for the rest of the day.	
CLITANDRE:	Provided I'm present at the King's retirement,	
	I've no engagements of significance.	
CÉLIMÈNE	(*to* ALCESTE):	
	You're joking, surely.	
ALCESTE:		Not by any means.
	We'll see if I'm the one you ask to leave.	
	(*Enter* BASQUE.)	
BASQUE	(*to* ALCESTE):	
	Monsieur, a gentleman would like to see you	
	About a matter which, he says, is urgent.	
ALCESTE:	Tell him there's no such thing as an urgent matter.	
BASQUE:	He wears a uniform with a swallow-tail,	
	And gold all over!	
CÉLIMÈNE:		Go and see what it is,
	Or have him enter.	
ALCESTE	(*speaking into wings*): What do you want with me?	
	Come in, come in.	
	(*Enter* OFFICER. *Exit* BASQUE.)	
OFFICER:		Sir, I've a message for you.
ALCESTE:	Speak up, sir; there's no need for secrecy.	
OFFICER:	The Court of Honor, of which I am the agent,	
	Commands, sir, your immediate appearance.	
ALCESTE:	Who, me, monsieur?	
OFFICER:		Yourself, sir.
ALCESTE:		And what for?
PHILINTE:	It's that ridiculous business with Oronte.	

CÉLIMÈNE: What's that?

PHILINTE: Oronte and he have had a quarrel
About some poetry he didn't approve.
The court desires to pacify the affair.

ALCESTE: I'll never make a base capitulation.

PHILINTE: You must obey the order; make up your mind.

ALCESTE: What do they want as reconciliation?
Will the decision of the court condemn me
To find the poetry in question good?
I won't unsay a single thing I've said.
The poem's bad.

PHILINTE: If you'll just take it easy—

ALCESTE: I won't retract. The poem's terrible.

PHILINTE: You'll have to act in a reasonable manner.
Come on!

ALCESTE: All right, I'll go; but nothing will force me
To take my words back.

PHILINTE: Come; we'll answer the summons.

ALCESTE: Unless a special order from the King
Orders me to approve the poem in question,
I will maintain forever it is bad,
And that the man who wrote it should be hanged!
(CLITANDRE *and* ACASTE *laugh*)
Zounds, gentlemen, I didn't realize
I was so funny!

CÉLIMÈNE: Hurry, make your appearance
Before the court!

ALCESTE: Madame, I'll do so; then
I'll come back here to finish our discussion.

ACT III

Enter CLITANDRE *and* ACASTE.

CLITANDRE: My dear Marquis, you're looking very cheerful!
Nothing upsets your equanimity!

　　　　　　Is it your own imagination merely,
　　　　　　Or is there reason for your satisfaction?
ACASTE:　　*Parbleu!* If I review my situation,
　　　　　　I see no reason to afflict myself.
　　　　　　I'm young and well-to-do; my family
　　　　　　Is noble, there's no argument about it.
　　　　　　And I am qualified by birth to hold
　　　　　　Almost any appointment at the court.
　　　　　　And as for bravery, which the world esteems,
　　　　　　I think I've given satisfactory proofs:
　　　　　　For I took on a little affair of honor,
　　　　　　And carried it decently to its conclusion.
　　　　　　Surely I have sufficient wit and taste
　　　　　　To treat all subjects with authority,
　　　　　　And at first nights, to take a seat on the stage,
　　　　　　And prove to the public I'm a connoisseur,
　　　　　　And clap my hands to indicate excellence,
　　　　　　And mark the good lines with "Oho! Aha!"
　　　　　　I've a good figure, an engaging manner;
　　　　　　I'm quick and deft; my teeth are really fine.
　　　　　　And as for taste in clothes, I shouldn't boast,
　　　　　　But how can one dispute the evidence?
　　　　　　It's clear I'm well regarded everywhere;
　　　　　　The ladies like me, and the King does too.
　　　　　　And so, my dear Marquis, it seems to me
　　　　　　I have some reason for self-satisfaction.
CLITANDRE:　But you can make many an easy conquest,
　　　　　　So why come here, to utter sighs in vain?
ACASTE:　　In vain? *Parbleu*, I'm not the kind of person
　　　　　　To endure the chilly blasts of a frozen beauty!
　　　　　　We'll let the common fellows, the out-of-fashion,
　　　　　　Display their constancy for a cruel belle,
　　　　　　Languish before her, obey her harsh commands,
　　　　　　And do the best they can with sighs and tears,

And try to obtain by long fidelity
What they can hardly gain by their own merits.
People like me, Marquis, are not the kind
To pay the costs of love on speculation.
The ladies may be very admirable,
But after all, we are worth something too;
And if they hold a heart like mine in thrall,
It isn't right that they should have it free.
And if you look at the matter fairly and squarely,
The advances should be made on equal terms.

CLITANDRE: Your standing here would seem to be excellent.

ACASTE: Indeed, Marquis, I have some grounds to think so.

CLITANDRE: I think, my friend, you are in total error.
I think you're blindly flattering yourself.

ACASTE: That's true, I'm blindly flattering myself!

CLITANDRE: What makes you sure that you're so fortunate?

ACASTE: I'm flattering myself!

CLITANDRE: What basis have you?

ACASTE: I'm blind!

CLITANDRE: But have you any kind of proof?

ACASTE: Oh, I must be mistaken!

CLITANDRE: Célimène,
Has she made any admission of her feelings?

ACASTE: No, she is brutal to me!

CLITANDRE: Won't you answer?

ACASTE: Nothing but snubs!

CLITANDRE: Let's drop the comedy;
Tell me what hope she may have given you.

ACASTE: I'm the unhappy one, and you are favored;
She actually has a loathing for my person.
One of these days I'll have to hang myself.

CLITANDRE: Marquis, to simplify our competition,
Suppose we both agree about one thing.
If one of us obtains clear indication

Of preference in Célimène's affections,
The other will yield the palm to the evident victor,
And free him from an annoying rivalry.

ACASTE: *Parbleu!* I like the idea very well.
I'll be extremely glad to make the deal.
But hush!

(*Enter* CÉLIMÈNE.)

CÉLIMÈNE: Still here?

CLITANDRE: It's love that holds us spellbound.

CÉLIMÈNE: I heard a carriage entering the court.
You don't know who—

CLITANDRE: Oh, no.

(*Enter* BASQUE.)

BASQUE: Madame, madame
Arsinoé is here.

CÉLIMÈNE: What does she want?

BASQUE: Madame Éliante is talking to her now.

(*Exit* BASQUE.)

CÉLIMÈNE: I wonder what inspired her to come here.

ACASTE: She passes as the epitome of the prude.
Her ardent piety—

CÉLIMÈNE: It's all a sham.
Her heart is still in the social world; she's trying
Forever to catch a man, without success.
She can see only with an envious eye
The avowed admirers of her lady friends.
Her poor attractions having lost their power,
She angrily attacks the oblivious world.
She tries to cover with a prudish veil
The fact that never a suitor sighs for her.
She treats as criminal all physical charm,
To vindicate the absence of her own.
And yet she'd find a lover very welcome;

She even has a weakness for Alceste.
She takes to heart his courtesies to me;
She thinks that I am thieving them from her.
Her jealous spite, which she can hardly hide,
She's always manifesting against me.
It is the silliest thing I've ever seen;
She really is outrageously indecent.
And—

(*Enter* ARSINOÉ)

Oh, what a lucky chance has brought you here!
Madame, to tell the truth, I've missed you sadly.

ARSINOÉ: I've come, from duty, to bring you information.

CÉLIMÈNE: Heavens, my dear, how happy I am to see you!

(ACASTE *and* CLITANDRE *laugh, bow, and exit.*)

ARSINOÉ: They leave, in fact, at a convenient moment.

CÉLIMÈNE: Shall we sit down?

ARSINOÉ: It isn't necessary,
Madame. True friendship ought to show itself
In matters that are really of importance.
And as no matters can be more important
Than those which touch one's standing in society,
I'll prove my friendship by informing you
Of something which affects your reputation.
Yesterday, at a most distinguished house,
The conversation chanced to turn on you.
Your—shall I say?—conspicuous behavior
Had the misfortune not to be approved.
The swarm of visitors whom you receive
And your coquettishness, as it was termed,
Aroused, I fear, excessive criticism,
Which was so harsh it caused me real distress.
You can imagine how I spoke to that;
In your defense I said all that I could,

And I insisted on your good intentions,
And vouched for your character's integrity.
And yet you know that some things in this life
Are hard to excuse, no matter how you wish to;
And so I found myself obliged to agree
Your way of life reflects a little on you.
It looks peculiar to the social world,
And stimulates some most regrettable stories.
In short, you might well alter your behavior
To give less cause for hostile criticism.
Not that I think there's anything really wrong—
Heaven preserve me from the very thought!—
But even the shadow of evil makes presumptions;
One cannot live sufficient to oneself.
Madame, I'm sure you're sensible enough
To take this good advice in the way it's meant,
And recognize that it is prompted only
By my concern for your best interests.

CÉLIMÈNE: Madame, I'm very deeply grateful to you.
I cannot take such information ill.
I can repay it only by telling you
Something which touches your own reputation.
And as you show your friendship by revealing
The tales in circulation about me,
I want to follow your excellent example
By warning you what people say of you.
I was just calling at a certain house
Where a most estimable group was gathered.
The conversation turning on the rules
For the good life, your name, madame, was men-
    tioned.
Your prudery and your excessive zeal
Were not regarded as the best of models.

Your affectation of a serious manner,
Your everlasting talk of good behavior,
Your screams at any hint of the indecent
Contained within a perfectly innocent word,
The high regard you evidence for yourself,
The pitying air you manifest to others,
Your frequent and embittered criticism
Of things which seem entirely chaste and pure—
All this, madame, if I may be so frank,
Was, by the general consent, condemned.
They said: "Her sage, demure, and modest manner,
Makes a strange contrast with the way she acts.
While she is most punctilious in her prayers,
She beats her servants, and she doesn't pay them.
She goes to church to show her piety,
But why does she have to paint her face so much?
She covers up the nudities of pictures,
But has a liking for the realities."
I came to your defense against them all;
It was all ugly slander, I maintained;
But everybody took the contrary view,
And their conclusion was, you would do well
To bother less with other people's actions
And make a closer scrutiny of your own.
One ought to make a self-examination
Before one ventures to admonish others.
Only a blameless life can authorize
One who assumes the post of general censor;
And still, that task might better be confided
To those whom Heaven has chosen for the purpose.
I think you too are sensible enough
To take this good advice in the way it's meant,
And recognize that it is prompted only

By my concern for your best interests.

ARSINOÉ: To give advice, I know, is dangerous;
And yet I am surprised by your reply.
Your acrid tone, madame, makes evident
That my sincerity has wounded you.

CÉLIMÈNE: Why, not at all, madame! If we were wise,
We'd make a practice of such mutual aid;
And thus, by frankness, we would put an end
To our sad ignorance about ourselves.
It rests with you whether we shall continue
To put this excellent device to service,
And make a point of telling all we know,
You about me, I about you, madame.

ARSINOÉ: Oh, about you, I can hear nothing, surely;
I am the one who should be criticized.

CÉLIMÈNE: Why, everything deserves both praise and blame,
And everyone is right—for his age and type.
There is a season for the game of love,
Another for the game of prudishness,
Which we may choose to play deliberately,
When once the natural bloom of youth is gone.
To hedge against unlucky accidents,
Some day, perhaps, I'll follow your example.
The years bring everything. And yet, madame,
Twenty is not the age to play the prude.

ARSINOÉ: How proud you are of a very small advantage!
You are unduly smug about your age!
I am not older by so many years
That one need make such a to-do about it!
I don't know why you seem to be impelled,
Madame, to make this strange assault upon me.

CÉLIMÈNE: And as for me, madame, I don't know why
You should attack me everywhere in public.

Why do you blame me for your own distresses?
If gentlemen don't court you, can I help it?
If I have something which makes people love me,
And if they come to offer me addresses
Which you may long to see eliminated,
It's not my fault; there's nothing I can do.
The field is open; and I don't prevent you
From having charms sufficient to allure.

ARSINOÉ: And do you think that I'm at all concerned
By the great swarm of suitors you're so proud of?
And do you think I don't know what's required
To keep them persevering, nowadays?
And do you think you can convince the world
That it's your merit which attracts that throng?
And that their love for you is honorable,
And that it is your virtues they are wooing?
The world is not so easily taken in;
We're not so stupid. There are plenty of women
With every quality to arouse affection,
But who discourage amorous young men.
From that I think we fairly may conclude
That one can't fish for lovers without bait,
And that it's not our beautiful eyes they sigh for,
And that one has to pay for their devotion.
You needn't be puffed up with vanity
For conquests hardly worthy of remark.
Your charms are not so mighty that you need
To treat the world with superciliousness.
Why, if we really envied you your victims,
I'm sure that we could imitate your system:
Let ourselves go. And thus we'd demonstrate
That if one wishes lovers, one can have them.

CÉLIMÈNE: By all means have some lovers, then, madame.

	You know the secret of allurement, so—
ARSINOÉ:	This conversation has gone far enough.
	We might say things we should be sorry for.
	Indeed, I should have taken leave long since,
	Had not my carriage been delayed, it seems.
CÉLIMÈNE:	Why, you may stop as long as you desire,
	Madame; don't be in any hurry at all.
	(ALCESTE *appears at door*)
	So, without making needless ceremony,
	I'm going to give you better company.
	This gentleman, whom happy chance has brought,
	Will be a better host to you than I.
	Alceste, excuse me; I must write a letter
	Which cannot be delayed another minute.
	Stay with Madame; and she will be so kind
	As to excuse my incivility.
	(*Exit* CÉLIMÈNE.)
ARSINOÉ:	You see, she wants me to converse with you
	For a moment or two, until my carriage comes.
	In point of fact, she couldn't offer me
	An opportunity I'd find more welcome.
	Really exceptional people must attract
	The affectionate regard of everyone;
	And your own quality is such, it moves me
	To sympathize with all your purposes.
	I wish the court would pay you more attention
	And better appreciate your genuine merit.
	You're badly treated, sir. It makes me angry
	To see you have no adequate reward.
ALCESTE:	Reward? What should I be rewarded for?
	What service have I rendered to the state?
	What are my brilliant deeds, to justify
	Complaints about the court's ingratitude?

ARSINOÉ: The people who enjoy the royal favor
             Have often rendered no particular service.
             Ability must find some circumstance
             To show itself; and your most evident merit
             Should really—
ALCESTE: Please, let's drop this talk of merit!
             How can the court concern itself with that?
             It certainly would be busy if it had to
             Discover and reveal the merit of men!
ARSINOÉ: Exceptional merit must reveal itself,
             And yours is much esteemed by many people.
             Why, only yesterday, in two great houses,
             I heard you praised by people of importance.
ALCESTE: Today, madame, one praises everybody.
             The present age has no distinctions left.
             With merit all are equally endowed,
             So it's no honor to be the subject of praise.
             Now everyone is smothered in compliments;
             Even my footman's in the society news.
ARSINOÉ: I wish your qualities were made more public,
             And that a court appointment might attract you.
             If you would manifest some interest,
             One might well pull the necessary strings.
             I have some friends whom I can put to work;
             They'll readily remove all difficulties.
ALCESTE: What would you have me do in such a post?
             I'm out of humor with the entire system.
             Madame, the character that I was born with
             Makes me unfit for the court's etiquette.
             I haven't got the necessary virtues
             To play its games and to succeed in them.
             My greatest talent is to be sincere;
             I don't know how to win by double talk.

A man who can't dissemble what he thinks
Cannot last long in this society.
Away from court, you won't get much support,
You won't get any honorary titles,
You won't achieve so much; but you won't have
The consciousness you're acting like a fool.
You needn't bear its spurns and insolence,
You needn't praise fine gentlemen's poetry,
Burn incense under a great lady's nose,
And laugh at our little lordlings' witticisms.

ARSINOÉ: Please, let us drop this matter of the court.
I want to say I'm sorry about your courtship.
To be entirely frank, I could have wished
You'd found another object of affection.
Certainly you deserve much better treatment.
Your charmer is not worthy of your love.

ALCESTE: When you say that, madame, do you remember,
I wonder, that the lady is your friend?

ARSINOÉ: Yes; but my conscience tells me to protest
Against the indecent treatment you receive.
I suffer deeply, seeing your situation;
And I must tell you that your love's betrayed.

ALCESTE: Why, this is very kind of you, madame.
A lover's much indebted for such news.

ARSINOÉ: Though she's my friend, I'm certain she is hardly
Fit to possess an honorable heart.
All her affection for you is a sham.

ALCESTE: That well may be; one cannot look in hearts.
And yet you might have had the charity
Not to put this suspicion in my own.

ARSINOÉ: Of course, if you don't want to know the facts,
It's easy enough not to say anything.

ALCESTE: No matter what one says on such a theme,
It's doubt which is the most distressing thing.

I wish that people would inform me only
Of things that they can definitely prove.

ARSINOÉ: Certainly, if you wish. You will receive
Considerable light upon the subject.
I want you to inspect the evidence.
If you will just conduct me to my home,
I will provide you with convincing proof
Of the disloyalty of your fair lady.
And if your heart can turn to other objects,
I'm sure that it will find its consolation.

ACT IV

Enter PHILINTE *and* ÉLIANTE.

PHILINTE: You never saw a man so hard to manage,
Or so much trouble in an arbitration!
Everyone tried in vain to work on him;
They couldn't make him alter his opinion.
I think it was the most peculiar quarrel
The Court of Honor ever had to settle.
"No, sirs," he said, "I won't take back a word.
I'll yield on everything except this point.
Why does he feel insulted anyway?
There's nothing shameful in not writing well.
What difference does my opinion make?
One can be virtuous and a wretched poet;
That's not a matter to affect one's honor.
I think him an accomplished gentleman,
A man of rank, merit, and character,
Whatever you like; but he's a dreadful author.
I'll praise his lavish getup if you like,
His horsemanship, his fencing, or his dancing,
But for his poetry, you must excuse me.

If that's the very best a man can do,
He ought to give up writing verse, unless
He's forced to, under penalty of death."
And finally, the only compromise
That he could force his principles to make
Was to express this handsome qualification:
"Sir, I'm distressed to be so difficult;
Out of regard for you, most heartily
I wish I could have found your sonnet better."
And so the case concluded; and the two
Principals were commanded to embrace.

ÉLIANTE: He's very singular in all his actions;
But I admit I think most highly of him.
In that sincerity that he's so proud of
There's something rather noble and heroic.
That's not a common virtue nowadays;
I'd like to see some more of it around.

PHILINTE: Well, as for me, the thing that seems most strange
Is the infatuation of his heart.
Considering his cast of character,
I don't know how he came to fall in love,
And even more I cannot understand
How it's your cousin that he fell in love with.

ÉLIANTE: That seems to indicate that love is not
Always affinity of character.
Let people talk of hidden sympathies;
Here's an example on the opposite side.

PHILINTE: But, from the look of things, you think she loves
him?

ÉLIANTE: That's not an easy matter to decide.
How can you settle if she really loves him?
Her heart is not quite sure of its own feelings.
A heart may love, denying that it loves,
Or think it loves, in ignorance of the truth.

PHILINTE: I think our friend, by fixing on your cousin,
Is building up more troubles than he knows.
And if he shared my feelings, the fact is
That he would look in a different direction,
And he'd have wit enough to take advantage
Of all your kindliness to him, madame.

ÉLIANTE: Well, I'll be frank about it; I believe
One ought to tell the truth about these matters.
I don't oppose his love for Célimène;
Indeed, I give it all encouragement.
If the affair were under my control,
I would unite him to the one he loves.
But if his love for her should run afoul
Of circumstances, as so well may happen,
If it falls out that she should wed another,
I should be ready to accept his suit.
I should not be offended by the fact
That he had been rejected by another.

PHILINTE: And for my part, madame, I have no quarrel
With all the kindness which you show to him.
And he can tell you, if he wishes to,
How I have counseled him upon the matter.
But if he were united with his loved one,
And thus debarred from paying you his suit,
I should attempt to capture for my own
That blissful favor which you show to him;
And if his heart can disregard it, I
Shall be most happy if it falls to me.

ÉLIANTE: My dear Philinte, you're joking.

PHILINTE: No, madame.
I speak sincerely; and I long to have
Freedom to make to you a formal offer,
And thus fulfill my uttermost desires.
(*Enter* ALCESTE.)

ALCESTE: Help me, madame, to get me vengeance for
            An insult which has robbed me of my strength!
ÉLIANTE: What is it that has so excited you?
ALCESTE: Why, it's a matter that it's death to think of!
            And the convulsion of all nature could
            Not overwhelm me like this circumstance.
            I'm done for. And my love—no, I can't speak!
ÉLIANTE: Alceste—do try to collect your wits a little.
ALCESTE: Heaven! How can such charm and grace be joined
            To the odious vices of the meanest souls!
ÉLIANTE: Once more, what is it—
ALCESTE: Oh, it's all destroyed!
            I am betrayed, I am assassinated!
            For Célimène—is it believable?—
            She has deceived me, she is a faithless creature!
ÉLIANTE: Have you good reason for believing this?
PHILINTE: Perhaps you form a fanciful suspicion;
            Sometimes your jealousy imagines things.
ALCESTE: *Morbleu,* monsieur! Please mind your own affairs!
            I have the best proof of her treachery
            Here in my pocket, written by her own hand.
            Yes, madame, yes! A letter to Oronte
            Has shown me my misfortune and her shame!
            Oronte! I thought that she avoided him.
            I feared him less than any of my rivals.
PHILINTE: A letter often gives a false impression.
            It may not be as guilty as it seems.
ALCESTE: Monsieur, again I ask you, leave me alone.
            Busy yourself with matters that concern you.
ÉLIANTE: You should control this outburst of ill temper—
ALCESTE: Madame, I put that task into your hands.
            It is to you my heart now has recourse
            To free itself from unendurable torment.
            Avenge me on your graceless, faithless cousin,

Who basely cheats my ardent constancy.
Avenge me for her despicable action!

ÉLIANTE: Avenge you? How do you mean?

ALCESTE: Accept my heart,

 ,   Madame: accept it; take the ingrate's place,
And thus I'll have my vengeance on the creature.
I'll punish her by the sincere engagement,
The genuine love and the respectful care,
The earnest regard, and the assiduous service
Which I am ready to consecrate to you.

ÉLIANTE: Surely, I sympathize with all you suffer;
I do not scorn the heart you offer me.
And yet perhaps the evil's not so great.
You may renounce your eagerness for vengeance.
When it's a charming person who offends us,
We make a lot of plans we don't fulfill.
Whatever reasons we may have for rupture,
A guilty dear one soon becomes innocent,
And all our rancor promptly dissipates.
We know well what a lover's anger is.

ALCESTE: No, no, madame. The offense is a deadly one,
And definitely we've come to the final break.
Nothing can change the purpose in my mind;
Never again can I give her my respect.
But here she is. It drives me mad to see her.
I shall reproach her for her villainous deed,
I shall expose her utterly, and then
Bring you a heart freed from her domination.
(*Enter* CÉLIMÈNE. *Exit* ÉLIANTE *and* PHILINTE)
God! Can I keep my righteous wrath in check?

CÉLIMÈNE: Dear me! You look as though you were upset!
What do you mean by your tremendous sighs?
What are you scowling at so frightfully?

ALCESTE: I mean that the worst sins of the human mind

Can't be compared with your disloyalty;
That fate and angry heaven and all the demons
Never produced your match in wickedness!

CÉLIMÈNE: These are some novel compliments indeed!

ALCESTE: Please don't be funny; this is no time to laugh.
Rather, you ought to blush; you've reason to.
I have sure testimony of your treason!
There were forebodings in my troubled mind;
My love with excellent reason took alarm.
And by my dark suspicions, which seemed shocking,
I sought the affliction which is now my lot.
In spite of all your care, your skill in feigning,
My star forewarned me what I had to fear.
But don't presume that I am going to suffer
This rude indignity without revenge!
I know one has no power over impulsions,
That love is free, rejecting all controls,
That not by main force can one take a heart,
That every soul elects its conqueror.
Thus I would have no reason to complain
If you had spoken openly to me,
Rejecting my advances from the first;
Then I would have only my fate to blame.
But to entice my love with false avowals
Is treachery, it's a perfidious act
Deserving the extremest punishment,
And I can give free rein to my resentment.
You are in danger, after such an outrage;
I am enraged, I can't restrain myself.
Since you have struck me with a mortal blow,
My senses are no longer ruled by reason.
I yield to the impulses of my anger;
I'm not responsible for what I do.

CÉLIMÈNE: Tell me, what is the reason for this frenzy?

	Have you perhaps gone totally insane?
ALCESTE:	Yes, I am crazy, since the day I took
	The drug you offered me, to my misfortune.
	I thought that there was some sincerity
	Lodged in the beauty that enraptured me.
CÉLIMÈNE:	What is this treachery that you complain of?
ALCESTE:	Oh, double heart that well knows how to feign!
	But I have means to put it to the test!
	Just look at this, and recognize your hand!
	This letter alone suffices to confound you;
	There is no answer to this testimony.
CÉLIMÈNE:	So that's the thing that has upset your wits!
ALCESTE:	You do not blush to see these written words?
CÉLIMÈNE:	Is there some reason why I ought to blush?
ALCESTE:	So! You are brazen in duplicity!
	Since there's no signature, you disavow it?
CÉLIMÈNE:	Why disavow a letter I have written?
ALCESTE:	And you can see it and not be confounded
	To recognize the crime which it reveals?
CÉLIMÈNE:	The fact is, you are really too absurd.
ALCESTE:	What! You defy conclusive evidence
	Which shows your inclination for Oronte?
	Doesn't this outrage me and prove your shame?
CÉLIMÈNE:	Oronte? You think the letter was for him?
ALCESTE:	That's what the person who gave it to me says.
	But never mind, suppose it's for another,
	I have as good a reason to reproach you,
	You're just as guilty and as false to me.
CÉLIMÈNE:	But if the letter's written to a woman,
	What's guilty in it? How does it offend you?
ALCESTE:	Oh, that's a splendid shift, a fine excuse!
	I grant you that I hadn't thought of that,
	So now you think I'm perfectly convinced!
	How do you dare employ such shabby tricks?

And do you think that people are so stupid?
I'm looking forward to the arguments
You'll use to bolster up a downright lie.
I want to see you fit to a woman friend
All of the phrases of this ardent letter.
Explain, to cover up your breach of faith,
What I'm about to read—

CÉLIMÈNE: No, I don't want to.
You have no business to be so high and mighty,
And dare to talk to me as you've been doing.

ALCESTE: Now, don't get angry; but just undertake
To justify to me these phrases here.

CÉLIMÈNE: I shall do nothing of the sort. Whatever
You choose to think concerns me not at all.

ALCESTE: Now please, just show me, I'll be satisfied,
How you explain this letter as to a woman.

CÉLIMÈNE: It's for Oronte; I want to have you think so.
I welcome his attentions with delight,
I love his talk, I think he's wonderful,
And I'll agree with anything you please.
So choose your course of action, go ahead,
And stop your shouting and don't bother me.

ALCESTE: God! Is there greater cruelty than this?
Was ever a lover treated in this way?
And I complain, and I'm the one who's scolded!
My pain, and my suspicions, are encouraged;
She leaves me to my doubt, and glories in it!
And yet my heart is still too cowardly
To rise and break the chains which fetter it,
To arm itself with a high-hearted scorn
Against the ingrate whom it loves too much!
How well you know, my faithless one, the way
To use against myself my utter weakness!

And turn to your advantage the excess
Of fatal love which you yourself inspired!
Make your defense at least against my charge,
And stop pretending that you're guilty toward me.
Prove, if you can, this letter innocent;
My love will even struggle to assist you.
If you endeavor only to seem true,
I shall endeavor to believe you so.

CÉLIMÈNE: Why, you are crazy in your jealous fits; .
You don't deserve to have a person love you.
I wonder what could force me to descend,
For your sake, to the meanness of pretending,
And why, if I should take another fancy,
I shouldn't tell it with all sincerity!
Doesn't the fact that I have given assurance
Of my affection answer your suspicions?
And is my word not of some weight against them?
In heeding them, aren't you insulting me?
And since a woman's heart must make an effort
When it resolves to make an avowal of love,
And since our honor is love's enemy,
And always is averse to such admissions,
The lover who sees this obstacle surmounted
Cannot with safety doubt his revelation.
Is he not guilty if he does not trust
What's only spoken after an inner conflict?
Oh, such suspicions well deserve my anger;
You are not worthy of my consideration.
I am a fool; I'm sorry I'm so simple
As still to preserve some charity for you.
I should transfer my favor to another,
And give you a proper reason for complaint.

ALCESTE: Faithless! How strange it is I love you still!

No doubt you cheat me with these easy words.
No matter; I must follow my destiny.
I have committed my spirit to your faith.
I must still watch to see what your heart's made of,
Whether it is so black it will betray me.

CÉLIMÈNE: You do not love me as a man should love.

ALCESTE: My love is too extreme for comparisons,
And in its eagerness to show itself,
It even imagines fantasies to your hurt.
Yes, I could wish that no one found you charming,
That you were reduced to some most wretched state,
That heaven had given you nothing at your birth,
Not rank, gentility, or property,
So that the public offering of my heart
Might then repair the injustice of your lot,
That I might have the glory and the joy
Of making you owe everything to my love.

CÉLIMÈNE: That's a peculiar way to wish me well!
May heaven preserve me from the chance occurring!
. . . But here's your man Du Bois! How odd he looks!

(*Enter* DU BOIS, *dressed in traveling costume, with high boots.*)

ALCESTE: What does this outfit mean? This frightened look? What's wrong?

DU BOIS: Monsieur—

ALCESTE: Well?

DU BOIS: Many mysteries!

ALCESTE: What is it?

DU BOIS: We're in a nasty situation!

ALCESTE: What?

DU BOIS: Shall I tell all?

ALCESTE: Yes, and be quick about it.

DU BOIS:	Isn't there someone here—
ALCESTE:	Oh, hurry up! Speak up!
DU BOIS:	Monsieur, we'll have to sound retreat!
ALCESTE:	How's that?
DU BOIS:	We must decamp, give ground, dislodge.
ALCESTE:	And why?
DU BOIS:	We must abandon our position.
ALCESTE:	What for?
DU BOIS:	We'll take the leave denoted French.
ALCESTE:	But tell me why you're giving this opinion.
DU BOIS:	Because, sir, we must fall back and re-form.
ALCESTE:	Oh, I will break your head in certainly, Unless you tell me what you mean, you rascal.
DU BOIS:	A man most dark, in costume and in manner, Came to our house and left on the kitchen table A paper couched in very barbarous style, Beyond the power of mortal man to fathom. It has to do, assuredly, with your lawsuit; But the devil himself could hardly understand it.
ALCESTE:	Villain, what has this paper got to do With the departure you've been talking of?
DU BOIS:	I mean to say, sir, a bare hour afterwards, A man who often pays his calls on you Came to inquire for you most urgently. And when he didn't find you, he ordered me, Knowing that I'm your very faithful servant, To give you a message—wait now, what's his name?
ALCESTE:	What did he tell you? Never mind his name.
DU BOIS:	Well, anyway, he's one of your good friends. He said that you're in danger, you must flee, And there's a chance that you may be arrested.
ALCESTE:	Didn't he tell you anything specific?

DU BOIS: No, he just asked to have some paper and ink,
              And wrote you a little note, which will reveal,
              As I suppose, the clue to the mystery.

ALCESTE: Then give it to me!

CÉLIMÈNE: What's at the bottom of this?

ALCESTE: I don't know yet; I hope to before long.
              Why can't you hurry, you damnable idiot?

DU BOIS   (*after a long search in his pockets*):
              Good faith, monsieur, I left it on your table.

ALCESTE: Why I don't hit you—

CÉLIMÈNE: Alceste, don't get angry.
              Hurry and find out what the trouble is.

ALCESTE: It seems that fate, in spite of my best efforts,
              Has sworn to interrupt our conversation.
              I won't be beaten; so, madame, permit me
              To see you again before the day is over.

ACT V

Enter ALCESTE *and* PHILINTE.

ALCESTE: I tell you I have quite made up my mind.

PHILINTE: However hard the blow may be, it needn't—

ALCESTE: There's no use talking, no use arguing;
              Nothing can turn me from my resolution.
              There's too much wickedness in the world today;
              I'm going to quit human society.
              What! Honor, justice, decency, and the law
              Are all arrayed against my adversary,
              And everyone proclaims my cause is just,
              And I'm at ease, in confidence of my rights—
              And yet I see myself betrayed by the outcome!
              Justice is on my side—I lose my case!
              A scoundrel, whose scandalous record is well known,

Triumphs, by means of filthy perjuries!
Thus honesty must yield to treachery!
He wins his victory by slaying me!
His false and grinning face he puts in the scales
To outweigh justice, upset equity!
He gets his crimes upheld by a court injunction!
And as if he hadn't done me harm enough,
There's a revolting book in circulation,
Which ought to be prohibited by law,
A book which deserves a pitiless punishment—
And he has the face to say that I'm the author!
And then we see Oronte nodding his head
And trying to substantiate the fraud!
Oronte, who plays the gentleman at court!
His only grievance is my sincerity.
He forced himself upon me, against my will,
To ask my judgment on his poetry;
And just because I use him honestly,
Unwilling to betray him, or truth either,
He helps to charge me with an imagined crime!
Now he's become my greatest enemy,
And never can I hope to have his pardon,
Because I would not call his sonnet good!
So that, *morbleu*, is the character of men!
These are the deeds their vanity inspires!
This is the virtue, the fidelity,
The justice and the honor of mankind!
I've suffered disillusion long enough;
It's time to leave this den of thieves and cutthroats.
Since men make here a society of wolves,
I shall not spend the rest of my life among them.

PHILINTE: Your verdict seems to me a little hasty;
The evil's not so great as you assume.
The imputations of your adversary

Have not availed to compass your arrest.
His perjury may well be undermined;
Perhaps this time he's overreached himself.

ALCESTE: Oh, he doesn't mind publicity for his tricks!
Roguery is his regular stock in trade,
And this adventure, far from injuring him,
Tomorrow will put him in a better posture.

PHILINTE: Anyway, people clearly don't much credit
The story he's maliciously invented.
You needn't be alarmed in that regard.
As for the lawsuit, you may properly grumble,
But you have legal grounds for an appeal
Against the judgment—

ALCESTE: No, I want to accept it.
Although the verdict does me injury,
I've no intention of getting it reversed.
It's a pure case of justice's miscarriage;
I want to leave it to posterity
To be a famous mark and testimony
To the scoundrelism of the present day.
It may well cost me twenty thousand francs,
But twenty thousand francs will give me the right
To curse the iniquity of human nature,
And cherish an unfailing hate for it.

PHILINTE: But after all—

ALCESTE: But after all, don't bother.
There's nothing on this theme that you can tell me.
You wouldn't go so far as to excuse
The horrors of the present situation?

PHILINTE: No, I'll agree with everything you please.
The world is run by selfish interest,
And trickery and graft are in the saddle,
And man should be a different kind of creature.
But is his guiltiness sufficient reason

To drive us out of his society?
These human failings furnish us with means
Of exercising our philosophy,
And that's the best employment for our virtue.
If truth and rectitude were universal,
If every heart were frank and reasonable,
Most of the virtues would be meaningless,
Because they enable us to bear serenely
The injustice of others, when our cause is just.
And even as an honorable heart—

ALCESTE: I know that you're a very brilliant talker;
You always have most wonderful arguments.
But now you're wasting both your talk and time.
It would be prudent for me to retire.
I cannot properly control my tongue.
I dare not answer for my spoken words;
I'd have a dozen squabbles on my hands.
Let me, without more talk, see Célimène.
She must consent to what I have in mind.
I shall discover if she really loves me;
This is the moment which will prove the case.

PHILINTE: We'd better wait in Éliante's apartment.

ALCESTE: No, I am too disquieted in mind.
You go and see her; leave me here alone
In this dark corner with my gloomy heart.
(*He sits in a shadowed corner of the room.*)

PHILINTE: That's no companion for your solitude.
I'll beg of Éliante that she come down.
(*Exit* PHILINTE. *Enter* CÉLIMÈNE *and* ORONTE.)

ORONTE: Madame, the choice is yours: to bind me to you
In love's delicious bonds, if that's your will.
But I must have assurance of your spirit;
A lover cannot bear uncertainty.
If I have moved you by my fervent passion,

You should not hesitate to let me know it.
And here's the evidence I ask of you:
No longer to permit Alceste to court you,
To sacrifice him to my love, madame,
And forthwith to forbid his presence here.

CÉLIMÈNE: But what's the reason for your irritation?
I've heard you talk so often of his merits.

ORONTE: Madame, it's not the time for explanations.
The essential thing to know is, what are your feelings?
So please decide to keep one man or the other;
For on your resolution mine depends.

ALCESTE   (*emerging from his retreat*):
The gentleman is right; you'll have to choose.
For his request and my desire agree.
My love, like his, demands an explanation;
My love requires an evidence of yours.
Things cannot drag on longer in this manner.
The time has come for you to declare yourself.

ORONTE: I do not wish, sir, by my urgencies
To bring disturbance to your happiness.

ALCESTE: I do not wish, sir, whether jealous or not,
To make division of her heart with you.

ORONTE: If she prefers your courtship to my own—

ALCESTE: If she has even a slight regard for you—

ORONTE: I swear that I shall make no claim upon her.

ALCESTE: I swear that I shall never see her again.

ORONTE: Madame, you're free to speak without reserve.

ALCESTE: Madame, explain yourself without a qualm.

ORONTE: You only need to say who has your heart.

ALCESTE: You only need to choose between us two.

ORONTE: What! The decision seems to embarrass you?

ALCESTE: What! You are wavering and disconcerted?

CÉLIMÈNE: But this insistence is quite out of place,
And both of you are most unreasonable!

Of course I know what my own preference is;
It's not my heart that's wavering, undecided.
It isn't balancing between you two,
And I could make my choice immediately.
But really, I am tortured at the thought
Of uttering such admissions to your face.
Such words as these are bound to be unpleasant;
They shouldn't be spoken in another's presence.
I think we show our feelings clearly enough
Without being forced to such crude revelations.
There are more kindly ways to break the news
To a lover that his addresses are unwelcome.

ORONTE: No, I am not afraid of a frank admission.
For my part, I consent.

ALCESTE: And I insist.
And what I ask for is an open statement;
I don't want any feelings to be spared.
You're too concerned with holding everyone.
So now, no more delay and uncertainty!
You must explain yourself upon this matter,
Or I shall take a refusal as a verdict;
Your silence I shall understand to mean
The confirmation of my worst suspicions.

ORONTE: I am obliged, sir, for your angry words.
I put to her the same request that you do.

CÉLIMÈNE: Oh, how you bore me with this freak of yours!
Can there be any sense in your demand?
Didn't I tell the motive which restrains me?
But here is Éliante; let her be judge.
(*Enter* ÉLIANTE *and* PHILINTE)
Cousin, I'm being persecuted here
By a pair of gentlemen with a fixed idea.
They both insist, with an excessive heat,
That I declare my preference between them,

That I forbid, by a public declaration,
One of the two to pay me courtesies.
Have people ever acted in this way?

ÉLIANTE: You needn't appeal to me upon the subject.
You might find my decision most unwelcome.
I am in favor of saying what one thinks.

ORONTE: Madame, you are defending yourself in vain.

ALCESTE: Your shifts and dodges get no countenance here.

ORONTE: You must declare yourself; stop paltering.

ALCESTE: If you persist in keeping silence, of course—

ORONTE: A single word's enough to settle things.

ALCESTE: Even without a word, I'll get my answer.

                (*Enter* ACASTE, CLITANDRE, *and* ARSINOÉ.)

ACASTE   (*to* CÉLIMÈNE):

Madame, we two have come, if you don't mind,
To get some light upon a little matter.

CLITANDRE: And gentlemen, your presence is convenient,
For you too are concerned in the affair.

ARSINOÉ: Madame, you'll be surprised to see me here,
But these two gentlemen are responsible.
They came to see me and they made a complaint
About a circumstance I couldn't believe.
For I esteem too much your character
To think you capable of such a misdeed.
I wouldn't credit the evidence they showed me;
My friendship disregards our little quarrel.
So I consented to accompany them,
To see you clear yourself of this calumny.

ACASTE: Let us be calm, madame, and let us see
How you will go about explaining this.
Here is a letter which you wrote Clitandre.

CLITANDRE: And here is a tender note you wrote Acaste.

ACASTE: Gentlemen, you must recognize this writing.

I do not doubt that she's been kind enough
To give you all examples of her hand.
But this is really worth being read aloud:
"You're a strange fellow, Clitandre, to complain
of my cheerfulness and to reproach me because
I'm never so happy as when I am not with you.
Nothing could be more unjust; and if you don't
come soon to ask my pardon for this offense, I
won't forgive you as long as I live. Our big
gawky vicomte—" He really should be here! "Our
big gawky vicomte, whom you complain about,
is a man I could never like; and since the time
I watched him, for a good three quarters of an
hour, spitting into a well to make rings, I have
never been able to hold a good opinion of him.
As for the little marquis—" If I may say so without vanity, that's me. "As for the little marquis,
who held my hand so long yesterday while escort-
ing me, I think he's about as insignificant as it is
possible to be; all his merit lies in his cloak and
sword. As for the man with the green ribbons—"
(*To* ALCESTE) Now it's your turn, sir. "As for the
man with the green ribbons, he sometimes amuses
me with his bluntness and his sour humors; but
there are many times when I find him most irri-
tating. And as for the man with the short coat—"
(*To* ORONTE) Here's your present. "As for the
man with the short coat, who is going in for in-
tellect and wants to be an author in spite of everybody, I can't take the trouble to listen to what he
says, and I find his prose as tiresome as his verse.
So please understand that I don't always have as
good a time as you think, and that I miss you

sorely in all the parties I am dragged to, and that
the presence of people one is really fond of is the
best seasoning for social amusements."

CLITANDRE: And now here I am.

"Your Clitandre, whom you mention, with his
cooing manner, is the last man I could really care
for. It is absurd for you to imagine that one could
be fond of him, and you are absurd to think that
one is not fond of you. To be reasonable, just reverse your opinions; and see me as much as you
can, to help me to bear the distress of being bored
by him."

So there's a noble character depicted.
You know the common name of it, madame?
Enough. We'll go together to pay some calls,
And show the glorious portrait of your heart.

ACASTE: There's plenty of subject here for my reproaches,
But I don't think you're worthy of my anger.
I'll show you that the little marquises
Can find more honest hearts for their consolation.
(*Exit* ACASTE *and* CLITANDRE.)

ORONTE: So this is the way I find myself traduced,
Despite the gulling words you've written me!
Your heart, displaying the tinsel shams of love,
Offers itself to the whole human race!
I was a dupe; I shall be dupe no more.
You do me a service by this revelation.
I gain my heart, which you return to me,
And in your loss of it my vengeance lies.
(*To* ALCESTE)
Sir, I remove an obstacle from your path.
You may conclude your business with Madame
(*Exit* ORONTE.)

ARSINOÉ: Really, I'm shocked by this unhappy business!

It makes me furious; I can't hold back.
Has anyone ever seen such strange behavior?
Disregarding the other gentlemen,
Alceste, whom your good fortune drew to you,
A gentleman of merit and of honor,
A gentleman who simply idolized you,
Did he deserve—

ALCESTE: Permit me, please, madame,
To handle my own interests in the case.
You needn't assume unnecessary burdens.
However much you may espouse my cause,
I can't repay your zeal with any affection;
And if in vengeance I should seek a heart
As substitute, the heart would not be yours.

ARSINOÉ: Ho! Do you think, sir, that I had that thought?
That one could be so eager to possess you?
I think you're overfull of vanity,
If you have flattered yourself with that belief!
The cast-offs of Madame are articles
With which no sensible woman could be pleased.
Open your eyes, don't be so high and mighty;
I'm not the sort of person that you need.
You will do better to dangle after her;
I'm looking forward to that glorious match!
(*Exit* ARSINOÉ.)

ALCESTE: Well, in despite of all, I have kept silence,
And I've allowed everyone else to speak.
Have I controlled myself sufficiently,
And may I now—

CÉLIMÈNE: Yes, you may say it all.
You have the right to make complaint of me,
And to reproach me for—whatever you wish.
I'm wrong, and I admit it. I'm confused.
I shall not try to find some vain excuse.

I can despise the anger of the others;
I must admit I have mistreated you.
Your bitterness is only reasonable;
I know too well how guilty I must seem,
How everything proclaims my treachery,
How, finally, you have good cause to hate me.
Hate me, then; I submit.

ALCESTE: Oh, faithless, can I?
Can I thus triumph over all my love?
However eagerly I wish to hate you,
Have I a heart that's ready to obey?
(*To* ÉLIANTE *and* PHILINTE)
You see the power of an unworthy love;
I make you both witnesses of my weakness.
But that's not all my weakness, I'm afraid;
You'll see me carry it to exaggeration,
And show how far from reasonable men are,
For man's essential frailty hides in the heart.
(*To* CÉLIMÈNE)
Yes, I will willingly forget your offenses
And find excuses for them in my mind,
I'll call them merely the infirmities
Which the conventions of our time encourage,
Provided you sincerely join with me
In my design, to flee society,
Provided you agree forthwith to share
My solitude, where I have vowed to live.
That is the only way you can repair
The hurt your words have done your reputation.
Thus, after this abominable scene,
My heart will have the right to love you still.

CÉLIMÈNE: What, leave society before I'm old,
And go and bury myself in your solitude?

ALCESTE: Why, if your passion corresponds with mine,

What do you care for all the rest of the world?
And can you not be satisfied with me?

CÉLIMÈNE: I'm only twenty; solitude terrifies me.
I fear that I am just not strong enough
To take upon myself so high a purpose.
But if our union can be recompense,
I can determine to accept its bonds;
And marriage—

ALCESTE: No. Now I have learned to hate you.
This is your one unpardonable deed.
Since you acknowledge that you cannot find
Your all in me, as I find all in you,
I shall not marry you. This last offense
Frees me forever from my long subjection.

(CÉLIMÈNE *goes upstage;* ALCESTE *turns his back
on her. She turns, curtsies, awaits a word from him,
then snaps open her fan resolutely, and exits. To*
ÉLIANTE)

Madame, you're virtuous and beautiful;
I recognize your frank sincerity.
Long have I honored and respected you.
Let my esteem remain the same, unaltered.
Suffer that in my manifold afflictions
I make no offering of my troubled heart.
I am not worthy. I begin to know
That heaven did not destine me for wedlock.
A heart refused by your inferior
Would be for you a most unworthy homage.

ÉLIANTE: Why, you may follow this thought to its conclusion;
And I may grant my favors where I will.
I might perchance find someone like our friend here
Who would accept my hand, if I should ask him.

PHILINTE: Madame, this honor is my sole desire;
I'd sacrifice my life, my blood, for it.

ALCESTE: May you forever keep this way of feeling
            One for the other, and gain true happiness.
            While I, betrayed, and loaded with injustice,
            Flee from this dunghill home of every vice,
            And seek some lonely cranny of the earth
            Where a man is free to be a man of honor.
            (*Exit* ALCESTE.)
PHILINTE: Madame, come, let us employ ourselves
            To thwart the purpose of his unruly heart.

The Physician
in Spite of Himself

Le Médecin malgré lui was staged on August 6, 1666, only two months after *The Misanthrope*. The most serious of Molière's plays was succeeded by the loudest and funniest. There is no reason to seek deep meanings in the contrast. The box office proved what the public wanted. Molière was tagged as a low comedian, and he could change his style only at his own peril and at that of his playhouse. Anyway, he loved farces, and in the part of Sganarelle he loved the big play-stopping laugh.

He took therefore (presumably) one of his early farces, now lost, and built it up with suggestions from a medieval French *fabliau*, from Rabelais, from the *commedia dell' arte*, to make a series of well-tested gags on a sufficient plot.

The play is included here as an example of Molière's popular farce, written only in the hope that it would make people laugh through the season. But its comic principles and tricks are so fundamental that it still makes people laugh. It runs second only to *Tartuffe* in the number of recorded performances of Molière's plays.

If the reader finds it almost too fantastic in its suppositions, structure, and characters, he should endeavor to picture it as a performance on a stage in his mind. The dialogue is not much more than a pretext for the business. If the reader thus co-operates, he should feel the play's dramatic vitality, which is surely an artistic merit. He would appreciate still better the universality of its humor if he should see it produced with noisy gusto, whether at the Comédie Française or on the stage of an American college dramatic society.

The Characters

SGANARELLE

MARTINE, his wife

MONSIEUR ROBERT, his neighbor

GÉRONTE

LUCINDE, his daughter

LÉANDRE, suitor of Lucinde

VALÈRE, steward of Géronte

LUCAS, peasant

JACQUELINE, his wife

THIBAUT, peasant

PERRIN, his son

ACT I

The scene is the exterior of SGANARELLE's *tumble-down house. Enter* SGANARELLE *and* MARTINE, *quarreling.*

SGANARELLE: I won't. I tell you I won't. And when I say something around here, it's an order.

MARTINE: And I tell you that I'll tell you how to behave. I didn't marry you in order to put up with your tricks and dodges.

SGANARELLE: Oh, what a burden is a wife, is it not indeed! How

287

right was Aristotle, when he said that a wife is worse than a demon!

MARTINE: What a smart fellow it is, with his half-wit Aristotle!

SGANARELLE: Yes, a smart fellow. You won't find another woodcutter who knows how to argue like me, and who worked for a famous doctor for six years, and who knew his First Latin Book by heart when he was a boy.

MARTINE: A plague on the champion fool!

SGANARELLE: A plague on the slut!

MARTINE: Cursed be the day and the hour when I took it into my head to say "I do!"

SGANARELLE: Cursed be the cuckold of a notary who made me sign my own destruction!

MARTINE: It's a nice thing for you to complain of that affair! Should you let a single minute go by without thanking heaven for having me for your wife? Did you deserve to marry a person like me?

SGANARELLE: Certainly you did me too much honor; and I had good reason to congratulate myself on our wedding night! Damnation! Don't get me going on that topic; I could say a few things—

MARTINE: And what could you say?

SGANARELLE: That's enough. We'll drop the subject. Just remember that we know what we know, and you were very lucky to find me.

MARTINE: What do you mean, lucky to find you? A man who is bringing me to the poorhouse, a drunkard, a good-for-nothing, who eats up everything I've got—

SGANARELLE: That's a lie. I drink part of it.

MARTINE: —who is selling off, bit by bit, everything in the house—

SGANARELLE: We mustn't let our possessions possess us.

MARTINE: —who has even got rid of my own bed—

SGANARELLE: You won't sleep so late.

MARTINE: —who won't leave a single stick of furniture in the house—

SGANARELLE: That makes moving easier.

MARTINE: —and who spends the whole day, from morning till night, drinking and gambling.

SGANARELLE: Well, I hate to be bored.

MARTINE: And while that goes on, what do you expect me to do with my family?

SGANARELLE: Anything you like.

MARTINE: I have four poor little children on my hands.

SGANARELLE: Put them on the floor.

MARTINE: And they keep forever crying out for bread.

SGANARELLE: Give them a good whipping. When I have had plenty to eat and drink, I like everyone in the house to have his bellyful.

MARTINE: And you expect, you drunken lout, that things are going to go on forever this way?

SGANARELLE: My dear wife, calm down.

MARTINE: And I'm to put up with your drink and debauchery to the end of time?

SGANARELLE: Now, let's not get excited, darling.

MARTINE: And I won't find some way to make you behave?

SGANARELLE: Sweetie, you know I'm not very patient, and I have a strong right arm.

MARTINE: I'm not afraid of your threats.

SGANARELLE: My little lollipop, you're itching for something, as usual.

MARTINE: I'll show you I'm not afraid of you.

SGANARELLE: My dainty pet, there's something you want me to give you.

MARTINE: You think you frighten me with your talk?

SGANARELLE: Fair object of my eternal vows, I'll knock your ears in.

MARTINE: Boozer!

SGANARELLE: I shall flog and flail you.

MARTINE: Souse!

SGANARELLE: I shall pummel and buffet.

MARTINE: Dirty no-good!

SGANARELLE: I shall administer the lash.

MARTINE: Rascal! Puppy! Deceiver! Coward! Scoundrel! Gallows-bird! Beggar! Waster! Rogue! Villain! Thief!

SGANARELLE (*takes a stick and beats her*): Well, you asked for it.

MARTINE: Oh, oh, oh, oh!

SGANARELLE: That's the best way to calm you down.

(*Enter* MONSIEUR ROBERT.)

M. ROBERT: Hello! Here, here, here! What's all this! This is an outrage! Confound the fellow, for beating his wife that way!

MARTINE (*her arms akimbo, forces* MONSIEUR ROBERT *backward step by step during the following dialogue*): And supposing I want to have him beat me?

M. ROBERT: Oh, well, then, I consent heartily.

MARTINE: What are you meddling for?

M. ROBERT: I was quite wrong.

MARTINE: Is it any business of yours?

M. ROBERT: No; no indeed.

MARTINE: Will you take a look at this butter-in, who wants to prevent husbands from beating their wives?

M. ROBERT: I take it all back.

MARTINE: Do you have some interest in the matter?

M. ROBERT: None at all.

MARTINE: Then why do you stick your nose in?

M. ROBERT: I'm sorry.

MARTINE: Mind your own business.

M. ROBERT: I will indeed.

MARTINE: I like to be beaten.

M. ROBERT: Excellent.

MARTINE: It doesn't hurt you any.

M. ROBERT: Quite right.

MARTINE: And you're a fool to come meddling in things which are no affair of yours.

> (MARTINE *slaps* MONSIEUR ROBERT's *face.* MONSIEUR ROBERT *escapes her, runs to center, and is confronted by* SGANARELLE.)

M. ROBERT: Comrade, with all my heart I ask your pardon. Go ahead, beat and drub your wife properly. I will help you, if you like.

> (*During the following dialogue,* SGANARELLE *forces* MONSIEUR ROBERT *backward, threateningly, paralleling the previous business with* MARTINE.)

SGANARELLE: But I don't like.

M. ROBERT: Oh, well, that's different.

SGNARELLE: I want to beat her if I want to; and I don't want to beat her if I don't want to.

M. ROBERT: Splendid!

SGANARELLE: She's my wife; she isn't your wife.

M. ROBERT: That's right.

SGANARELLE: You can't give me any orders.

M. ROBERT: I agree; I agree.

SGANARELLE: I don't need any help from you.

M. ROBERT: Absolutely not.

SGANARELLE: And you're an insolent meddler, to come and interfere in other people's affairs. Learn that Cicero says: "Put not the bark between thy finger and the tree." (SGANARELLE *beats* MONSIEUR ROBERT, *and drives him off the stage. He returns to* MARTINE.) Well now, let's make peace. Shake hands.

MARTINE: Yes, indeed! After beating me that way!

SGANARELLE: That's nothing. Shake hands.

MARTINE: I don't want to.

SGANARELLE: Eh?

MARTINE: No.

SGANARELLE: My sweet little wife!

MARTINE: I won't.

SGANARELLE: Oh, come on!

MARTINE: Nothing of the sort.

SGANARELLE: Come on, come on!

MARTINE: No. I'd rather be angry.

SGANARELLE: What, for just a trifle? Come on!

MARTINE: Let me alone.

SGANARELLE: Shake hands, I tell you.

MARTINE: You hurt me too much.

SGANARELLE: All right then, I ask your pardon. Give me your hand.

MARTINE: Oh, very well. I pardon you. (*Aside*) But you'll pay for it!

SGANARELLE: You're silly to take the matter seriously. Those little flare-ups are sometimes necessary to true friendship; and five or six good wallops, between lovers, merely stimulate affection. Now I'm off to the woods. I promise to bring in today more than a hundred bundles of kindling wood.

(*Exit* SGANARELLE.)

MARTINE: Well, no matter how I pretend, I can't forget how you hurt me. I'd like to find a good way to punish you for that beating. I know that a woman always has a way to take revenge on her husband. But that's too dainty a punishment for that scalawag; it wouldn't be satisfaction enough for the way he's treated me. I want a revenge he'll feel down to his bones.

(*Enter* VALÈRE *and* LUCAS. *They do not immediately perceive* MARTINE.)

LUCAS: By gosh and by gum! Ain't that a queer job we took on! I be switched if I know how she's going to turn out.

VALÈRE: Well, Uncle Lucas, what can we do? We have to obey our master. And besides, we both have an interest in the recovery of his daughter, the young mistress. No doubt we'll get some good presents at her marriage, which is postponed by her illness. Horace is quite likely to be accepted as a suitor, and he's free with his money. And although she has shown her preference for a certain Léandre, you know very well that her father has always refused to accept him as a son-in-law.

MARTINE (*who has been absorbedly meditating, without noticing* VALÈRE *and* LUCAS):   I wonder if I can't cook up some scheme to get my revenge.

LUCAS: But what kind of fool idea has the master took into his noodle, now the doctors say they're all up a tree?

VALÈRE: Well, sometimes, by just hunting, one finds unexpected help; and often among simple people in out-of-the-way places . . .

MARTINE: Yes, I'm going to get my revenge, at any price. Those cudgel blows still smart; I won't stand for them. (*In her distraction, she bumps into the newcomers*) Oh, gentlemen, I ask your pardon. I didn't see you; I was trying to think out an answer to some troubles of mine.

VALÈRE: Everyone has his troubles in this world. In fact, we were trying to find an answer to some troubles of our own.

MARTINE: Would it be anything I could help you in?

VALÈRE: Possibly. We are trying to find a gifted man, a special sort of doctor, who might bring some relief to our master's daughter. She has been attacked by a disease which suddenly deprived her of all power of speech. Several physicians have already exhausted all their science on her. But sometimes one runs across people who possess some wonderful secrets of nature, certain special remedies, which accomplish what the regular doctors can't do. That's what we're looking for.

MARTINE (*aside*):   Heaven inspires me with a great idea for getting revenge on my rapscallion husband! (*Aloud*) You couldn't land on a better person to give you a tip. There's a fellow around here who is just wonderful for desperate cases.

VALÈRE: Do tell me, where could we find him?

MARTINE: You can find him now in that little wood over yonder. He's amusing himself by cutting wood.

LUCAS: A doctor cutting wood!

VALÈRE: Amusing himself by gathering herbs, you mean?

MARTINE: No; he's a very peculiar man who enjoys doing that. He's queer, fantastic, crotchety; you'd never take him for what he is. He goes around dressed in funny old clothes, and sometimes he pretends to be ignorant; he keeps all his knowledge hidden, and he always hates to exercise the marvelous talents for medicine which heaven has given him.

VALÈRE: It's a remarkable thing that great men always have some fantasticality, some little touch of folly mingled with their knowledge.

MARTINE: This man's folly is greater than you'd believe. Sometimes it goes so far that he has to be beaten before he'll admit his abilities; and I warn you that if he's in that mood you'll never make him admit he's a doctor, unless you both take sticks and pound him well until he finally confesses what he'll hide from you at first. That's what we do around here when we need his services.

VALÈRE: What a strange folly!

MARTINE: True enough; but afterwards, you'll see that he can do real marvels.

VALÈRE: What's his name?

MARTINE: His name is Sganarelle. It's easy to recognize him. He has a big black beard, and he wears a ruff, and a green and yellow coat.

LUCAS: Green and yaller! He's a doctor for parrots, then?[1]

VALÈRE: But is it really true that he's so clever as all that?

MARTINE: Why, he's a man who works miracles! Six months ago there was a woman here given up by all the other doctors. They thought she was dead, and were getting ready to lay her

[1] Physicians invariably wore black gowns.

out. And six hours afterwards the man I'm telling about was dragged in by main strength. He looked her over and put a little drop of something or other in her mouth, and right away she got up off her bed and started walking around the room as if nothing had happened.

LUCAS: Aha!

VALÈRE: It must have been a drop of potable gold.

MARTINE: You may be right. And only three weeks ago a twelve-year-old boy fell down from the top of the belfry, and he landed on the pavement and broke his arms, his legs, and his head. Well, as soon as they brought in this fellow, he rubbed the boy all over with a certain ointment he knows how to make. And immediately the boy stood right up, and ran off to shoot marbles.

LUCAS: Aha!

VALÈRE: That man must have the universal panacea.

MARTINE: No doubt about it.

LUCAS: By gee and by golly! That's just the man we're alookin' for. Let's go git him.

VALÈRE: We are much obliged to you for your useful suggestion.

MARTINE: But anyhow, remember the warning I gave you.

LUCAS: Dad-burn and dad-blast! Trust us! If all he needs is a beating up, we've got the pig in the poke.

(*Exit* MARTINE.)

VALÈRE: We were very lucky to run into that good woman. She really gives me some high hopes.

(*Enter* SGANARELLE, *brandishing a bottle and singing.*)

SGANARELLE: La, la, la.

VALÈRE: I heard someone cutting wood; and now he's singing.

SGANARELLE: La, la, la . . . That's enough work for a while. Let's take a little breather. (*He drinks*) Nothing like wood-cutting to dry a man out. (*He sings*)

　　　　Oh, how pretty

> Is my little brown jug!
> Oh, how pretty
> Is your glug-glug-glug!
> But everybody else would be jealous of me
> If you were always as full as can be;
> So little brown jug, let me give you a hug,
> Turn your pretty bottom up, little brown jug!

God's truth, we must defend ourselves against morbid melancholia.

VALÈRE: That's the man himself.

LUCAS: I reckon you're right; we've landed smack onto him.

VALÈRE: Let's get closer.

SGANARELLE: Naughty little bottle! How I love my little cutie! (*Perceives* LUCAS *and* VALÈRE; *watches them, turning alternately toward one and the other; lets his voice die away*) Everybody else . . . would be . . . jealous of me . . . What the devil! Have those fellows got it in for somebody?

VALÈRE: That's the man, certainly.

LUCAS: It's his spit and image, like they told us.

SGANARELLE: They are whispering to each other. What's the idea?

> (*He puts his bottle on the ground. As* VALÈRE *makes him a deep bow,* SGANARELLE *suspects him of designs on the bottle, whisks it to the other side. When* LUCAS *makes a similar bow,* SGANARELLE *seizes the bottle and holds it against his stomach.*)

VALÈRE: I beg your pardon, sir. Aren't you the gentleman named Sganarelle?

SGANARELLE: What's all this?

VALÈRE: I am asking you if your name isn't Sganarelle.

SGANARELLE (*after making a close inspection of* VALÈRE, *and then of* LUCAS): Well, yes and no. Depends on what you want.

VALÈRE: All we want is to pay him our warmest respects.

SGANARELLE: In that case, my name is Sganarelle.

VALÈRE: Sir, we are delighted to meet you. We have been re-
ferred to you for our present purposes; so we have come to
implore your assistance in our present need.

SGANARELLE: If it is something, gentlemen, which pertains to
my little business, I am prepared to render you every service.

VALÈRE: Sir, you are all too kind. But, sir, put on your hat, I
beg you; you might find the sunshine too strong.

LUCAS: Yes, kindly put your lid on.

SGANARELLE (*aside*):   Polite, anyhow.

VALÈRE: Sir, you must not find it strange that we have recourse
to you. Men of ability are always sought out; and we have been
informed of your exceptional capacities.

SGANARELLE: It is true, gentlemen, that I am probably the first
man in the world in the kindling-wood line.

VALÈRE: Ah, sir—

SGANARELLE: I spare no pains or trouble. I go so far as to say
that no criticism of my kindling wood is possible.

VALÈRE: Sir, that matter is not in question.

SGANARELLE: But observe that I sell it at a hundred and ten
sous for a hundred sticks.

VALÈRE: We needn't discuss that.

SGANARELLE: I assure you that I can't give it to you for less.

VALÈRE: Sir, we have been informed—

SGANARELLE: If you have been informed, you know that that
is the price.

VALÈRE: Sir, please don't be ridiculous.

SGANARELLE: Nothing ridiculous about it. I can't take off a
penny.

VALÈRE: Let's take another approach—

SGANARELLE: Of course you can get it cheaper elsewhere. There
is kindling wood and kindling wood. But as for my kindling
wood—

VALÈRE: Sir, let's drop this subject—

SGANARELLE: I swear to you that you can't have it for a farthing less.

VALÈRE: Damn!

SGANARELLE: No, on my conscience, that's the price you'll have to pay. I am speaking with all sincerity, and I'm not the kind of man who would overcharge.

VALÈRE: Why, sir, should a person like you indulge in these clumsy pretenses? Why degrade yourself to talk in such a way? Why should a learned man, a physician like you, try to disguise himself before the public, and keep his great talents hidden?

SGANARELLE (*aside*):   He's crazy.

VALÈRE: Sir, kindly do not dissimulate with us.

SGANARELLE: What?

LUCAS: No use fiddlin' around with us; we know what's what.

SGANARELLE: What! What are you trying to give me? What do you take me for?

VALÈRE: We take you for what you are: a great physician.

SGANARELLE: Physician yourself. I'm no physician, and I never have been.

VALÈRE (*to* LUCAS):   There's his mania. (*To* SGANARELLE) Sir, kindly make no further denials. Do not force us to extreme and painful measures.

SGANARELLE: What do you mean?

VALÈRE: To expedients which would be distressing to us.

SGANARELLE: 'Struth! Use any expedients you like. I'm not a physician, and I don't know what you're talking about.

VALÈRE (*to* LUCAS):   I can see that we'll have to employ the usual system. (*To* SGANARELLE) Once more, sir, I beg you to admit you are what you are.

LUCAS: Gol-ding and gol-darn! No more messin' around! Come clean and spit it out and say you're a doctor!

SGANARELLE (*aside*):   They give me a pain!

VALÈRE: Why deny what everyone knows?

LUCAS: What's the use of all this flimflam? What good does it do you?

SGANARELLE: Gentlemen, I tell you simply and flatly: I am not a doctor.

VALÈRE: You are not a doctor?

SGANARELLE: No.

LUCAS: You ain't no doctor?

SGANARELLE: No, I tell you.

VALÈRE: Since you insist, we'll have to go through with it.

(VALÈRE *and* LUCAS *pick up sticks and beat* SGANA-RELLE.)

SGANARELLE: Oh, oh, oh! Gentlemen, I am anything you like!

VALÈRE: Why, sir, do you oblige us to resort to this violence?

LUCAS: Why do you bullyrag us into beating you up?

VALÈRE: Let me assure you of my profoundest regrets.

LUCAS: B'jeez, I'm sorry, Doc.

SGANARELLE: What the devil is all this, anyway? Is it a joke? Or are you both crazy, to insist I'm a doctor?

VALÈRE: What? You still won't surrender? You won't admit you're a doctor?

SGANARELLE: Like the devil I'm a doctor!

LUCAS: It ain't true you're a doc, hey?

SGANARELLE: No, plague take me! (VALÈRE *and* LUCAS *beat* SGANARELLE) Oh, oh! All right, gentlemen, all right! I'm a doctor, if that's what you want! I'm a physician, and an apothecary too, if you like. I'll consent to everything rather than be beaten to death.

VALÈRE: Why, that's excellent, sir. I am delighted to see you in a reasonable mood.

LUCAS: I sure am tickled to hear you talk thataway.

VALÈRE: I ask your most sincere pardon.

LUCAS: Please excuse me for takin' the liberty.

SGANARELLE (*aside*):   Hey, hey! Maybe I'm the one who was

mistaken! Maybe I've become a doctor without knowing it.

VALÈRE: Sir, you will have no reason to regret revealing your true self. I am sure you will have every reason for satisfaction.

SGANARELLE: But, gentlemen, tell me, couldn't you be mistaken yourselves? Is it quite certain that I'm a physician?

LUCAS: Yes, by ding and by dog!

SGANARELLE: Honestly?

VALÈRE: Unquestionably.

SGANARELLE: The devil take me if I knew it!

VALÈRE: What do you mean? You're the cleverest doctor on earth!

SGANARELLE: Aha!

LUCAS: A doc who's cured I don't know how many ails and complaints.

SGANARELLE: Bless my soul!

VALÈRE: A woman was considered dead for six hours; they were ready to lay her out, when you gave her a drop of something and she came to and began walking around the room.

SGANARELLE: I'll be hanged!

LUCAS: A twelve-year-old boy fell down off the top of a belfry, and he got his arms and legs and head busted; and you put some kind of salve onto him, and he stood right up on his feet and went off and shot marbles!

SGANARELLE: Marbles!

VALÈRE: In short, sir, you will be well satisfied with our treatment; and you will earn whatever you like, if you let us take you to a certain place.

SGANARELLE: I will earn whatever I like?

VALÈRE: Yes.

SGANARELLE: Oho! I'm a physician! No question about it. It had slipped my mind; but now I remember. What is the trouble? Where do we have to go?

VALÈRE: We'll take you there. We are to see a girl who has lost her speech.

SGANARELLE: Faith, I haven't found it.

VALÈRE: He likes his little joke. Come on, sir.

SGANARELLE: Without a doctor's gown?

VALÈRE: We'll get one.

SGANARELLE (*solemnly presents his bottle to* VALÈRE):   Take that. That's what I keep my potions in. (*Turns to* LUCAS; *spits on the ground*) Now, you walk in front. Doctor's orders.

LUCAS: By gosh and by golly! There's the kind of doctor I like! I think he'll do all right, because he's funny.[2]

ACT II

A room in GÉRONTE's *house.* GÉRONTE, VALÈRE, LUCAS, *and* JACQUELINE *are discovered.*

VALÈRE: Yes, sir, I think you will be satisfied. We have brought you the greatest physician on earth.

LUCAS: Yes, by dad and by dang; he's a feller who can't be beat. All the others ain't knee-high to him.

VALÈRE: He's a man who has made some marvelous cures.

LUCAS: He even cured some who was dead.

VALÈRE: He's a little eccentric, as I told you. And sometimes he has spells when his wits wander and he doesn't seem quite himself.

LUCAS: Yes, he likes to be funny; and sometimes, pardon the liberty, you might say he'd been hit on the head with an ax.

VALÈRE: But under it all, he's a man of profound knowledge. Sometimes he says some very remarkable things.

LUCAS: When he puts his mind to it, he spits it out as if he was reading right off a book.

VALÈRE: His reputation has spread about the region, and everyone goes to consult him.

GÉRONTE: I am dying to see him. Bring him to me right away.

2 Some critics see in this phrase a covert reference to Molière's pique at the relative ill success of *The Misanthrope.*

VALÈRE: I'll go and fetch him.

(*Exit* VALÈRE.)

JACQUELINE: Land's sake, sir, this man won't do no more than the others. It'll be six of one and half a dozen of the other. The best medicine you could give your daughter, if you'll heed me, would be a fine likely husband she'd be sweet on.

GÉRONTE: Well, well, my good nurse! You have a lot of opinions to express!

LUCAS: Shut up, old girl! You got no call to stick your nose in.

JACQUELINE: I vow and declare that all these doctors won't do no more good than so much plain water; and your daughter needs something else than rhubarb and senna; and a husband is a poultice who cures all a young girl's troubles.

GÉRONTE: Is she in any state now to be saddled with a husband, with her present affliction? And when I proposed to marry her off, didn't she oppose my wishes?

JACQUELINE: Sure and certain she did. You wanted to rig her out with a husband she couldn't abide. Why didn't you pick that Monsieur Léandre she was crazy about? She would have been fine and obedient; and I bet you he'd take her right now, the way she is, if you wanted to give her to him.

GÉRONTE: That Léandre is not the right person. He is much poorer than the other man.

JACQUELINE: He's got a rich uncle, and he's the heir.

GÉRONTE: All these great expectations seem to me very chancy. There's nothing like having your own money in your own hands. It's very risky to count on property which someone else intends for you. Death doesn't always listen to the prayers and pleas of the heirs; and a man has time to starve, while he is waiting for someone else to die so that he may live his own life.

JACQUELINE: Well, I've always heard folks tell that in marriage, like in everything else, it's better to be happy than rich. Fathers and mothers have that confounded habit of always asking "How much has he got?" and "How much has she got?" Old

Uncle Pierre married his daughter Simonette to big Thomas because he had a quarter of a vineyard more than young Robin, who she'd set her heart on. And now the poor critter has turned as yellow as a lemon, and she ain't been hearty and chipper since. There's a fine example for you, sir. All we've got in this world is our pleasure; and I'd rather give my daughter to a good husband she'd cotton to than have all the farms of La Beauce.

GÉRONTE: Pest and plague! My good nurse, how your tongue runs away with you! Silence, please! You take too much interest in my affairs; and you'll curdle your milk.

LUCAS (*to* JACQUELINE):   By heck and by hang! Shut up! You're too fresh and uppity! (*Tapping smartly on* GÉRONTE'S *breast*) Master here ain't got no call for your advice; he knows what he's got to do. You stick to giving the baby a good suck, and don't go in for argufyin'. Master here is the father of his own daughter, and he's got sense enough to see what's good for her.

GÉRONTE: Easy there! Take it easy!

LUCAS: Master, sir, I want to mortify her a little and teach her fittin' respect.

GÉRONTE: Yes, but you don't need such vivid demonstrations.

(*Enter* VALÈRE.)

VALÈRE: Sir, prepare yourself. Here is our doctor coming in.

(*Enter* SGANARELLE, *in a doctor's gown, with a tall pointed hat.*)

GÉRONTE: Sir, I am delighted to see you in my house. We are in great need of your services.

SGANARELLE: Hippocrates says . . . that we should both put on our hats.

GÉRONTE: Hippocrates says that?

SGANARELLE: Yes.

GÉRONTE: In what chapter, if you please?

SGANARELLE: In his chapter on hats.

GÉRONTE: Since Hippocrates says to, we must do it.

SGANARELLE: Doctor, having learned of the marvelous things—
GÉRONTE: Whom are you addressing, if you please?
SGANARELLE: You.
GÉRONTE: I'm not a doctor.
SGANARELLE: You aren't a doctor?
GÉRONTE: No, really.
SGANARELLE (*takes a stick and beats him*):   Positively?
GÉRONTE: Positively! Oh, oh, oh!
SGANARELLE: You're a doctor now. That's the only diploma I ever had.
GÉRONTE (*to* VALÈRE):   What kind of madman have you brought me?
VALÈRE: Well, I told you he was a rather whimsical doctor.
GÉRONTE: Yes; but deuce take his whimsicalities.
LUCAS: Don't pay it no mind, sir; it's just his fun.
GÉRONTE: I don't like that kind of fun.
SGANARELLE: Sir, I ask your pardon for the liberty I took.
GÉRONTE: I am at your service, sir.
SGANARELLE: I am sorry.
GÉRONTE: Not at all, not at all.
SGANARELLE: The little beating up—
GÉRONTE: No harm was done.
SGANARELLE: —which I had the honor to bestow upon you—
GÉRONTE: Let's drop the subject. Sir, I have a daughter who has fallen into a strange illness.
SGANARELLE: I am overjoyed, sir, that your daughter has some need of me. I could go farther, and wish with all my heart that you also needed me, you and your entire family, so that I might give evidence of my eagerness to be of use to you.
GÉRONTE: I am much obliged to you for your kind attentions.
SGANARELLE: I assure you that I speak with the utmost sincerity.
GÉRONTE: You do me too much honor.
SGANARELLE: What is your daughter's name?

GÉRONTE: Lucinde.

SGANARELLE: Lucinde! There is an excellent name for medication! Lucinde!

GÉRONTE: I'll go and see what she is up to.

SGANARELLE: Who is that fine big woman?

GÉRONTE: She is the wet nurse of my small boy.

(*Exit* GÉRONTE.)

SGANARELLE: Pest and pox! What a handsome article! Ah, wet nurse, charming wet nurse, all my medicine is the very humble slave of your wet-nursery! How I should like to be the fortunate little babe who is imbibing the milk of your good graces! (*He pats her breast*) All my remedies, all my knowledge, all my capacities are at your service, and—

LUCAS: With your kind permission, Doctor, sir, leave my wife be, if you please.

SGANARELLE: What! She's your wife?

LUCAS: Yes.

SGANARELLE (*opens his arms, preparatory to embracing* LUCAS, *but turns and enclasps* JACQUELINE): Oh, really, I didn't know that, but I'm delighted, for the love of you both.

LUCAS (*pulling at* SGANARELLE): Take it easy, if you please.

SGANARELLE: I assure you that I rejoice that we are thus bound together. (*He starts to embrace* LUCAS, *dodges, throws his arms about* JACQUELINE) I felicitate her for having such a husband as you; and I felicitate you for having such a beautiful and modest wife, and so well built.

LUCAS (*pulling at* SGANARELLE): By gum and by gravy! No more compliments, I pray and plead.

SGANARELLE: Don't you want me to rejoice with you about your happy marriage?

LUCAS: With me, all you like; but with my wife, you needn't be so dum polite.

SGANARELLE: But I am equally concerned with the happiness of both of you. (*Same business*) And if I embrace you to demonstrate my joy, I must, in all fairness, make the same demonstration to her.

LUCAS (*pulling him again*):   By jeez and by jingo! Doctor, what a lot of blather!

(*Enter* GÉRONTE.)

GÉRONTE: Doctor, my daughter will be here in a moment.

SGANARELLE: I await her, sir, with all my medicines at hand.

GÉRONTE: Where are they?

SGANARELLE (*tapping his forehead*):   Here.

GÉRONTE: Very good.

SGANARELLE (*trying to feel* JACQUELINE's *breast*):   But as I take a deep interest in the entire family, I must test your nurse's milk, and I must therefore examine her breast.

LUCAS (*pulling* SGANARELLE *away and making him spin around*): Not on your life; we won't have no truck with that.

SGANARELLE: It is a physician's business to inspect the nurses' breasts.

LUCAS: None of that business here, thanking you kindly.

SGANARELLE: Are you so brazen as to oppose a medical man? Out! Away!

LUCAS: I don't care a hoot.

SGANARELLE (*menacingly*):   I shall give you a case of fever!

JACQUELINE (*takes* LUCAS *by the arm, and spins him around*): Get out! Ain't I big enough to stand up for myself, if he tries to do something that ain't right?

LUCAS: I don't want him to go pawing you.

SGANARELLE: Shame on the jealous rascal!

GÉRONTE: Here comes my daughter.

(*Enter* LUCINDE.)

SGANARELLE: Is this the patient?

GÉRONTE: Yes. She is my only daughter, and I should be heartbroken if she should die.

SGANARELLE: She'd better not; she can't die without a doctor's prescription.

GÉRONTE: Come, bring a chair for the doctor.

SGANARELLE: There is a patient who is by no means repulsive. I think that a sound man could put up with her very nicely.

(LUCINDE *laughs.*)

GÉRONTE: You made her laugh, sir.

SGANARELLE: Excellent. When the doctor makes the patient laugh at him, that's a very good sign. (*To* LUCINDE) Well now, what's the trouble? What's the matter with you? Do you feel any pains?

LUCINDE (*pointing to her mouth, head, and throat*):   Ank, eek, onk, ank.

SGANARELLE: What did you say?

LUCINDE (*gesturing*):   Ank, eek, onk, ank, ank, eek, onk.

SGANARELLE: How's that?

LUCINDE: Ank, eek, onk.

SGANARELLE (*imitating her*):   Ank, eek, onk, ank, ank. I don't get you. What the devil kind of language is that?

GÉRONTE: Monsieur, that is just her trouble. She has become dumb, and so far no one has been able to discover the cause. Her misfortune has caused the postponement of her marriage.

SGANARELLE: What for?

GÉRONTE: The man she is to marry wants to wait for her to be cured before concluding the affair.

SGANARELLE: And who is the fool who doesn't want his wife to be dumb? I wish to God mine had that disease! I'd take good care not to cure her.

GÉRONTE: Anyway, sir, we beg you to make all your best efforts to relieve her of her malady.

SGANARELLE: Don't worry. Tell me, does this illness distress her very much?

GÉRONTE: Yes, sir.

SGANARELLE: Good. Does she feel much pain?

GÉRONTE: Very much.

SGANARELLE: Splendid! Does she go—you know where?

GÉRONTE: Yes.

SGANARELLE: Copiously?

GÉRONTE: As to that, I am unable to say.

SGANARELLE: The results are . . . salubrious?

GÉRONTE: I am unfamiliar with such matters.

SGANARELLE (*to* LUCINDE): Give me your arm . . . There is a pulse which indicates . . . that your daughter is dumb.

GÉRONTE: Why yes, sir, that is exactly her trouble. You discovered it immediately.

SGANARELLE: Aha!

JACQUELINE: Look how quick he guessed it!

SGANARELLE: A really good doctor knows things right away. An ignoramus would have been confused; he would have said, "Maybe it's this, maybe it's that." But I go right to the heart of the matter, and I tell you that your daughter is dumb.

GÉRONTE: Yes; but I wish you could tell me how that comes about.

SGANARELLE: Nothing is easier. That comes from the fact that she has lost her power of speech.

GÉRONTE: Very good. But what, if you please, is the cause of her losing her power of speech?

SGANARELLE: All the best authors will tell you . . . that it is an obstruction to the tongue's action.

GÉRONTE: But further, what is your opinion about this obstruction to the tongue's action?

SGANARELLE: Aristotle, on that head, says . . . some very fine things.

GÉRONTE: I can well believe it.

SGANARELLE: Oh, he was a big man!

GÉRONTE: Assuredly.

SGANARELLE (*raising his arm*): A really big man! Bigger than me—by so much. To return to our diagnosis, then, I maintain that this obstruction to the tongue's action is caused by certain humors, which we scientists call peccant humors. Peccant, that is to say . . . peccant humors. Since the vapors caused by the exhalation of the influences which arise in the diseased area, arriving . . . you might say . . . at . . . Do you understand Latin?

GÉRONTE: Not a word.

SGANARELLE (*jumping up*): You don't understand Latin?

GÉRONTE: No.

SGANARELLE (*gesturing*): Cabricias arci thuram, catalamus, singulariter, nominativo haec Musa—or "the Muse"—bonus, bona, bonum, Deus sanctus, estne oratio latinas? Etiam, yes. Quare—why? Quia substantivo et adjectivum concordat in generi, numerum, et casus.[3]

GÉRONTE: Oh, why did I never study?

JACQUELINE: There's a smart man for you!

LUCAS: Yes, that's so grand I don't catch on to a single word.

SGANARELLE: Now these vapors I refer to, making a passage from the left side, where the liver is, to the right side, where the heart is, it comes about that the lungs, which we call in Latin *armyan*, having a communication with the brain, which we term in Greek *nasmus*, by means of the vena cava, which we denominate in Hebrew *cubile*, encounter on their path the aforesaid vapors, which fill the ventricles of the scapula; and because the aforesaid vapors—give close heed to this argument, please—because the aforesaid vapors have a certain malignity—I beg you to pay the closest attention.

GÉRONTE: Yes.

SGANARELLE: Because they have a certain malignity, which is caused—I must ask you to be attentive—

GÉRONTE: Oh, I am.

SGANARELLE: —which is caused by the acridity of the humors engendered in the concavity of the diaphragm, it then happens

---

[3] According to the traditional stage business, Sganarelle works himself up into violent excitement during this speech, then throws himself into a chair, which falls over backward. Scholars are delighted because his last word, *casus*, means both *case* (of a noun) and *fall*.

that the vapors—ossabundus, nequeys, nequer, potarinum, quipsa milus. And that is exactly how it comes about that your daughter is dumb.

JACQUELINE: Oh, wasn't that lovely, husband!

LUCAS: Why ain't I got that gift of gab!

GÉRONTE: I am sure that no one could argue the case better. There is just one thing that bothers me: the position of the liver and the heart. It seems to me that you place them wrongly; and the heart is on the left side, and the liver on the right.

SGANARELLE: Yes, that is the way it used to be. But we have changed all that; now we use an entirely new method in medicine.

GÉRONTE: Oh, I didn't know that. I ask your pardon for my ignorance.

SGANARELLE: No harm done. You aren't obliged to be as well informed as we are.

GÉRONTE: Assuredly. But, sir, what do you think we ought to do for this disease?

SGANARELLE: What I think we ought to do?

GÉRONTE: Yes.

SGANARELLE: My opinion is that we should put her back to bed, and give her as treatment a quantity of bread soaked in wine.

GÉRONTE: Why is that, sir?

SGANARELLE: Because in wine and bread united there is a sympathetic virtue which makes people talk. Don't you know that that is what they give parrots, and thus they learn to speak?

GÉRONTE: That's true. Oh, the great man! Quick! Get some bread and wine!

SGANARELLE: I will come back this evening and see how she's doing. (*Exit* LUCINDE *and* LUCAS. JACQUELINE *starts to go;* SGANARELLE *stops her*) Wait a minute, you. (*To* GÉRONTE) Sir, there is a wet nurse who needs some of my little remedies.

JACQUELINE: Who, me? I'm feeling fine.

SGANARELLE: That's bad, nurse, very bad. Such good health is alarming. It wouldn't be a bad idea to give you a nice little bloodletting, or a nice little emollient enema.

GÉRONTE: But, sir, that is something I don't understand. Why should you be bled when you aren't sick?

SGANARELLE: Never mind; it's a very salutary system. As we drink for fear of being thirsty, we should be bled for the illness which hasn't yet arrived. That's preventive medicine.

JACQUELINE: Land's sakes, I won't have none of that. I don't want to turn my body into no drug store.

SGANARELLE: You are rebellious toward medicine; but we'll get you down in the end. (*Exit* JACQUELINE) I bid you good day, sir.

GÉRONTE: Wait a minute, please.

SGANARELLE: What do you want to do?

GÉRONTE: Give you some money, sir.

SGANARELLE (*hoisting his gown and thrusting his hand backward, as* GÉRONTE *opens his purse*):   I won't take money, sir.

GÉRONTE: But, sir—

SGANARELLE: Not at all.

GÉRONTE: But just a moment!

SGANARELLE: By no means.

GÉRONTE: But please!

SGANARELLE: Don't be absurd.

GÉRONTE: There you are.

SGANARELLE: I'll do nothing of the sort.

GÉRONTE: Oh!

SGANARELLE: Money is not my motive.

GÉRONTE: I believe you.

SGANARELLE (*weighing the coins*):   They aren't short weight?

GÉRONTE: No, sir.

SGANARELLE: I am not a mercenary physician.

GÉRONTE: I am well aware of it.

SGANARELLE: I don't seek personal advantage.

GÉRONTE: I never had such an idea.

(*Exit* GÉRONTE. SGANARELLE *brings his hand forward and looks at the money.*)

SGANARELLE: Well, not so bad, not so bad! If only—

(*Enter* LÉANDRE.)

LÉANDRE: Sir, I have been watching my chance to see you for a long time. I have come to implore your assistance.

SGANARELLE (*seizing* LÉANDRE's *wrist*):   The pulse is very bad.

LÉANDRE: I am not sick, sir; that is not my reason for coming to see you.

SGANARELLE: If you aren't sick, why the devil didn't you say so?

LÉANDRE: Please! To put it briefly, my name is Léandre, and I'm in love with Lucinde, whom you've just examined. And since I have no access to her, because of her father's animosity, I have ventured to ask you to aid my love, and to play a little trick, to give me the chance of saying to her a couple of words, on which my happiness and my life absolutely depend.

SGANARELLE (*angrily*):   What do you take me for? How do you dare address yourself to me to help you in a love affair, and to degrade the dignity of a physician to such base employments!

LÉANDRE: Sir, please don't make so much noise!

SGANARELLE (*thrusting him backward*):   I'll make all the noise I like! You are an impertinent puppy!

LÉANDRE: Calm down, sir.

SGANARELLE: A blundering fool!

LÉANDRE: Please, sir—

SGANARELLE: I'll show you that I'm not that kind of a man, and it is the height of insolence—

LÉANDRE (*pulling out a purse and handing it to* SGANARELLE):   But, sir—

SGANARELLE: —to make such a proposition . . . I'm not referring to you personally, for you're a good fellow, and I should be delighted to do you a service. But there are some impertinent puppies around who misjudge people entirely; and I freely grant that that sort of thing makes me angry.

LÉANDRE: I ask your pardon, sir, for the liberty—

SGANARELLE: Not at all, not at all. What is the story?

LÉANDRE: You must know then, sir, that this illness you are trying to cure is only pretended. The doctors have argued about it in due form. They have given their opinions; some say it comes from the brain; others, from the intestines, or from the spleen, or from the liver. But the fact is that love is the real cause, and that Lucinde has invented this affliction only to escape from a threatening marriage. But I am afraid we may be overseen together; let's leave this spot, and I'll tell you as we go what I want from you.

SGANARELLE: Let's be on our way, sir. You have given me an almost inconceivable sympathy for your love. The patient will either die, or she'll be yours—or I'm no doctor.

ACT III

The scene is a sylvan setting, near GÉRONTE's *house.*
(*In modern stage productions the scene commonly remains the same as in Act II.*)
LÉANDRE, *disguised as an apothecary, and* SGANA-RELLE *are discovered.*

LÉANDRE: It seems to me I'm rather good as an apothecary; and as the father never saw much of me, I think this gown and wig will be a sufficient disguise.

SGANARELLE: By all means.

LÉANDRE: The only thing is, I'd like to know a few big medical terms, to decorate my speech and make me sound professional.

SGANARELLE: Go on, that's not necessary. All you need is the costume. In fact, I don't know any more than you do.

LÉANDRE: What?

SGANARELLE: I'm damned if I know anything about medicine! You're a good fellow, and I'm willing to confide in you, as you have confided in me.

LÉANDRE: What! You aren't in fact—

SGANARELLE: No, I tell you. I was kicked into the medical profession. I never had any idea of being a scholar; I didn't get beyond the third grade. I don't know how they got this maggot in their heads; but when I saw they were bound and determined that I was a physician, I decided to be one, no matter who got hurt. Still, you wouldn't believe how the idea has got around, and how pigheaded everybody is in taking me for a great healer. People come from all over to consult me. If things go on this way, maybe I'll stick to medicine for the rest of my life. I think it's the best trade there is, for whether you do well or badly, you get paid just the same. We never get blamed for doing a bad job; and we cut the cloth we work on to please ourselves. A cobbler making shoes can't spoil a piece of leather without paying for the damage; but in this job we can spoil a man without its costing us a penny. The blunders aren't our fault; they're always the fault of the man who dies. In short, the nice thing about this profession is that dead men have a most marvelous decency and discretion; you never hear a dead man complain of the doctor who killed him.

LÉANDRE: It is true that the dead are uncommonly polite on this subject.

(*Enter* THIBAUT *and* PERRIN.) [4]

SGANARELLE: Here are some fellows who look as though they are coming for a consultation. You go and wait for me near your lady's house.

(*Exit* LÉANDRE.)

THIBAUT: Doctor, sir, me and my son, we've come to see you.

SGANARELLE: What's the matter?

---

[4] The following scene with Thibaut and Perrin is commonly omitted in modern productions.

THIBAUT: His poor mother, her name is Perrette, she's been sick abed going on now six months.

SGANARELLE (*thrusting out his hand*):   And what do you expect me to do about it?

THIBAUT: We'd like for you to give us some little dohickus for to cure her.

SGANARELLE: I'd have to know the kind of illness she has.

THIBAUT: She's sick with hypocrisy, sir.

SGANARELLE: Hypocrisy?

THIBAUT: Yes; I mean to say she's all swole up; and they do tell it's a lot of seriosities she's got inside, and her liver, her stomach, her spleen, or what you may call it, is just amakin' water instead of blood. Every two days she gits the fever and shakes, with lastitudes and miseries in the leg mussicles. You can hear in her throat phlegm like to choke her, and now and then she has syncopations and compulsions, so I'm afeared she's goin' to pass away. We've got in our village a pothecary, pardon the expression, who has give her a lot of messes, and I've paid out more than a dozen good crowns in enemies, begging your pardon, and setatives to make her set better, and infections and cordialities. But all that, as the feller says, has just been water down the train. He wanted to give her a kind o' physic called a medic wine, but to tell you the honest truth, I was scared it would finish her. I hear tell the big doctors have killed off a terrible lot ot folks with that invention.[5]

SGANARELLE (*irritably wiggling his thrust-out hand*):   Come to the point, my friend, come to the point.

THIBAUT: The point is, sir, that we've come to ask you what we ought for to do.

SGANARELLE: I don't understand you at all.

PERRIN: Sir, my mother is ailing; and here's two crowns we've brung you to give us a cure.

---

[5] The efficacy of emetic wine, containing antimony, was then the subject of a fierce medical controversy.

SGANARELLE: Ah, I understand you perfectly! There is a young man who speaks clearly, and knows how to express himself. You say your mother is ill with dropsy, that her whole body is swollen up, that she has fever, and pains in the legs, that she has syncopes and convulsions, or, that is, fainting fits?

PERRIN: Oh, yes, sir, that's it perzackly.

SGANARELLE: I understood you immediately. Your father doesn't know what he's talking about. And now you want a remedy?

PERRIN: Yes, sir.

SGANARELLE: A remedy to cure her?

PERRIN: That's the way we kind o' look at it.

SGANARELLE: Look, here's a piece of cheese you must make her swallow.

PERRIN: Cheese, sir?

SGANARELLE: Yes, it's a specially prepared cheese, with gold, coral, pearls, and other precious substances ground up in it.

PERRIN: Sir, we are much beholden to you; we'll make her swaller it straight off.

SGANARELLE: That's right. And if she dies, don't fail to give her the best possible burial.

(*Exit* PERRIN *and* THIBAUT. *The scene changes to a room in* GÉRONTE's *house, as in Act II. Enter* SGANARELLE *and* JACQUELINE.)

SGANARELLE: Ah, here is the lovely wet nurse! Ah, wet nurse of my heart, I am delighted to see you again! The vision of you is the rhubarb, cassia; and senna which purge all the melancholy of my soul!

JACQUELINE: My stars alive! Doctor, sir, that's too fine talk for me, and I don't understand any of your Latin.

SGANARELLE: Fall ill, nurse, I pray you. Fall ill, for love of me. I would be only too delighted to cure you.

(*Enter* LUCAS. *He approaches the speakers stealthily and unobserved.*)

JACQUELINE: Much obliged. I'd liefer not take none of your cures.

SGANARELLE: How I pity you, fair wet nurse, for having such a jealous, troublesome husband!

JACQUELINE: Ah, well, sir, it's penance for my sins. Where the goat is tied, there she has to graze.

SGANARELLE: What, such a bumpkin, a hick! A man who watches you every minute, and won't let anyone even speak to you!

JACQUELINE: Oh, dear, you ain't seen nothing yet. That's just a sample of his jealous turn of mind.

SGANARELLE: Is it possible! That a man should have so base a character as to mistreat a person like you! Ah, lovely wet nurse, I know some people, not very far from here, who would think themselves happy even to kiss the sweet utensils of your trade! How could it happen that a beautiful creature like you should fall into such hands as his! That such a coarse lout, brutal, stupid, a fool—pardon me, nurse, if I speak in this way of your husband—

JACQUELINE: Ah, sir, I know very well he deserves all them names.

SGANARELLE: Yes, certainly, nurse, he deserves them. He would further deserve that you plant a certain adornment on his brow, to punish him for his suspicions.

JACQUELINE: It's true that if I only thought about what's good for him, he might drive me to some pretty goings-on.

SGANARELLE: On my word, you wouldn't do badly to revenge yourself on him, with someone's help. He's the kind of man, I tell you, who deserves exactly that. And if, fair nurse, I were fortunate enough to be chosen as the instrument—

> (*Both become aware of* LUCAS's *presence behind them. Both escape to opposite sides of the stage, and exit. Enter* GÉRONTE.)

GÉRONTE: Hello, Lucas. You haven't seen our doctor around?

LUCAS: Yes, by gee and by jiminy! I seen him, and my wife too!

GÉRONTE: I wonder where he can be.

LUCAS: I don't know; but I wisht he was in hell's fire.

GÉRONTE: Go and find out what my daughter is doing.

(*Exit* LUCAS. *Enter* SGANARELLE *and* LÉANDRE)

Ah, monsieur, I was just asking where you were.

SGANARELLE: I was dallying in the courtyard. (*Aside*) Expelling the superfluity of my potations. (*Aloud*) And how is our patient doing?

GÉRONTE: A little worse, since she took your medicine.

SGANARELLE: Good; good! That's a sign it's working.

GÉRONTE: Yes; but while it's working, I'm afraid it will undo˙ her completely.

SGANARELLE: Don't worry. I have remedies which are proof against everything. I am waiting for her to come to her death agony.

GÉRONTE: Who is that man with you?

SGANARELLE (*imitating an apothecary administering an enema*): He's—

GÉRONTE: What?

SGANARELLE: He's the man—

GÉRONTE: Eh?

SGANARELLE: The man who—

GÉRONTE: Oh, I understand.

SGANARELLE: Your daughter will need him.

(*Enter* LUCINDE *and* JACQUELINE.)

JACQUELINE (*to* GÉRONTE):   Sir, here's your daughter. She wants to walk around a bit.

SGANARELLE: That will do her good. Apothecary, feel her pulse, while I discuss her illness with you, sir. (*Exit* JACQUELINE. LÉANDRE *draws* LUCINDE *to one side of the stage.* SGANARELLE *pulls* GÉRONTE *to the other side, puts his arm over* GÉRONTE'*s shoulders, his hand under* GÉRONTE'*s chin. As* GÉRONTE *tries to see what his daughter and* LÉANDRE *are doing,* SGANARELLE *turns* GÉRONTE'*s face toward his own. In current productions,* SGANARELLE *resorts to every burlesque device to block* GÉ-RONTE'*s view, even standing on a chair and spreading his gown wide as a screen*) Sir, it is a great and subtle question among the learned, whether women are easier to cure than men. I beg you to listen attentively to this. Some say yes; others say no; and I say yes and no. Inasmuch as the incongruity of the opaque humors which are to be found in the natural temperament of women are the reason that the grosser nature forever attempts to overmaster the sensitive nature, we see that the variation of their opinions depends upon the oblique movement of the moon's circle; and as the sun, which casts its rays upon the concavity of the earth, finds—

LUCINDE: No, I am entirely incapable of ever changing my feelings.

GÉRONTE: My daughter is speaking! Oh, what power was in the remedy! Oh, what a wonderful doctor! How indebted I am to you, sir, for this marvelous cure! How can I reward you for your services!

SGANARELLE (*walking to and fro, and wiping his brow*): There is a case which caused me a lot of trouble.

LUCINDE: Yes, Father, I have recovered my power of speech; but I have recovered it in order to tell you that I will never have any other husband than Léandre, and there's no use in your trying to give me to Horace.

GÉRONTE: But—

LUCINDE: Nothing can shake my resolution.

GÉRONTE: What—

LUCINDE: You can argue all you please.

GÉRONTE: If—

LUCINDE: All your talk will do no good.

GÉRONTE: I—

LUCINDE: I have made up my mind about it.

GÉRONTE: But—

LUCINDE: There is no parental authority which can force me to marry in spite of myself.

GÉRONTE: I have—

LUCINDE: Do whatever you like; it's no good.

GÉRONTE: He—

LUCINDE: My heart can never submit to such tyranny.

GÉRONTE: There—

LUCINDE: And I will take refuge in a convent rather than marry a man I don't love.

GÉRONTE: But—

LUCINDE (*in a deafening·shout*): No! By no manner of means! Absolutely not! You're wasting your time! I won't do it! It's all settled!

GÉRONTE: What a flood of talk! I can't stand up against it. Doctor, I beg you to make her dumb again.

SGANARELLE: That, I fear, is impossible. All I can do, to serve you, is to make you deaf, if you like.

GÉRONTE: No, thanks. (*To* LUCINDE) So you think—

LUCINDE: No. All your arguments will do no good.

GÉRONTE: You will marry Horace, and you will do it this very day.

LUCINDE: I'll die first.

SGANARELLE: Good Lord, stop! Let me medicate the affair. The woman is still sick, and I know the remedy we must employ.

GÉRONTE: Is it possible, sir, that you can also cure this malady of the mind?

SGANARELLE: Yes. Let me handle it. I have remedies for everything, and our apothecary will help in this cure. (*To* LÉANDRE) A word with you. You perceive that her infatuation with Léandre is entirely contrary to her father's wishes, and that there is no time to lose; her humors are much inflamed, and it is necessary to find very promptly a remedy for this disease, which might easily get worse with delay. Personally, I see only one cure, which is a dose of purgative getawayum, which you will combine properly with two drachms of matrimonium in pill form. She may make some difficulty about taking this medicine, but as you're a clever man at your trade, you will have to persuade her, and make her swallow the dose the best way you can. Now you two go and take a turn around the garden, in order to prepare her humors, while I have a talk with her father. But above all don't lose time. The remedy, quickly, the panacea!

(*Exit* LÉANDRE *and* LUCINDE.)

GÉRONTE: Doctor, what are those drugs you just mentioned? I don't think I have ever heard of them.

SGANARELLE: They are drugs one uses only in critical cases.

GÉRONTE: Did you ever hear of such insolence as hers?

SGANARELLE: Girls are sometimes a little headstrong.

GÉRONTE: You can't imagine how mad she is about that Léandre.

SGANARELLE: The heat of the blood has that effect on young minds.

GÉRONTE: Ever since I discovered the violence of my daughter's attachment, I've kept her locked up.

SGANARELLE: Very wise.

GÉRONTE: And I've kept them from having any communication with each other.

SGANARELLE: Excellent.

GÉRONTE: If I'd allowed them to see each other, some folly would have resulted.

SGANARELLE: No doubt.

GÉRONTE: I think she'd have been capable of running away with him.

SGANARELLE: Sensibly argued.

GÉRONTE: I've been warned that he's been making all sorts of efforts to speak to her.

SGANARELLE: The scoundrel!

GÉRONTE: But he's wasting his time.

SGANARELLE: Ha, ha!

GÉRONTE: I'll keep him from seeing her, all right.

SGANARELLE: He's not dealing with a simpleton. You know

more tricks than he does. Anyone will have to get up early to catch you napping.

(*Enter* LUCAS.)

LUCAS: By cripes and by crikey, sir, hell's apoppin'! Your daughter has gone and run off with her Léandre! The pothecary, it was him; and that there doctor was the one who done the trick!

GÉRONTE: What! I'm ruined! Call the police! Don't let him escape! Traitor! I'll have you punished by the law!

(*Exit* GÉRONTE.)

LUCAS: Dad-burn, dad-blame, and dad-rot! Doctor, sir, you're going to git hung; so don't move.

(*Enter* MARTINE.)

MARTINE: Oh, dear, what a lot of trouble I had finding this house! (*To* LUCAS) Why, how do you do? Tell me, what happened to the doctor I recommended to you?

LUCAS: There he is, there. He's going to git hung.

MARTINE: What! My husband is going to get hung? Oh, dear! What did he do, then?

LUCAS: He got our master's daughter kidnaped.

MARTINE: Alas, my dear husband, is it true they're going to hang you?

SGANARELLE: Well, you see. Oh!

MARTINE: Are you going to let yourself die in front of everybody?

SGANARELLE: And what can I do about it?

MARTINE: If you'd even finished cutting our wood, it would be some consolation.

SGANARELLE: Get out of here; you're breaking my heart.

MARTINE: No, I'm going to stay in order to cheer you up. I won't leave until I've seen you hung.

SGANARELLE: Ah!

(*Enter* GÉRONTE.)

GÉRONTE (*to* SGANARELLE):   The police chief will be here soon; they'll put you in a place where you'll be good and secure.

SGANARELLE (*kneeling, hat in hand*):   Alas! You couldn't change it to a little flogging?

GÉRONTE: No, no; the law must take its course. But what's this? (*Enter* LÉANDRE, LUCINDE, *and* JACQUELINE.)

LÉANDRE (*to* GÉRONTE):   Sir, I am Léandre, come to present myself to you, and to entrust Lucinde to your power. We had proposed to flee together, and to get married; but we have given up this purpose in favor of more honorable behavior. I do not wish to steal your daughter from you; I desire to receive her only from your own hands. I have further news for you, sir; I have just received letters informing me that my uncle is dead, and I inherit all his property.

GÉRONTE (*who has been threatening* LÉANDRE *with a stick, now throws it away*):   Sir, your merits are most worthy of consideration; and I give you my daughter with the utmost joy.

SGANARELLE: The art of medicine had a narrow escape.

MARTINE (*to* SGANARELLE):   Since you aren't going to be hung, do me the favor of being a doctor; I am the one who gained this honor for you.

SGANARELLE: Yes, you are the one who gained me some fine beatings.

LÉANDRE: The result is so happy that you shouldn't bear her any ill will.

SGANARELLE: All right. I pardon you the beatings in consideration of the dignity to which you have elevated me. But prepare yourself from now on to treat with great respect a man of my importance; and remember that a doctor's anger is terrible!

The Would-Be Gentleman

A COMEDY-BALLET

In the winter of 1669-70, the Turks were in the news. Suleiman Aga, envoy of the Sultan, appeared at Versailles. Louis XIV went out of his way to impress the Turk, and had a costume made, coruscating with fourteen million francs' worth of diamonds. Suleiman Aga and his small escort, wearing markedly dirty turbans, presented themselves to His Majesty; whether from Oriental calm or Oriental good manners, they seemed not to notice the magnificence of Versailles or the Sun-King's diamond coat. The King never forgave the Turks, as one does not forgive a guest who gobbles the caviar without recognizing it. According to a story which seems authentic, the King suggested to Molière that the Turks would make a fine funny theme for comedy, and sent him a returned traveler to help with the language, costumes, and local color.

A royal patron's ideas are always good ideas. Molière prepared a comédie-ballet, or musical comedy, in which the songs and dances are incorporated in the story and justified by it. (The King was a balletomane, and himself danced in some of Molière's *divertissements*, until reproved by the Church.) The celebrated musician, Jean-Baptiste Lulli, wrote the music for *Le Bourgeois gentilhomme*, directed the choreography, and took the part of the

Mufti. There is no doubt that in 1670 *Le Bourgeois gentilhomme* was regarded as primarily a song-and-dance show; as in any musical comedy, the librettist was the servant of the composer.

In such circumstances and under such restrictions, Molière's play is a triumphant tour de force. According to any rules of dramatic construction, it is deplorable. *"C'est un monstre que cette comédie,"* says René Bray.[1] The first two acts are a series of gags, with no suggestion of a plot. The love interest appears in the third act, to be resolved by the gigantic burlesque of the Turkish ceremony in Act IV. The fifth act prolongs the misunderstanding while the dancers change their costumes and prepare the final ballet. The two pairs of lovers are united in the final moments; but Monsieur Jourdain's disillusionment, the logical terminus, is left to the spectator's imagination. But let the critics complain; the spectators do not.

The première of the play took place on October 14, 1670, at the royal castle of Chambord, near Blois. What an enterprise, to amuse the King and his courtiers after a day's hunting! To carry actors, singers, dancers, orchestra, stagehands, scenery, costumes, properties, instruments on a four-day journey to Chambord was a task worthy of a King's magnificence, and certainly a problem to his transport service and his finance minister.

Citizens of a different world, a different time, are likely to feel a certain sour aftertaste on reading the play. The immense mockery of the Bourgeois, whose only offense is that he wants to be a gentleman, seems to us, who are not gentlemen either, excessive, even repellent. Monsieur Jourdain's desire for instruction, for excellence, is admirable rather than ridiculous. We note that the representative of the nobility is a thoroughgoing scoundrel, who belongs in jail and not in the King's suite. We sympathize with Madame Jourdain's candor and with Cléante's manly statement of his pride in the bourgeois tradition. Are such reactions due merely to the changed social situation, or did Molière consciously hint at

---

[1] *Molière homme de théâtre* (1954), page 254.

social criticism? The spectator of the play has no time for such reflections; the reader has a right to say that Molière's words have taken on a new meaning which he could not have intended. Perhaps; but I think Molière knew what he was saying.

The Characters

MONSIEUR JOURDAIN, bourgeois

MADAME JOURDAIN, his wife

LUCILE, his daughter

CLÉONTE, in love with Lucile

DORIMÈNE, a marquise

DORANTE, a count

NICOLE, servant of Monsieur Jourdain

COVIELLE, manservant of Cléonte

A MUSIC MASTER

THE MUSIC MASTER'S PUPIL

A DANCING MASTER

A FENCING MASTER

A PHILOSOPHY MASTER

A MERCHANT TAILOR

A JOURNEYMAN TAILOR

TWO LACKEYS, several SINGERS, INSTRUMENTALISTS, DANCERS, COOKS, TAILOR'S APPRENTICES, and other characters in the ballets.

The scene is in Paris, in Monsieur Jourdain's house.

ACT I

After the overture, the curtain rises. The MUSIC MASTER'S PUPIL *is working at a table. He may rise, strike*

*some notes on a harpsichord, and return to his com-
position. He hums his tune, trying both the men's
and women's parts.*

Enter the MUSIC MASTER, *three* SINGERS, *and two*
VIOLINISTS.

MUSIC MASTER (*to his musicians*):   All right, come in here, and
take a rest until he comes.
    (*Enter from the opposite side the* DANCING MASTER
    and four DANCERS.)

DANCING MASTER (*to his dancers*):   Come in this way.

MUSIC MASTER (*to* PUPIL):   All done?

PUPIL: Yes.

MUSIC MASTER: ·Let me see it a minute. (*Inspects composition*)
That will do nicely.

DANCING MASTER: Is it something new?

MUSIC MASTER: Yes; it's the music for a serenade I've had him
working on here, while we're waiting for our man to get up.

DANCING MASTER: May I take a look?

MUSIC MASTER: You will hear it, with the words, when he
comes. He won't be long.

DANCING MASTER: We're certainly occupied now, both of us.

MUSIC MASTER: That's right. We've both found the man we've
been looking for. This Monsieur Jourdain is a very nice property, with his visions of nobility and gallantry. In the interests
of your art of dance and mine of music, we could well wish
there were many more like him.

DANCING MASTER: Well, not exactly like him. I could wish he
had more appreciation of the things we do for him.

MUSIC MASTER: It's true he doesn't know much about them.
But he pays well; and that's what our arts need more than anything else right now.

DANCING MASTER: Well, personally, I admit I enjoy a little rec-
ognition. Applause really stimulates me. And I find it an actual

torture to perform for idiots, and to bear their uncouth comments on our creations. There is genuine pleasure, confess it, in working for people who can recognize the fine points of our art, and reward us for our work with heart-warming approval. Yes, the best payment we can receive is to see our work appreciated, and welcomed with the applause which does us honor. There is no better return for all our labor and fatigue; and enlightened praise gives exquisite delight.

MUSIC MASTER: I agree; I enjoy such praise as much as you do. Certainly nothing gratifies us like that kind of applause. But you can't live on applause; praise alone won't pay the rent. We need something a bit more solid; the best hand people can give us is a hand with cash in it. True enough, our man has no cultivation; he gets everything all wrong, and he is sure to applaud the wrong thing; but his money purifies his bad taste. His fat purse is full of critical insight; his approval is convertible into cash; and this ignorant commoner is a lot more useful to us, as you are well aware, than that noble amateur of the arts who introduced us to him.

DANCING MASTER: There is some truth in what you're saying. But I think you dwell on money a little too much. Material advantage is so base a thing that a man of character should never show any concern for it.

MUSIC MASTER: Still, you seem to accept the money our man hands you.

DANCING MASTER: By all means; but I don't make my happiness depend upon it; and I could wish that with all his wealth he had some tincture of good taste.

MUSIC MASTER: Naturally I should like that too. That's what we're both laboring to bring about, as best we can. But at any rate, he is helping us to get a reputation; he will underwrite the things that others will applaud for him.

DANCING MASTER: Here he is now.

(*Enter* MONSIEUR JOURDAIN *and two* LACKEYS. MON-

SIEUR JOURDAIN *wears a gorgeous striped dressing gown, lined with green and orange.*)

M. JOURDAIN: Well, sirs, how's things? You're going to show me your little thingamajig?

DANCING MASTER: What? What little thingamajig?

M. JOURDAIN: Why, the—what d'you call it? Your prologue or dialogue of song and dance.

DANCING MASTER: Ha, ha!

MUSIC MASTER: We are quite ready, sir.

M. JOURDAIN: I've held you up a little. But the fact is I'm dressing today in court style; and my tailor sent me some silk stockings I thought I'd never get on.

MUSIC MASTER: We are here only to await your leisure.

M. JOURDAIN: I'll ask you both not to leave until they've brought my coat, so you can see it.

DANCING MASTER: Whatever you wish.

M. JOURDAIN: You'll see me turned out properly from head to foot.

MUSIC MASTER: We don't doubt it.

M. JOURDAIN: I've just had this dressing gown made.

DANCING MASTER: It is very handsome.

M. JOURDAIN: My tailor told me that people of quality are like this in the morning.

MUSIC MASTER: It looks very well on you.

M. JOURDAIN: Lackeys! Hey, my two lackeys!

FIRST LACKEY: What do you wish, sir?

M. JOURDAIN: Nothing. I just wanted to see if you hear me all right. (*To the two* MASTERS) What do you think of my servants' liveries?

DANCING MASTER: Magnificent.

M. JOURDAIN (*opens his dressing gown, displaying tight red velvet breeches and a short green velvet jacket*): And here's a little sports costume to do my exercises in, in the morning.

MUSIC MASTER: Very smart.

M. JOURDAIN: Lackey!

FIRST LACKEY: Yes, sir?

M. JOURDAIN: Other lackey!

SECOND LACKEY: Yes, sir?

M. JOURDAIN: Here, hold my gown. (*He removes his gown*) How do you like me this way?

DANCING MASTER: Splendid. It couldn't be more perfect.

M. JOURDAIN: Now let's have your little business.

MUSIC MASTER: First, I should like to have you hear a composition which this young man here has just done for the serenade you ordered. He is one of my pupils; he is very gifted for this sort of thing.

M. JOURDAIN: Yes; but you shouldn't have had it done by a pupil. You aren't too good to do the job yourself.

MUSIC MASTER: Don't let the word "pupil" put you off, sir. Such pupils as this know as much as the greatest masters; and the melody is as lovely as it can be. Just listen.

M. JOURDAIN: Give me my dressing gown so I can listen better . . . Wait a minute, I think it will be better without the dressing gown . . . No, give it back to me. It'll be better that way.

A WOMAN SINGER:

Ah, grievous is my woe, I languish night and day
Since thy imperious eye has brought me 'neath thy sway;
If thus thou deal'st, my fair, with one who loves thee so,
Ah, what must be the fate of one who is thy foe?

M. JOURDAIN: That song seems to me rather dismal. It puts you to sleep. I wish you could brighten it up a little here and there.

MUSIC MASTER: It is necessary, sir, that the music fit the words.

M. JOURDAIN: I learned a very pretty one a little while ago. Wait a minute . . . now . . . how did it go?

DANCING MASTER: Really, I don't know.

M. JOURDAIN: Something about a sheep.

DANCING MASTER: A sheep?

M. JOURDAIN: Yes. Aha! (*He sings*)

I thought my dear Jeannette
Was just a little lamb;
I thought my dear Jeannette
Was sweet as currant jam.
Oh, dear, oh, dear, oh, dear!
I must have made a bungle!
She's crueler, it's clear,
Than a tiger in the jungle!
Isn't that pretty?

MUSIC MASTER: Extremely pretty.

DANCING MASTER: And you sing it well.

M. JOURDAIN: And I never studied music!

MUSIC MASTER: You ought to learn music, sir, as you are learning the dance. The two arts have a very close connection.

DANCING MASTER: And they open a man's mind to things of beauty.

M. JOURDAIN: Do people of quality study music too?

MUSIC MASTER: Oh, yes, sir.

M. JOURDAIN: Well, then, I'll study it. But I don't know how I'll find the time; for not to mention the fencing master who's giving me lessons, I have hired a philosophy professor; he's to begin this morning.

MUSIC MASTER: Philosophy is very fine; but music, sir, music—

DANCING MASTER: Music and the dance; music and the dance, that's all you really need.

MUSIC MASTER: There is nothing so useful in a state as music.

DANCING MASTER: There is nothing so necessary to men as the dance.

MUSIC MASTER: Without music, a state can hardly persist.

DANCING MASTER: Without the dance, a man is totally helpless.

MUSIC MASTER: All the disorders and wars in the world come about because men haven't learned music.

DANCING MASTER: All men's misfortunes, and the appalling disasters of history, the blunders of statesmen and the errors of great generals, they have all occurred for lack of knowledge of dancing.

M. JOURDAIN: How is that?

MUSIC MASTER: Doesn't war come from discords among men?

M. JOURDAIN: That's true.

MUSIC MASTER: And if everybody should learn music, wouldn't that be a way to harmonize everything, and to bring universal peace to the world?

M. JOURDAIN: You're right.

DANCING MASTER: When a man has made some blunder, whether in his family affairs, or in government, or in generalship, don't we always say: "So-and-so has made a false step in such a matter"?

M. JOURDAIN: Yes, we say that.

DANCING MASTER: And taking a false step, can that result from anything else than not knowing how to dance?

M. JOURDAIN: That's true. You're both right!

DANCING MASTER: It's just to show you the excellence and utility of dancing and music.

M. JOURDAIN: I understand that now.

MUSIC MASTER: Do you want to see our productions?

M. JOURDAIN: Yes.

MUSIC MASTER: I have already told you, this is a little effort of mine to delineate the various emotions that music can express.

M. JOURDAIN: Very good.

MUSIC MASTER (*to the* SINGERS): Step forward, please. (*To* MONSIEUR JOURDAIN) You must imagine that they are dressed as shepherds.

M. JOURDAIN: Why are they always shepherds? All I ever see around is shepherds.

MUSIC MASTER: When one wants to make people speak in music, one must always put them in a pastoral setting. That's what we call verisimilitude. Singing has always been the specialty of shepherds and shepherdesses. It is hardly natural, in a dramatic dialogue, that princes or commoners should sing their emotions.

M. JOURDAIN: All right, all right. Let's hear it.

WOMAN SINGER:

A heart that tyrant love's dictation captures
Is filled with turbulence incessantly.
They say that languishing and sighs are raptures,
But still our dearest boon is liberty!

FIRST MALE SINGER:

Nought is so sweet as tender ardors thronging
To make twin hearts blend in a lover's kiss.
There is no happiness without love's longing;
Take love from life, you cancel all its bliss.

SECOND MALE SINGER:

It would be sweet to enter love's domain,
If one could find in love true steadfastness;
But oh, alas! Oh, cruelty and pain!
How can one find a faithful shepherdess?
The sex is fickle and inconstant; hence
One must renounce for aye love's blandishments!

FIRST MALE SINGER:

Dear love is revealed—

WOMAN SINGER:

How delightful to yield—

SECOND MALE SINGER:

But love is a cheat!

FIRST MALE SINGER:

My darling, my sweet!

WOMAN SINGER (*to* SECOND MALE SINGER):

Dear love, I adjure you—

SECOND MALE SINGER:

I cannot endure you!

FIRST MALE SINGER (*to* SECOND MALE SINGER):

Ah, learn to love, forget your peevishness!

WOMAN SINGER:

> And I shall gladly tell you where you'll see
>   A faithful shepherdess!

SECOND MALE SINGER:

> Where to discover such a prodigy?

WOMAN SINGER (*to* SECOND MALE SINGER):

> Just in defense of womankind,
>   I offer here my heart to you!

SECOND MALE SINGER:

> Sweet shepherdess, and shall I find
> That it will be forever true?

WOMAN SINGER:

> Let us essay, and make a test
> Which of us two can love the best!

SECOND MALE SINGER:

> And may the one accursèd be
> Who first shall fail in constancy!

THE THREE SINGERS:

> The power that kindles deathless fires
>   Now let us all pay tribute to!
> How sweet it is when love inspires
>   Two hearts that ever shall be true!

M. JOURDAIN: Is that all?

MUSIC MASTER: Yes.

M. JOURDAIN: A neat job. Very neat. There were some remarks in it that weren't bad.

DANCING MASTER: Now, as my part of the performance, here is a little effort to display the most beautiful postures and evolutions with which a dance may be varied.

M. JOURDAIN: More shepherds?

DANCING MASTER: They are anything you please.

> (*Four* DANCERS *execute various steps and evolutions at the* DANCING MASTER's *order. This is the first* Interlude, *marking the division of the play into acts.*)

ACT II

The action is continuous. After the Interlude, *the dancers retire, leaving* MONSIEUR JOURDAIN, *the* MUSIC MASTER, *the* DANCING MASTER, *and the two* LACKEYS.

M. JOURDAIN: No nonsense about that! Those boys cut some fine capers.

MUSIC MASTER: When the dance is combined with the music, it will be much more effective. You will find very gallant the little ballet we have organized for you.

M. JOURDAIN: Have it ready soon, anyhow. The person I've ordered all this for is to do me the honor of coming to dinner[2] today.

DANCING MASTER: It's all ready.

MUSIC MASTER: Incidentally, sir, you should go farther. A person like you, doing things in a big way, and with a taste for the finer things of life, should have a musicale at home every Wednesday or Thursday.

M. JOURDAIN: Do people of quality have that?

MUSIC MASTER: Yes, sir.

M. JOURDAIN: I'll have it, then. It will be nice, will it?

MUSIC MASTER: Certainly. You will need three voices: a soprano, a counter-tenor, and a basso; they will be accompanied by a bass viol, a theorbo or archlute, and a harpsichord for the sustained bass, with two violins to play the refrains.

M. JOURDAIN: You ought to put in an accordion too. The accordion is an instrument 1 like; it's harmonious.

MUSIC MASTER: Just let us arrange things.

M. JOURDAIN: Anyway, don't forget to send me some singers by and by, to sing at the dinner.

MUSIC MASTER: You will have everything you need.

M. JOURDAIN: And especially, be sure the ballet is nice.

2 Dinner commonly occurred about midday.

MUSIC MASTER: You will be pleased, I am sure; especially with certain minuets you will see.

M. JOURDAIN: The minuet! That's my dance! You should see me dance the minuet! Come on, dancing master!

DANCING MASTER: A hat for the gentleman, please! (MONSIEUR JOURDAIN *seizes a lackey's hat, claps it on over his nightcap, removing it to make the sweeping bows required by the dance; the* DANCING MASTER *sings the music, and also his instructions*) La, la, la; La, la, la, la, la, la. La, la, la, repeat. La, la, la; La, la. Keep in tune—if you please. La, la, la, la. Right leg stiff, la, la, la. Don't move shoulders—quite so much. La, la, la, la, la; La, la, la, la, la. Both your arms—are they crippled? La, la, la, la, la. Lift your head—turn toe out. La, la, la. Stand up straight.

M. JOURDAIN (*with an intonation between "I'm done in!" and "How's that?"*):   Uh!

MUSIC MASTER: Splendid! Splendid!

M. JOURDAIN: This reminds me. Teach me how to make a bow to salute a marquise. I'm going to need it soon.

DANCING MASTER: A bow to salute a marquise?

M. JOURDAIN: Yes. A marquise named Dorimène.

DANCING MASTER: Give me your hand.

M. JOURDAIN: No, you do it alone. I'll get the idea.

DANCING MASTER: If you want to make a very respectful salute, you must first make a bow stepping backward, then advance toward the lady with three forward bows, and at the last you bow down to the level of her knees.

M. JOURDAIN: Show me . . . Good.

(*Enter a* LACKEY.)

LACKEY: Monsieur, here is your fencing master who's come.

M. JOURDAIN: Tell him to come in and give me my lesson. (*Exit* LACKEY) I want you two to watch how I do it.

(*Enter* FENCING MASTER. *He salutes and hands* MONSIEUR JOURDAIN *a foil.*)

FENCING MASTER: Now, sir; first make your bow . . . Body straight . . . Weight a little more on the left thigh. Legs not so wide apart. Feet on the same line. Your wrist in line with your forward hip. The point of your weapon on the level of your shoulder. The arm not quite so straight out. The left hand at the level of the eye. Left shoulder drawn back a little more. Head up. Put on a confident look. . . . Advance . . . Keep the body tense. Engage my foil in quart, and carry through . . . One, two . . . Recover . . . Thrust again, keeping feet in same position . . . Backward jump . . . When you make your thrust, sir, the sword should start before the foot, and you must keep your body protected . . . One, two . . . Now, touch my sword in tierce, and carry through . . . Advance . . . Body firm . . . Advance . . . Thrust from that position. One, two . . . Recover . . . Thrust . . . Backward jump . . . On guard, sir, on guard! (*Penetrating* MONSIEUR JOURDAIN's *guard, he pinks his breast.*)

M. JOURDAIN: Uh?

MUSIC MASTER: You're doing marvelously.

FENCING MASTER: As I have already told you, the whole secret of swordplay consists in two things: to give; and not to receive. And as I proved the other day, with demonstrative logic, it is impossible for you to receive, if you know how to divert your enemy's weapon from the line of your body; and that depends only on a simple twist of the wrist, either inward or outward.

M. JOURDAIN: So a person who may not be very brave can be sure of killing his man, and not getting killed?

FENCING MASTER: Exactly. Didn't you see the demonstration?

M. JOURDAIN: Yes.

FENCING MASTER: Thus we can see how highly we swordsmen should be esteemed in a state, and how far the science of fencing is superior to the useless branches of knowledge, like dancing, music, and—

DANCING MASTER: Wait a minute, swordsman; please speak of the dance with respect.

MUSIC MASTER: And learn, I beg of you, to treat music with proper consideration.

FENCING MASTER: You're a funny pair, trying to compare your subjects with mine!

MUSIC MASTER: Look at the great man, will you?

DANCING MASTER: He's a comic sight, with his padded chest protector!

FENCING MASTER: My little dancing master, I'll show you some new steps. And you, my little musician, I'll make you sing—but small!

DANCING MASTER: My good blacksmith, I'll teach you your trade!

M. JOURDAIN (*to the* DANCING MASTER): Are you crazy, to pick a fight with him, who knows all about tierce and quart, and can kill a man by demonstrative logic?

DANCING MASTER: Little I care for his demonstrative logic, and his tierce and quart.

M. JOURDAIN: Take it easy, I tell you.

FENCING MASTER (*to* DANCING MASTER): What, you impertinent puppy!

M. JOURDAIN: Now, now, fencing master.

DANCING MASTER: What, you big cart horse!

M. JOURDAIN: Now, now, dancing master.

FENCING MASTER: If I let myself go—

M. JOURDAIN: Easy, easy there!

DANCING MASTER: If I lay a finger on you—

M. JOURDAIN: Gently, gently!

FENCING MASTER: I'll beat you to a pulp!

M. JOURDAIN: Please!

DANCING MASTER: I'll trim you down to size!

M. JOURDAIN: I beg and pray you!

MUSIC MASTER: We'll teach him how to talk!

M. JOURDAIN: Dear God! Stop, stop! (*Enter* PHILOSOPHY MASTER) Hello, Monsieur Philosopher, you arrive in the nick of time with your philosophy. Come and make peace among these people.

PHILOSOPHY MASTER: What is it? What is the matter, good sirs?

M. JOURDAIN: They have got angry about the standing of their professions, to the point of calling each other names and starting to fight.

PHILOSOPHY MASTER: Dear, dear! My friends, should you let yourselves get so excited? Haven't you read the learned treatise Seneca composed upon anger? Is anything more base and shameful than that passion, which turns man into a wild beast? Should not reason be the mistress of all our actions?

DANCING MASTER: Why, sir, he goes and insults us both, sneering at my trade, the dance; and at music, which is *his* profession!

PHILOSOPHY MASTER: A wise man is superior to any insult he may hear. The proper reply one should make to all affronts is moderation and patience.

FENCING MASTER: They have both had the audacity to compare their professions to mine.

PHILOSOPHY MASTER: Should such a thing move you? Men should not dispute about vainglory and precedence; what truly distinguishes men one from another is wisdom and virtue.

DANCING MASTER: I am simply telling him that dancing is a science which can hardly be sufficiently honored.

MUSIC MASTER: And I was saying that music is a science revered throughout history.

FENCING MASTER: And I was pointing out that the science of arms is the most beautiful and necessary of all sciences.

PHILOSOPHY MASTER: And what, then, is the place of philosophy? I find all three of you very impudent, to speak before me with this arrogance, and to give brazenly the name of science to things which one should not even honor with the title of craft, and which can be grouped only under the denomination of wretched trades of gladiator, minstrel, and posturer!

FENCING MASTER: Get out, you pig of a philosopher!

MUSIC MASTER: Get out, you half-wit highbrow!

DANCING MASTER: Get out, you crackpot professor!

PHILOSOPHY MASTER: What, you yokels!

(*He throws himself upon them; the other three unite to beat him.*)

M. JOURDAIN: Philosopher, sir!

PHILOSOPHY MASTER: The insolent scoundrels! The rascals!

M. JOURDAIN: Philosopher, sir!

FENCING MASTER: Devil take the swine!

M. JOURDAIN: Dear sirs!

PHILOSOPHY MASTER: Impudent rogues!

M. JOURDAIN: Philosopher, sir!

DANCING MASTER: To hell with the jackass!

M. JOURDAIN: My friends!

PHILOSOPHY MASTER: Blackguards!

M. JOURDAIN: Philosopher, sir!

MUSIC MASTER: Damn him and his insolence!

M. JOURDAIN: My dear sirs!

PHILOSOPHY MASTER: Villains! Beggars! Traitors! Impostors!

M. JOURDAIN: Philosopher, sir! Dear sirs! Philosopher, sir! My friends! Philosopher, sir! (*Exit the four* MASTERS, *fighting*) Oh, fight all you like. There's nothing I can do about it, and I won't get my dressing gown dirty trying to separate you. I'd be crazy to get into that mess; I might get a nasty bang.

(*Enter* PHILOSOPHY MASTER, *tidying his clothing.*)

PHILOSOPHY MASTER: And now let's have our lesson.

M. JOURDAIN: Ah, sir, I'm sorry for the blows you've received.

PHILOSOPHY MASTER: That's nothing. A philosopher knows how to take things as they come; and I am going to compose a satire against them, in the style of Juvenal, which will settle their hash. We'll drop the matter. What do you want to learn?

M. JOURDAIN: Everything I can, for I am crazy to be a scholar. It makes me furious that my father and mother didn't make me study all the branches of knowledge when I was young.

PHILOSOPHY MASTER: That is a very laudable sentiment. *Nam sine doctrina vita est quasi mortis imago.* You understand that; you know Latin, of course.

M. JOURDAIN: Yes; but let's pretend I don't know it. Explain to me what that means.

PHILOSOPHY MASTER: That means: "Without knowledge, life is almost an image of death."

M. JOURDAIN: That Latin is right.

PHILOSOPHY MASTER: Don't you have some basic elements, some beginnings in the fields of study?

M. JOURDAIN: Oh, yes; I know how to read and write.

PHILOSOPHY MASTER: Now where would you like to begin? Would you like to have me teach you logic?

M. JOURDAIN: Just what is that logic?

PHILOSOPHY MASTER: Logic teaches the three operations of the mind.

M. JOURDAIN: What are these three operations of the mind?

PHILOSOPHY MASTER: The first, the second, and the third. The first is true conception by means of the universals. The second is true judgment by means of categories; and the third, the true drawing of logical consequences by means of the figures Barbara, Celarent, Darii, Ferio, Baralipton, and so forth.

M. JOURDAIN: Those words sound kind of repulsive. I don't like that logic. Let's learn something prettier.

PHILOSOPHY MASTER: Would you like to learn ethics?

M. JOURDAIN: Ethics?

PHILOSOPHY MASTER: Yes.

M. JOURDAIN: What do they do?

PHILOSOPHY MASTER: Ethics treats of the nature of happiness, teaches men to moderate their passions, and—

M. JOURDAIN: No, none of that. I have a devilish excitable nature; no ethics for me. When I want to get mad, I want to get good and mad.

PHILOSOPHY MASTER: Would you like to learn physics?

M. JOURDAIN: Physics? Why not leave them to the doctors?

PHILOSOPHY MASTER: Physics is the science which explains the principles of the natural world and the properties of matter. It treats the nature of the elements, of the metals, of minerals, stones, plants, and animals, and teaches us the causes of meteors, rainbows, shooting stars, comets, lightning, thunder and thunderbolts, rain, snow, hail, winds and whirlwinds.

M. JOURDAIN: There's too much rowdydow in that; too much rumpus and ruckus.

PHILOSOPHY MASTER: Well, then, what do you want me to teach you?

M. JOURDAIN: Teach me spelling.

PHILOSOPHY MASTER: Gladly.

M. JOURDAIN: And afterwards, you can teach me the almanac, so I'll know when there's a moon and when there isn't.

PHILOSOPHY MASTER: Very well. To follow your idea and to treat this subject from a philosophical point of view, one must proceed according to the natural order of things, by an exact understanding of the nature of the letters, and of the different manner of pronouncing them. I shall first inform you that the letters are divided into vowels, from the Latin meaning "vocal," so called because they express the voiced sounds; and into consonants, meaning "with-sounding," so called because they "sound with" the vowels, and merely mark the various articulations of the voiced sounds. There are five vowels, or voiced sounds: A, E, I, O, U.

M. JOURDAIN: I understand all that.

PHILOSOPHY MASTER: The vowel A, pronounced *ah,* is formed by opening the mouth wide: *Ah.*

M. JOURDAIN: *Ah, ah.* Yes, yes.

PHILOSOPHY MASTER: The vowel E, pronounced *euh,* is formed by bringing the lower jaw closer to the upper jaw: *Euh. Ah, euh.*

M. JOURDAIN: *Ah, euh; ah, euh.* Bless my soul, yes! Oh, how beautiful that is!

PHILOSOPHY MASTER: The vowel I, pronounced *Ee,* is made by bringing the jaws still closer together, and by widening the mouth, or extending its corners toward the ears: *Ee. Ah, euh, ee.*

M. JOURDAIN: *Ah, euh, ee, ee, ee.* That's true! Hurrah for science!

PHILOSOPHY MASTER: The vowel O is formed by opening the jaws again, and by bringing the corners of the mouth closer together: *Oh.*

M. JOURDAIN: *Oh, oh.* Nothing could be truer! *Ah, euh, ee, oh, ee, oh.* That's wonderful! *Ee, oh, ee, oh!*[3]

PHILOSOPHY MASTER: The opening of the mouth makes, as it happens, a small circle which represents an O.

M. JOURDAIN: *Oh, oh, oh.* You're right: *oh.* Oh, what a fine thing it is to know something!

PHILOSOPHY MASTER: The vowel U[4] is formed by bringing the teeth close together, without their quite touching, and by thrusting out the lips, thus making a small aperture: *U.*

M. JOURDAIN: *U, u.* It couldn't be truer! *U!*

PHILOSOPHY MASTER: The lips are extended as if you are pouting; hence it comes that if you want to make this sound at someone, expressing contempt, all you say to him is *U.*[5]

M. JOURDAIN: *U, u.* That's right! Oh, why didn't I study sooner, to learn all that?

PHILOSOPHY MASTER: Tomorrow we shall take up the other letters, the consonants.

M. JOURDAIN: Are they as remarkable as these vowels?

---

[3] Traditionally, the actor here imitates an ass braying.
[4] The French U, like a German ü.
[5] The sound is used by the French for booing.

PHILOSOPHY MASTER: Certainly. The consonant D, for example, is pronounced by touching the tip of the tongue to the hard palate, just above the teeth: *Da.*

M. JOURDAIN: *Da, da.* Yes. Oh, how wonderful, wonderful!

PHILOSOPHY MASTER: The F is pronounced by applying the upper teeth to the lower lip: *Fa.*

M. JOURDAIN: *Fa, fa.* It's the truth! Oh, Father and Mother, how I blame you!

PHILOSOPHY MASTER: And the R, by placing the tip of the tongue against the upper palate, so that it is brushed by the air, forcefully expelled, and yields to it, and returns constantly to the same position, making a kind of vibration: *Rra.*

M. JOURDAIN: *R, r, ra; R, rr, rrra.* That's right! Oh, what a clever man you are! And how much time I've lost! *Rrrra.*

PHILOSOPHY MASTER: I shall explain to you all these important facts in detail.

M. JOURDAIN: Please do. And by the way, I must take you into my confidence. I am in love with a person of very high rank, and I should like to have your help in writing something in a little note I want to drop at her feet.

PHILOSOPHY MASTER: I shall be delighted.

M. JOURDAIN: It will be in the gallant style, yes?

PHILOSOPHY MASTER: Certainly. Is it poetry you want to write her?

M. JOURDAIN: No, no; no poetry.

PHILOSOPHY MASTER: You want only prose?

M. JOURDAIN: No; I don't want either poetry or prose.

PHILOSOPHY MASTER: Well, it has to be either one or the other.

M. JOURDAIN: Why?

PHILOSOPHY MASTER: For the reason, sir, that we have no means of expression other than prose and poetry.

M. JOURDAIN: There's nothing but prose or poetry?

PHILOSOPHY MASTER: Quite so, sir. All that is not prose is poetry; and all that is not poetry is prose.

M. JOURDAIN: And when a man talks, what's that?

PHILOSOPHY MASTER: Prose.

M. JOURDAIN: What? When I say: "Nicole, bring me my slippers and give me my nightcap," that's prose?

PHILOSOPHY MASTER: Yes, sir.

M. JOURDAIN: Well, I'll be hanged! For more than forty years I've been talking prose without any idea of it; I'm very much obliged to you for telling me that. So, I'd like to put in a letter: "Beautiful Marquise, your lovely eyes make me die of love." But I'd like to have it put in the gallant style; neatly turned, you know.

PHILOSOPHY MASTER: Put it, then, that the rays of her eyes reduce your heart to ashes; that for her sake you suffer night and day the tortures of—

M. JOURDAIN: No, no, no. I don't want all that. I just want what I told you: "Beautiful Marquise, your lovely eyes make me die of love."

PHILOSOPHY MASTER: Well, you ought to stretch it out a little.

M. JOURDAIN: No, I tell you. I just want only those words in the letter; but elegantly put, properly arranged. So I'm asking you to tell me, out of curiosity, the different ways you could write them.

PHILOSOPHY MASTER: Well, firstly, you could put them the way you said: "Beautiful Marquise, your lovely eyes make me die of love." Or else: "Of love, beautiful Marquise, your beautiful eyes make me die." Or else: "Your eyes, lovely, of love, Marquise beautiful, make die me." Or else: "Die, beautiful Marquise, of love your lovely eyes me make." Or else: "Me your lovely eyes of love make die, beautiful Marquise."

M. JOURDAIN: But of all those ways, which one is the best?

PHILOSOPHY MASTER: The one you said: "Beautiful Marquise, your lovely eyes make me die of love."

M. JOURDAIN: And nevertheless I have never studied; I did that straight off! I thank you with all my heart; please come again tomorrow early.

PHILOSOPHY MASTER: I won't fail to.

(*Exit* PHILOSOPHY MASTER.)

M. JOURDAIN (*to his* LACKEYS): Look here, hasn't my new suit come yet?

SECOND LACKEY: No, sir.

M. JOURDAIN: That damned tailor makes me wait until a day when I have so much to do! He makes me furious. May the quartan fever take that hangbird tailor! To the devil with the tailor! May the galloping plague seize the tailor! If I had him here now, that infernal tailor, that dog of a tailor, that pig of a tailor, I'd . . . (*Enter* MERCHANT TAILOR *and his* APPRENTICE, *carrying* M. JOURDAIN'*s suit*) Oh, here you are! I was on the point of getting angry with you.

MERCHANT TAILOR: I couldn't come sooner; I have had twenty journeymen working on your coat.

M. JOURDAIN: The silk stockings you sent me were so tight that I had a terrible time getting them on, and already there are a couple of stitches broken.

MERCHANT TAILOR: They will get looser.

M. JOURDAIN: Yes, if all the stitches break. And what's more, you made me some shoes which hurt frightfully.

MERCHANT TAILOR: Not at all, sir.

M. JOURDAIN: What do you mean, not at all?

MERCHANT TAILOR: They don't hurt you.

M. JOURDAIN: I tell you they do hurt me!

MERCHANT TAILOR: You just imagine it.

M. JOURDAIN: I imagine it because I feel it. What kind of talk is that?

MERCHANT TAILOR: Now look, here is the finest coat in all the court, the most harmoniously matched. It is a great achievement to have invented a formal coat which is not black. I defy the most eminent tailors to equal it in a dozen tries.

M. JOURDAIN: What's this? You've got the flowers upside down

MERCHANT TAILOR: You didn't tell me you wanted them righ side up.

M. JOURDAIN: Did I have to tell you that?

MERCHANT TAILOR: Yes, indeed. All the people of quality wear them this way.

M. JOURDAIN: People of quality wear the flowers upside down?

MERCHANT TAILOR: Yes, sir.

M. JOURDAIN: Oh, well, it's all right then.

MERCHANT TAILOR: If you prefer, I'll turn them right side up.

M. JOURDAIN: No, no.

MERCHANT TAILOR: You have only to say so.

M. JOURDAIN: No, I tell you. You did all right . . . Do you think the costume will look well on me?

MERCHANT TAILOR: What a question! I defy any artist to paint a finer ensemble. I have a workman who, for assembling a wide trouser, is the greatest genius on earth; and another who, for confecting a doublet, is the hero of our age.

M. JOURDAIN: The peruke and the plumes, are they all right?

MERCHANT TAILOR: Perfect.

M. JOURDAIN (*noticing the tailor's coat*): Ah, master tailor, there is some material from the last coat you made me! I recognize it perfectly.

MERCHANT TAILOR: The fact is, the material seemed to me so beautiful that I made a coat for myself from it.

M. JOURDAIN: Yes, but you shouldn't have made it with my material.

MASTER TAILOR: Do you want to try on your coat?

M. JOURDAIN: Yes; give it to me.

MERCHANT TAILOR: Wait a moment. That's not the way to do it. I have brought some men to dress you to music; that kind of costume has to be put on with ceremony. Holà! Come in, you men. (*Enter four* JOURNEYMEN TAILORS) Put this coat on the gentleman, in the way you do for persons of quality.

> (*Two* TAILORS *remove* MONSIEUR JOURDAIN's *breeches, two others remove his jacket. They try on his new coat.* MONSIEUR JOURDAIN *promenades*

*among them for their inspection. All takes place to
the music of the entire orchestra.*)

A TAILOR: Gentleman, sir, will you give a little tip to the work-
men?

M. JOURDAIN: What did you call me?

TAILOR: Gentleman, sir.

M. JOURDAIN: Gentleman, sir! That's what comes from dressing like a person of quality. If you go around always dressed as
a commoner, no one will say to you: "Gentleman, sir!" Here;
that's for "gentleman, sir."

TAILOR: Monsignor, we are very much obliged to you.

M. JOURDAIN: Monsignor! Oh, oh, Monsignor! Wait a bit, my
friend; "Monsignor" deserves a little something. Here; that's
a present from Monsignor.

TAILOR: Monsignor, we shall all drink to the health of Your
Grace.

M. JOURDAIN: Your Grace! Oh, oh, oh! Wait; don't go away.
"Your Grace"—to me! Faith, if he goes as far as Royal High-
ness he'll have my whole purse! . . . Here; that's for My
Grace.

TAILOR: Monsignor, we thank you very humbly for your gener-
osity.

M. JOURDAIN: A good thing he stopped there. I was going to
give him the whole business.

(*The four* JOURNEYMEN TAILORS *express their joy
in a dance, which forms the second* Interlude.)

ACT III

The MERCHANT TAILOR *and his assistants exit, leaving* MONSIEUR JOURDAIN *and his two* LACKEYS *on
the stage.*

M. JOURDAIN: Follow me, while I take a little walk to show my
new suit around town. And especially, both of you be sure to

walk directly behind me, so that everybody can see that you belong to me.

LACKEYS: Yes, sir.

M. JOURDAIN: Get Nicole for me. I want to give her some orders. No, don't move. Here she is now. (*Enter* NICOLE) Nicole!

NICOLE: Yes, what is it?

M. JOURDAIN: Listen to me.

NICOLE: He, he, he, he, he!

M. JOURDAIN: What is there to laugh at?

NICOLE: He, he, he, he, he, he!

M. JOURDAIN: What does the rascal mean?

NICOLE: He, he, he! How funny you look! He, he, he!

M. JOURDAIN: What's the matter?

NICOLE: Oh, oh, good Lord! He, he, he, he, he!

M. JOURDAIN: You scamp! Are you trying to make fun of me?

NICOLE: Oh, no, sir. I'd hate to do that. He, he, he, he, he, he!

M. JOURDAIN: I'll land one on your nose, if you laugh any more.

NICOLE: Monsieur, I can't help it. He, he, he, he, he, he!

M. JOURDAIN: You won't stop?

NICOLE: Monsieur, I beg your pardon. But you look so funny, I can't keep from laughing. He, he, he!

M. JOURDAIN: I never saw such impudence.

NICOLE: You're so comical like that. He, he!

M. JOURDAIN: I'm going to—

NICOLE: I beg you to excuse me. He, he, he, he!

M. JOURDAIN: Look here, if you laugh once more, I swear I'll apply to your cheek the biggest slap that has ever been slapped.

NICOLE: It's all over, sir. I won't laugh any more.

M. JOURDAIN: Make sure you don't. Now, I want you to clean up, in preparation for—

NICOLE: He, he!

M. JOURDAIN: To clean up properly—

NICOLE: He, he!

M. JOURDAIN: I say I want you to clean up the parlor, and—

NICOLE: He, he!

M. JOURDAIN: What, again!

NICOLE: Look here, sir, I'd rather have you beat me and let me laugh myself out. That will do me more good. He, he, he, he, he!

M. JOURDAIN: You'll drive me crazy!

NICOLE: Please, monsieur, I beg you to let me laugh. He, he, he!

M. JOURDAIN: If I catch you—

NICOLE: Monsieu-eur, I'll blow-ow-ow up, if I don't laugh. He, he, he!

M. JOURDAIN: Has anyone ever seen such a hussy! She comes and laughs insolently in my face, instead of obeying my orders!

NICOLE: What do you want me to do, sir?

M. JOURDAIN: I want you, you rogue, to see to getting the house ready for the company that is due to come soon.

NICOLE: Well, my sakes, I've lost all fancy to laugh. Your company always makes such a mess around here that the mere mention of it is enough to put me out of humor.

M. JOURDAIN: So, for your convenience, I ought to shut my door to everybody?

NICOLE: At least, you ought to shut it to certain people.

(*Enter* MADAME JOURDAIN.)

MME JOURDAIN: Aha, here's something new! Tell me, my good husband, what's this getup of yours? Are you crazy, to go and rig yourself out that way? Do you want people to mock you everywhere?

M. JOURDAIN: My good wife, only the fools, male and female, will mock me.

MME JOURDAIN: Well, they haven't waited for this occasion to start. Your behavior has been making everybody laugh for quite some time.

M. JOURDAIN: Everybody! What do you mean by everybody, if you please?

MME JOURDAIN: I mean everybody who knows what's what, and who has got more sense than you. For my part, I am scandalized by the kind of life you are leading. I vow I don't recognize our own house. You'd say it was carnival time here every day; and to make sure of it, from early morning on there's nothing but a great row of fiddlers and singers, enough to disturb the whole neighborhood.

NICOLE: Madame is quite right. I can never keep the house clean any more, with all that gang of people you bring in here. They've got big feet which go and hunt for mud in every quarter of the city, in order to bring it back here. And poor Françoise is worn almost to a shadow, scrubbing the floors that your fine folks dirty up regularly every day.

M. JOURDAIN: Now, now, Nicole, you've got to be quite a speech-maker for a peasant servant girl.

MME JOURDAIN: Nicole is quite right; she's got more sense than you. I'd like to know what you think you're doing with a dancing teacher, at your age.

NICOLE: And with a great big bully of a fighter, who stamps so he shakes the whole house, and loosens up all the tiles on the parlor floor.

M. JOURDAIN: Shut up, servant; and shut up, wife.

MME JOURDAIN: You want to learn how to dance, for when you won't be able to walk?

NICOLE: You want to kill somebody?

M. JOURDAIN: Shut up, I tell you! You are both ignorant fools; you don't know the prerogatives of all that.

MME JOURDAIN: You ought to think rather of marrying off your daughter. She's of an age to have a husband now.

M. JOURDAIN: I'll think of marrying my daughter when a proper match for her appears. But I also want to think of learning the finer things of life.

NICOLE: I've also heard, madame, that to top it off he took on a philosophy teacher today.

M. JOURDAIN: Quite right. I want to sharpen my wits, and be able to discuss things among intelligent people.

MME JOURDAIN: One of these days you'll be going to school to get yourself whipped, at your age.

M. JOURDAIN: Why not? I wish to heaven I could be whipped now, in front of everybody, if I could know what one learns in school.

NICOLE: Yes, my faith! Much good that would do you!

M. JOURDAIN: It would indeed.

MME JOURDAIN: A lot of use that would be for running your house.

M. JOURDAIN: You're right, it would. You both talk like simpletons, and I'm ashamed of your ignorance. (*To* MADAME JOURDAIN) For example, do you know what you're saying now?

MME JOURDAIN: Yes, I know that what I am saying is very well said, and you ought to think of changing your way of life.

M. JOURDAIN: I'm not talking of that. I ask you, what are the words that you are saying now?

MME JOURDAIN: They are very sensible words, and that's what your conduct is not.

M. JOURDAIN: I'm not talking of that, I tell you. I ask you; what I'm speaking to you, what I'm saying to you now, what is it?

MME JOURDAIN: Stuff and nonsense.

M. JOURDAIN: No, no, not at all. What we are both saying, the language we are talking now?

MME JOURDAIN: Well?

M. JOURDAIN: What is that called?

MME JOURDAIN: That is called whatever you've a mind to call it.

M. JOURDAIN: It is called prose, ignorant woman!

MME JOURDAIN: Prose?

M. JOURDAIN: Yes, prose. Everything which is prose is not poetry; and everything which is not poetry is not prose. Ha, that's what comes of studying! (*To* NICOLE) And you, do you know what you have to do to make an U?

NICOLE: How's that?

M. JOURDAIN: Yes. What do you do when you make an U?

NICOLE: What?

M. JOURDAIN: Just say U, for example.

NICOLE: All right, U.

M. JOURDAIN: Now what are you doing?

NICOLE: I'm saying U.

M. JOURDAIN: Yes, but when you say U, what are you doing?

NICOLE: I'm doing what you tell me.

M. JOURDAIN: Oh, what a dreadful thing it is to have to deal with idiots! You thrust your lips outward, and you bring the upper jaw down close to the lower jaw: U. You see, U. I pout: U.

NICOLE: Yes, that's right pretty.

MME JOURDAIN: Wonderful!

M. JOURDAIN: It's quite different, if you'd seen O, and Da, da, and Fa, fa.

MME JOURDAIN: What's all this rubbish?

NICOLE: What does all that cure you of?

M. JOURDAIN: It makes me sick to see such ignorant women.

MME JOURDAIN: You ought to kick all those fellows out, with their moonshine.

NICOLE: And especially that big gawk of a fencing master, who fills the whole house with dust.

M. JOURDAIN: Yes, that fencing master worries you a lot. I'll show you how stupid you are, right away. (*He has a lackey bring him the foils, takes one, and hands one to* NICOLE) Take this. Logical demonstration, the line of the body. When you thrust in quart, this is all you have to do. And when you thrust in tierce, that's what you do. In this way, you can never get killed. Isn't it fine, to be assured of the result, when you're fighting with someone? There now, just make a thrust, to try it out.

NICOLE: All right. (*She makes several lunges, pricking* MONSIEUR JOURDAIN.)

M. JOURDAIN: Hold on! Hey, easy there! The devil take the wench!

NICOLE: You told me to thrust.

M. JOURDAIN: Yes, but you thrust in tierce before thrusting in quart; and you wouldn't wait for me to parry.

MME JOURDAIN: You're crazy, my poor husband, with your fancy ideas. It's all happened since you took it into your head to hang around with the nobility.

M. JOURDAIN: When I hang around with the nobility, I show my good judgment. It's a lot finer thing than to hang around with your bourgeoisie.

MME JOURDAIN: Really now! There's a lot to be gained by associating with your nobles! You've done some nice business with that Monsieur le Comte you're so fascinated with.

M. JOURDAIN: Quiet! Think what you're saying. Are you aware, wife, that when you mention him, you don't know who he really is? He is a person of greater importance than you think, a lord who is highly considered at court. He speaks to the King just the way I am speaking to you. Isn't it a very honorable thing for people to see a person of such quality come to my house so often, calling me his dear friend, and treating me as if I were his equal? He has done me some kindnesses you would never guess; and in front of everybody he shows me such special regards that I am embarrassed myself.

MME JOURDAIN: Yes, he does you kindnesses, and he shows you special regards; but he borrows your money.

M. JOURDAIN: Well, isn't it an honor for me to lend money to a man of that rank? And can I do any less for a lord who calls me his dear friend?

MME JOURDAIN: And this lord, what does he do for you?

M. JOURDAIN: He does things that would astonish people, if they were known.

MME JOURDAIN: What things, for instance?

M. JOURDAIN: Enough; I won't explain. Let it suffice that if I have lent him money, he will repay me well, and that soon.

MME JOURDAIN: Yes; you can expect it any minute.

M. JOURDAIN: Certainly; didn't he tell me so?

MME JOURDAIN: Yes, yes; he won't fail to do nothing of the sort.

M. JOURDAIN: He gave me his word as a gentleman.

MME JOURDAIN: Nonsense!

M. JOURDAIN: You are very obstinate, wife. I tell you he'll keep his word. I'm sure of it.

MME JOURDAIN: And I tell you he won't; and all the attentions he shows you are just to take you in.

M. JOURDAIN: Shut up; here he is.

MME JOURDAIN: That's the last straw. Perhaps he's coming to get another loan from you. The sight of him takes away my appetite.

M. JOURDAIN: Shut up, I tell you.
            (*Enter* DORANTE.)

DORANTE: My dear friend Monsieur Jourdain, and how are you?

M. JOURDAIN: Very well, sir, at your humble service.

DORANTE: And Madame Jourdain here, how is she doing?

MME JOURDAIN: Madame Jourdain is doing the best she can.

DORANTE: Well, well, Monsieur Jourdain! How elegantly you're gotten up!

M. JOURDAIN: Well, you see.

DORANTE: You look very brave in that suit; we have no young sprigs at court better turned out than you are.

M. JOURDAIN: He, he!

MME JOURDAIN (*aside*):   He scratches him where he itches.

DORANTE: Turn around. It's really stylish.

MME JOURDAIN (*aside*):   Yes; as silly behind as in front.

DORANTE: 'Pon my word, Monsieur Jourdain, I have been extraordinarily anxious to see you. I have a higher opinion of you than of absolutely anyone else. I was talking about you this very morning in the King's bedchamber.

M. JOURDAIN: You do me too much honor, sir. (*To* MADAME JOURDAIN) In the King's bedchamber!

DORANTE: Come, come; put on your hat.

M. JOURDAIN: Monsieur, I know the respect I owe you.

DORANTE: Good Lord, put it on! Let's have no ceremony between us, please.

M. JOURDAIN: Monsieur . . .

DORANTE: Cover, I tell you, Monsieur Jourdain; you are my friend.

M. JOURDAIN: Monsieur, I am your humble servant.

DORANTE: I won't cover, if you don't.

M. JOURDAIN (*covering*):   I'd rather be unmannerly than troublesome.

DORANTE: I am your debtor, as you know.

MME JOURDAIN (*aside*):   Yes, we know it only too well.

DORANTE: You have generously lent me money on several occasions, and you have obliged me with the best grace in the world, most assuredly.

M. JOURDAIN: You're joking, sir.

DORANTE: But I make a point of repaying all loans, and recognizing the kindnesses that are done me.

M. JOURDAIN: I don't doubt it, sir.

DORANTE: I want to clean matters up between us. I've come so we can go over our accounts together.

M. JOURDAIN (*to* MADAME JOURDAIN):   See how unjust you were!

DORANTE: I am the kind of fellow who likes to pay off his debts as soon as possible.

M. JOURDAIN (*to* MADAME JOURDAIN):   I told you so!

DORANTE: Let's see now how much I owe you.

M. JOURDAIN (*to* MADAME JOURDAIN):   You and your ridiculous suspicions!

DORANTE: Do you remember exactly how much you lent me?

M. JOURDAIN: I think so. I made a little memorandum. Here it is. On one occasion, given to you, two hundred louis.

DORANTE: That's right.

M. JOURDAIN: Another time, one hundred twenty.

DORANTE: Yes.

M. JOURDAIN: And another time, a hundred and forty.

DORANTE: You're right.

M. JOURDAIN: These three items add up to four hundred and sixty louis, which makes five thousand and sixty francs.

DORANTE: The accounting is excellent. Five thousand and sixty francs.

M. JOURDAIN: One thousand eight hundred and thirty-two francs to your feather supplier.

DORANTE: Exactly.

M. JOURDAIN: Two thousand seven hundred and eighty francs to your tailor.

DORANTE: True enough.

M. JOURDAIN: Four thousand three hundred seventy-nine francs twelve sous and eight farthings to your haberdasher.

DORANTE: Excellent. Twelve sous eight farthings. Very exact accounting.

M. JOURDAIN: And one thousand seven hundred forty-eight francs seven sous and four farthings to your saddler.

DORANTE: That's all correct. How much does it come to?

M. JOURDAIN: Sum total, fifteen thousand eight hundred francs.

DORANTE: The sum total is quite correct: fifteen thousand eight hundred francs. Now add two hundred pistoles you can give me now; that will make exactly eighteen thousand francs, which I will pay you at the earliest possible moment.

MME JOURDAIN (*to* MONSIEUR JOURDAIN): Well, didn't I guess it?

M. JOURDAIN (*to* MADAME JOURDAIN): Silence!

DORANTE: Would it be inconvenient for you to give me that amount?

M. JOURDAIN: No, no.

MME JOURDAIN (*to* MONSIEUR JOURDAIN): That fellow is milking you like a cow.

M. JOURDAIN (*to* MADAME JOURDAIN): Shut up!

DORANTE: If it's inconvenient, I can get it somewhere else.

M. JOURDAIN: No, indeed.

MME JOURDAIN (*to* MONSIEUR JOURDAIN): He won't be satisfied until he's ruined you.

M. JOURDAIN (*to* MADAME JOURDAIN): Shut up, I tell you!

DORANTE: If it embarrasses you, you have only to say so.

M. JOURDAIN: Not at all, sir.

MME JOURDAIN (*to* MONSIEUR JOURDAIN): He's nothing but a crook.

M. JOURDAIN (*to* MADAME JOURDAIN): Will you shut up?

MME JOURDAIN (*to* MONSIEUR JOURDAIN): He'll suck you dry, down to your last penny.

M. JOURDAIN (*to* MADAME JOURDAIN): I tell you to shut your mouth!

DORANTE: There are plenty of people who would be delighted to lend it to me; but since you're my best friend, I thought I would be doing you an injury if I asked anyone else.

M. JOURDAIN: You do me too much honor, my dear sir. I'll go and fetch what you want.

MME JOURDAIN (*to* MONSIEUR JOURDAIN): What! You're going to give it to him?

M. JOURDAIN (*to* MADAME JOURDAIN): What can I do? Do you expect me to refuse a man of such rank, who talked of me this very morning in the King's bedchamber?

MME JOURDAIN (*to* MONSIEUR JOURDAIN): Go on, you're just an easy mark!

(*Exit* MONSIEUR JOURDAIN.)

DORANTE: You seem cast down about something. What is the matter, Madame Jourdain?

MME JOURDAIN: I've cut my eyeteeth; I wasn't born yesterday.

DORANTE: And your charming daughter, I don't see her. Where is she?

MME JOURDAIN: My charming daughter is all right where she is.

DORANTE: How is she getting along?

MME JOURDAIN: She is getting along on her two legs.

DORANTE: Wouldn't you like to bring her some day to see the command performance of the ballet and comedy before the King?

MME JOURDAIN: Oh, yes, we certainly need a good laugh; a good laugh is certainly what we need.

DORANTE: I think, Madame Jourdain, you must have had many admirers in your youth; you must have been so pretty and of such a charming humor.

MME JOURDAIN: Good land, sir, is Madame Jourdain doddering already? She's got one foot in the grave, maybe?

DORANTE: 'Pon my soul, Madame Jourdain, I ask your pardon. I didn't realize you're still young; I'm so unobservant. I beg you to excuse my impoliteness.

(*Enter* MONSIEUR JOURDAIN.)

M. JOURDAIN: Here are two hundred louis exactly.

DORANTE: I assure you, Monsieur Jourdain, that I am very much at your service; I am most eager to do you some good turn at court.

M. JOURDAIN: I am very deeply obliged to you.

DORANTE: If Madame Jourdain wants to see the performance before His Majesty, I shall get the best seats in the house for her.

MME JOURDAIN: Madame Jourdain kisses your hands with gratitude.

DORANTE (*aside to* MONSIEUR JOURDAIN):   As I told you in my note, our lovely Marquise will come here soon for the ballet and the refreshments. I have finally persuaded her to accept the party you want to give her.

M. JOURDAIN (*aside to* DORANTE):   Let's move farther off, for good reason.

DORANTE: I haven't seen you for a week, and I haven't given you any news of the diamond ring you asked me to present to her in your name. But the fact is I had all sorts of trouble in overcoming her scruples, and it's only today she made up her mind to accept it.

M. JOURDAIN: How did she find it?

DORANTE: Marvelous! And unless I'm much mistaken, the beauty of the diamond will work wonders for you.

M. JOURDAIN: Would to God it were so!

MME JOURDAIN (*to* NICOLE): When he once gets with that Count, he can't leave him.

DORANTE (*to* MONSIEUR JOURDAIN): I played up to her properly the value of the present and the greatness of your love.

M. JOURDAIN: Your kindness overwhelms me, sir. I am embarrassed beyond words to see a person of your rank lower himself to do what you are doing for me.

DORANTE: Are you joking? Between friends, does one worry about scruples of that sort? Wouldn't you do the same thing for me, if the occasion should arise?

M. JOURDAIN: Oh, assuredly; with the utmost willingness.

MME JOURDAIN (*to* NICOLE): I can't abide seeing that fellow around.

DORANTE: Personally, I stick at nothing when it's a question of serving a friend. And when you confided to me your passion for my friend, the charming Marquise, you saw that I immediately offered to aid your love.

M. JOURDAIN: That's true. I am confounded by your kindnesses.

MME JOURDAIN (*to* NICOLE): Won't he ever go away?

NICOLE: They just like each other's company.

DORANTE: You have taken the right course to touch her heart. Women love above all things to have people spend money on them; and your frequent serenades, and the continual offerings of flowers, and the superb fireworks on the lake, and the diamond ring she received in your name, and the party you are preparing for her—that sort of thing speaks far better in favor of your love than all the words you might utter to her in person.

M. JOURDAIN: There are no expenditures I wouldn't make, if

they would help me find the way to touch her heart. A lady of quality has ravishing charms for me; I would pay any price for the honor of her love.

MME JOURDAIN (*to* NICOLE): What can they be argufying so much about? Sneak over and see if you can't pick up something.

DORANTE: Very soon you will enjoy at your ease the pleasure of seeing her; and your eyes will have plenty of time to satisfy their longing.

M. JOURDAIN: To get free, I have arranged that my wife shall go and dine with her sister, and she'll spend the whole afternoon there.

DORANTE: That's very prudent. Your wife might have made trouble. I have given all the directions to the caterer, in your name; and I've done everything necessary for the ballet. I worked out the scheme for it myself; if the execution comes up to my idea, I am sure it will be found—

M. JOURDAIN (*perceiving that* NICOLE *is listening, gives her a box on the ear*): What's this, saucebox! (*To* DORANTE) Please, let's get out of here.

(*Exit* MONSIEUR JOURDAIN *and* DORANTE.)

NICOLE: My stars, madame, curiosity cost me something. But I think there's more here than meets the eye. They're talking about some affair they don't want you to know about.

MME JOURDAIN: Well, Nicole, this isn't the first time I've had some suspicions about my husband. Unless I am very much mistaken, he's setting his cap at someone, and I'm trying to find out who it is. But let's think about my daughter a moment. You know how Cléonte loves her. He's a man I like, and I want to help his suit, and give Lucile to him, if I can.

NICOLE: Really, madame, I am just delighted to know you feel that way; for if you like the master, I like the manservant just as much, and it would make me very happy if our marriage could take place in the shadow of theirs.

MME JOURDAIN: Go and give him a message from me. Tell him to come and see me soon, and we'll go together to my husband and ask my daughter's hand.

NICOLE: I'll do so right away, madame, and very gladly. I couldn't do a pleasanter errand. (*Exit* MADAME JOURDAIN) I think I'm going to make some people very happy. (*Enter* CLÉONTE *and* COVIELLE) Ah, here you are, by a lucky chance! I bring you good news. I've come—

CLÉONTE: Withdraw, perfidious creature! Don't try to distract me with your treacherous words!

NICOLE: So that's the way you take—

CLÉONTE: Withdraw, I tell you! And go straightway and tell your faithless mistress that she will never befool the too confiding Cléonte!

NICOLE: What kind of a fit is this? My dear Covielle, do tell me what this means.

COVIELLE: Your dear Covielle! You scoundrel! Quick, out of my sight, villain! Leave me in peace!

NICOLE: What! You too—

COVIELLE: Out of my sight, I tell you! Never speak to me again!

NICOLE (*aside*): Ouch! What's biting them both? I'd better go right away and tell my mistress of this fine to-do.

(*Exit* NICOLE.)

CLÉONTE: What! To treat in such a way a lover, the most faithful and ardent of all lovers!

COVIELLE: It's appalling, how they treat us both.

CLÉONTE: I display for a certain person all the ardor and affection conceivable. I love only her in all the world; I have her alone in my thought; she has all my devotion, all my desires, all my joy; I speak only of her, I think only of her, I dream only of her, I breathe only for her, my heart exists only for her; and here is the fit reward for so much love! I pass two days without seeing her, which are to me two frightful centuries; I meet her by chance; and at the sight my heart is utterly transported, my joy manifests itself upon my countenance. Ravished with delight, I fly to her; and the faithless one turns her face from me, and passes grimly by, as if she had never seen me in her life!

COVIELLE: I say—exactly the same thing.

CLÉONTE: Has anything, Covielle, ever matched the perfidy of the ingrate Lucile?

COVIELLE: Or that, sir, of the hussy Nicole?

CLÉONTE: After so many devout sacrifices, sighs, and vows that I have offered to her charms!

COVIELLE: After so many attentions, services, and helping hands I have extended to her in her kitchen!

CLÉONTE: So many tears I have shed at her knees!

COVIELLE: So many buckets of water I have pulled up out of the well for her!

CLÉONTE: So much ardor I have evidenced, in cherishing her more than my own self!

COVIELLE: So much heat I have endured in turning the spit for her!

CLÉONTE: She flees me with contempt!

COVIELLE: She turns her back on me with an uppity air!

CLÉONTE: It is perfidy deserving the utmost chastisement.

COVIELLE: It is treason deserving a thousand slaps in the face.

CLÉONTE: Never, I beg you, take it into your head to speak in her defense.

COVIELLE: I, sir? Heaven forbid!

CLÉONTE: Don't try to excuse the action of the faithless one.

COVIELLE: Don't be afraid, I won't.

CLÉONTE: No. For you see, all your efforts to defend her will avail nothing.

COVIELLE: Defend her? Who could have that idea?

CLÉONTE: I want to keep my resentment fresh, and break off all relations with her.

COVIELLE: I give my consent.

CLÉONTE: That Monsieur le Comte who goes to her house dazzles her perhaps; and I can see that she may let herself be allured by rank and quality. But, for my own honor, I must forestall the public revelation of her inconstancy. I can see her moving in the direction of a change of heart, and I want to keep step with her, and not let her have all the credit for quitting me.

COVIELLE: That's very well said. I share in all your feelings.

CLÉONTE: Come to the aid of my rancor, and support my resolution against any lingering remains of love that might speak in her favor. Tell me, please, all the evil you can about her; paint me a portrait of her person which will make her despicable to me; and to complete my disillusionment, point out all the defects you can see in her.

COVIELLE: What, in her, sir? She's a fine poser, an affected show-off, for you to fall in love with! She seems very ordinary to me; you could find a hundred girls worthier of you. In the first place, her eyes are too small.[6]

CLÉONTE: That's true; her eyes are small. But they are full of fire, very brilliant and sparkling, and unusually touching.

COVIELLE: She has a big mouth.

CLÉONTE: Perhaps. But one sees in it graces that are not in ordinary mouths. That mouth, when one looks at it, inspires desires. It is the most attractive and amorous mouth on earth.

COVIELLE: For her figure, it isn't a tall one.

CLÉONTE: No; but it's dainty and flexible.

COVIELLE: She affects a kind of carefree speech and behavior.

CLÉONTE: True; but she does so gracefully, and her manners are engaging; she has a certain charm which insinuates itself into the heart.

COVIELLE: As for wit—

CLÉONTE: Ah, that she has, Covielle, the keenest and most delicate.

6 According to tradition, the description is of Molière's wife, who played Lucile.

COVIELLE: Her conversation—

CLÉONTE: Her conversation is delightful.

COVIELLE: She is always serious.

CLÉONTE: Well, do you want broad gaiety, everlasting outbursts of glee? Is there anything more tiresome than those
women who are always laughing at everything?

COVIELLE: But finally, she's as capricious as anybody alive.

CLÉONTE: Yes, she's capricious, I agree. But that suits a beauty.
We can bear anything from a beauty.

COVIELLE: Since that's the way of it, I can see that you want to
love her forever.

CLÉONTE: I? I'd rather die. I am going to hate her as much as
I have loved her.

COVIELLE: And how will you do that, if you find her so perfect?

CLÉONTE: That is exactly how my revenge is going to be so
sensational, and how I'm going to show so clearly the resolution of my heart, in hating and leaving her, beautiful, attractive, and lovable as she is . . . But here she is.

(*Enter* LUCILE *and* NICOLE.)

NICOLE (*to* LUCILE):   As for me, I was quite scandalized.

LUCILE: The only explanation, Nicole, is what I was telling you
. . . But there he is.

CLÉONTE (*to* COVIELLE):   I won't even speak to her.

COVIELLE: I'll do just like you.

LUCILE: What is it, Cléonte? What is the matter?

NICOLE: What's got into you, Covielle?

LUCILE: Why this distress of mind?

NICOLE: Why are you so sulky?

LUCILE: Are you dumb, Cléonte?

NICOLE: Has the cat got your tongue, Covielle?

CLÉONTE (*to* COVIELLE):   What an outrageous way to act!

COVIELLE: Just a couple of Judases!

LUCILE (*to* CLÉONTE):   I see that our recent encounter has
troubled you.

CLÉONTE (*to* COVIELLE):   Aha! She realizes what she has done.

NICOLE (*to* COVIELLE):   Our greeting this morning has got your goat.

COVIELLE (*to* CLÉONTE):   They've guessed where the shoe pinches.

LUCILE: Isn't it true, Cléonte, that that is the cause of your ill humor?

CLÉONTE: Yes, perfidious one, it is, since I must speak. And I have this information for you: that you won't laugh off your infidelity as you expect, that I intend to be the first to break with you, and that you won't have the satisfaction of dismissing me. No doubt I shall have trouble in conquering my love for you. That will cause me some pain; I shall suffer for a time. But I shall overmaster it, and I'll sooner pierce my own heart than be so weak as to return to you.

COVIELLE: With me, ditto.

LUCILE: That's a lot of fuss about nothing, Cléonte. I want to tell you why I avoided your greeting this morning.

CLÉONTE (*turning his back*):   No, I don't want to hear a word.

NICOLE (*to* COVIELLE, *who turns his back*):   I want to tell you the reason we went by so quick.

COVIELLE: I won't listen.

LUCILE: Know, then, that this morning—

CLÉONTE: No, I tell you.

NICOLE: Here are the facts—

COVIELLE: No, traitor.

LUCILE: Listen—

CLÉONTE: There's no use talking.

NICOLE: Let me tell you—

COVIELLE: I'm deaf.

LUCILE: Cléonte!

CLÉONTE: No.

LUCILE: Covielle!

COVIELLE: I won't!

LUCILE: But stop—

CLÉONTE: Rubbish!

NICOLE: Listen to me!

COVIELLE: Fiddlededee!

LUCILE: Just a moment!

CLÉONTE: Not at all!

NICOLE: Be patient.

COVIELLE: Applesauce!

LUCILE: Just two words—

CLÉONTE: No, it's all over.

NICOLE: Just one word—

COVIELLE: I'll have no truck with you.

LUCILE: Well, since you won't listen to me, think what you please, and do what you please.

> (LUCILE *and* NICOLE, *who have been following* CLÉ-ONTE *and* COVIELLE *about the stage, cease their pursuit. The business is reversed, the men interceding with the girls.*)

NICOLE: Since that's the way you behave, take it any way you like.

CLÉONTE (*to* LUCILE): You might as well tell me why you greeted me so coldly.

LUCILE: I don't feel like telling you now.

COVIELLE: Go on, tell us the story.

NICOLE: I don't want to any more.

CLÉONTE: Tell me—

LUCILE: No, I won't say a thing.

COVIELLE: Go ahead; speak up.

NICOLE: Not a word.

CLÉONTE: Please!

LUCILE: No, I tell you.

COVIELLE: Oh, be nice—

NICOLE: Nothing doing.

CLÉONTE: I beg you—

LUCILE: Let me alone.

COVIELLE: I beseech you—

NICOLE: Get out!

CLÉONTE: Lucile!

LUCILE: No.

COVIELLE: Nicole!

NICOLE: Not on your life.

CLÉONTE: In heaven's name!

LUCILE: I don't want to.

COVIELLE: Speak to me!

NICOLE: I won't.

CLÉONTE: Explain my doubts away!

LUCILE: I'll do nothing of the sort.

COVIELLE: Cure my ailing mind!

NICOLE: I don't feel like it.

CLÉONTE: Well, since you care so little about relieving my suffering and justifying yourself for the unworthy way you have treated my devotion, you see me, ingrate, for the last time. I am going far away to die of grief and love.

COVIELLE: And I'll be right behind you.

(COVIELLE *and* CLÉONTE *start for the exit.*)

LUCILE: Cléonte!

NICOLE: Covielle!

CLÉONTE: Eh?

COVIELLE: What is it?

LUCILE: Where are you going?

CLÉONTE: Where I told you.

COVIELLE: We're going to die!

LUCILE: You are going to die, Cléonte?

CLÉONTE: Yes, cruel beauty, since that is what you wish.

LUCILE: You mean I wish you to die?

CLÉONTE: Yes, you wish it.

LUCILE: Who told you so?

CLÉONTE: Don't you wish my death, if you refuse to clear up my suspicions?

LUCILE: Is that my fault? If you had been willing to listen to me, wouldn't I have told you that the occurrence this morning, which you're complaining about, was caused by the presence of my old aunt, who is convinced that the mere approach of a man dishonors a girl? She lectures us perpetually on this theme, and she pictures all men to us as devils we must flee from.

NICOLE: That's the secret of the whole business.

CLÉONTE: You aren't deceiving me, Lucile?

COVIELLE: You aren't trying to bamboozle me?

LUCILE: It's absolutely true.

NICOLE: That's just the way things happened.

COVIELLE (*to* CLÉONTE):   Do we surrender to that?

CLÉONTE: Ah, Lucile, how a word from your lips can appease my heart's tumult! How readily one lets oneself be convinced by a loved one!

COVIELLE: How easily a man is hooked by those confounded creatures!

(*Enter* MADAME JOURDAIN.)

MME JOURDAIN: I am very glad to see you, Cléonte; you are here at just the right moment. My husband is coming; so take this chance to ask him for Lucile's hand.

CLÉONTE: Ah, madame, how sweet are these words! How they flatter my desires! Could I receive a more delightful order? A more precious favor? (*Enter* MONSIEUR JOURDAIN) Sir, I did not wish to get any intermediary to make to you a request I have been long meditating. This request touches me so closely that I have chosen to undertake it myself. Without further preamble, I shall tell you that the honor of being your son-in-law would be a glorious favor which I beg you to bestow upon me.

M. JOURDAIN: Before giving you an answer, sir, I ask you to tell me if you are a gentleman.

CLÉONTE: Sir, most people do not hesitate long at such a question. The word is easily spoken. People assume the appellation without scruple, and common usage today seems to authorize its theft. But as for me, I freely grant, I have somewhat more delicate feelings on the subject. I think that any imposture is unworthy of a decent man, and I think it is mean and base to conceal the state to which it has pleased God to call us, and to adorn oneself in the world's eye with a stolen title, and to try to pass oneself off for what one is not. Certainly, I am the son of a line which has held honorable offices. In the army I acquired the merit of six years of service; and I am possessed of sufficient wealth to sustain a very respectable position in society. But with all that, I am unwilling to give myself a name which others, in my place, would feel justified in assuming; and I will tell you frankly that I am not a gentleman.

M. JOURDAIN: Shake hands, sir; my daughter is not for you.

CLÉONTE: What?

M. JOURDAIN: You are not a gentleman; you won't have my daughter.

MME JOURDAIN (*to* MONSIEUR JOURDAIN):   What do you mean, with this gentleman business? Are we descended from the rib of Saint Louis?

M. JOURDAIN: Shut up, wife. I see what you're driving at.

MME JOURDAIN: Were our ancestors anything but good bourgeois?

M. JOURDAIN: Slander!

MME JOURDAIN: And wasn't your father a merchant, just like mine?

M. JOURDAIN: Drat the woman! She never misses a chance! If your father was a merchant, so much the worse for him; but as for my father, it's only the ignorant who say so. All I have to tell you is that I want a son-in-law who's a gentleman.

MME JOURDAIN: What your daughter needs is a husband who suits her, and she'd much better have an honorable man who is rich and handsome than some ugly gentleman without a penny.

NICOLE: That's right. There's the son of the gentleman in our village, he's the biggest booby and ninny ever seen.

M. JOURDAIN: Shut up, saucebox. You're always sticking your oar in the conversation. I have enough property for my daughter; all I need is honor; and I want to make her a marquise.

MME JOURDAIN: Marquise?

M. JOURDAIN: Yes, marquise.

MME JOURDAIN: Alas, God forbid!

M. JOURDAIN: It's something I've made up my mind to.

MME JOURDAIN: As for me, it's something I'll never consent to. Alliances with people above our own rank are always likely to have very unpleasant results. I don't want to have my son-in-law able to reproach my daughter for her parents, and I don't want her children to be ashamed to call me their grandma. If she should happen to come and visit me in her grand lady's carriage, and if by mistake she should fail to salute some one of the neighbors, you can imagine how they'd talk. "Take a look at that fine Madame la Marquise showing off," they'd say. "She's the daughter of Monsieur Jourdain, and when she was little, she was only too glad to play at being a fine lady. She wasn't always so high and mighty as she is now, and both her grandfathers sold dry goods besides the Porte Saint Innocent. They both piled up money for their children, and now perhaps they're paying dear for it in the next world; you don't get so rich by being honest." Well, I don't want that kind of talk to go on; and in short, I want a man who will feel under obligation to my daughter, and I want to be able to say to him: "Sit down there, my boy, and eat dinner with us."

M. JOURDAIN: Those views reveal a mean and petty mind, that wants to remain forever in its base condition. Don't answer back to me again. My daughter will be a marquise in spite of everyone; and if you get me angry, I'll make her a duchess.

(*Exit* MONSIEUR JOURDAIN.)

MME JOURDAIN: Cléonte, don't lose courage yet. Lucile, come

with me; and tell your father straight out that if you can't have him, you won't marry anybody.

(*Exit* MADAME JOURDAIN, LUCILE, *and* NICOLE.)

COVIELLE: You've got yourself into a nice mess with your high principles.

CLÉONTE: Well, what can I do? I have serious scruples on that point, that can't be overcome by the example others set us.

COVIELLE: It's foolish to take your scruples seriously with a man like that. Don't you see he's crazy? Would it have cost you anything to fall in with his fancies?

CLÉONTE: No doubt you're right. But I didn't think one had to give proofs of nobility to be the son-in-law of Monsieur Jourdain.

COVIELLE: Ha, ha, ha!

CLÉONTE: What are you laughing at?

COVIELLE: At an idea I had to take the fellow in, and get you what you want.

CLÉONTE: How's that?

COVIELLE: It's rather funny.

CLÉONTE: What is it, then?

COVIELLE: There's been a comic performance recently which would fit in perfectly here. I could work the troupe into a practical joke we could play on our joker. It would be rather on the burlesque side, perhaps; but with him you can go to any lengths; you don't have to be too fussy. He could act his own part in it perfectly; he'd play up to all the farce. I can get the actors, and they have the costumes all ready. Just let me manage it.

CLÉONTE: But tell me—

COVIELLE: I'll tell you everything. But he's coming back; let's get out.

(*Exit* COVIELLE *and* CLÉONTE. *Enter* MONSIEUR JOURDAIN.)

M. JOURDAIN: What the devil! The only thing they have to reproach me for is my noble friends; and as for me, I think there's nothing so splendid as to associate with noble lords. They have the monopoly of honor and civility. I'd gladly give two fingers off my hand, to have been born a count or a marquis.

(*Enter a* LACKEY.)

LACKEY: Monsieur, here is Monsieur le Comte, and a lady on his arm.

M. JOURDAIN: Oh, good God! I have some orders to give. Tell them I'll be here right away.

(*Exit* MONSIEUR JOURDAIN. *Enter* DORANTE *and* DORIMÈNE.)

LACKEY: The master has just gone and said he'd be here right away.

DORANTE: Very well.

(*Exit* LACKEY.)

DORIMÈNE: I don't know, Dorante; it seems to me rather peculiar, to let you bring me into a house where I don't know anyone.

DORANTE: Well, my dear lady, what place can my love find to entertain you properly, since, to avoid gossip, you won't let me use either your house or mine?

DORIMÈNE: Yes, but you don't say that I am becoming involved every day, by accepting such excessive evidences of your devotion. I do my best to refuse, but you wear down my resistance; and you show a polite obstinacy which makes me yield gently to anything you like. The frequent visits began it; and then the impassioned declarations; and they brought along the serenades and the parties; and then came the presents. I made opposition to everything; but you don't let yourself be discouraged, and step by step you are breaking down my resolutions. Really, I can no longer be quite sure of myself; and I think that in the end you will drag me into marriage, in spite of my reluctance.

DORANTE: My word, madame, you ought to be already in that happy state. You are a widow; you have no obligations to anyone but yourself. I am independent; and I love you more than my life. What obstacle is there to your making me immediately the happiest of men?

DORIMÈNE: Good heavens, Dorante, for a happy married life many qualities are necessary in both parties; and the most reasonable pair of people alive often have much trouble in forming a quite satisfactory union.

DORANTE: You are absurd, my dear, in imagining so many difficulties. From one unfortunate experience you should not draw conclusions about all the others.

DORIMÈNE: Anyway, I keep coming back to the same point. I am disturbed by the expenditures I see you making for me, and for two reasons: one, that they obligate me more than I like; and two, that I am sure—if you will forgive me—that you aren't making them without embarrassment; and I don't want that.

DORANTE: Ah, madame, they are mere trifles! It is not by such means—

DORIMÈNE: I know what I am saying. Among other things, the diamond you forced me to accept is of such value—

DORANTE: Oh, madame, please! Don't rate so highly something my love regards as all unworthy of you! And permit— But here comes the master of the house.

>   (*Enter* MONSIEUR JOURDAIN. *He makes two sweeping bows, stepping forward. He finds himself close to* DORIMÈNE.)

M. JOURDAIN: Stand back a little, madame.

DORIMÈNE: What?

M. JOURDAIN: One step back, please.

DORIMÈNE: What for?

M. JOURDAIN: Back up a little, for the third.

DORANTE: Madame, Monsieur Jourdain knows his etiquette.

M. JOURDAIN: Madame, it is a very great distinction to me to find myself so fortunate as to be so happy as to have the happiness that you have had the kindness to grant me the grace of doing me the honor of honoring me with the favor of your presence; and if I had also the merit of meriting a merit like yours, and if heaven . . . envious of my bliss . . . had granted me . . . the privilege of finding myself worthy . . . of the . . . .

DORANTE: Monsieur Jourdain, that is enough. Madame does not care for high compliments, and she knows that you are an intelligent man. (*Aside to* DORIMÈNE) He is a good bourgeois, and rather ridiculous in his behavior, as you see.

DORIMÈNE (*aside to* DORANTE): That's not hard to recognize.

DORANTE: Madame, this is the best of my friends.

M. JOURDAIN: You do me too much honor.

DORANTE: A man of the world, absolutely.

DORIMÈNE: I have much esteem for him.

M. JOURDAIN: I have done nothing as yet, madame, to deserve such kindness.

DORANTE (*aside to* MONSIEUR JOURDAIN): Be sure, anyway, you don't mention the diamond ring you've given her.

M. JOURDAIN (*aside to* DORANTE): Couldn't I even ask her how she likes it?

DORANTE (*aside to* MONSIEUR JOURDAIN): Not by any means. That would be horribly vulgar. As a man of the world, you must act as if you hadn't made the present at all. (*To* DORIMÈNE) Madame, Monsieur Jourdain says he is overjoyed to see you in his house.

DORIMÈNE: He honors me deeply.

M. JOURDAIN (*aside to* DORANTE): How much obliged I am to you for speaking to her in such a way!

DORANTE (*aside to* MONSIEUR JOURDAIN): I had a dreadful time getting her to come here.

M. JOURDAIN (*aside to* DORANTE): I don't know how to thank you.

DORANTE: He says, madame, that he thinks you are the most beautiful person on earth.

DORIMÈNE: It is very kind of him.

M. JOURDAIN: Madame, the kindness is all on your side, and . . .

(*Enter a* LACKEY.)

DORANTE: Let's think about dinner.

LACKEY: Everything is ready, sir.

DORANTE: Then let's sit down; and send in the musicians.

(*Six* COOKS *enter dancing. They bring in a table covered with various dishes. This makes the third* Interlude.)

ACT IV

After the Interlude, DORIMÈNE, DORANTE, MONSIEUR JOURDAIN, *two* MALE SINGERS, *a* WOMAN SINGER, *and several* LACKEYS *remain on the stage.*

DORIMÈNE: Why, Dorante! What a magnificent repast!

M. JOURDAIN: You are joking, madame. I wish it were more worthy of being offered to you.

(DORIMÈNE, DORANTE, MONSIEUR JOURDAIN *and the* SINGERS *sit at table.*)

DORANTE: Monsieur Jourdain is quite right, madame, in speaking in that way, and he puts me under a deep obligation by doing so well the honors of his house. I agree with him that the repast is unworthy of you. As it was I who ordered it, and as I have not the finesse of some of our friends on this subject, you will not find here a culinary symphony, and you will perhaps notice some gastronomic incongruities, some solecisms of good taste. If Damis had had a hand in it, the rules would be strictly observed; you would recognize a mingling of elegance and erudition. He would not fail to call your attention to the dishes he would serve; he would make you applaud his high capacity in the science of cookery. He would mention the rolls, cooked golden-brown on the hearth's edge with a uniform crust, crumbling delicately under the tooth; the wine with a velvet bouquet, somewhat young and saucy, but not to the point of impudence; a breast of lamb pinked with parsley; a loin of riverside veal from Normandy, no longer than that, white, dainty, like almond paste on the tongue; partridges prepared with a special spice and mushroom sauce; and for his crowning triumph, a young fat turkey flanked by squabs, crested with white onions blended with chicory, swimming in a pearl bouillon. But for my part, I must admit my ignorance; and as Monsieur Jourdain has very well said, I could wish that the repast was more worthy of being offered you.

DORIMÈNE: I reply to this compliment by devouring the dinner as I do.

M. JOURDAIN: Oh, what beautiful hands!

DORIMÈNE: The hands are ordinary hands, Monsieur Jourdain; but you notice the diamond, which is indeed beautiful.

M. JOURDAIN: I, Madame? God forbid that I should mention it. That would not be the action of a man of the world. The diamond is nothing much.

DORIMÈNE: You are hard to please.

M. JOURDAIN: You are too kind—

DORANTE (*with a cautionary gesture to* MONSIEUR JOURDAIN): Come, some wine for Monsieur Jourdain, and for our musical guests, who will give us the pleasure of singing us a drinking song.

DORIMÈNE: There's no better seasoning for good cheer than to combine it with music. I am being magnificently regaled here.

M. JOURDAIN: Madame, it is not—

DORANTE: Monsieur Jourdain, let us lend an ear to the musicians; their songs will express our feelings better than we could in words.

(*The* SINGERS *take glasses in hand, and sing two drinking songs, accompanied by the orchestra.*)

DUET

Phyllis, a drop of wine, to make the moment pass!
How daintily your hand holds the delightful glass!
Ah, Phyllis, you and wine, you lend each other arms,
For wine and love together increase each other's charms.
So you and wine and I, come let us vow to be
    A constant trinity.
The wine that wets your lip itself doth beautify;
And yet your lovely lip is lovelier thereby.
The lips, they bid me drink; the wine, it bids me kiss!
Ah, what intoxication can ever equal this!
So you and wine and I, come let us vow to be
    A constant trinity.

DUET

Drink, my comrades, drink;
    The hour's propitious.
Let your glasses clink;
    The wine's delicious.
Too swift our steps we bend
    To the dark shore,
Where love is at an end,
    And we drink no more.
The scholars can't agree
    Where lives the soul;
By our philosophy
    It's in the bowl.
Not glory, wealth, nor wit
    Chase care away;
But wine doth still permit
    Man to be gay.

CHORUS

Come, wine for all, my lads; and never cease to pour,

And pour and pour again, while men can ask for more!

DORIMÈNE:　That couldn't be better sung; it's really lovely.

M. JOURDAIN:　I can see something even lovelier around here.

DORIMÈNE:　Oho! Monsieur Jourdain is more gallant than I thought.

DORANTE:　Why, madame, what do you take Monsieur Jourdain for?

M. JOURDAIN:　I wish she would take me for something I could suggest.

DORIMÈNE:　You're still at it?

DORANTE (*to* DORIMÈNE):　You don't know him.

M. JOURDAIN:　She can know me better whenever she likes.

DORIMÈNE:　Oh, I give up!

DORANTE:　He always has an answer ready. But you haven't noticed, madame, that Monsieur Jourdain eats all the bits that your spoon has touched in the serving dish.

DORIMÈNE:　Monsieur Jourdain is a man who ravishes me.

M. JOURDAIN:　If I could ravish your heart, I would be—

(*Enter* MADAME JOURDAIN.)

MME JOURDAIN:　Aha! I find some fine company here, and I can see that I wasn't expected. So, it's for this pretty business, my good husband, that you were so anxious to send me off to dine with my sister? I've just seen a kind of a theatre downstairs; and here I see a kind of a wedding feast. So that's how you spend your money? And that's the way you put on a big party for ladies in my absence, and you give them music and a play, while you send me to Jericho?

DORANTE:　What do you mean, Madame Jourdain? You must have hallucinations, to get it into your head that your husband is spending his own money, and that he's the one who is giving the party for Madame. Let me inform you that I'm footing the bill. He is merely lending me his house; you ought to be more careful about what you say.

M. JOURDAIN: Yes, insolence! It's Monsieur le Comte who is giving all this to Madame, who is a lady of quality. He does me the honor to borrow my house, and to ask me to join him.

MME JOURDAIN: Stuff and nonsense! I know what I know.

DORANTE: Madame Jourdain, you need some new spectacles.

MME JOURDAIN: I don't need any spectacles at all, monsieur; I can see all right without them. I've known what's up for quite some time now; I'm not such a fool. It's a very cheap business for you, a great lord, to encourage my husband's follies the way you're doing. And you, madame, for a great lady, it's neither pretty nor decent for you to bring trouble into a family, and to allow my husband to be in love with you.

DORIMÈNE: What is the meaning of all this? Dorante, you're unpardonable, to expose me to the delusions of this fantastic creature. (*She starts to leave.*)

DORANTE (*following* DORIMÈNE):   Madame, look here! Madame, where are you running off to?

(*Exit* DORIMÈNE.)

M. JOURDAIN: Madame! . . . Monsieur le Comte, make my apologies to her, and try to bring her back. (*Exit* DORANTE. *To* MADAME JOURDAIN) Impudence! These are nice tricks of yours! You come and insult me before everybody, and you drive people of quality out of the house!

MME JOURDAIN: I don't care a straw for their quality.

M. JOURDAIN: You cursèd troublemaker, I don't know why I don't crack your skull with the leftovers of the dinner you ruined!

(*The* LACKEYS *carry out the table and dishes.*)

MME JOURDAIN: I don't care a pin. I'm defending my rights; and every woman will be on my side. (*She starts for the door.*)

M. JOURDAIN: You do well to escape my anger. (*Exit* MADAME JOURDAIN) What a time she picked to interrupt! I was just in the mood to say some very neat things. I never felt myself so bubbling over with inspiration . . . But what's all this?

(*Enter* COVIELLE, *wearing an Oriental costume and a long beard.*)

COVIELLE: Monsieur, I don't know if I have the honor of being known to you.

M. JOURDAIN: No, sir.

COVIELLE: I last saw you when you weren't any bigger than that. (*Holds his hand a foot from the floor.*)

M. JOURDAIN: Me?

COVIELLE: Yes, you were the prettiest child ever seen, and all the ladies would take you in their arms to kiss you.

M. JOURDAIN: To kiss me!

COVIELLE: Yes. I was a great friend of your late honorable father.

M. JOURDAIN: My late honorable father?

COVIELLE: Yes. He was a very worthy gentleman.

M. JOURDAIN: What did you say?

COVIELLE: I said he was a very worthy gentleman.

M. JOURDAIN: My father?

COVIELLE: Yes.

M. JOURDAIN: You knew him well?

COVIELLE: Certainly.

M. JOURDAIN: And you knew him to be a gentleman?

COVIELLE: Of course.

M. JOURDAIN: The world is certainly a funny place!

COVIELLE: How is that?

M. JOURDAIN: There are some stupid people who try to tell me he was a merchant.

COVIELLE: He, a merchant? It's pure slander; he never was anything of the sort. The fact is, he was very obliging, very helpful by nature. And as he was a remarkable judge of woolens, he used to go here and there and pick them out, and have them brought to his house; and then he would give them to his friends—for money.

M. JOURDAIN: I am delighted to know you, and to have your testimony that my father was a gentleman.

COVIELLE: I will testify to the fact before everyone.

M. JOURDAIN: That's very kind. And what brings you here?

COVIELLE: Since the time when I knew your late honorable father, that worthy gentleman, I have been roving the wide world.

M. JOURDAIN: The wide world!

COVIELLE: Yes.

M. JOURDAIN: That must be quite a trip.

COVIELLE: It is, certainly. I returned from my far journeys only four days ago; and because of my interest in everything that concerns you, I have come to announce to you some excellent news.

M. JOURDAIN: What's that?

COVIELLE: You know that the son of the Grand Turk is here?

M. JOURDAIN: Me? No.

COVIELLE: Really! He has come with a magnificent retinue. Everyone goes to see him; and he was received in this country as a noble lord of great importance.

M. JOURDAIN: Bless me! I didn't know that.

COVIELLE: And what concerns you, to your great advantage, is that he has fallen in love with your daughter.

M. JOURDAIN: The son of the Grand Turk?

COVIELLE: Yes. And he wants to be your son-in-law.

M. JOURDAIN: My son-in-law? The son of the Grand Turk?

COVIELLE: The son of the Grand Turk wants to be your son-in-law. I went to call on him; and as I understand his language perfectly, he said to me, after discussing various matters: "Acciam croc soler ouch alla moustaph gidelum amanahem varahini oussere carbulath."[7] That is, "Have you by chance seen a beautiful girl, the daughter of Monsieur Jourdain, a Parisian gentleman?"

M. JOURDAIN: The son of the Grand Turk said that about me?

COVIELLE: Yes. When I replied that I had a particular acquaint-

---

[7] Molière's Turkish is a mingling of genuine Turkish, Arabic, and Hebrew with mere gibberish.

ance with you, and that I had chanced to see your daughter, he said: "Ah! marababa sahem!" That means: "Oh, how much I love her!"

M. JOURDAIN: "Marababa sahem" means "Oh, how much I love her?"

COVIELLE: Yes.

M. JOURDAIN: Bless my soul, I'm glad you told me, for personally I would never have imagined that "marababa sahem" could mean "Oh, how much I love her." Turkish is certainly a wonderful language.

COVIELLE: More wonderful than you would think. Do you know what "cacaracamouchen" means?

M. JOURDAIN: "Cacaracamouchen?" No.

COVIELLE: That means "my darling."

M. JOURDAIN: "Cacaracamouchen" means "my darling"?

COVIELLE: Yes.

M. JOURDAIN: That's really marvelous. "Cacaracamouchen; my darling." Can you imagine? You amaze me.

COVIELLE: In short, to fulfill the purpose of my embassy, he wants to ask the hand of your daughter in marriage. And to have a father-in-law of a rank suitable for him, he wants to make you a mamamouchi, which is a certain high dignity of his own country.

M. JOURDAIN: A mamamouchi?

COVIELLE: Yes, a mamamouchi. That is to say, in our language, a paladin. The paladins, they were those old-time—well, in short, paladins. There is nothing nobler than that anywhere. You will be the equal of the greatest lords on earth.

M. JOURDAIN: The son of the Grand Turk honors me very profoundly. I beg you to take me to his presence so that I can express my thanks.

COVIELLE: It's unnecessary. He is coming here.

M. JOURDAIN: He's coming here?

COVIELLE: Yes. And he's bringing everything needful for the ceremony of your ennoblement.

M. JOURDAIN: He certainly works fast.

COVIELLE: His love is such that he can bear no delay.

M. JOURDAIN: There's just one awkward thing. My daughter is very stubborn, and she's gone and set her mind on a certain Cléonte, and she swears she won't marry anyone else but him.

COVIELLE: She will change her views when she sees the son of the Grand Turk. And also—a very remarkable fact—the son of the Grand Turk has a striking resemblance to Cléonte. I've just seen this Cléonte; I had him pointed out to me. Her love for the one may easily shift to the other; and . . . But I think I hear him coming. Indeed, here he is.

> (*Enter* CLÉONTE *in Turkish costume, with three* PAGES *carrying his train.*)

CLÉONTE: Ambousahim oqui boraf, Jordina salamalequi!

COVIELLE (*to* MONSIEUR JOURDAIN):   That is, "Monsieur Jourdain, may your heart be all year long like a rosebush in bloom!" That is a courteous expression in those countries.

M. JOURDAIN: I am the very humble servant of his Turkish Highness.

COVIELLE: Carigar camboto oustin moraf.

CLÉONTE: Oustin yoc catamalequi basum base alla moran!

COVIELLE: He says: "May Heaven give you the strength of lions and the prudence of serpents!"

M. JOURDAIN: His Turkish Highness does me too much honor, and I wish him every kind of prosperity.

COVIELLE: Ossa binamen sadoc babally oracaf ouram.

CLÉONTE: Bel-men.

COVIELLE: He says you must go with him right away to make preparations for the ceremony, and afterwards you'll see your daughter and conclude the marriage.

M. JOURDAIN: All that in two words?

COVIELLE: Yes, the Turkish language is like that. It says a great deal in very few words. You go where he wants you to, quickly.

> (*Exit* MONSIEUR JOURDAIN, CLÉONTE, *and* PAGES.)

COVIELLE: Ha, ha, ha! That was a good one! What a dupe he is!

He couldn't play his part better if he'd learned it by heart! Ha, ha, ha! (*Enter* DORANTE) I beg you, sir, to help us out in a little performance we're staging.

DORANTE:　Ha, ha! Covielle, I would never have recognized you! What kind of getup is this?

COVIELLE:　Well, take a look. Ha, ha!

DORANTE:　What are you laughing at?

COVIELLE:　At something, sir, which deserves a laugh.

DORANTE:　How's that?

COVIELLE:　You'd never guess, sir, the trick we're playing on Monsieur Jourdain, to induce him to give his daughter to my master.

DORANTE:　I can't guess the trick, but I can guess that it is pretty sure to work, since you are organizing it.

COVIELLE:　Evidently, sir, you are a judge of character.

DORANTE:　Tell me the story.

COVIELLE:　Be so kind as to come to one side, and give room to what I see coming in. You will see a part of the story, and I will tell you the rest.

> (*The Turkish ceremony of the ennobling of* MON-
> SIEUR JOURDAIN, *performed with music and dance,
> forms the fourth* Interlude.
>
> *Six* DANCING TURKS *enter gravely, two by two, to
> the full orchestra. They carry three long carpets,
> with which they make various evolutions, and fi-
> nally raise them high. The* TURKISH MUSICIANS *and
> other instrumentalists pass beneath. Four* DERVISHES,
> *accompanying the* MUFTI, *or legal-religious digni-
> tary, close the procession.*
>
> *The* TURKS *spread the carpets on the ground and
> kneel upon them. The* MUFTI, *standing in the
> middle, makes an invocation with contortions and
> grimaces, turning up his face, and wiggling his
> hands outward from his head, like wings. The*

TURKS *bow forward, touching their foreheads to the floor, singing "Ali"; they resume the kneeling position, singing "Allah." They continue thus to the end of the invocation; then they all stand, singing "Allah akbar."*

Then the DERVISHES *bring before the* MUFTI MONSIEUR JOURDAIN, *dressed in Turkish costume, cleanshaven, without turban or sword. The* MUFTI *sings in solemn tones.*)

MUFTI:

Se ti sabir,
Ti respondir;
Se non sabir,
Tazir, tazir.

Mi star muphty;
Ti qui star ti?
Non intendir:
Tazir, tazir.[8]

(*Two* DERVISHES *lead out* MONSIEUR JOURDAIN. *The* MUFTI *questions the* TURKS *as to the candidate's religion.*)

MUFTI:

Dice, Turque, qui star quista?
Anabatista, anabatista?[9]

TURKS:

Ioc.[10]

---

[8] "If you know, answer; if you don't know, keep still, keep still. I am a mufti; you, who are you? You don't understand; keep still, keep still." Most of the language of the Turkish ceremony is *lingua franca*, once used for commercial and diplomatic purposes around the Mediterranean, still known to sailors and harbor men. It is a blend mostly of French, Spanish, Italian, and Arabic. All grammatical forms are simplified; verbs have only the infinitive form. (A sort of Basic Romance.) Any Frenchman, or Spaniard or Italian, could understand the Mufti well enough.

[9] "Tell me, Turks, what is this man? An Anabaptist?"

[10] "No." An authentic Turkish word.

MUFTI:
Zwinglista?[11]

TURKS:
Ioc.

MUFTI:
Coffita?[12]

TURKS:
Ioc.

MUFTI:
Hussita? Morista? Fronista?[13]

TURKS:
Ioc. Ioc. Ioc.

MUFTI:
Ioc, Ioc, Ioc!
Star pagana?

TURKS:
Ioc.

MUFTI:
Luterana?

TURKS:
Ioc.

MUFTI:
Puritana?

TURKS:
Ioc.

MUFTI:
Bramina? Moffina? Zurina?[14]

TURKS:
Ioc. Ioc. Ioc.

---

[11] Follower of Zwingli, Protestant reformer.
[12] Member of the Coptic Church.
[13] A Hussite, follower of Bohemian reformer John Huss. The meaning of the other two words is obscure.
[14] Brahmin; "Moffina" and "Zurina" are apparently invented words.

MUFTI:

Ioc. Ioc. Ioc.

Mahametana? Mahametana?

TURKS:

Hey valla! Hey valla![15]

MUFTI:

Como chamara? Como chamara?[16]

TURKS:

Giourdina, Giourdina.

MUFTI:

Giourdina! (*He leaps high, and peers in all directions*)
Giourdina? Giourdina? Giourdina?

TURKS:

Giourdina! Giourdina! Giourdina!

MUFTI:

Mahameta per Giourdina

Mi pregar sera e matina;

Voler far un paladina

De Giourdina, de Giourdina.

Dar turbanta e dar scarcina

Con galera e brigantina

Per deffender Palestina.

Mahameta per Giourdina

Mi pregar sera e mattina.[17]

(*Questioning the* TURKS)

Star bon Turca Giourdina?

Star bon Turca Giourdina?

TURKS:

Hey valla, hey valla!

Hey valla, hey valla!

[15] "Yes, by Allah!" (Arabic.)
[16] "What is his name?"
[17] "I pray to Mahomet for Jourdain night and morning. I want to make a paladin of Jourdain, of Jourdain. Give a turban and a scimitar, with a galley and a brigantine, to defend Palestine. I pray to Mahomet for Jourdain night and morning."

MUFTI (*dancing*):

Hu la ba ba la chou ba la ba ba la da!

(*The* MUFTI *exits; the* TURKS *dance and sing.*)

TURKS:

Hu la ba ba la chou ba la ba ba la da!

> (*The* MUFTI *returns, wearing an enormous cere-*
> *monial turban, adorned with four or five rows of*
> *blazing candles. Two* DERVISHES *accompany him,*
> *wearing pointed hats, also adorned with lighted*
> *candles. They solemnly bear the Koran. The two*
> *other* DERVISHES *conduct* MONSIEUR JOURDAIN, *who*
> *is terrified by the ceremony. They make him kneel*
> *down with his back to the* MUFTI: *then they make*
> *him bend forward till his hands rest on the floor.*
> *They put the Koran on his back, which serves as a*
> *reading desk for the* MUFTI. *The* MUFTI *makes a*
> *burlesque invocation, scowling and opening and*
> *shutting his mouth without uttering a word. Then he*
> *speaks vehemently, now muttering, now shouting*
> *with terrifying passion, slapping his sides as if to*
> *force out his words, occasionally striking the Koran,*
> *turning its leaves briskly. He finally raises his hands*
> *and exclaims loudly: "Hou!"*[18] *During this invoca-*
> *tion, the* TURKS *sing, "Hou, hou, hou!" bending for-*
> *ward three times, then straightening up, singing,*
> *"Hou, hou, hou!" They continue doing so through-*
> *out the* MUFTI's *invocation. After the invocation, the*
> DERVISHES *remove the Koran from* MONSIEUR
> JOURDAIN's *back. He exclaims, "Ouf!" with relief.*
> *The* DERVISHES *raise him to his feet.*)

MUFTI (*to* MONSIEUR JOURDAIN):

Ti non star furba?[19]

---

[18] *He,* or *God,* in Arabic.
[19] "You aren't an evildoer?"

TURKS:

No, no, no.

MUFTI:

Non star forfanta?[20]

TURKS:

No, no, no.

MUFTI (*to the* TURKS):

Donar turbanta, donar turbanta.[21]

> (*Exit the* MUFTI. *The* TURKS *repeat the* MUFTI's *words, and with song and dance present the turban to* MONSIEUR JOURDAIN. *The* MUFTI *re-enters with a scimitar, which he presents to* MONSIEUR JOURDAIN.)

MUFTI:

Ti star nobile, non star fabola.

Pigliar schiabola.[22]

> (*Exit the* MUFTI. *The* TURKS *draw their scimitars and repeat the* MUFTI's *words. Six of them dance around* MONSIEUR JOURDAIN, *feigning to strike him with their weapons. The* MUFTI *returns.*)

MUFTI:

Dara, dara bastonara, bastonara, bastonara.[23]

> (*Exit the* MUFTI. *The* TURKS *repeat his words, beating* MONSIEUR JOURDAIN *to music. Re-enter the* MUFTI.)

MUFTI:

Non tener honta;

Questa star l'ultima affronta.[24]

> (*The* TURKS *repeat the* MUFTI's *words. The* MUFTI, *leaning on the* DERVISHES, *makes another invocation, to the full orchestra. Evidently fatigued by the*

[20] "You aren't a rascal?"
[21] "Give the turban."
[22] "You're a noble, it's no lie. Take this sword."
[23] "Give him a beating."
[24] "Feel no shame; this is the last affront."

ceremony, he is respectfully supported by the DER-
VISHES. The TURKS. leaping, dancing, and singing
around the MUFTI, conduct him off-stage to the
sound of Turkish musical instruments.)

ACT V

After the Interlude, *all retire except* MONSIEUR
JOURDAIN. *Enter* MADAME JOURDAIN.

MME JOURDAIN: Lord have mercy on us! What's all this? What
a figure of fun! You're dressing up for Hallowe'en at this time
of year? Tell me, what's going on? Who rigged you up that
way?

M. JOURDAIN: Insolent creature, to talk that way to a mamamouchi!

MME JOURDAIN: How's that?

M. JOURDAIN: Yes, now you've got to show me some respect.
I've just been made a mamamouchi.

MME JOURDAIN: What do you mean with your mamamouchi?

M. JOURDAIN: Mamamouchi, I tell you! I'm a mamamouchi!

MME JOURDAIN: What kind of a creature is that?

M. JOURDAIN: Mamamouchi! That is, in our language, a
paladin.

MME JOURDAIN: Aballadin'!²⁵ You're going to go around aballadin', at your age?

M. JOURDAIN: Such ignorance! I said a paladin. That's a dignity that just has been conferred upon me, with due ceremony.

MME JOURDAIN: What kind of ceremony?

M. JOURDAIN: Mahameta per Giourdina!

MME JOURDAIN: What does that mean?

M. JOURDAIN: Giourdina, that is, Jourdain.

MME JOURDAIN: Well, what of it, Jourdain?

²⁵ The pun is better in French.

M. JOURDAIN: Voler far un paladina de Giourdina.

MME JOURDAIN: What?

M. JOURDAIN: Dar turbanta con galera.

MME JOURDAIN: What sense is there in that?

M. JOURDAIN: Per deffender palestina.

MME JOURDAIN: What are you trying to say?

M. JOURDAIN: Dara dara bastonara.

MME JOURDAIN: What's all that gibberish?

M. JOURDAIN: Non tener honta; questa star l'ultima affronta.

MME JOURDAIN: What's the idea, anyway?

M. JOURDAIN (*singing and dancing*): Hou la ba ba la chou ba la ba ba la da.

MME JOURDAIN: Alas, dear God! My husband has gone crazy!

M. JOURDAIN: Silence, insolent woman! Show proper respect to a noble mamamouchi.

(*Exit* MONSIEUR JOURDAIN.)

MME JOURDAIN: How has he gone and lost his wits? I must keep him from going out. Oh, dear, oh, dear, this is the last straw! There's nothing but trouble everywhere!

(*Exit* MADAME JOURDAIN. *After a moment, enter* DORANTE *and* DORIMÈNE.)

DORANTE: Yes, madame, you will see a very amusing sight. I don't think you will ever find a crazier man than he is. And besides, madame, we must try to aid Cléonte's love affair, and fall in with his masquerade. He's a very decent fellow, who deserves our interest and help.

DORIMÈNE: I think very highly of him; he merits good fortune in his enterprise.

DORANTE: Besides, we have a ballet due us. We shouldn't let it be wasted. And I want to see if my scheme for the performance works out well.

DORIMÈNE: I've just seen some of the preparations; they are magnificent. And I must tell you, Dorante, that I simply cannot allow this sort of thing. I must put a stop to your lavishness; and to check your mad spending of money on me, I have decided to marry you very soon. That's the best solution; with marriage, all the extravagances stop.

DORANTE: Ah, madame, is it possible that you have made so welcome a resolution in my favor?

DORIMÈNE: It's only to prevent you from ruining yourself. Otherwise, I can see that soon you wouldn't have a penny.

DORANTE: What an obligation I have, my dear, to your concern for preserving my property! It is all yours, and my heart is too; you can do with them what you will.

DORIMÈNE: I shall take proper care of both of them . . . But here is our good man; he certainly looks extraordinary.

(*Enter* MONSIEUR JOURDAIN.)

DORANTE: Sir, madame and I have come to render homage to your new dignity, and to felicitate you on the proposed marriage of your daughter to the son of the Grand Turk.

M. JOURDAIN (*after making obeisances in the Turkish style*): Sir, I wish you the strength of serpents and the wisdom of lions.

DORIMÈNE: I am happy to be one of the first, Monsieur, to congratulate you upon the high degree of glory you have attained.

M. JOURDAIN: Madame, I wish your rosebush may be in bloom all year long. I am infinitely obliged to you for your sympathetic interest in the honors which have come to me, and I take great joy in seeing you here again, so that I may make my very humble apologies for my wife's excesses.

DORIMÈNE: It was nothing at all; I can readily excuse her impulse. Your heart is no doubt precious to her; it is not strange that the possession of a man like you may expose her to some alarms.

M. JOURDAIN: The possession of my heart is entirely yours to dispose of.

DORANTE: You see, madame, that Monsieur Jourdain is not one

of those people who are dazzled by prosperity. Even in his glory, he does not forget his old friends.

DORIMÈNE: That is the character of a really noble soul.

DORANTE: But where is His Turkish Highness? As your friends, we should like to pay him our respects.

M. JOURDAIN: There he is, coming now. I have sent for my daughter, in order to give him her hand.

(*Enter* CLÉONTE, *in Turkish costume.*)

DORANTE (*to* CLÉONTE):   Sir, as friends of your honorable father-in-law, we have come to make obeisance to Your Highness, and to respectfully assure Your Highness of our humble service.

M. JOURDAIN: Where is the interpreter, to tell him who you are, and make him understand what you are saying? You'll see that he'll answer you; he speaks Turkish wonderfully. Hello, hello! Where the deuce did he go to? (*To* CLÉONTE) Strouf, strif, strof, straf. This gentleman is a *grande segnore, grande segnore, grande segnore;* and Madame is a *granda dama, granda dama.* (*Recognizing that he fails to make himself understood*) Oh, dear! Sir, him French mamamouchi; Madame here, French female mamamouchi. I can't make it any clearer . . . Good! Here's the interpreter! (*Enter* COVIELLE) Where did you get off to? We can't say a thing without you. Just tell him that the gentleman and lady are persons of high rank, who have come to salute him, as my friends, and to assure him of their regards. (*To* DORIMÈNE *and* DORANTE) You'll see how he'll answer you.

COVIELLE: Alabala crociam acci boram alabamen.

CLÈONTE: Catalequi tubal ourin soter amalouchan.

M. JOURDAIN: You see?

COVIELLE: He says: "May the rain of prosperity forever sprinkle the garden of your family."

M. JOURDAIN: Didn't I tell you he spoke Turkish?

DORANTE: It's certainly amazing.

(*Enter* LUCILE.)

M. JOURDAIN: Come here, daughter, come here. Come and give your hand to the gentleman, who does you the honor of asking to marry you.

LUCILE: Father! How you're gotten up! Are you acting in a play?

M. JOURDAIN: No, no; it isn't a play. It's a very serious matter, and one that does you the greatest honor you could conceive. Here is the husband I'm giving you.

LUCILE: Husband—to me, Father?

M. JOURDAIN: Yes, to you. Go on, shake hands with him, and thank heaven for your good fortune.

LUCILE: I don't want to get married.

M. JOURDAIN: Well, I want you to, and I'm your father.

LUCILE: Well, I won't.

M. JOURDAIN: Oh, talk, talk! Come on, I tell you. Here, give me your hand.

LUCILE: No, Father, I have told you, no power on earth can force me to take any other husband than Cléonte; and I'll go to any lengths, rather than— (*She recognizes* CLÉONTE) It is true that you are my father, and I owe you entire obedience, and it is your right to dispose of me according to your decision.

M. JOURDAIN: Ah, I'm delighted to see you recognize your duty so quickly. It's always a pleasure to have an obedient daughter.

(*Enter* MADAME JOURDAIN.)

MME JOURDAIN: What's this? What in the world is up? They say you're trying to marry your daughter to a circus clown!

M. JOURDAIN: Will you shut up, impertinence? You always come sticking your oar into everything, and there's no way to teach you to be reasonable.

MME JOURDAIN: You're the one there's no getting any sense into; you go from one crazy fool trick to another. What's your idea? And what are you trying to do with this tomfool marriage?

M. JOURDAIN: I want to marry our daughter to the son of the Grand Turk.

MME JOURDAIN: The son of the Grand Turk!

M. JOURDAIN: Yes. You can have the interpreter there pay him your compliments for you.

MME JOURDAIN: I don't care a hoot for any interpreter, and I'll tell him myself to his face that he won't have my daughter.

M. JOURDAIN: Once more, will you shut up?

DORANTE: What, Madame Jourdain, you are opposing such a happy opportunity as this? You refuse His Turkish Highness for a son-in-law?

MME JOURDAIN: My good sir, mind your own business.

DORIMÈNE: It's a glorious honor, hardly to be turned down.

MME JOURDAIN: Madame, I shall beg you also not to interfere in matters with which you have no concern.

DORANTE: It is our friendly feeling for you which makes us take an interest in your welfare.

MME JOURDAIN: I don't need any of your friendly feelings.

DORANTE: But your daughter has yielded to her father's wishes.

MME JOURDAIN: My daughter consents to marry a Turk?

DORANTE: Certainly.

MME JOURDAIN: She can forget Cléonte?

DORANTE: Ah, well, what won't a girl do to be a great lady?

MME JOURDAIN: I would strangle her with my own hands, if she ever did a trick like that.

M. JOURDAIN: Talk, talk, talk! I tell you that this marriage will take place.

MME JOURDAIN: And I tell you it won't.

M. JOURDAIN: Gabble, gabble, gabble!

LUCILE: Mother!

MME JOURDAIN: You're a nasty girl!

M. JOURDAIN (*to* MADAME JOURDAIN):   You're scolding her because she obeys me?

MME JOURDAIN: Yes; she belongs to me as well as to you.

COVIELLE (*to* MADAME JOURDAIN):   Madame!

MME JOURDAIN: What are you trying to tell me, you?

COVIELLE: Just a word—

MME JOURDAIN: I don't want to hear any "just a word" out of you.

COVIELLE (*to* MONSIEUR JOURDAIN):   Sir, if she will listen to me a moment in private, I promise you I'll make her consent to your desires.

MME JOURDAIN: I won't consent.

COVIELLE: But just listen to me!

MME JOURDAIN: I won't.

M. JOURDAIN: Listen to him!

MME JOURDAIN: I don't want to listen to him.

M. JOURDAIN: He will tell you—

MME JOURDAIN: I don't want him to tell me anything.

M. JOURDAIN: How obstinate women are! Will it do you any harm to hear what he says?

COVIELLE (*to* MADAME JOURDAIN):   Just listen to me; and afterwards you can do whatever you please.

MME JOURDAIN: Well, all right. What?

COVIELLE (*to* MADAME JOURDAIN):   We've been trying to signal to you for the last half-hour. Don't you see that we're doing all this just to fall in with your husband's mania, and we're fooling him under this disguise, and it's Cléonte himself who is the son of the Grand Turk?

MME JOURDAIN: Aha!

COVIELLE: And I'm Covielle!

MME JOURDAIN (*aside to* COVIELLE):   Oh, well, in that case, I surrender.

COVIELLE: Don't give anything away.

MME JOURDAIN (*to* M. JOURDAIN):   Well, all right. I consent to the marriage.

M. JOURDAIN: Ah, now everybody's reasonable at last. You wouldn't listen to me. But I knew very well he would explain to you what it means to be the son of the Grand Turk.

MME JOURDAIN: He's explained it to me very nicely, and I'm satisfied. Let's send out for a notary.

DORANTE: That's very well said. And Madame Jourdain, in order that you may have your mind entirely at ease, and dismiss any suspicion you may have conceived about your husband, Madame Dorimène and I shall make use of the same notary for our own marriage contract.

MME JOURDAIN: I consent to that too.

M. JOURDAIN (*aside to* DORANTE): That's just to throw dust in her eyes, I suppose?

DORANTE (*aside to* MONSIEUR JOURDAIN): It's a good thing to play her along with this pretense.

M. JOURDAIN (*aside*): Good, good. (*Aloud*) Have the notary sent for, right away.

DORANTE: While we're waiting for him to come and draft the contracts, let's have a look at our ballet. It will be a nice entertainment for His Turkish Highness.

M. JOURDAIN: A very good idea. Let's take our seats.

MME JOURDAIN: How about Nicole?

M. JOURDAIN: I'll give her to the interpreter; and my wife to anyone that wants her.

COVIELLE: Sir, I thank you. (*Aside*) If anyone can find a madder madman, I'll go to Rome and tell it to the world.

        (*The play concludes with the Ballet of the Nations. As this has nothing to do with the previous action and characters, it is here omitted.*)